Champions of Access to Knowledge

All digital forms of access to our high-quality open texts are entirely FREE! All content is reviewed for excellence and is wholly adaptable; custom editions are produced by Lyryx for those adopting Lyryx assessment. Access to the original source files is also open to anyone!

We have been developing superior online formative assessment for more than 15 years. Our questions are continuously adapted with the content and reviewed for quality and sound pedagogy. To enhance learning, students receive immediate personalized feedback. Student grade reports and performance statistics are also provided.

Access to our in-house support team is available 7 days/week to provide prompt resolution to both student and instructor inquiries. In addition, we work one-on-one with instructors to provide a comprehensive system, customized for their course. This can include adapting the text, managing multiple sections, and more!

Additional instructor resources are also freely accessible. Product dependent, these supplements include: full sets of adaptable slides and lecture notes, solutions manuals, and multiple choice question banks with an exam building tool.

Contact Lyryx Today!
info@lyryx.com

Intermediate Financial Accounting
by Glenn Arnold & Suzanne Kyle
Edited by Athabasca University

Version 2018 — Revision A

BE A CHAMPION OF OER!

Contribute suggestions for improvements, new content, or errata:
A new topic
A new example
An interesting new question
Any other suggestions to improve the material

Contact Lyryx at info@lyryx.com with your ideas.

Lyryx Learning Team

Bruce Bauslaugh
Peter Chow
Nathan Friess
Stephanie Keyowski
Claude Laflamme

Martha Laflamme
Jennifer MacKenzie
Tamsyn Murnaghan
Bogdan Sava
Ryan Yee

LICENSE

Creative Commons License (CC BY): This work is licensed under a Creative Commons Attribution 4.0 International License.

To view a copy of this license, visit http://creativecommons.org/licenses/by/4.0/

Table of Contents

Table of Contents iii

12 Current Liabilities 1

Chapter 12 Learning Objectives 2

Introduction 3

Chapter Organization 4

12.1 Definition 5

12.2 Classification 5

12.3 Current Financial Liabilities 7

    12.3.1 Trade Accounts Payable 7

    12.3.2 Lines of Credit 8

    12.3.3 Notes Payable 8

    12.3.4 Customer Deposits 9

    12.3.5 Sales Tax Payable 10

    12.3.6 Employee Payables 11

12.4 Current Non-Financial Liabilities 15

    12.4.1 Unearned Revenues 15

    12.4.2 Product Warranties 17

    12.4.3 Customer Loyalty Programs 18

12.5 Provisions and Contingencies 20

    12.5.1 Product Warranties 22

    12.5.2 Decommissioning Costs 24

12.6 Commitments and Guarantees 25

12.7 Presentation and Disclosure 27

12.8 Analysis 28

12.9 IFRS/ASPE Key Differences 29

Chapter Summary 30

Exercises 33

13 Long-Term Financial Liabilities   41

Chapter 13 Learning Objectives 42

Introduction 42

Chapter Organization 43

13.1 Long-Term Financial Liabilities: Overview 43

13.2 Notes Payable 44

    13.2.1 Long-Term Notes Payable, Interest, and the Time Value of Money . 46

    13.2.2 Subsequent Measurements and Derecognition 60

13.3 Bonds Payable 66

    13.3.1 Initial and Subsequent Measurement, at Par, at a Discount, and at a Premium 68

    13.3.2 Repayment Before Maturity Date 77

13.4 Fair Value Option, Defeasance, and Off-Balance Sheet Financing 78

13.5 Disclosures of Long-Term Debt 80

13.6 Long-Term Debt Analysis 81

13.7 IFRS/ASPE Key Differences 83

Chapter Summary 84

Exercises 88

14 Complex Financial Instruments   97

Chapter 14 Learning Objectives 98

Introduction 99

Chapter Organization 99

14.1 Complex Financial Instruments: Overview 100

14.2 Long-Term Debt and Equity Instruments: A Review 101

14.3 Complex Financial Instruments 103

    14.3.1 Convertible Debt and Preferred Shares Classification: Two Methods 104

    14.3.2 Presentation of Convertible Debt and Preferred Shares 111

14.4 Options, Warrants, Forwards, and Futures 112

14.5 Stock Compensation Plans 116

    14.5.1 Employee Stock Options Plans 116

    14.5.2 Compensatory Stock Options Plans 117

    14.5.3 Stock Appreciation Rights and Performance-Based Plans 119

    14.5.4 Disclosures of Compensation Plans 119

14.6 Analysis 120

14.7 IFRS/ASPE Key Differences 120

Chapter Summary 121

Exercises 124

15 Income Taxes — 131

Chapter 15 Learning Objectives 132

Introduction 132

Chapter Organization 134

15.1 Current Income Taxes Payable 134

15.2 Differences Between Accounting and Taxable Profit 136

15.3 Deferred Tax: Effect of Temporary Differences 138

    15.3.1 Calculation of Deferred Tax 140

    15.3.2 A More Complex Example 142

15.4 Tax Rate Changes 145

15.5 Unused Tax Losses and Tax Credits 147

15.6 Deferred Tax Assets 150

15.7 Presentation and Disclosure 151

15.8 IFRS/ASPE Key Differences 152

15.9 Appendix A: Accounting for Income Taxes under ASPE 153

Chapter Summary 154

Exercises 157

16 Pensions and Other Employment Benefits — 165

Chapter 16 Learning Objectives 166

Introduction 167

Chapter Organization 167

16.1 Definition 168

16.2 Types of Pension Plans 168

16.3 Defined Contribution Plans 168

16.4 Defined Benefit Plans 169

      16.4.1 Accounting for Defined Benefit Plans 173

      16.4.2 Net Defined Benefit Asset 179

16.5 Other Post-Employment Benefits 179

16.6 Other Employment Benefits 179

16.7 Presentation and Disclosure 180

16.8 IFRS/ASPE Key Differences 182

16.9 Appendix A: Accounting for Post-Employment Benefits Under ASPE 183

Chapter Summary 185

Exercises 189

17 Leases   **195**

Chapter 17 Learning Objectives 196

Introduction 197

Chapter Organization 197

17.1 Leases: Overview 198

17.2 Classification Criteria for Capitalization 198

17.3 Accounting Treatment for Capitalized Leases 203

17.4 Sales and Leaseback Transactions 221

17.5 Leasing: Disclosures 223

17.6 IFRS/ASPE Key Differences 225

Chapter Summary 225

References 228

Exercises 228

18 Shareholders' Equity — 235

Chapter 18 Learning Objectives 236

Introduction 236

Chapter Organization 237

18.1 What is Equity? 237

    18.1.1 Funds Contributed by Shareholders 238

    18.1.2 Retained Earnings 241

    18.1.3 Reserves 241

18.2 Issuing Shares 241

18.3 Reacquiring Shares 245

18.4 Dividends 248

    18.4.1 Preferred Share Dividends 252

18.5 Presentation and Disclosure 253

18.6 IFRS/ASPE Key Differences 257

Chapter Summary 257

Exercises 260

19 Earnings per Share — 267

Chapter 19 Learning Objectives 267

Introduction 268

Chapter Organization 268

19.1 Earnings per Share: Overview 269

19.2 Basic and Diluted Earnings per Share: A Review 270

    19.2.1 Basic Earnings per Share 271

    19.2.2 Diluted Earnings per Share 277

19.3 Other Issues 285

19.4 Comprehensive Illustration 286

19.5 Earnings per Share Analysis 292

19.6 IFRS/ASPE Key Differences 293

Chapter Summary 293

Exercises 296

20 Statement of Cash Flows   303

Chapter 20 Learning Objectives 304

Introduction 304

Chapter Organization 305

20.1 Financial Reports: Overview 306

20.2 Statement of Cash Flows: Indirect Method Review 308

    20.2.1 Differences Between IFRS and ASPE 312

    20.2.2 Preparing a Statement of Cash Flows: Indirect Method 313

20.3 Statement of Cash Flows: Direct Method 327

    20.3.1 Preparing a Statement of Cash Flows: Direct Method 328

20.4 Interpreting the Results 334

20.5 Disclosures 337

20.6 Analysis 337

20.7 Comprehensive Example: Both Methods 339

    20.7.1 Preparing the Statement of Cash Flows: Indirect Method 343

    20.7.2 Operating Activities Section: Direct Method 353

20.8 Specific Items 354

20.9 IFRS/ASPE Key Differences 357

Chapter Summary 357

Exercises 361

21 Changes and Errors   373

Chapter 21 Learning Objectives 374

Introduction 374

Chapter Organization 375

21.1 IAS 8 375

21.2 Changes in Accounting Policies 376

    21.2.1 Applying Voluntary Accounting Policy Changes 377

    21.2.2 Impracticability 380

21.3 Changes in Accounting Estimates 381

21.4 Correction of Errors 382

21.5 Presentation and Disclosure 385

21.6 Examples 386

21.7 IFRS/ASPE Key Differences 387

Chapter Summary 388

Exercises 390

22 Putting It All Together: Disclosures and Analysis Overview 397

Chapter 22 Learning Objectives 397

Introduction 398

Chapter Organization 399

22.1 Disclosures and Analysis: Overview 399

22.2 Disclosure Issues 400

    22.2.1 Full Disclosure 401

    22.2.2 Related Party Transactions 403

    22.2.3 Subsequent Events – After the Reporting Period 406

22.3 Auditor's Reports 407

22.4 Financial Statement Reporting and Analysis 410

    22.4.1 Interim Reporting 410

    22.4.2 Segmented Reporting 412

    22.4.3 Analysis Techniques 415

22.5 IFRS/ASPE Key Differences 420

Chapter Summary 420

Exercises 423

Chapter 12

Current Liabilities

Toyota Applies the Brakes

On March 19, 2014, Toyota Motor Corporation agreed to settle an outstanding legal issue with the U.S. Department of Justice by paying a $1.2 billion (USD) penalty. This amount represented approximately 1/3 of the company's total profit in 2013. The issue related to a problem of unintended acceleration in various Toyota vehicles and the subsequent investigation of those problems. These problems received widespread media attention between November 2009 and January 2010, when Toyota recalled over 9 million vehicles worldwide to replace faulty floor mats and repair sticking accelerator pedals. The effect of this problem, and the resulting media frenzy, was significant: in one week of trading in January 2010, Toyota's share price dropped by 15%. The total cost to the company is difficult to determine, but is likely several billion dollars when the effects of lost sales, repairs, and the settled and outstanding lawsuits are combined with the above penalty.

Companies like Toyota that manufacture complex consumer products can face significant product liabilities. Automobiles are likely to carry warranties that may require service over a period of several years. The costs of providing this service may be significant if there are product quality issues. As well, automobile manufacturers engage in a process of voluntary recalls when product faults potentially impact public safety. When product faults cause injury or death, the company faces further liabilities in the form of legal actions taken by the survivors.

From an accounting perspective, the question is whether these warranty and product safety costs represent liabilities and, if so, how can they be measured? On Toyota's March 31, 2015, financial statement, an amount of 1,328,916 million yen was accrued as a "liability for quality assurance." Note 13 describes this amount as a combination of estimated warranty costs and costs for recalls and other safety measures. Since 2013, this amount had risen by 15% from the previous year by 32%.

Toyota has recognized both the warranty costs and the recall costs as liabilities at the time of sale, based on the terms of the warranty contract and past experience. Although past experience can certainly provide a base for these estimations, there is no precise way to predict future expenditures, as there are numerous variables that affect product quality.

With respect to legal actions taken by customers, these are even more difficult to predict, as the results are determined through the due process of the legal system.

> As a consequence of the unintended acceleration issue, Toyota faced hundreds of lawsuits, both individual and class action, claiming a wide range of damages. Note 23 of Toyota's March 31, 2015, financial statements indicated that the company was "unable to estimate a reasonably possible loss" beyond the amounts accrued.
>
> It is clear that companies like Toyota face significant challenges in accounting for product warranty and product safety issues. These amounts do, however, need to be accrued and disclosed when possible, as the amounts can be material to the operation of the business.
>
> (Sources: Douglas & Fletcher, 2014; Toyota Motor Corporation, 2016)

Chapter 12 Learning Objectives

After completing this chapter, you should be able to:

LO 1: Define *current liabilities* and account for various types of current liabilities.

LO 2: Differentiate between financial and non-financial current liabilities.

LO 3: Explain the accounting treatment of different types of current, financial liabilities.

LO 4: Explain the accounting treatment of different types of current, non-financial liabilities.

LO 5: Discuss the nature of provisions and contingencies and identify the appropriate accounting treatment for these.

LO 6: Discuss the nature of commitments and guarantees and identify the appropriate accounting disclosure for these items.

LO 7: Describe the presentation and disclosure requirements for various types of current liabilities.

LO 8: Use ratio analysis of current liabilities to supplement the overall evaluation of a company's liquidity.

LO 9: Identify differences in the accounting treatment of current liabilities between IFRS and ASPE.

Introduction

If you recall our discussion about financial statement elements from Chapter 1, one of the key components of financial statements identified by the conceptual framework is the liability. The proper management of liabilities is an essential feature of business success. Liabilities can impose legal and operational constraints on a business, and managers need to be prudent and strategic in the management of these obligations. Shareholders and potential investors are also interested in the composition of a company's liabilities, as the restrictions created by these obligations will have a significant effect on the timing and amount of future cash flows. Creditors, of course, have a direct interest in the company's liabilities, as they are the ultimate beneficiaries of these obligations. Because of the broad interest in these types of accounts, it is important that the accountant have a thorough understanding of the issues in recognition, measurement, and disclosure of liabilities.

Liabilities can take many forms. The most obvious example would be when a company borrows money from a bank and agrees to repay it later. Another common situation occurs when companies purchase goods on credit, agreeing to pay the supplier within a specified time period. These types of examples are easy to understand, but there are situations where the existence of the liability may not be so clear. When a retail store offers loyalty points to its customers, does this create a liability for the store? Or, when you purchase a new car and the manufacturer offers a five-year warranty against repairs, does this create a liability and, if so, how much should be recorded?

In this chapter we will examine current liabilities, provisions, and contingent liabilities. We will look at the recognition, measurement, and disclosure requirements for these types of accounts. Long-term financial liabilities will be discussed in Chapter 13.

Chapter Organization

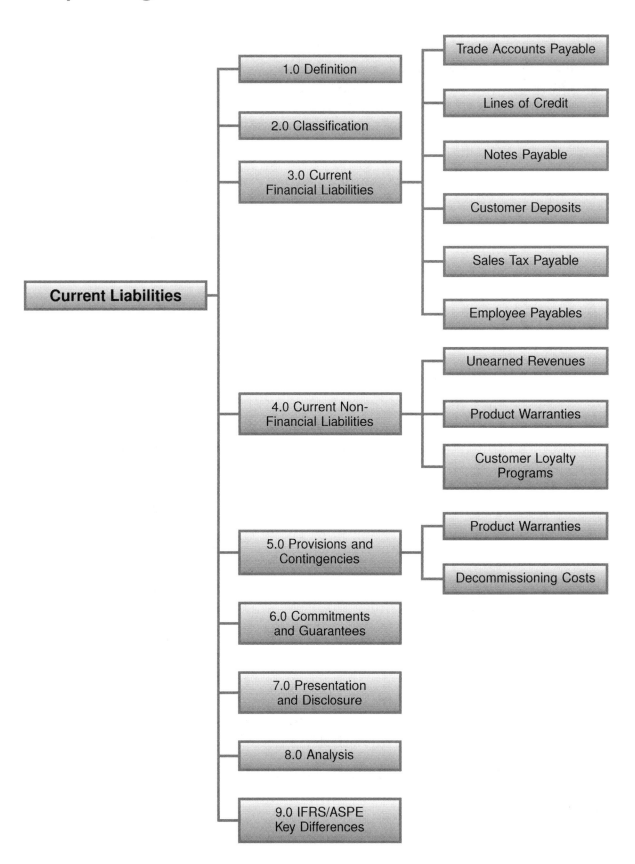

12.1 Definition

From Chapter 2: Why Accounting? recall that the definition of *liability* is "a present obligation of the entity arising from past events, the settlement of which is expected to result in an outflow from the entity of resources embodying economic benefits" (CPA Canada, 2016, 4.4 b). This definition embodies three essential concepts.

First, the liability needs to be a present obligation. This means that at the financial reporting date the entity must have some legal or constructive force that will compel it to settle the obligation. This suggests that the company has no effective way to avoid the obligation. Although this often is the result of the ability of the creditor to legally enforce payment, liabilities can still exist even in the absence of a legal authority. The concept of a constructive obligation suggests that as a result of a company's past business practice, its desire to maintain a good reputation, or even its desire to simply act (and be seen as acting) in an ethical manner, a liability may be created even in the absence of legal enforceability.

Second, the obligation must be the result of a past event. Two common examples of events that would give rise to a liability include the purchase of goods on credit or the receipt of loan proceeds from a bank. The events, which result in economic benefits being delivered to the company, clearly create an obligation. On the other hand, if a company plans to purchase goods in the future, this does not create an obligation, as no event has yet occurred. Although these examples are quite straightforward, we will see later in this chapter that in some situations it is more difficult to ascertain whether a past event has created a present obligation.

The third criterion requires a future outflow of economic benefits. Although we can easily understand the repayment of an outstanding account payable as a use of economic resources, there are other ways that liabilities can be settled that don't involve the payment of cash. These can include the future delivery of goods or services to customers or other parties. In some cases, there may be difficulties in determining the values of the goods or services to be delivered in the future. We will examine several examples of liabilities that are settled with non-cash resources.

12.2 Classification

When classifying liabilities, we need to assess two conditions: is the liability financial or non-financial, and is the liability current or non-current.

Financial or Non-Financial

IAS 32.11 defines one type of financial liability to be a contractual obligation:

I. to deliver cash or another financial asset to another entity; or

II. to exchange financial assets or financial liabilities with another entity under conditions that are potentially unfavourable to the entity (CPA Canada, 2016, IAS 32.11).

A key feature of this definition is that the obligation is created by a contract. This means that there needs to be some type of business relationship between the parties. Liabilities that are created by laws, such as taxation liabilities, do not meet this definition. Other types of non-financial liabilities include unearned revenues, warranty obligations, and customer loyalty programs. These are non-financial because the obligation is to deliver goods or services in the future, rather than cash.

Financial liabilities will normally be initially measured at their fair value, and many will be subsequently measured at their amortized cost. (Note: this definition will be expanded in a later chapter covering complex financial instruments.) Non-financial liabilities are normally measured at the amount the entity would pay to settle the obligation, or to transfer it to a third party. This definition presumes that the entity would act in rational manner (i.e., the presumed settlement is arm's length, non-distressed, and orderly). The determination of this amount will be discussed in more detail later in this chapter.

Current or Non-Current

One of the essential characteristics of a classified balance sheet is the distinction between current and non-current items. This distinction is useful to readers of the financial statements as it helps them to understand the demands on the entity's resources and the potential timing of future cash flows. This information may have an effect on the readers' decisions, so an understanding of this classification is important.

IAS 1 requires the use of current and non-current classifications for both assets and liabilities, unless a presentation in order of liquidity is reliable and more relevant. IAS 1.69 defines *liability* as current when:

- The entity expects to settle the liability in its normal operating cycle.

- The entity holds the liability primarily for the purpose of trading.

- The liability is due to be settled within 12 months after the reporting period.

- The entity does not have an unconditional right to defer settlement of the liability for at least 12 months after the reporting period. Terms of a liability that could, at the option of the counterparty, result in its settlement by the issue of equity instruments do not affect its classification. (CPA Canada, 2016, IAS 1.69).

One of the key components of this definition is the operating cycle. A company's operating cycle is the time from the acquisition of raw materials, goods, and other services for processing, to the time when cash is collected from the sale of finished goods and services. This cycle can vary greatly between industries. For example, a grocery store, which sells perishable food products, would have a very short operating cycle, perhaps only a few weeks, while a shipbuilding company may take several years to complete and sell a single vessel. For those liabilities that are part of the company's working capital, the operating cycle would be the primary determinant of the current classification, even if settlement occurs more than 12 months after the year-end. For other liabilities that are not part of the company's working capital, the other elements of the definition would be applied. In some cases, the operating cycle may not be obvious or well defined. In these cases, the operating cycle would normally be assumed to be 12 months. Keep the criteria for current classification in mind as we examine more detailed examples of these current liabilities.

12.3 Current Financial Liabilities

12.3.1 Trade Accounts Payable

Trade accounts payable are likely the most common current liability presented in company financial statements. The balance results from the purchase of goods and services from suppliers and other entities on account. A typical business arrangement would first involve the supplier approving the purchasing company for credit. Once this is done, the purchasing company would be allowed to purchase goods or services up to a maximum amount, with payment required within some specified period of time. Typical terms would require payment within 30 to 60 days from the date of purchase. Many suppliers will also encourage early payment by offering a discount if payment is received within a shorter time period, often as little as 10 days. These types of arrangements were previously discussed in the cash and receivables chapter. From the perspective of the purchaser, the amount of any discount earned by early payment should be deducted directly from the cost of the inventory purchased or any other asset/expense account debited in the transaction.

One issue that accountants need to be concerned with is ensuring that accounts payable are recorded in the correct accounting period. A basic principle of accrual accounting is that expenses should be recorded in the period in which the goods or services are consumed or received. This means that the liability for those purchases must also be recorded in the same period. For this reason, accountants will be very careful during the period immediately before and after a reporting date to ensure that the cut off of purchase transactions has been properly completed. The issue of goods-in-transit at the reporting date was previously discussed in detail in the inventory chapter.

12.3.2 Lines of Credit

Management of operating cash flows is an essential task that must be executed efficiently and effectively in all companies. The nature of the company's operating cycle will determine how long the company needs to finance its operations, as cash from sales will not be immediately collected. Many companies will negotiate an agreement with their banks that allows them to borrow funds on a short-term basis to finance operations. A line of credit essentially operates as a regular bank account, but with a negative balance. A company will make disbursements of cash through the line of credit to purchase goods, pay employees, and so on, and when money is received from customers, it will be used to pay down the balance of the line of credit. At the end of any particular reporting period, the company's bank balance may be positive, in which case it would be reported in the current asset section as cash. If it is negative, for example if the line of credit has been drawn upon, it would be reported as bank indebtedness in the current liability section.

The line of credit will be governed by a contract with the bank that specifies fees and interest charged, collateral pledged, reporting requirements, and certain other covenant conditions that must be maintained (such as maintenance of certain financial ratios). Because of these contractual conditions, there are a number of disclosure requirements under IFRS for these types of bank indebtedness. These will be discussed later in the chapter.

Note as well that another lender related current financial liability is the current portion of long-term debt. This represents the principal portion of a long-term liability that will be paid in the next reporting period, and will be covered in more detail in the long-term financial liabilities chapter.

12.3.3 Notes Payable

In the cash and receivables chapter, we discussed the accounting entries and calculations for short-term notes receivable. In the case of notes payable, the journal entries are a mirror of those, as we are simply taking the perspective of the other party in the transaction. In the example used in the cash and receivables chapter, the note was issued in exchange for the cancellation of an outstanding trade payable. As well, notes may sometimes be issued directly for loans received.

If we revisit the Ripple Stream Co. example from the cash and receivables chapter, the journal entries required by the debtor would be as follows:

General Journal				
Date	Account/Explanation	PR	Debit	Credit
Mar 14	Accounts payable................................		5,000	
	Note payable................................			5,000

The entry for payment of the note 90 days at maturity on June 12 would be:

General Journal				
Date	Account/Explanation	PR	Debit	Credit
Jun 12	Note payable..................................		5,000	
	Interest expense............................		98.63	
	Cash....................................			5,098.63
	For Interest expense: ($5,000 × 0.08 × 90 ÷ 365)			

If financial statements are prepared during the period of time that the note payable is outstanding, then interest will be accrued to the reporting date of the balance sheet. For example, if the company's year-end was April 30, then the entry to accrue interest from March 14 to April 30 would be:

General Journal				
Date	Account/Explanation	PR	Debit	Credit
Apr 30	Interest expense............................		51.51	
	Interest payable...........................			51.51
	($5,000 × 0.08 × 47 ÷ 365) (Mar 14 to 31 = 17 days; Apr = 30 days)			

When the cash payment occurs at maturity on June 12, the entry would be:

General Journal				
Date	Account/Explanation	PR	Debit	Credit
Jun 12	Note payable..................................		5,000.00	
	Interest payable............................		51.51	
	Interest expense............................		47.12	
	Cash....................................			5,098.63
	For Interest expense: [($5,000 × 0.08 × 90 ÷ 365) − $51.51]			

IFRS requires the use of the effective interest method for the amortization of zero interest notes and other financial instruments classified as loans and receivables. Thus, the journal entries from the perspective of the debtor for these different types of notes will simply be the reverse of those presented in the cash and receivables chapter. They will follow a similar pattern, as outlined above.

12.3.4 Customer Deposits

Businesses may sometimes require customers to pay deposits in advance of the delivery of the service or good for which it is contracted. These deposits serve a variety of purposes. A common example is a landlord requiring a security deposit that will be refundable at the end of the lease, if there is no damage to the property. If the property is damaged, then the deposit will be retained to cover the cost of repairs. Another type of deposit may be required for special order or custom designed goods. As the vendor may not be able to fully recover its costs on such contracts if the customer were to cancel, the deposit is required to ensure the commitment of the customer. As well, utility companies will often require deposits from customers to cover the cost of any unpaid balances that may arise if the customer were to move out of premises prior to receiving the final invoice.

Although the circumstances that create these deposits may be different, the accounting treatment still follows the same basic rules for classification described in Section 12.2. If the company expects the liability to be settled within the operating cycle, or if the company has no unconditional right to defer settlement beyond 12 months, then the liability would be classified as current. If these conditions are not true, then the liability would be classified as non-current. The individual conditions of the contract would need to be examined to determine the proper classification.

12.3.5 Sales Tax Payable

Many countries and tax jurisdictions levy sales taxes on the sale of certain products and services. These types of taxes are often referred to as value-added taxes (VAT) or goods and services taxes (GST). Although the tax rules in each jurisdiction will vary, the general approach to these types of taxes will be similar in any location. A sales tax collected by an entity on the sale of goods or services represents a liability, as the tax is being collected on behalf of the relevant government authority. To use a simple example, assume a company sells $500 of professional services to a customer in a jurisdiction that requires a sales tax of 10% be charged. The journal entry would look like this:

General Journal				
Date	Account/Explanation	PR	Debit	Credit
	Accounts receivable............................		550	
	Service revenue			500
	Sales tax payable			50

When the sales tax is remitted to the government authority, the sales tax payable account would be reduced accordingly. These liabilities will usually be classified as current, as the relevant government authority would normally require payment within a fairly short time period (usually monthly or quarterly).

When we look at this transaction above, we should also consider the accounting for the purchaser of the service. The treatment of the tax paid will depend on the rules in the relevant jurisdiction. If the sales tax is *refundable*, the payer can claim a credit for the amount paid. If the sales tax is *non-refundable*, then the payer simply absorbs this cost into the operations of the business.

Using the example above, the journal entries for the purchaser would be as follows:

Refundable Sales Tax Jurisdiction

	General Journal			
Date	Account/Explanation	PR	Debit	Credit
	Professional fee expense		500	
	Sales tax recoverable		50	
	Accounts payable			550

Non-Refundable Sales Tax Jurisdiction

	General Journal			
Date	Account/Explanation	PR	Debit	Credit
	Professional fee expense		550	
	Accounts payable			550

When the sales tax is non-refundable, it simply gets included in the relevant expense account. If the purchase were related to an inventory or a property, plant, and equipment item, then the tax would be included in the initial cost of acquisition for the asset. In some jurisdictions, it is possible that both refundable and non-refundable sales taxes will apply to a particular purchase. In those cases, the two tax amounts will need to be separated and treated accordingly.

12.3.6 Employee Payables

There are a number of current liabilities reported with respect to the employees of the business. Some of these liabilities will be discussed below.

Salaries and Wages Payable

Any amounts owing to employees for work performed up to the end of the accounting period need to be accrued and reported. For employees who are paid an hourly wage, the amount is simply determined by multiplying the hourly rate by the number of hours worked since the last pay date, up to the reporting date. For salaried employees, the calculation is usually performed by determining a daily or weekly rate and then applying that rate to the appropriate number of days. Consider the following example: an employee receives an annual salary of $60,000 and is paid every two weeks. The last pay period ended on May 26, and the company reports on a May 31 year-end. The amount of salary to accrue would be calculated as follows:

Annual salary	$ 60,000
Bi-weekly salary (÷ 26 weeks)	$2,307.69
Amount accrued, May 27–31 (5 days)	$1,153.85

Note that when an employee is paid a bi-weekly salary, it is normally presumed that the work week is 5 days and that the pay period is 10 days (i.e., 2 work weeks). Thus, we accrue one-half of the regular bi-weekly pay in this example. The accrued amount would be reversed in the following accounting period when the next salary payment is made.

Payroll Deductions

Payroll deductions, also referred to as source deductions, are a common feature in most jurisdictions. Government authorities will often levy income taxes on employment income and will require the employer to deduct the required amount directly from the employee's pay. Thus, the amount is deducted at the source. The amount deducted by the employer represents a type of trust arrangement, as the employer is agreeing to submit the funds to the government on behalf of the employee. As these deductions are required to be submitted in a timely manner to the relevant government authority, they are reported as current liabilities. Additionally, aside from income taxes, government authorities may require other deductions. In Canada, for example, most employees must also pay Canada Pension Plan and Employment Insurance premiums. For these types of deductions, the employer must submit a further amount, based on a proportion of the amount the employee pays. Thus, the company will report a liability greater than the amount deducted from the employee, with the difference, the employer's share, representing an expense for the company.

There are other types of deductions taken from employee's pay that are not the result of a government levy. Examples include these instances: employers may provide private pension plans that require monthly contributions, employees may belong to unions that require dues payments based on the level of earnings, employees may have extended health benefits that require payment, or employees may have to pay a monthly fee for parking. There are numerous examples of employee deductions, and the accounting treatment of these items will depend on their natures. If the item is deducted in trust for another party, then the company must report it as a liability. If the amount is not submitted to a third party, then the employer may report it as either a cost recovery or a revenue item. Calculations of various types of source deductions can become fairly complex and, as a result, most companies will employ staff with specialized training to take care of the accounting for payroll matters.

Paid Absences

Many employers allow their employees time off from work with pay. IAS 19 describes these kinds of arrangements as paid absences and classifies them into two types: accumulating and non-accumulating.

Accumulating paid absences are those that can be carried forward into a future accounting period if they are not fully used in the current period. An annual vacation entitlement is a common example of this type of paid absence. Employment law in many jurisdictions requires employers to give a certain amount of time off with pay each year to its employees. Employers may choose to grant more than the legally required minimum vacation time as a way to attract and retain high-quality employees. Because the employees earn the paid vacation time based on the time they work, an obligation and expense is created, even if the employees haven't taken the vacation. IAS 19 further distinguishes accumulating paid absences as being either vesting or non-vesting. Vesting benefits are those for which the employee is entitled to a payment upon termination of employment, while non-vesting benefits are those for which no such entitlement exists. In the case of paid vacation, the minimum legally required vacation time would be considered a vesting benefit, while any additional vacation granted by the employer may or may not be considered vesting, depending on the terms of the employment contract. IAS 19 requires that a liability be established for both vesting and non-vesting accumulating benefits. This means that the entity needs to make an estimate of the additional amount that needs to be paid at the end of the reporting period for the unused entitlement to accumulating paid absences. For those paid absences that are non-vesting, the entity would need to estimate the amount that won't be paid out due to employee termination. This could be done by examining past employee turnover patterns or other relevant data.

Consider the following example. Norstar Industries employs 100 people who are each paid $1,000 per week. By December 31, 2015, each employee has earned two weeks of vacation that are considered vesting and a further week of vacation that is considered non-vesting. Note that no vacation was taken by the employees during 2015. Based on past history, the company estimates that 5% of its employees will leave before taking their vacation, thus losing their entitlement to the non-vesting portion. As well, the company has budgeted for a 3% salary increase to take effect on January 1, 2016. The liability for vacation pay would be calculated as follows:

Vesting benefit:	100 employees × $1,030 per week × 2 weeks =	$206,000
Non-vesting benefit:	95 employees × $1,030 per week × 1 week =	97,850
Total obligation	=	$303,850

Note that the calculation is based on the pay rate that is expected to be in effect when the employees take their vacation. The total obligation would be reported as a current liability and an expense on the December 31, 2015 financial statements. In 2016, as the employees take their vacation, the liability would be reduced. If the estimates of employee terminations or salary increases were incorrect, then the expense in 2016 would be adjusted to reflect the actual result. No adjustment to the previous year's accrual would be made.

Non-accumulating paid absences refer to those entitlements that are lost if they are not used. Sick days often fall into this category. Employees may be allowed a certain number of sick days per month or year, but these do not accumulate beyond the end of the relevant period. Additionally, employees are not entitled to a cash payment for unused amounts if their employment is terminated. Other common examples of non-accumulating paid absences include the following: parental leave (maternity, paternity, or adoption), leave for public service (e.g., jury duty), and some short-term disability leaves. In these cases, the company does not accrue any expense or liability until the absence actually occurs. This makes sense as it is not the employee's service that creates the obligation, but rather the event itself.

Profit-Sharing and Bonus Plans

In addition to regular salary payments, companies often establish bonus plans for their employees. These plans may be made available to all employees, or there may be different schemes for different groups. The purpose of a bonus plan is to motivate employees to work toward the best interests of the company and of its shareholders. Bonus plans and profit-sharing arrangements are, therefore, intended to act as a method to relieve the agency theory problem that was discussed in Chapter 1.

Bonuses will usually be based on some measurable target and often rely on accounting information for their calculation. A common example would be to pay out employee bonuses as a certain percentage of reported profit. The individual employee's entitlement to a bonus will be based on some measurable performance objective that should be determined and communicated at the start of the year. As bonuses are really just another form of employee remuneration, IAS 19 requires them to be accrued and expensed in the year of the employee's service, assuming they can be reasonably estimated. IAS 19 also notes that bonuses may result from both legal and constructive obligations. Thus, even though the company's employment contracts may not specify a bonus calculation, consistent past practices of paying bonuses may create a constructive obligation. The calculation used in the past would then form the basis for the current accrual. IAS 19 also requires accrual of the amount expected to be paid out for the bonuses. That is, if a bonus payment is only paid to employees who are still employed at the end of the year, the calculation of the accrued bonus will need to consider the number of employees who leave before the end of the year.

Consider the following example. A company with 25 employees has historically paid out a bonus each year of 5% of the pre-tax profit. The current year's pre-tax profit is $1,000,000. The bonus will be paid out two months after the year-end, but employees will only receive the bonus if they are still employed at that time. In prior years, the company has experienced, on average, the departure of two employees between the year-end and the bonus payment. Bonuses not paid to departed employees are retained by the company and not redistributed to the other employees. The amount to be accrued at year-end would be calculated as follows:

Total bonus:	$1,000,000 × 5%	= $50,000
Bonus per employee:	$50,000 ÷ 25	= $ 2,000
Actual bonus expected to be paid:	$2,000 × 23 employees	= $46,000

The company would then make the following journal entry at its year-end:

General Journal				
Date	Account/Explanation	PR	Debit	Credit
	Employee bonus expense....................		46,000	
	Employee bonus payable................			46,000

12.4 Current Non-Financial Liabilities

As described in Section 12.2, non-financial liabilities are those liabilities that are settled through the delivery of something other than cash. Often, the liability will be settled by the delivery of goods or services in a future period. Examples include: unearned revenues, product warranties, and customer loyalty programs. For these types of liabilities, the determination of the amount to be settled, and the timing of the settlement, may not always be clear. However, because a present obligation exists, the liability must still be recorded. We will examine several examples of non-financial liabilities and consider the related measurement and accounting issues.

12.4.1 Unearned Revenues

One of the most common non-financial liabilities is unearned revenue. Unearned revenue results when a customer makes a payment in advance of receiving a good or a service. Examples include the following: prepayment for a magazine subscription, purchase of season tickets for a sports team, prepayment for airline flights that will be taken in the future, annual dues for a recreational club, prepaid maintenance contracts, and gift cards sold by retail stores. In all of these examples, the key feature is that the money is paid by the customer prior to receiving any goods or services from the vendor. Because the vendor has an obligation to provide these items in the future, the amount received must be recorded as a liability, usually described as unearned revenue. The unearned revenue should be reported at the fair value of the outstanding obligation and will be reclassified as revenue as the goods or services are provided. In most cases, the fair value will be equal to the cash received, as the transaction is normally presumed to be negotiated by arm's length parties and is not expected to extend far into the future, that is, no discounting is required. For unearned revenues resulting from the sale of gift cards by retail stores, an estimate will need to be made of the number of gift cards that will not be redeemed, as some customers will never use the cards and, therefore, the store will never deliver the goods or services. This estimate affects the fair value of the total obligation and can usually be determined by examining historical redemption patterns.

Consider the following example of a magazine subscription. *Motoring Monthly* sold 1,000 one-year subscriptions to its magazine in June 2015, and a further 2,000 one-year subscriptions in September 2015. The magazine is published monthly, and the price of a one-year subscription is $40. Delivery of the magazines commences in the month following payment. The following journal entries would be recorded in 2015:

General Journal				
Date	Account/Explanation	PR	Debit	Credit
Jun 2015	Cash		40,000	
	Unearned subscription revenue			40,000
	(1,000 × $40 = $40,000)			

The entry above records the initial payment of the first group of subscriptions.

General Journal				
Date	Account/Explanation	PR	Debit	Credit
Jul 2015	Unearned subscription revenue		3,333.33	
	Subscription revenue			3,333.33
	($40,000 ÷ 12 months = $3,333.33)			

The entry above recognizes one month of subscription revenue and would be repeated for the months starting August 2015 to June 2016, when the subscription expires.

General Journal				
Date	Account/Explanation	PR	Debit	Credit
Sept 2015	Cash		80,000	
	Unearned subscription revenue			80,000
	(2,000 × $40 = $80,000)			

The entry above records the initial payment of the second group of subscriptions.

General Journal				
Date	Account/Explanation	PR	Debit	Credit
Oct 2015	Unearned subscription revenue		6,666.66	
	Subscription revenue			6,666.66
	($80,000 ÷ 12 months = $6,666.66)			

The entry above recognizes one month of subscription revenue and would be repeated for the months starting November 2015 to September 2016, when the subscription expires.

To summarize, the company will report the following amount as a current liability on its balance sheet as at December 31, 2015:

$$\text{Unearned subscription revenue} \quad \$80{,}000$$
$$(\$40{,}000 \times 6 \div 12 + \$80{,}000 \times 9 \div 12)$$

The company will also report the following amount as revenue on its income statement for the year ended December 31, 2015:

$$\text{Subscription revenue} \quad \$40{,}000$$
$$(\$40{,}000 \times 6 \div 12 + \$80{,}000 \times 3 \div 12)$$

On the income statement, the company would also report the costs to produce and distribute the magazine to properly convey the gross margin earned on the sales.

12.4.2 Product Warranties

As a way to promote sales and develop customer loyalty, many businesses will offer a warranty on their products. A warranty will obligate the company to repair the product if it doesn't function correctly, or replace it if it cannot be fixed. While there are many limitations to warranty arrangements, including time limits, the contract with the customer does obligate the company to deliver the goods or services in the future, assuming the requisite conditions have been met. As a result, the company is required to recognize this obligation as a liability on the balance sheet. As before, the obligation should be reported at its fair value. In some cases, the value of the warranty may be explicitly stated, as is the case with extended warranties that require separate payment from the product itself, such as those sold by automobile retailers. In other cases, however, the price of the warranty may be implicitly included with the total sale price of the product. This is essentially a bundled sale, which was discussed previously in the revenue chapter. If you recall the treatment of bundled sales, the value of each component should be determined using the relative fair value method, and then recorded as revenue or unearned revenue as appropriate.

Consider the following example. Calvino Cars manufactures and sells new automobiles. Included with every sale is a two-year comprehensive warranty that will cover the cost of any repairs due to mechanical failure. The company recently sold a unit of its most popular model, the Cosimo, for $30,000. This price includes the two-year warranty. Based on analysis of similar arrangements at other car companies that sell separate warranties, Calvino Cars estimates that the fair value of this warranty is $1,500. The company has also estimated that 25% of the cost of warranty repairs will be incurred in the first year of the warranty term and 75% in the second year. The journal entry at the time of sale would be:

General Journal				
Date	Account/Explanation	PR	Debit	Credit
	Cash		30,000	
	Sales revenue – automobiles			28,500
	Unearned revenue – warranty............			1,500

In the first year, repair costs of $304 are actually incurred for this vehicle. Two journal entries are required in this case:

General Journal				
Date	Account/Explanation	PR	Debit	Credit
	Unearned revenue – warranty...............		375	
	Sales revenue – warranty			375
	($1,500 × 25% = $375)			

General Journal				
Date	Account/Explanation	PR	Debit	Credit
	Warranty expense...........................		304	
	Cash			304

The first journal entry recognizes the revenue from the warranty, based on the expected pattern of costs to service the warranty. The second journal entry records the actual costs of the repairs made. In the second year, the remaining revenue ($1,500 × 75% = $1,125) will be recognized and any repair costs incurred will be recorded in a similar fashion. If, after the first year, it is estimated that future repair costs would exceed the remaining unearned revenue, then an additional liability would need to be established. This is referred to as an *onerous contract,* a concept that will be discussed later in the chapter.

The approach above, which is the preferred technique under IFRS, is often referred to as the *revenue approach*. However, if it were not possible to estimate the revenue component of the warranty, then a different approach, referred to as the *expense approach*, would be used. This will be discussed later in this chapter under the provisions and contingencies section.

12.4.3 Customer Loyalty Programs

As a method of encouraging repeat business and customer loyalty, many companies offer loyalty rewards. Often denominated in points, they can be redeemed later for additional goods or services. For example, many grocery and other retail stores allow customers to collect points that can be applied against future purchases. Also, airlines quite often encourage their passengers to collect travel miles that can be applied to future flights.

Because there is the potential for an obligation to deliver goods or services in the future, these loyalty rewards need to be accounted for as a liability.

The general principles of the IAS 18 revenue recognition standard are applied in these cases, which results in the loyalty reward being considered a separate component of the sales transaction. In addition, IFRIC 13, *Customer Loyalty Programmes*, provides specific guidance on the treatment of these transactions. The key feature of IFRIC 13 is that it requires the loyalty rewards to be reported at their fair values. It is quite likely that an active market for the loyalty points does not exist, so some type of estimation technique is required to determine the fair value of the rewards. IFRIC 13 suggests that the fair value of the loyalty points should be based on the fair values of the awards for which the points could be redeemed, and should take into account:

- the amount of the discounts or incentives that would otherwise be offered to customers who have not earned award credits from an initial sale
- the proportion of award credits that are not expected to be redeemed by customers
- non-performance risk

If customers can choose from a range of different awards, the fair value of the award credits reflect the fair values of the range of available awards, weighted in proportion to the frequency with which each award is expected to be selected. (CPA Canada, 2016, IFRIC 13.AG2)

Obviously there is some judgment required in making these fair value determinations. Let's look at an example involving a premium car wash. Sudz offers car wash and detailing services for all types of passenger vehicles. To encourage repeat business, the company awards points for each car wash, which can be redeemed in the future for additional car washes or for upgraded services, such as glass repair and scratch buffing. In 2015, the company earned $2,000,000 in revenue from car washes and awarded 10,000 points. Based on an examination of the awards chosen by customers in the past, the company has estimated the fair value of the points awarded at $12,150. As well, the company expects that 10% of the award points will never be redeemed. In 2016, 7,000 points are redeemed and in 2017, 2,000 points are redeemed. The journal entries to record these transactions are as follows:

General Journal				
Date	Account/Explanation	PR	Debit	Credit
2015	Cash		2,000,000	
	Sales revenue – car washes			1,987,850
	Unearned revenue – loyalty points			12,150
2016	Unearned revenue – loyalty points		9,450	
	Sales revenue – loyalty points			9,450
	$12,150 ÷ (10,000 × 90%) = $1.35 per point; $1.35 × 7,000 = $9,450			
2017	Unearned revenue – loyalty points		2,700	
	Sales revenue – loyalty points			2,700
	$12,150 ÷ (10,000 × 90%) = $1.35 per point; $1.35 × 2,000 = $2700			

Note that the value per point is based on the total estimated fair value divided by the number of points expected to be redeemed, rather than the total number of points awarded. If the estimates turn out to be incorrect, the revenue will simply be adjusted prospectively in the current year.

12.5 Provisions and Contingencies

IAS 37 deals specifically with provisions, contingent liabilities, and contingent assets. The standard defines a *provision* as a "liability of uncertain timing or amount" (CPA Canada, 2016, IAS 37.10). These uncertainties can create problems for accountants, as the questions of whether or not the item should be recorded, and what amount should be used if it is recorded, do not always have clear answers. In this section we will examine the general criteria to be used in evaluating provisions and contingencies, and we will look at two specific examples: product warranties and decommissioning costs.

The key feature of the definition of a provision is the existence of uncertainty. The standard distinguishes provisions from other current liabilities, such as trade payables and accruals, on the basis of this uncertainty. In comparison, there is no uncertainty regarding trade payables, as these are usually supported by an invoice with a due date. Even an accrual for a monthly utility expense does not contain sufficient uncertainty to be classified as a provision, as this amount can normally be estimated fairly accurately through examination of past utility bills. Although there is some uncertainty in this process of estimation, the uncertainty is far less than in the case of a provision. It is for this reason that IAS 37 requires separate disclosure of provisions, but not regular accruals.

The standard also defines a contingent liability as:

a. possible obligation that arises from past events and whose existence will be confirmed only by the occurrence or non-occurrence of one or more uncertain future events not wholly within the control of the entity; or

b. A present obligation that arises from past events but is not recognised because:

   i. It is not probable that an outflow of resources embodying economic benefits will be required to settle the obligation; or

   ii. The amount of the obligation cannot be measured with sufficient reliability. (CPA Canada, 2016, IAS 37.10).

A careful reading of this definition will lead us to the conclusion that a contingent liability does not meet the general definition of a liability. The obligation may not be present due to the uncertainty of future events, or the uncertainty may make it impossible to determine if or how many economic resources will be outflowing in the future. For these reasons, the standard does not allow contingent liabilities to be recognized. A common example of a contingent liability would be a legal action taken against the company where the outcome cannot yet be predicted. The court's decision to be rendered is the uncertain future event that is not within the entity's control. However, in some cases, the company's legal counsel may conclude that the decision is fairly certain based on the facts, in which case, recognition of a provision may be warranted. Significant judgment may be required in evaluating the correct accounting treatment of these situations. Contingent assets, which are also defined in relation to an uncertain future event, are also not recognized under the standard. However, there are disclosure requirements for contingent assets and liabilities, which will be discussed later. If an inflow of economic resources were *virtually certain*, however, then the asset would be recognized, as it is no longer considered contingent. The standard doesn't define virtual certainty, but in practice it has come to mean a very high level of probability, usually greater than 95%.

In assessing whether an outflow of resources is *probable*, the standard defines this term as meaning that the event is more likely than not to occur. In mathematical terms, this would mean that the event has a greater than 50% probability of occurring. The standard also states that no disclosure is required if the probability of the outflow of resources is remote. This term is not defined in the standard. In practice, when making this determination most professional accountants will use a guideline of 5–10% maximum probability.

We can think of the guidance offered by IAS 37 in terms of a decision tree:

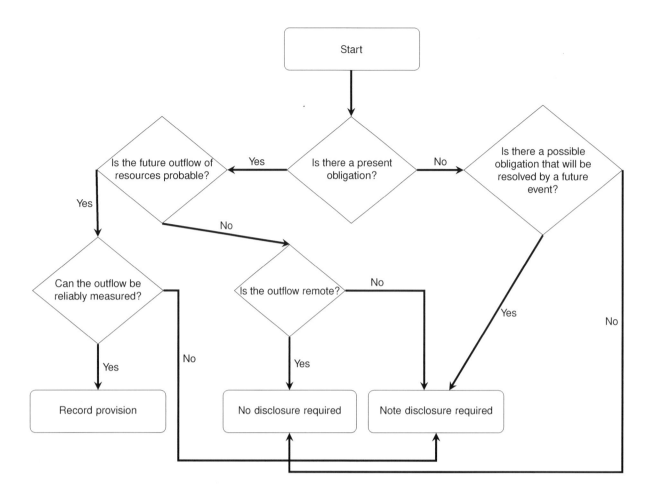

12.5.1 Product Warranties

In Section 12.4, we looked at an example where the warranty contract was considered part of a bundled sale and the warranty revenue was recognized separately. In some cases, it may not be possible to separate the warranty amount from the total sales revenue being recorded. In these cases, the warranty revenue would be recognized immediately as part of the total sale. However, this creates an accounting problem, as there are still potential future costs that will be incurred in servicing the warranty. In this situation, a provision needs to be established for those future warranty costs. This provision will help by reporting the expense in the same period as the related revenue. Let's return to our example of Calvino Cars, but this time we will assume that it is not possible to estimate the fair value of the warranty component. As before, the company estimates that 25% of the warranty repair costs will be incurred in the first year, and 75% in the second year. As well, based on prior experience with this car model, the company has estimated that the total cost of repairs for the warranty term will be $1,100. The journal entries that would be recorded at the time of sale would be:

General Journal				
Date	Account/Explanation	PR	Debit	Credit
	Cash		30,000	
	Sales revenue – automobiles			30,000

General Journal				
Date	Account/Explanation	PR	Debit	Credit
	Warranty expense...........................		1,100	
	Provision for warranty liability			1,100

In the first year, repair costs of $304 are actually incurred for this vehicle. The journal entry required in this case is:

General Journal				
Date	Account/Explanation	PR	Debit	Credit
	Provision for warranty liability................		304	
	Cash, parts inventory, etc.			304

At the end of the first year, the company will report a current liability of $796 ($1,100 − $304), which represents the unused portion of the warranty provision. If the warranty period extended beyond the end of the next operating cycle, then the provision would need to be separated into current and long-term portions. As it is possible that the actual warranty costs will not be the same as the predicted costs, an additional adjustment to profit or loss will be required when the warranty term expires in order to reduce the provision to zero.

One question the accountant will need to face is how to estimate the future warranty costs. IAS 37 suggests that the obligation should be reported at the value that the entity would rationally pay to settle it at the end of the reporting period. This requires some judgment; however, the standard does supply some guidance on how to estimate this amount. When the population being estimated contains a large number of items, such as a warranty plan, the accountant should use the *expected value* method to determine the amount. This method looks at all the possible outcomes and applies a probability weighting to each. For example, if Calvino Cars were to determine the warranty obligation for all of the cars it sells, it may use the following calculation. If all of the cars sold were to contain minor defects, then the total cost to repair these defects would be $8,000,000. If all of the cars sold were to contain major defects, then the total repair costs would be $30,000,000. Based on experience and engineering studies, the company has determined that 80% of the cars it sells will have no defects, 17% will have minor defects, and 3% will have major defects. The warranty provision would then be calculated as follows: $(80\% \times \$0) + (17\% \times \$8,000,000) + (3\% \times \$30,000,000) = \$2,260,000$.

The standard also suggests that when estimating a provision for a single item, the most likely outcome should be used. However, if the range of possible outcomes is not evenly distributed, it may be appropriate to accrue a provision that takes this skewed distribution into account. In making these judgments, the accountant will need to be aware that the subjective nature of these estimates may lead to earnings management or other attempts to manipulate the result. As always, the integrity of the reported amounts depends on the accountant's skillful and professional application of the standard.

12.5.2 Decommissioning Costs

In our chapter on property, plant, and equipment, we briefly discussed the accounting treatment of decommissioning and site restoration costs. The general approach is to capitalize these costs as part of the asset's carrying value and report an obligation, sometimes referred to as an *asset retirement obligation*. This obligation represents a provision and is covered by IAS 37.

The requirement to clean up and restore an industrial site often results from regulation. In order to obtain permission to operate a business that alters the natural condition of an area, a government authority may include restrictions in the operating license that require the restoration of the site, once the industrial activity is concluded. Common examples include: mineral extraction operations, oilfield drilling, nuclear power plants, gas stations, and any other businesses that might result in contamination of water or soil. In addition to the regulatory requirement, IAS 37 also considers the *constructive obligation* that may exist as a result of the company's own actions. If a company has a publicly stated policy or past practice of restoring industrial sites to a condition beyond the requirements of legislation, then the company is creating an expectation of similar future performance. As a result, the amount of the obligation will need to include the costs required to meet the constructive, as well as the legal, obligations.

Let's look at an example. Icarus Aviation Ltd. has just purchased a small, existing airport that provides local commuter flights to downtown businesses in Edwardston. Although the airport is already 50 years old, the company believes that it can still operate profitably for another 20 years until it is replaced by a newer airport, at which time the land will be sold for residential development. To obtain the operating license from the local government, the company had to agree to decontaminate the site before selling it. It is expected that this process will cost $10,000,000 in 20 years' time as the site is heavily polluted with aviation fuel, de-icing solutions, and other chemicals. Also, the company has publicly stated that, when the airport is sold, part of the land will be converted into a public park and returned to the city. It is estimated that the park will cost an additional $2,000,000. As the company has both legal and constructive obligations, the total site restoration costs of $12,000,000 need to be recorded as an obligation. Because the costs are to be incurred in the future, the obligation should be reported at its present value. IAS 37 requires the use of a discount rate that reflects current market conditions and the risks specific to the liability. If we assume a 10% discount rate in this case, the present value of the $12,000,000 obligation is $1,783,724.

At the time of the acquisition of the property, the following journal entry is required:

General Journal				
Date	Account/Explanation	PR	Debit	Credit
	Airport..		1,783,724	
	Obligation for future site restoration......			1,783,724

As the site restoration cost is included in the property, plant, and equipment balance, it needs to be depreciated each year. Assuming straight-line depreciation, the following journal entry would be required each year:

General Journal				
Date	Account/Explanation	PR	Debit	Credit
	Depreciation expense........................		89,186	
	Accumulated depreciation – airport......			89,186
	($1,783,724 ÷ 20 years)			

Additionally, interest on the obligation needs to be recorded. This will be calculated based on the carrying amount of the obligation each year. For the first two years, the journal entries will be:

General Journal				
Date	Account/Explanation	PR	Debit	Credit
Year 1	Interest expense.............................		178,372	
	Obligation for future site restoration......			178,372
	($1,783,724 × 10%)			

General Journal				
Date	Account/Explanation	PR	Debit	Credit
Year 2	Interest expense.............................		196,210	
	Obligation for future site restoration......			196,210
	(($1,783,724 + $178,372) × 10%)			

The interest expense will increase each year as the obligation increases. At the end of 20 years, the balance in the obligation account will be $12,000,000. Over the 20-year period, the total amount expensed (interest plus depreciation) will also equal $12,000,000. Thus, the cost of the site restoration will have been matched to the accounting periods in which the asset was used.

12.6 Commitments and Guarantees

We have seen in our previous discussions that IFRS requires recognition of assets and liabilities when certain criteria have been met. In many business transactions, companies will enter into contracts that commit them to future actions. If neither party has executed any part of these contracts at the reporting date, then we would normally not recognize any asset or liability. However, because the contract will require future actions by both parties, there is a justification for disclosure, as financial statement readers are interested in the future profits and cash flows of the business. As such, there are disclosure requirements for certain types of commitments, and, in some cases, there are even recognition criteria.

An unexecuted contract to purchase property, plant, and equipment is a common commitment that requires disclosures. Even if the contract has not yet been fully executed, IAS 16.74 requires disclosure of the commitment. As PPE expenditures are often irregular and material, this disclosure helps the financial statement reader understand the potentially significant effect of the contract on future cash flows.

We previously discussed the concept of an *onerous contract*. This is a contract for which the unavoidable future costs of the contract exceed the economic benefits that are expected. This result is clearly not what the entity originally intended when it entered into the contract, but circumstances can change and can result in contracts turning into unprofitable ventures. In determining the unavoidable future costs, the entity should use the least net cost of exiting the contract, which may be either the cost of fulfilling the contract or the payment of penalties under the contract for non-performance. When an onerous contract exists, IAS 37.66 requires the entity to recognize a liability for the amount of the obligation.

Consider the following example. Rapid Rice Inc., a wholesale distributor of bulk rice to food manufacturers, has entered into a contract to purchase 1,000,000 kg of rice at $0.40 per kilogram. The company intends to resell the rice to its customers at $0.50 per kilogram. If Rapid Rice Inc. cancels the purchase contract before it is fulfilled, it must pay a penalty of 30% of the total contract value. One month after the contract is signed, but before any rice is delivered, the vendor reduces the price of rice to $0.30 per kilogram, due to weak market conditions. Also as a result of these weak market conditions, Rapid Rice Inc. is forced to reduce the price it charges its customers to $0.37 per kilogram. Rapid Rice Inc. has the choice of fulfilling the contract and selling at the adjusted price to its customers, or cancelling the contract and purchasing at the current price to fill its orders. The following analysis is required to determine if this is an onerous contract:

	Fulfill Contract	Cancel Contract
Expected benefit (1,000,000 × $0.37/kg)	$370,000	$370,000
Unavoidable costs (1,000,000 × $0.40/kg)	$400,000	
or (1,000,000 × $0.30/kg)		$300,000
Penalty (1,000,000 × $0.40/kg) × 30%		$120,000
Net Cost	$(30,000)	$(50,000)

A third option would be to simply cancel the contract and not purchase any rice, but this would result in a net cost of $120,000 (i.e., the penalty). Since all options result in a loss, this is an onerous contract. The least costly option is to fulfill the contract. The company will then need to record a provision as follows:

	General Journal			
Date	Account/Explanation	PR	Debit	Credit
	Loss on onerous contract................		30,000	
	Provision for onerous contract...........			30,000

A guarantee is a special type of commitment that requires some type of future performance or payment if another party defaults on an obligation. This type of arrangement often occurs when two or more companies are under common control. A parent company may guarantee the bank debt of a subsidiary company. Although the subsidiary company is the debtor, the guarantee provides additional security to the bank should a default occur. IAS 39 requires such financial guarantees to be measured initially at the fair value of the guarantee. Subsequently, the guarantee will be measured at the higher of the best estimate to settle the obligation and the unamortized premium received by the guarantor. (It is common for the guarantor to receive a fee for its guarantee.) A discussion of the measurement of these amounts is beyond the scope of this text. However, it is important to know that, aside from the measurement issues, there are significant disclosure requirements for guarantees as these arrangements do have the potential to significantly affect future cash flows.

12.7 Presentation and Disclosure

The topics discussed in this chapter are encompassed by a number of different IFRSs. As a result, there are a significant number of different disclosure requirements regarding current liabilities, contingent liabilities, provisions, and guarantees. A guiding principle that companies should follow when disclosing current liabilities is that there should be sufficient information to allow the reader to identify the current requirement for cash. This means that sufficient detail needs to be provided about major types of current liabilities, including amounts owing to related parties and amounts secured by assets of the company. As well, there are further detailed disclosure requirements for contingencies, commitments, and guarantees.

IAS 1 (Presentation of Financial Statements) does not specify the order in which current liabilities should be presented or where on the balance sheet they should be presented. The standard allows for different formats of presentation as long as information disclosed is sufficient for the reader to understand the nature and function of the items, and their impact on the financial position of the company. As a result, an examination of several companies reporting under IFRS will reveal different orders of presentation and different levels of aggregation.

Consider the following two examples, adapted from the balance sheets of a multinational energy company, and an international chain of grocery stores and hypermarkets. The energy company presents its current liabilities as the first section in the liabilities and equity section of the balance sheet, while the grocery chain presents its current liabilities as the last section. The order of presentation within the classification is different for each company as well. The grocery chain presents bank debt, or short-term borrowings, first, while the energy company presents trade and other payables first. These two examples provide typical disclosures of current liabilities under IFRS, and demonstrate that a variety of formats are allowable, as long as sufficient and meaningful information is disclosed.

Grocery Chain	NOTE	2016	2015
Short-term borrowings	28	2,106	2,251
Suppliers and other creditors	29	12,502	15,444
Short term consumer credit	33	3,211	4,165
Income tax payable		1,075	1,158
Other payables	31	2,613	2,948
Liabilities for assets held-for-sale		256	–
Total current liabilities		21,763	25,966

Energy Company	NOTE	2016	2015
Current liabilities			
Trade and other payables	21	45,112	44,251
Derivative financial instruments	23	2,165	2,799
Accruals		8,498	6,284
Finance debt	24	7,155	10,147
Current income tax payable		1,813	2,567
Provisions	26	5,163	7,616
		69,906	73,664
Liabilities related to assets held-for-sale	6	–	913
		69,906	74,577

12.8 Analysis

From our previous discussion in the cash and receivables chapter, recall that one way to evaluate a company's liquidity is to calculate the quick ratio. This ratio relates the company's highly liquid assets ("quick" assets) to its current liabilities. This is an important measure because a company's credit rating and reputation can suffer if it cannot pay its current obligations when they come due. Recall from Chapter 5 that our analysis of Best Coffee and Donuts Inc. revealed a quick ratio of 0.45 in 2016. Ratios in isolation are not particularly meaningful as they need to be compared to a benchmark. However, in this case, a quick ratio of 0.45 is not to be viewed as a positive result, as it implies that the company does not have enough highly liquid assets to cover its currently maturing obligations.

Another measure that can be used to evaluate liquidity is the **days' payables outstanding** ratio. This ratio is the mirror image of the days' sales uncollected ratio calculated previously. The days' payables outstanding ratio measures how long it takes the company to pay its outstanding payables. The ratio is calculated using the following formula:

$$\text{Days' payables outstanding} = (\text{Trade accounts payable} \div \text{Purchases on credit}) \times 365$$

Purchases on credit is usually not separately disclosed on the financial statements. Often, the cost of sales figure can be used as an estimate of this amount. However, the individual characteristics of the company would need to be examined to determine if this is a reasonable assumption. If we assume that Best Coffee and Donuts Inc.'s cost of sales in 2016 is $1,594,739, then the ratio is calculated as follows:

$$\text{Days' payable outstanding} = (\$204,514 \div \$1,594,739) \times 365 = 46.81 \text{ days}$$

Although it is difficult to make any conclusive statement, this calculation shows that the company has been paying its outstanding payables somewhat slowly. To be fully meaningful, we would need to know the creditors' normal credit terms and industry averages, and we would want to calculate the trend over several years. However, it is common for many creditors to allow 30 days for payment, so it would appear that Best Coffee and Donuts Inc. is exceeding these terms. Further analysis is needed to determine why this is happening, and whether this is damaging the company's relationship with its creditors.

For ratio analysis to be meaningful, a deeper understanding of the business is required. Best Coffee and Donuts Inc. primarily sells fast food and settles most of its transactions in cash or near cash (i.e., debit and credit cards). In this industry, inventory items would be converted fairly quickly to cash, as perishable items cannot be held for long periods of time. Thus, although the quick ratio appears low, this may not be a serious problem due to the rapid conversion of inventory to cash. However, the fact that the company has been paying its accounts payable slowly may indicate a problem. It is important to consider broader data, including historical trend analysis and industry averages, before drawing further conclusions, though.

12.9 IFRS/ASPE Key Differences

IFRS	ASPE
Contingent assets and liabilities are not recognized because they do not meet the recognition criteria.	Contingent losses are recognized when it is likely that a future event will confirm the existence of a liability and the amount can be reasonably estimated. Contingent gains are not accrued.
A provision is a liability of uncertain timing or amount. It is accrued when the future outflow of economic resources is probable and a reliable estimate can be made. Although not defined, "probable" is usually interpreted as being greater than a 50% probability.	Contingent losses that are "likely" are accrued. A "likely" event is defined as one whose probability of occurrence, or non-occurrence, is "high." This is usually interpreted as being a higher level of probability than the equivalent IFRS condition.
Provisions are accrued based on the expected value approach, which assigns probabilities to each possible outcome.	Where a range of possible outcomes exist, the amount accrued will be the most likely amount in the range. If no amount is more likely than another, then the lowest amount of the range is accrued.
IFRIC 13 provides specific guidance on customer loyalty programmes.	ASPE does not contain specific guidance on customer loyalty programmes.
Both legal and constructive obligations for decommissioning costs are recognized.	Only legal obligations are recognized as asset retirement obligations.
Decommissioning costs related to the asset are recognized as part of property, plant, and equipment. Decommissioning costs related to subsequent production are included in inventory.	All costs, both capital and production, are included in property, plant, and equipment.
Disclosure requirements are detailed, and are included in IAS 1, 19, 32, 37, 39, IFRS 7, and IFRIC 13.	Disclosure requirements are less detailed. Disclosure requirements are included in sections 1510, 3110, 3280, 3290, 3856, and AcG 14.

Chapter Summary

LO 1: Define *current liabilities* and account for various types of current liabilities.

A liability is a present obligation of the entity arising from past events, the settlement of which is expected to result in an outflow from the entity of resources embodying economic benefits. A current liability is one that is expected to be settled within the normal operating cycle, or within 12 months, of the balance sheet date. A liability may also be current if it is held for trading, or if the company does not have the unconditional right to defer settlement beyond one year. Common current liabilities include accounts payable, lines of credit, notes payable, customer deposits, and sales tax payable.

LO 2: Differentiate between financial and non-financial current liabilities.

A financial liability is a contractual obligation to deliver cash or another financial asset to another entity, or to exchange financial assets or liabilities under conditions that are unfavourable to the entity. Non-financial liabilities are those that do not meet this definition.

LO 3: Explain the accounting treatment of different types of current, financial liabilities.

With accounts payable, an important accounting procedure is ensuring that the liability is reported in the correct period. Lines of credit usually require a formal agreement with a lender and, as such, certain disclosures will be required. Notes payable should be accounted for using the effective interest method. The conditions of individual contracts with customers need to be examined carefully to determine the correct classification of deposits received. Sales tax collected on behalf of a government agency represents a liability, but the liability may be offset for sales tax paid in certain cases. Employee-related liabilities can include salaries and wages payable, payroll deductions, paid absences, profit-sharing, and bonus plans. For paid absences, IAS 19 distinguishes between accumulating and non-accumulating absences, and only requires accrual of accumulating amounts.

LO4: Explain the accounting treatment of different types of current, non-financial liabilities.

Unearned revenues represent an obligation to provide goods or services in the future to customers. Unearned revenues are reported as liabilities until such time as they are recognized as revenues, that is, when the goods or services are provided. Unearned revenues should be reported at their fair values, and are normally not discounted. A product warranty is a promise to provide future repairs or replacement if a product has defects. The preferred accounting approach is to treat this as a bundled sale and recognize the warranty component as unearned revenue. The revenue will then be recognized over the term of the warranty, matched against the actual expenses incurred to service the warranty. If the revenue component of the warranty cannot be determined, then the liability for future repairs is treated as a provision. A customer loyalty program represents a separate component of revenue that should be reported at its fair value and deferred as appropriate. Estimation will likely be required to determine the fair value.

LO 5: Discuss the nature of provisions and contingencies and identify the appropriate accounting treatment for these.

A provision is a liability of uncertain timing or amount. A provision will be accrued when the future outflow of resources is probable and the amount can be reliably measured. If one of these conditions is not present, then no amount is accrued but disclosure is required (except when the probability is remote). When the revenue portion of a product warranty cannot be determined, a provision for future expected warranty expenditures is required. The provision will be based on the expected value of the obligation, and will be accrued at the time of sale of the product. As warranty costs are incurred, the provision will be reduced. A provision for decommissioning costs needs to be accrued based on the legal and constructive obligations of the company (only the legal obligation under ASPE). As the costs may be incurred far into the future, discounting of the obligation is appropriate. The value of the initial obligation will be added to the cost of the relevant asset. Every year, interest calculated will be added to the balance of the obligation. Each year the asset will be depreciated and the interest expense recorded. At the end of the asset's life, the balance of the obligation will equal the amount estimated to complete the decommissioning.

LO 6: Discuss the nature of commitments and guarantees and identify the appropriate accounting disclosure for these items.

A commitment represents a future action to be taken by the company under an unexecuted contract. Commitments are not normally accrued, as no part of the contract has yet been executed. However, if they are material, commitments should be disclosed because they do represent a potential effect on future cash flows. If a contractual commitment becomes onerous, the least amount required to execute or withdraw from the contract should be accrued, as this future expenditure cannot be avoided.

Guarantees represent possible future outflows of resources on behalf of another party. Guarantees are initially measured and recorded at their fair value, and are subsequently recorded at the greater of the amount required to settle the obligation and the unamortized premium.

LO 7: Describe the presentation and disclosure requirements for various types of current liabilities.

As current liabilities have a direct impact on immediate cash flows, significant disclosure requirements are detailed in several sections of the IFRSs. The standards do not specify the precise format of current liability disclosure on the balance sheet, so companies have adopted a variety of practices regarding the order of presentation and terminology used.

LO 8: Use ratio analysis of current liabilities to supplement the overall evaluation of a company's liquidity.

The days' payables outstanding ratio can be used in conjunction with the current and quick ratios to draw some conclusions about a company's liquidity. However, a broader understanding of the nature of the business, industry standards, historical trends, and other factors is required to draw proper conclusions.

LO 9: Identify differences in the accounting treatment of current liabilities between IFRS and ASPE.

There are some differences between IFRS and ASPE with respect to contingencies and provisions, customer loyalty programmes, and decommissioning costs. ASPE disclosure requirements are less detailed than IFRS requirements.

References

CPA Canada. (2016). *CPA Canada handbook.* Toronto, ON: CPA Canada.

Douglas, D., & Fletcher, M. A. (2014, March 19). Toyota reaches $1.2 billion settlement to end probe of accelerator problems. *Washington Post.* Retrieved from `https://www.washingtonpost.com/business/economy/toyota-reaches-12-billion-settlement-to-end-criminal-probe/2014/03/19/5738a3c4-af69-11e3-9627-c65021d6d572_story.html`

Toyota Motor Corporation. (2016). *Year ended March 31, 2015.* Retrieved from `http://www.toyota-global.com/investors/ir_library/sec/`

Exercises

EXERCISE 12-1

For each of the following items, identify whether it should be reported as a current liability (CL), a non-current liability (NCL), both a current and non-current liability, or not recorded at all.

a. A bank overdraft

b. Refundable sales tax collected on sales

c. Accounts payable

d. Accrued vacation pay

e. A bank loan with a five-year term that requires monthly payments

f. A commitment under a purchase contract that is not onerous

g. Unearned revenue

h. Decommissioning costs

i. A claim against the company filed under a lawsuit

j. Income taxes payable

k. Unremitted payroll deductions

l. A five-year warranty on the sale of an automobile

m. Notes payable

n. A deposit received from a customer

o. Loyalty points awarded by a hotel chain

EXERCISE 12–2

On October 5, Bendel Ltd. renegotiated the terms of an $8,000 outstanding account payable with a supplier. The supplier agreed to replace the outstanding amount with a 120-day, 9% note. Bendel Ltd. has a December 31 year-end.

Required:

a. Prepare the journal entry made by Bendel Ltd. on October 5.

b. Prepare any journal entries required by Bendel Ltd. on December 31.

c. Prepare the journal entry required by Bendel Ltd. on the note's maturity date.

EXERCISE 12–3

Baldwin Inc. operates in a jurisdiction that levies two types of sales taxes: a federal, 6%, refundable goods and services tax and a provincial, 4% non-refundable sales tax. Both taxes are calculated on the base cost of the item, that is, there is no tax on the tax, and apply to all transactions. During the current year, the following transactions occurred:

a. Inventory was purchased on account at a cost of $10,000, plus applicable taxes.

b. Equipment was purchased for cash at a cost of $3,000, plus applicable taxes.

c. Sales on account were made for proceeds of $16,000 plus applicable taxes.

d. Cash sales were made for proceeds of $5,000 plus applicable taxes.

e. At the end of the year, the net amounts of all sales taxes owing were remitted to the federal and provincial government authorities.

Required: Prepare journal entries to record the transactions detailed above.

EXERCISE 12–4

Mandler Inc.'s payroll clerk unexpectedly quit on December 24, one week before the end of the fiscal year. At that time, employees had not been paid for the most recent pay period. Management issued total cash advances of $50,000 to the employees until payroll could be properly prepared. These advances were recorded in the Employee receivable account. In early January, the company hired a new payroll clerk who determined the following:

Gross employee pay, December 10 – 24	$73,000
Income tax withheld from employees	$19,000
Government pension withheld from employees	$ 1,000
Additional government pension to be paid by employer	$ 1,200

The new payroll clerk also determined that no year-end accrual had been made for the payroll from December 25 to 31. The clerk has determined that the pay for this period should be accrued at the same rate as the previous pay period.

Required:

a. Record the journal entry to correct the December 24 payroll amounts.

b. Record the journal entry to accrue the payroll amount from December 25 to 31.

EXERCISE 12–5

Wightman WaxWorks Ltd. offers repair and maintenance services for premium turntables and other audio equipment. Service contracts may be purchased for one, two, or three years. Prices are $120 for a one-year contract, $200 for a two-year contract, and $280 for a three-year contract. All contract fees must be paid at the start of the term. In 2016, three sales promotion events occurred that generated sales in the following months:

	January 2016	July 2016	December 2016
One-year subscription	17	18	12
Two-year subscription	24	20	30
Three-year subscription	30	22	36

Service begins immediately in the month of purchase. No amount of the service contract is refundable.

Required:

a. Determine the amount of revenue recognized in the year ended December 31, 2016.

b. Determine the amount of deferred revenue reported as a current liability at December 31, 2016.

c. Determine the amount of deferred revenue reported as a non-current liability at December 31, 2016.

EXERCISE 12–6

Wilder Watersports Inc. sells luxury yachts and related equipment. The sale price of each yacht includes a three-year comprehensive warranty that covers all repairs and maintenance for the period. Each yacht sells for $3,000,000. A review of competitor pricing indicates that a similar warranty, if sold separately, would be valued at $10,000. On January 1, 2016, Wilder Watersports Inc. sold seven yachts. Repair costs actually incurred for these yachts were as follows:

Year ended December 31, 2016	$12,000
Year ended December 31, 2017	$30,000
Year ended December 31, 2018	$35,000

Required:

a. Prepare all the necessary journal entries for 2016, 2017, and 2018 to reflect the above transactions.

b. Calculate the amount of unearned revenue to be reported at December 31, 2017.

EXERCISE 12-7

Lofft Furniture Mfg. currently employs 10 people on its assembly line, each of whom earn $160 per day. Each employee is entitled to 15 days of vacation per year and one sick day per month. Vacation days accumulate each month, but cannot be taken until after the end of the current year. Sick days do not accumulate, and if they are not taken in a given month they are forfeited. The company is planning to give a 3% raise to its employees in the next fiscal year. The 10 employees worked for the entire year and took a total of 96 sick days. No vacation was taken during the year.

Required:

a. Prepare the journal entries for the current year with respect to the vacation and sick pay.

b. Calculate the amount of liability to be reported at the end of the current year with respect to the vacation pay and sick pay.

EXERCISE 12-8

Sarkissian Specialties sells premium gelato from a portable trailer located in a busy public park. To promote sales, the business has created a loyalty program. If a customer buys nine cups of gelato, the tenth cup will be free. Each cup of gelato sells for $2.70. In 2015, the business sold 36,000 cups of gelato and redeemed 1,000 free cups. The business expects that another 1,000 free cups will be redeemed in the future. They also expect that any remaining free cups will be forfeited as the loyalty card expires one year after the first purchase, and past experience has indicated that only approximately 50% of the customers redeem their free cup.

Required:

a. Prepare the journal entries for the current year with respect to the sales and loyalty program.

b. Calculate the amount of liability to be reported at the end of the current year with respect to the loyalty program.

EXERCISE 12–9

Lupinetti Industries Ltd. has begun manufacturing a specialized cardiopulmonary bypass machine used to maintain the respiration and blood flow of patients during open-heart surgery. The company expects to continue manufacturing this machine for another 10 years, until such time that competitive products render the current technology obsolete. The company has agreed to vacate its current factory in 10 years' time. The local government granted the land for the facility on the condition that it will be returned to its original state when vacated. The company has also agreed to build a public park on the site once the remediation is complete. The company has estimated that the total cost of the site remediation to be $3 million and the cost of constructing the park to be $500,000. The interest rate appropriate for this type liability is 11%.

Required:

a. Prepare the journal entry to initially record the decommissioning cost.

b. Prepare the journal entries required for the first two years after the initial recognition of the decommissioning cost.

EXERCISE 12–10

Braden Bonnet Technologies manufactures sewing and pressing machines that are used in the manufacture of felt hats. Each machine sold includes a three-year limited warranty that guarantees repairs if the machine should fail. The warranty is an integral part of the sale price and there is no reasonable way to determine its fair value. In 2016, 3,000 machines were sold at a price of $11,000 each. Based on past experience, the company has estimated that the expected value of the warranty repairs will be $600 per machine. Actual repair costs on the machines sold in 2016 were incurred as follows:

Year	Costs Incurred
2016	$975,000
2017	$345,000
2018	$425,000

Required:

a. Prepare all the journal entries to record the sale and warranty transactions for 2016 to 2018.

b. Determine the warranty liability balance that will be reported at each year-end from 2016 to 2018.

EXERCISE 12-11

Kercher Imports Inc. purchases large quantities of precious minerals in Asia that are then resold to various European end-use customers. The company has recently entered into a contract to purchase 10,000 grams of a particular mineral at a price of $50 per gram. The company intends to resell the mineral to its customers at $90 per gram. Soon after the contract was signed, the civil war in the mineral's source country ended and a stable government was installed. This result calmed the markets, and the spot price for the mineral dropped to $31 per gram. Kercher Imports Inc. examined the contract and determined that to exit the arrangement early would result in a penalty of $75,000. As a result of the change in the market price, Kercher Imports Inc. can now only sell the product to its end-users at $45 per gram.

Required:

a. Determine if this is an onerous contract. Prepare the journal entry required to report this contract.

b. Repeat part (a) assuming that the penalty for contract cancellation is $150,000 instead of $75,000.

EXERCISE 12-12

The financial statements for Stuewe Enterprises Ltd. are presented below:

Stuewe Enterprises Ltd.
Balance Sheet
As at December 31, 2016

	2016	2015
Current Assets		
Cash	$ 35,000	$ 56,000
Accounts receivable	175,000	150,000
Inventory	113,000	88,000
	323,000	294,000
Property, plant and equipment	475,000	510,000
	$798,000	$804,000
Current Liabilities		
Accounts payable	$229,000	$201,000
Current portion of long-term debt	55,000	60,000
	284,000	261,000
Long-term debt	216,000	270,000
	500,000	531,000
Equity		
Share capital	10,000	10,000
Retained earnings	288,000	263,000
	298,000	273,000
	$798,000	$804,000

Stuewe Enterprises Ltd.
Income Statement
For the year ended December 31, 2016

	2016	2015
Sales	$975,000	$950,000
Cost of goods sold	595,000	610,000
Gross profit	380,000	340,000
Operating expenses	275,000	195,000
Income before tax	105,000	145,000
Income tax	21,000	30,000
Net income	$ 84,000	$115,000

Required:

a. Calculate the current ratio, quick ratio, days' sales uncollected, and days' payable outstanding ratios. Assume that all sales are made on credit and the only purchases made on credit are inventory purchases, that is, no operating expenses. Use period-end values rather than averages for your calculations.

b. Using the ratios from part (a), evaluate the liquidity of Stuewe Enterprises Ltd.

Chapter 13

Long-Term Financial Liabilities

Leveraging and Debt – Can it be a Smart Move?

In simple terms, leveraging is borrowing to invest, in the hopes that the investment will generate a higher rate of return than the interest rate of the debt. The investment that is financed by debt may be intended to increase a company's corporate wealth by expanding its market share, or adding new product lines to increase net income. It can also involve investing in other companies' shares to enhance a special relationship or receive share dividends and capital appreciation of the shares as a return on investment. No matter the reason, there are important aspects of leveraging that must be considered before entering into such an arrangement.

1. Does the company currently generate enough net income and hold enough assets to service the proposed leveraging strategy?

2. Is leveraging the best strategy, given alternative financing arrangements such as increasing equity by issuing more shares?

3. Does management clearly understand the risks of taking on a leveraging strategy or is the decision driven more by emotions than by careful consideration?

4. Since leveraging increases the debt burden, will this impact any existing restrictive debt covenants from other creditors?

5. Does the company have sufficient business processes in place to adequately monitor and measure the return of the investment funded by the additional debt? This must be done to ensure that the return from the investment exceeds the interest rate of the debt itself.

6. If the investment's return is less than expected, does the company have enough net income and other resources to keep the investment in hopes of an improvement in the future?

7. Is the company diversified enough to achieve a balance between the leveraged investment and its other sources of funds and operations?

(Source: HSBC, 2013)

Chapter 13 Learning Objectives

After completing this chapter, you should be able to:

LO 1: Describe long-term financial liabilities and their role in accounting and business.

LO 2: Describe notes payable, and explain how they are classified and how they are initially and subsequently measured and reported.

LO 3: Describe bonds payable, and explain how they are classified and how they are initially and subsequently measured and reported.

LO 4: Define and describe other accounting and valuation issues such as the fair value option, defeasance, and off-balance sheet financing.

LO 5: Explain how long-term debt is disclosed in the financial statements.

LO 6: Identify the different methods used to analyze long-term liabilities; calculate and interpret three specific ratios used to analyze long-term liabilities.

LO 7: Explain the similarities and differences between ASPE and IFRS regarding recognition, measurement, and reporting of long-term payables.

Introduction

This chapter will focus on the basics of long-term debt, such as bonds and long-term notes payable. Each of these will be discussed in terms of their use in business, their recognition, measurement, reporting and analysis. Other, more complex types of financial liabilities such as convertible debt, pension liabilities, and leasing obligations, will be discussed in future chapters.

Chapter Organization

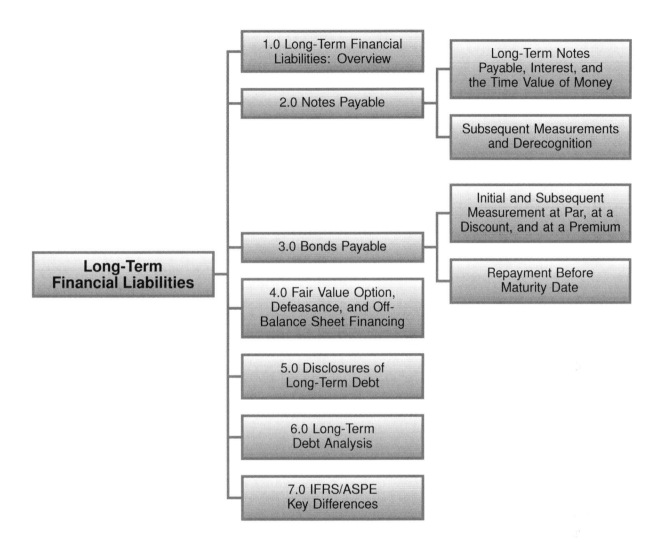

13.1 Long-Term Financial Liabilities: Overview

Most businesses will incur debt at some point during their existence. For example, new businesses may be required to borrow start-up cash to purchase revenue-generating assets as they do not yet have any cash holdings accumulated from profits. Or, existing companies may want to expand their operations, or they may want to replenish depleted cash holdings that resulted from a temporary downturn in business. Additionally, companies with large infrastructures, such as airlines or railways, may require more cash for their capital projects than what can be generated from normal operations. Whatever the case, businesses can obtain the additional cash they need through various financing activities. Three sources of such financing are:

1. **Using internally generated free cash flow:** *Cash from previous sales cycles* ⟶ *Purchase assets* ⟶ *Sales* ⟶ *Accounts receivable* ⟶ *Cash*
   Source of cash from within operations

2. **Borrowing from creditors:** *Cash from borrowings* ⟶ *Purchase assets* ⟶ *Sales* ⟶ *Accounts receivable* ⟶ *Cash*
   Source of cash from acquiring debt (short-term or long-term)

3. **Issuing capital shares**: *Cash from borrowings* ⟶ *Purchase assets* ⟶ *Sales* ⟶ *Accounts receivable* ⟶ *Cash*
   Source of cash from investors (equity)

As shown above, cash obtained from any of the three financing sources can be invested into assets that a company hopes will generate sales and, ultimately, a cash profit. Additionally, each source of financing has its own advantages. For example, using internally-generated funds is the easiest to access but it misses the opportunity to maximize profits through leveraging, as explained in the opening story. As previously discussed, leveraging means using a creditor's cash to generate a profit where the interest rate from the creditor is less than the return generated by operating profits. However, care must be taken to ensure that the best method is used from the choices available on a case-by-case basis. Consider that while borrowing from creditors can result in desirable leveraging, it can also increase the liquidity and solvency risk, as borrowings are obligations that must be repaid. Also, while issuing shares doesn't affect liquidity or solvency, as they are not repayable obligations, issuing more shares results in diluted ownership for the shareholders, which could result in less dividends or a lower market price for the shares. There are also tax implications when choosing between debt and equity sourced financing since interest expense from holding debt is deductible for tax purposes while dividends paid for shares are not.

Long-term debt, such as bonds and long-term notes (including mortgages payable) are examples of financial liabilities. Financial liabilities are the financial obligation to deliver cash, or other assets, in a determinable amount to repay an obligation. They are also monetary liabilities because they represent a claim to cash where the amount is fixed by contract. Financial assets and liabilities share the same mirror image characteristic: that a long-term note payable reported on the balance sheet of the borrowing company will be reported as a long-term note receivable on the balance sheet of the creditor company.

13.2 Notes Payable

Recognition and Measurement of Notes Payable

A note payable is an unconditional written promise to pay a specific sum of money to the creditor, on demand or on a defined future date. It is supported by a formal written promissory note. These notes are negotiable instruments in the same way as cheques and bank drafts.

Notes payable are initially recognized at the fair value on the date that the note is legally executed (usually upon signing). Subsequent valuation is measured at amortized cost using the effective interest rate.

Characteristics

A typical note payable requires payment of a specified face amount, also called **principal**, and interest, that is paid as a single lump sum at maturity, as a series of payments, or as a combination of both. (This topic will be discussed later in this chapter.)

Secured notes payable identify collateral security in the form of assets belonging to the borrower that the creditor can seize if the note is not paid at the maturity date.

Notes may be referred to as interest bearing or non-interest bearing:

- Interest-bearing notes have a stated rate of interest that is payable in addition to the face value of the note.

- Notes that are zero-bearing or non-interest bearing do not have a stated rate of interest. Although, while they may appear at first glance not to have any interest, in actual fact there is an interest component embedded in the note. The interest component will be equal to the difference between the borrowed and repaid amounts.

Cash payments vary and can be a single payment of principal and interest upon maturity, or payment of interest only throughout the term of the note with the principal portion payable upon maturity, or a mix of interest and principal throughout the term of the note.

Transaction Costs

It is common for notes to incur transaction costs, especially if the note payable is acquired using a broker as they will charge a commission for their services. For a company using either ASPE or IFRS, the transaction costs associated with financial liabilities, such as notes payable that are carried at amortized cost, are to be **capitalized**, meaning that the costs will reduce the note payable amount. If the debt is subsequently classified and measured at its fair value, the transaction costs are to be expensed. This is referred to as the fair value option and will be discussed later in this chapter.

Classification

Notes may be classified as short-term (current) or long-term payables on the SFP/BS:

- Short-term notes are current liabilities payable within the next 12 months, or within the business's operating cycle if longer than 12 months.

- Long-term notes are notes that do not meet the definition of a current (short-term) liability. For example, notes with due dates greater than one year.

As previously discussed, the difference between a short-term note and a long-term note is the length of time to maturity. Also, the process to issue a long-term note is more formal, and involves approval by the board of directors and the creation of legal documents that outline the rights and obligations of both parties. These include the interest rate, property pledged as security, payment terms, due dates, and any restrictive covenants. Restrictive covenants are any quantifiable measures that are given minimum threshold values that the borrower must maintain. Additionally, restrictions on minimum working capital (current assets minus current liabilities), management remuneration, capital expenditures, or dividends paid to shareholders are often found in covenant conditions. Maintenance of certain ratio thresholds, such as the current ratio or debt to equity ratios, are all common measures identified in restrictive covenants.

As the length of time to maturity of the note increases, the interest component becomes increasingly more significant. As a result, any notes payable with greater than one year to maturity are to be classified as long-term notes and require the use of present values to estimate their fair value at the time of issuance. A review of the time value of money, or present value, is presented in the following to assist you with this learning concept.

13.2.1 Long-Term Notes Payable, Interest, and the Time Value of Money

Long-term notes payable are to be measured initially at their fair value, which is calculated as the present value amount. But what is present value? It is a discounted cash flow concept, which we will discuss next.

It is common knowledge that money borrowed from a bank will accrue interest that the borrower will pay to the bank, along with the principal. The present value of a note payable is equivalent to the amount of money deposited today, at a given rate of interest, which will result in the specified future amount that must be repaid upon maturity. The cash flow is discounted to a lesser sum that eliminates the interest component—hence the term **discounted cash flows**. The future amount can be a single payment at the date of maturity, a series of payments over future time periods, or a combination of both. Put into context for notes payables, if a creditor must wait until a future date to receive repayment for its lending, then the note payable's face value at maturity will not be an exact measure of its fair value today (transaction date) because of the embedded interest component.

For example, assume that a company purchases equipment in exchange for a two-year, $5,000 note payable, and that notes of a similar risk have a market rate of 9%. The face value of the note is therefore $5,000. The note's present value, without the interest component, is $4,208.40, not $5,000. The $4,208.40 is the amount that, if deposited today at an interest rate of 9%, would equal exactly $5,000 at the end of two years. Using a variables string, the present value of the note can be expressed as:

> PV = (9% I/Y, 2N, 5000FV) = $4,208.40
> Where I/Y is interest of 9% each year for two years;
> N is for the number of years that the interest is compounded;
> FV is the payment at the end of two years' time (future value) of $5,000.

To summarize, the present value (discounted cash flow) of $4,208.40 is the fair value of the $5,000 note at the time of the purchase. The additional amount received of $791.60 ($5,000.00 – $4,208.40) is the interest component paid to the creditor over the life of the two-year note.

Note: The symbols PV, I/Y, N, FV, and PMT are intended to be a generic reference to the underlying variables string. Each brand of financial calculator will have its own owner's manual that will identify the set of keys for inputting the variables above.

After issuance, long-term notes payable are measured at amortized cost. As illustrated next, determining present values requires an analysis of cash flows using interest rates and time lines

Present Values and Timelines

The following timelines will illustrate present value using discounted cash flows. Below are three different scenarios:

1. Assume that on January 1, Maxwell lends some money to Nictonia in exchange for a $5,000, five-year note payable as a lump-sum amount at the end of five years. Notes of similar risk have a market interest rate of 5%. Additionally, Maxwell's year-end is December 31. The first step is to identify the amount(s) and timing of all the cash flows as illustrated below on the timeline. Inputting the variables into a financial calculator, the amount of money that Maxwell would be willing to lend to the borrower using the present value calculation of the cash flows would be $3,917.63.

48 ■ Long-Term Financial Liabilities

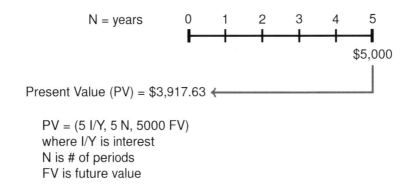

PV = (5 I/Y, 5 N, 5000 FV)
where I/Y is interest
N is # of periods
FV is future value

In this case, Maxwell would be willing to lend $3,917.63 today in exchange for a payment of $5,000 at the end of five years, at an interest rate of 5% per annum. Nictonia's entry for the note payable at the date of issuance would be:

	General Journal			
Date	Account/Explanation	PR	Debit	Credit
Jan 1	Cash		3,917.63	
	Notes payable			3,917.63

Notes of this nature are often referred to as zero-interest or non-interest-bearing notes. This is a misnomer, however, as all debt transactions between unrelated third parties will bear interest based on market interest rates. For example, note that Maxwell lends $3,917.63 now and collects $5,000 at the end of five years. The difference of $1,082.37 represents the interest component over the five years.

2. Now assume that on January 1, Maxwell lends an amount of money in exchange for a $5,000, five-year note. The current market rate for similar notes is 5%. The repayment of the note is $1,000 at the end of each year for the next five years (present value of an ordinary annuity). The amount of money that Maxwell would be willing to lend Nictonia using the present value calculation of the cash flows would be $4,329.48, as follows:

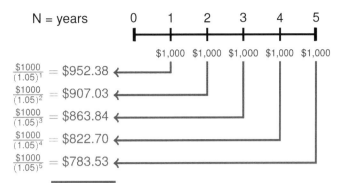

Present Value of an Ordinary Annuity = $4,329.48

PV = (1000 PMT, 5 I/Y, 5 N, 0 FV)
where PMT is the payment amount
I/Y is the interest
N is the # of periods
FV is the single payment at maturity.

Nictonia's entry for the note payable at the date of issuance would be:

	General Journal			
Date	Account/Explanation	PR	Debit	Credit
Jan 1	Cash		4,329.48	
	Note payable			4,329.48

Note that in this example Maxwell is willing to lend more money, $4,329.48 as compared to $3,917.63, to Nictonia. Another way of looking at it would be that the interest component embedded in the note is less in this case. This makes sense as the principal amount of the note is being slowly reduced over its five-year term due to of the yearly payments of $1,000. In other words, the higher the frequency of payments, the lower the interest component will be. This is the same concept as with a mortgage owing for a house. It is common for financial advisors to say that a mortgage payment paid twice a month, instead of a single payment once a month, will result in a significant reduction in interest costs over the term of the mortgage. The bottom line is that if the principal amount owing at any time over the life of a note is reduced, then there will be less interest charged overall. Another name for a note with equal payments of interest and principal is an instalment or blended payment note.

3. How would the amount of the loan and the entries above differ if Maxwell received five equal payments of $1,000 at the beginning of each year (present value of an annuity due) instead of at the end of each year, as shown in example 2? The amount of money that Maxwell would be willing to lend Nictonia using the present value calculation of the cash flows paid at the beginning of the period (P/AD generic symbol) would be $4,545.95, as follows:

50 ■ Long-Term Financial Liabilities

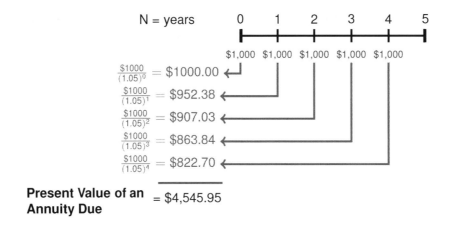

Present Value of an Annuity Due = $4,545.95

PV = (1000 P/AD, 5 I/Y, 5 N, 0 FV)
where P/AD is the payment at the beginning of the period
I/Y is interest
N is # of periods
FV is a single payment at maturity.

Nictonia's entry for the note payable at the date of issuance would be:

	General Journal			
Date	Account/Explanation	PR	Debit	Credit
Jan 1	Cash		4,545.95	
	Note payable			4,545.95

Again, the interest component will be less because a payment is paid immediately upon execution of the note, which causes the principal amount to be reduced sooner than a payment made at the end of each year.

Below is a comparison of the three scenarios:

	Scenario 1	Scenario 2	Scenario 3
	Single payment at maturity	Five payments of $1,000 at the end of each month	Five payments of $1,000 at the beginning of each month
Face value of the note	$ 5,000	$ 5,000	$ 5,000
Less: present value of the note	3,918	4,329	4,546
Interest component	$ 1,082	$ 671	$ 454

Note that the interest component decreases for each of the scenarios even though the total cash repaid is $5,000 in each case. This is due to the timing of the cash flows, as discussed earlier. In scenario 1, the principal is not reduced until maturity and interest would accrue for the full five years of the note. In scenario 2, the principal is being reduced at the end of each year, so the interest will decrease due to the decreasing balance owing. In scenario 3, there is an immediate reduction of principal as a result of the first payment of $1,000 made upon issuance of the note. The remaining four payments are made at the beginning of each year instead of at the end. This results in a faster reduction in the principal amount owing as compared with scenario 2.

Present Values With Unknown Variables

As is the case with any algebraic equation, if all variables except one are known, then the final unknown variable can be calculated, or derived In the case of present value calculations, if any four of the five variables in the following equation

$PV = (PMT, I/Y, N, FV)$

are known, then the fifth unknown variable amount can be determined using a financial calculator or an Excel net present value function. For example, if the interest rate (I/Y) is not known, it can be derived if all the other variables in the variables string are known. This will be illustrated when non-interest-bearing long-term notes payable are discussed later in this chapter.

Present Values: When Stated Interest Rates Are Different Than Effective (Market) Interest Rates

Differences between the stated interest, or face rate, and the effective, or market, rate at the time a note is issued can have accounting consequences as follows:

- If the stated interest rate of the note, (i.e., the interest rate that the note pays) is 10% at a time when the effective interest rate (also called the market rate or yield) is 10% for notes with similar characteristics and risk, then the note is initially recognized as:

  Face value = Fair value = Present value of the note

  This makes intuitive sense since the stated rate of 10% is equal to the market rate of 10%.

- If the stated interest rate is 10%, and the market rate is 11%, then the stated rate is lower than the market rate and the note is trading at a discount.

- If the stated interest rate is 10%, and the market rate is 9%, then the stated rate is higher than the market rate and the note is trading at a premium.

The premium or discount amount is to be amortized over the term of the note.

Below are the acceptable methods to amortize discounts or premiums:

- If a company follows IFRS, then the effective interest method of amortization is required, which we will discuss in the next section.
- If a company follows ASPE, the amortization method is not specified, so either straight-line amortization or the effective interest method is appropriate as an accounting policy choice.

Here are some examples with journal entries involving various face value, or stated rates, compared to market rates.

1. **Notes issued at face value**

    Assume that on January 1, Carpe Diem Ltd. lends $10,000 to Fascination Co. in exchange for a $10,000, three-year note, bearing interest at 10% payable annually at the end of each year (ordinary annuity). The market interest rate for a note of similar risk is also 10%. The note's present value is calculated as:

Face value of the note	$10,000
Present value of the note principal and interest:	
Payment = $10,000 × 10% = $1,000 PMT	
PV = (1000 PMT, 10 I/Y, 3 N, 10000 FV)	10,000
Difference	$ 0

    In this case, the note's face value and present value, or fair value, are the same ($10,000) because the effective, or market, and stated interest rates are the same. Fascination Co.'s entry on the date of issuance is:

General Journal				
Date	Account/Explanation	PR	Debit	Credit
Jan 1	Cash		10,000	
	Notes payable			10,000

    If Fascination Co.'s year-end was December 31, the accrued interest each year would be:

General Journal				
Date	Account/Explanation	PR	Debit	Credit
Dec 31	Interest expense		1,000	
	Interest payable			1,000
	(10,000 × 10%)			

2. **Stated rate lower than market rate – a discount**

    Assume that Anchor Ltd. makes a loan to Sizzle Corp. in exchange a $10,000, three-year note, bearing interest at 10% payable annually. The market rate of interest for a note of similar risk is 12%. Recall that the stated rate of 10% determines the amount of the cash paid for interest. However, the present value uses the effective (market) rate to discount all cash flows to determine the amount to record as the note's value at the time of issuance. The note's present value is calculated as:

Face value of the note	$10,000
Present value of the note principal and interest:	
Payment = $10,000 × 10% = $1,000 PMT	
PV = (1000 PMT, 12 I/Y, 3 N, 10000 FV)	9,520
Discount amount	$ 480

As shown above, the note's stated rate (10%) is less than the market rate (12%), so the note is issued at a discount.

Sizzle Corp.'s entry to record the issuance of the note payable would be:

General Journal				
Date	Account/Explanation	PR	Debit	Credit
Jan 1	Cash		9,520	
	Note payable			9,520

Even though the face value of the note is $10,000, the amount of money lent to Sizzle Corp. would only be $9,520. This takes into account the discount amount due to the difference between the stated and market interest rates discussed earlier. In return, Sizzle Corp. will pay to Anchor Ltd. an annual cash payment of $1,000 for three years, plus a lump sum payment of $10,000 at the end of the third year when the note matures. The total cash payments will be $13,000 over the term of the note, and the interest component of the note would be:

Cash paid	$13,000	
Present value (fair value)	9,520	
Interest component	3,480	(over the three-year term)

As mentioned earlier, if Sizzle Corp. follows IFRS, then the $480 discount amount would be amortized using the effective interest rate method. If Sizzle Corp. follows ASPE, then there would be a choice between the effective interest method and the straight-line method.

Below is a schedule that calculates the cash payments, interest expense, discount amortization, and the carrying amount (book value) of the note at the end of each year using the effective interest method:

$10,000 Note Payment and Amortization Schedule
Effective Interest Method
Stated rate of 10% and Market Rate of 12%

	Cash Paid	Interest Expense @ 12%	Amortized Discount	Carrying Amount
Date of issue				$ 9,520
End of year 1	$ 1,000	$ 1,142*	$ 142	9,662
End of year 2	1,000	1,159	159	9,821
End of year 3	1,000	1,179	179	10,000
End of year 3 final payment	10,000	-	-	0
	$ 13,000	$ 3480	$ 480	

* $9,520 × 0.12 = $1,142

Note that the total discount amortized of $480 in the schedule is equal to the discount originally calculated as the difference between the face value of the note and the present value of the note principal and interest. Also, the amortization amount calculated each year is added to the note's carrying value, thereby increasing its carrying amount until it reaches its maturity value of $10,000. As a result, the carrying amount at the end of each period is always equal to the present value of the note's remaining cash flows discounted at the 12% market rate. This is consistent with the accounting standards for the subsequent measurement of long-term notes payable at the *amortized cost*.

Assuming that Sizzle Corp.'s year-end was the same date as the note's interest paid, at the end of year 1, using the schedule above, Sizzle Corp.'s entry would be:

General Journal

Date	Account/Explanation	PR	Debit	Credit
End of year 1	Interest expense................................		1,142	
	Note payable (discount amortized amount)			142
	Cash...			1,000
	For Interest expense: (9,520 × 12%)			

Alternatively, if Sizzle Corp. followed ASPE then the straight-line method of amortizing the discount is simple to apply. The total discount of $480 is amortized over the three-year term of the note in equal amounts. The annual amortization of the discount is $160 ($480 ÷ 3 years) for each of the three years, as shown in the following entry:

General Journal

Date	Account/Explanation	PR	Debit	Credit
End of year 1	Interest expense................................		1,160	
	Note payable....................................			160
	Cash...			1,000

Comparing the three years' entries for both the effective interest and the straight-line methods, the following pattern for amortization over the life of the note payable is shown below:

	Effective Interest	Straight-Line
End of year 1	$ 142	$ 160
End of year 2	159	160
End of year 3	179	160
	$ 480	$ 480

The amortization of the discount using the effective interest method results in increasing amounts of interest expense that will be recorded in the adjusting entry (decreasing amounts of interest expense for amortizing a premium) compared to the equal amounts of interest expense using the straight-line method. The straight-line method is easier to apply but its shortcoming is that the interest rate (yield) for the note is not held constant at the 12% market rate as it is with the effective interest method. This is because the amortization of the discount is in equal amounts and does not take into consideration what the carrying amount of the note was at any given period of time. However, at the end of year 3, the notes payable balance is $10,000 for both methods, and so the same entry is recorded for the payment of the cash.

| General Journal ||||||
Date	Account/Explanation	PR	Debit	Credit
End of year 3	Note payable................................		10,000	
	Cash..			10,000

3. **Stated rate more than market rate – a premium**

   Had the note's stated rate of 10% been greater than a market rate of 9%, then the present value of $10,253 would be greater than the face value of the note due to the premium. The same types of calculations and entries as shown in the previous illustration would be used. Note that the premium amortized each year would decrease the carrying amount of the note at the end of each year until it reaches its face value amount of $10,000.

$10,000 Note Payemnt and Amortization Schedule Effective Interest Method Stated rate of 10% and Market Rate of 9%					
	Cash Paid	Interest Expense @ 9%	Amortized Premium	Carrying Amount
Date of issue				$ 10,253
End of year 1	$ 1,000	$ 923*	$ 77	10,176
End of year 2	1,000	916	84	10,092
End of year 3	1,000	908	92	10,001
End of year 3 final payment	10,000	-	-	0
	$13,000	$ 2,747	$ 253	

* $10,253 × 0.09 = $923

Sizzle Corp.'s entry on the note's issuance date is for the present value amount (fair value):

General Journal				
Date	Account/Explanation	PR	Debit	Credit
Jan 1	Cash		10,253	
	Note payable			10,253

Assuming that the company's year-end was the same date as the note's interest paid at the end of year 1, using the schedule above, the entry would be:

General Journal				
Date	Account/Explanation	PR	Debit	Credit
End of year 1	Interest expense		923	
	Note payable (premium amortized amount)..		77	
	Cash			1,000

The entry when paid at maturity would be:

General Journal				
Date	Account/Explanation	PR	Debit	Credit
End of year 3	Note payable		10,000	
	Cash			10,000

4. **Zero-interest-bearing notes**

Some companies will issue zero-interest-bearing notes as a sales incentive. While they do not state an interest rate, the term *zero-interest* is inaccurate as the notes do include an interest component that is equal to the difference between the cash lent and the higher amount of cash repaid at maturity. Even though the interest rate is not stated, the implied interest rate can be derived because the cash amounts lent and received are both known. In most cases, the transaction between the issuer and acquirer of the note is at arm's length, so the implicit interest rate would be a reasonable estimate of the market rate.

Assume that on January 1, Eclipse Corp. received a five-year, $10,000 zero-interest-bearing note from Galaxy Ltd. The amount of cash lent to Galaxy Ltd., which is equal to the present value, is $7,835 (rounded). Galaxy Ltd.'s year-end is December 31. Looking at the cash flows and the timeline:

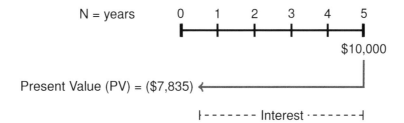

I/Y = (+/-7835 PV, 5 N, 10000 FV)
where I/Y is interest
PV is the amount of cash lent
N is # of periods
FV is the future cash received

Interest = 5% (rounded), or $2,165

Note that the sign for the $7,835 PV is preceded by the +/- symbol, meaning that the PV amount is to have the opposite symbol to the FV amount. Also, FV is the cash paid at maturity, while the PV is the amount of cash lent to the note issuer. Many financial calculators require the use of a +/- sign for one value, and no sign for the other, to correctly calculate imputed interest rates. Consult your calculator manual for further instructions regarding zero-interest note calculations.

The implied interest rate is calculated to be 5% and the note's interest component (rounded) is $2,165 ($10,000 - $7,835), which is the difference between the cash lent and the higher amount of cash repaid at maturity. Below is the schedule for the interest and amortization calculations using the effective interest rate method:

Non-Interest-Bearing Note Payment and Amortization Schedule
Effective Interest Method

	Cash Paid	Interest Income @ 5%	Amortized Discount	Carrying Amount
Date of issue				$7,835.26
End of year 1	$ 0	$ 391.76*	$ 391.76	8,227.02
End of year 2	0	411.35	411.35	8,638.37
End of year 3	0	431.92	431.92	9,070.29
End of year 4	0	453.51	453.51	9,523.80
End of year 5	0	476.20**	476.20	10,000
End of year 5 payment	$10,000	-	-	0
		$ 2,164.74	$ 2164.74	

* $7,835.26 × 0.05 = $391.76
** rounding

Galaxy Ltd.'s entry for the note payable when issued would be:

58 ■ Long-Term Financial Liabilities

General Journal				
Date	Account/Explanation	PR	Debit	Credit
Jan 1	Cash		7,835.26	
	Note payable			7,835.26

At Galaxy Ltd.'s year-end on December 31, the accrued interest at the end of the first year using the effective interest method would be:

General Journal				
Date	Account/Explanation	PR	Debit	Credit
Dec 31	Interest expense (discount amortized amount)		391.76	
	Note payable			391.76
	(7,835.26 × 5%)			

At maturity when the cash payment is made, Galaxy Ltd.'s entry would be:

General Journal				
Date	Account/Explanation	PR	Debit	Credit
End of year 5	Note payable................................		10,000	
	Cash			10,000

If Galaxy Ltd. followed ASPE instead of IFRS, then the entry using the straight-line method for amortizing the discount is calculated as the total discount of $2,164.74, amortized over the 5-year period term of the note resulting in equal amounts each year. Therefore, the annual amortization is $432.95 ($2,164.74 ÷ 5 years) each year:

General Journal				
Date	Account/Explanation	PR	Debit	Credit
End of year 1	Interest expense (discount amortized amount)		432.95	
	Note payable			432.95

5. **Notes Payable in Exchange for Property, Goods, or Services**

   When property, goods, or services are exchanged for a note, and the market rate and the timing and amounts of cash paid are all known, then the present value of the note can be determined. For example, assume that on May 1, Hudson Inc. receives a $200,000, 5-year note from Xertoc Corp. in exchange for land that originally cost $120,000. If the market rate for a note with similar characteristics and risks is 8%, the present value is calculated as follows:

   $$PV = (8 \text{ I/Y}, 5 \text{ N}, 200000 \text{ FV})$$
   $$PV = \$136,117$$

   Xertoc Corp.'s entry upon issuance of the note and purchase of the land would be:

General Journal				
Date	Account/Explanation	PR	Debit	Credit
May 1	Land...		136,117	
	Note payable			136,117

However, if the market rate is not known, either of following two approaches can be used to determine the fair value of the note:

1. **Determine the fair value of the property, goods, or services received.** As was discussed for zero-interest-bearing notes where the interest rate was not known, the implicit interest rate can still be derived because the cash amount lent and the timing and amount of the cash flows paid from the issuer are both known. In this case the amount lent is the fair value of the property, goods, or services given up. Once the interest is calculated, the effective interest method can be applied.[1]

    For example, on June 1, Mayflower Consulting Ltd. receives a $40,000, three-year note from Norfolk Ltd. in exchange for some land. The market rate cannot be accurately determined due to some credit risks regarding Norfolk Ltd. The land fair value on the transaction date is $31,750. The imputed interest rate is calculated as follows:

    $$I/Y = (+/- 31750 \text{ PV}, 3 \text{ N}, 40000 \text{ FV})$$
    $$I/Y = 8\%$$

    and the interest expense component is $8,250 over three years ($40,000 − $31,750). Norfolk Ltd.'s entry upon issuance of the note would be:

General Journal				
Date	Account/Explanation	PR	Debit	Credit
Jun 1	Land...		31,750	
	Note payable			31,750

2. **Determine an imputed interest rate**. An imputed interest rate is an estimated interest rate used for a note with comparable terms, conditions, and risks between an independent borrower and lender.

---

[1] According to IAS (2013) "IFRS 13 Fair Value Measurement applies to IFRSs that require or permit fair value measurements or disclosures and provides a single IFRS framework for measuring fair value and requires disclosures about fair value measurement. The Standard defines fair value on the basis of an 'exit price' notion and uses a 'fair value hierarchy', which results in a market-based, rather than entity-specific, measurement. IFRS 13 was originally issued in May 2011 and applies to annual periods beginning on or after 1 January 2013" (para 1). IFRS 13 is beyond the scope of this course. For simplicity, the fair value of the property, goods, or services given up, as explained in the chapter material, assumes that IFRS 13 assumptions and hierarchy to determine fair values have been appropriately considered.

On June 1, Edmunds Co. receives a $30,000, three-year note from Virginia Simms Ltd. in exchange for some swamp land. The land has a historic cost of $5,000 but neither the market rate nor the fair value of the land can be determined.

In this case, a risk-adjusted rate of return must be determined and then used to determine the note's present value (fair value). For companies that follow IFRS, the fair value hierarchy identified in IFRS 13 Fair Value Measurement would be used to determine the appropriate risk adjusted rate of return and the subsequent fair value of the land. In the absence of a directly comparable market, level 2 or level 3 inputs are used. This can include present value calculations based on expected future cash flows. In this case, the future cash flow is the $30,000 note payment. The discount rate should be determined based on the risk-free rate of return, adjusted for the risk factors of the transaction. Alternately, use risk-adjusted cash flows, discounted at the risk free rate. The calculated PV then becomes the fair value used. In this case, the risk free rate of return adjusted for the risk factors for this transaction is determined to be 7%. The present value is calculated as follows:

$$PV = (7 \text{ I/Y}, 3 \text{ N}, 30000 \text{ FV})$$
$$PV = \$24,489$$

Virginia Simms Ltd.'s entry upon issuance of the note would be:

General Journal				
Date	Account/Explanation	PR	Debit	Credit
Jun 1	Land..		24,489	
	Note payable			24,489

13.2.2 Subsequent Measurements and Derecognition

As previously discussed, under ASPE and IFRS, long-term notes payable that are held by debtors are subsequently accounted for at amortized cost, which is calculated as:

- present value of the cash flows, including commissions or fees if any

- +/- reductions in principal or for any adjustments for amortization of the discount or premium

- derecognition of the debt through retirement or settlement. All premiums or discounts will be fully amortized by the maturity date. The carrying amount at maturity will be the same as the note's face value so there will be no gain or loss at maturity unless the debt is settled early.

Impairment

If a debtor runs into financial difficulties and is unable to pay, or fully repay, the note, then the estimated impaired cash flows become an important reporting disclosure for the lender. If the lender can reasonably estimate the impaired cash flows then an entry is made to record the debt impairment. The impairment amount is calculated as the difference between the carrying value at amortized cost and the present value of the estimated impaired cash flows.

For example, on January 1, 2016, Empire Construction Ltd. signed a $200,000, four-year, non-interest-bearing note payable with Second National Bank. The required yield for the bank was 8%. During 2018, Empire Construction Ltd. experienced some serious financial difficulties. Based on the information provided by Empire Construction Ltd. management, the bank estimated that it was probable that it would receive only 75% of the 2018 balance at maturity. Additionally, the current market rate of interest in 2018 is 7%.

Below are the effective interest schedule and entries for Second National Bank:

Second National Bank
Note with Empire Construction Ltd.
Effective Interest Rate Schedule
8% year, non-interest-bearing note, due Jan 1, 2020

	Payment	Interest @ 8%	Carrying Value	
Jan 1, 2016			$ 147,006	
Jan 1, 2017	0	$11,760	158,766	
Jan 1, 2018	0	12,701	171,468	← Impairment date
Jan 1, 2019	0	13,717	185,185	
Jan 1, 2020	0	14,815	200,000	

For the lender, the entries for 2016 and 2017 would be:

	General Journal			
Date	Account/Explanation	PR	Debit	Credit
Jan 1, 2016	Note receivable		147,006	
	Cash			147,006
	PV = (8 I/Y, 4N, 200,000 FV) = 147,006			
Jan 1, 2017	Note receivable		11,760	
	Interest income			11,760

The interest schedule and amounts entered would be the same for Empire Construction Ltd. who would record the entries to interest expense and to notes payable as a long-term liability. In 2018, the impairment would be calculated and recorded by the lender as calculated and shown below:

Note receivable balance as at January 1, 2018 $171,468
Present value of impaired cash flows:
(At the original required yield of 8%)
PV = (8 I/Y, (4 − 2) N, 128,601 FV*)   110,255
Impairment loss $ 61,213

* $171,468 × 75% probability = $128,601

\multicolumn{6}{c}{General Journal}
Date	Account/Explanation		PR	Debit	Credit
2018	Bad debt expense............................			61,213	
	Allowance for doubtful accounts...........				61,213
	(AFDA is contra to the note receivable.)				

Empire Construction Ltd. (debtor) makes no entry since it still legally owes the debt amount, unless the impairment results in a troubled debt restructuring, which is discussed next.

Troubled Debt Restructurings

A troubled debt restructuring occurs if a lender grants concessions such as a reduced interest rate, an extended maturity date, or a reduction in the debts' face amount. These can take the form of a settlement of the debt or a modification of the debt's terms.

1. **Settlement of Debt**

    This occurs when the debt is derecognized and all amounts relating to the debt, and any unamortized discounts or premiums, are removed from the debtor's accounts. A gain by the debtor is usually recorded, since the creditor grants a concession when there is a troubled debt restructuring. The creditor will also remove the debt from the accounts and will record a loss.

    The debtor will settle the account by transferring assets such as property, plant, or equipment that may have been used to secure the note (a loan foreclosure), by issuing shares, or using the cash proceeds received for a new debt obtained from a new creditor.

    To illustrate, continuing with the example of Empire Construction Ltd.'s note with Second National Bank, assume that by January 1, 2019, financial troubles have continued to plague Empire Construction Ltd. to the point where it could no longer pay the loan when it matured the following year. On January 1, 2019, Second National Bank agrees to accept a building with a fair value of $160,000 from Empire Construction Ltd. in full settlement of the note. The building had an original cost of $185,000 and accumulated depreciation of $5,000. The bank's (creditor) entry for the settlement is recorded below:

General Journal				
Date	Account/Explanation	PR	Debit	Credit
Jan 1, 2019	Building...		160,000	
	Allowance for doubtful accounts.............		61,213	
	Gain on impairment.......................			40,925
	Note receivable...........................			180,288
	Note receivable (Jan 1, 2019 carrying value): $171,468 + ($110,255 \times 8\%)$			

The fair value of the building is the valuation used to record the asset. The note receivable and related doubtful account is derecognized, or removed, from the accounts, and a further gain of $40,925 is recorded. If the bank had not previously used an allowance account, then the loss on impairment would be $20,288 ($61,213 − 40,925). At this point, the bank has fully recovered the loan and made a net profit of $12,994: $11,760 + 12,701 + 8,821 = $33,282 interest − $61,213 impairment loss + $40,925 impairment gain. If the note had originally been secured by the building, then the bank could have applied to the courts to legally seize ownership of the building to satisfy the loan obligation.

The debtor's entries are shown below:

General Journal				
Date	Account/Explanation	PR	Debit	Credit
Jan 1, 2019	Accumulated depreciation.....................		5,000	
	Loss on sale of building*.....................		20,000	
	Note payable.................................		185,185	
	Building			185,000
	Gain on restructuring of debt..............			25,185
	*(fair value minus carrying value) (160,000 − (185,000 − 5,000))			

Note that there is a separate asset loss recorded of $20,000, as well as a gain recorded of $25,185, which is required for the restructuring of the note.

Had Second National Bank agreed to accept Empire Construction Ltd.'s shares, with a market value of $160,000 in full settlement of the note, then the entry would have been similar:

General Journal				
Date	Account/Explanation	PR	Debit	Credit
2019	Investment in shares − HFT..................		160,000	
	Allowance for doubtful accounts.............		61,213	
	Gain on impairment.......................			40,925
	Note receivable...........................			180,288

The entry for Empire Construction Ltd. would be:

General Journal				
Date	Account/Explanation	PR	Debit	Credit
2019	Note payable.................................		185,185	
	Common shares...........................			160,000
	Gain on restructuring of debt.............			25,185

2. **Modification of Terms**

    If the creditor grants concessions such as a reduced interest rate, an extended maturity date, a reduction in the debt's face amount, or accrued interest, then there is a 10% threshold that is used to determine if the concession is minor or substantial.

3. **Modification of Terms Less Than 10%**

    If the present value of the new terms, using the historic interest rate for consistency and comparability, is less than 10% different from the present value of the remaining cash flows of the old debt, then it is considered a modification of terms. The old debt amount remains but is restated using the new terms. In addition, a new effective interest rate is determined as the rate that equates the old debt with the revised cash flows resulting from the concessions made, such as the changed interest rate, due date, and face value. No gain from restructuring of the debt is recorded by the debtor.

    For example, on January 1, 2016, Lehry Ltd. owed $50,000, with interest payments to be made annually to Freeman Financial Trust. However, it ran into financial difficulties before any payments were made. On January 1, 2016, Freeman Financial Trust agrees to make the following concessions:

    - Reduce the interest rate from 5% to 4%, with annual payments remaining at $2,500.
    - Extend the due date from January 1, 2016, to January 1, 2019.
    - Reduce the face value from $50,000 to $45,000.

    Applying the 10% threshold to the present value calculations:

    Carrying value of old debt, due January 1, 2016 (present value) $50,000
    The present value, using the historic rate of 5% for the new terms:
    PV = (2,500 PMT, 5%, 3 N, 45,000 FV) = $45,681
    Concession amount $ 4,319

    The present value of $45,681 has a concession amount of $4,319, which is less than the 10% of the present value of the old debt of $50,000 that is now due. As a result, the concession is treated as a modification of terms. The old debt remains as the carrying value of the note but with a new effective interest rate and reduced face value of $45,000 at maturity. The new effective interest rate is calculated the same way as was done for a non-interest-bearing note where the present value, payment amount, number of years, and future value are known:

I/Y = (+/- 50,000 PV, 2,500 PMT, 3 N, 45,000 FV) = 1.72 % (rounded)

The new effective interest rate schedule is shown below:

	Payment	Interest @ 1.72%	Amortization	Balance
Jan 1, 2016				$50,000
Jan 1, 2017	$2,500	$860	$1,640	48,360
Jan 1, 2018	2,500	832	1,668	46,692
Jan 1, 2019	2,500	808*	1,692	45,000

*rounded

Assuming a year-end date of December 31, Lehry Ltd. would make the following adjusting entry:

	General Journal			
Date	Account/Explanation	PR	Debit	Credit
Dec 31, 2016	Interest expense.............................		860	
	Notes payable................................		1,640	
	Cash...			2,500

At maturity, Lehry Ltd. would make the following entry to settle and derecognize the note:

	General Journal			
Date	Account/Explanation	PR	Debit	Credit
Jan 1, 2019	Notes payable................................		45,000	
	Cash...			45,000

Freeman Financial Trust would account for the restructuring of the note as an impairment, which was discussed in the previous section of this chapter.

4. **Modification of Terms Greater Than 10%**

    Modifications to a debt would be considered substantial if either of the following conditions is present:

    - The present value of the new terms (using the historic interest rate) is more than 10% different than the present value of the remaining cash flows of the old debt.
    - There is a change in creditor and the original debt is legally discharged (CPA Canada, 2016, Part II, Section 3856.A52 and IAS 39.40/AG62).

    If either condition exists, then the modification is substantial and will be considered a settlement of the old debt, and a new debt with the new terms is assumed.

    Going back to the Lehry Ltd. example, on January 1, 2016, Lehry Ltd. owed $50,000 to Freeman Financial Trust but has run into financial difficulties. On January 1, 2016, Freeman Financial Trust agrees to make the following concessions:

- Reduce the interest rate from 5% to 3%. Payments are to remain at $2,500.
- Extend the due date from January 1, 2016, to January 1, 2018.
- Reduce the face value from $50,000 to $40,000.

Applying the 10% threshold to the present value calculations:

Carrying value of old debt, due January 1, 2016 (present value)	$50,000
The present value, using the historic rate of 5% for the new terms:	
PV = (2,500 PMT, 5%, 2 N, 40,000 FV) =	$40,930
Concession amount	$ 9,070

The present value of $40,930 has a concession amount of $9,070, which is more than the 10% of the present value of the old debt of $50,000, which is now due. As a result, the concession is treated as a substantial modification of terms. The old debt is settled, a gain is recorded by the debtor, and a new debt with the new terms is recorded as shown in the following entry:

	General Journal			
Date	Account/Explanation	PR	Debit	Credit
Jan 1, 2016	Note payable...............................		50,000	
	Notes payable			42,488
	Gain on restructuring of debt............			7,512

The present value of the new debt is calculated as follows:

PV = (2,500 PMT, 3 I/Y, 2 N, 40,000 FV) = $42,488

Freeman Financial Trust would account for the restructuring of the note as an impairment, a term previously discussed in this chapter, except that no allowance account would be used since this modification is considered to be a settlement and not simply an adjustment.

	General Journal			
Date	Account/Explanation	PR	Debit	Credit
Jan 1, 2016	Bad debt expense..........................		9,070	
	Note receivable..........................			9,070

13.3 Bonds Payable

When the amount to be borrowed is significant, bonds can provide a source of cash that is compiled from many investors. The process to issue bonds is initiated by a bond indenture that contains details such as the denomination or face value of the bonds, the annual interest rate and payment dates (usually twice per year), and the face amount payable at maturity. Each bond is issued as a certificate with a specific denomination or face value, and bonds are usually issued in multiples of $100 or $1,000.

Many bond issuances are sold to an underwriter or broker who acts as the seller in the marketplace. Brokers can buy the entire issue and resell, thereby assuming all the risks in the marketplace, or they can sell on behalf of the issuing company on a commission basis. Each bond issuance has a credit rating assigned to it by independent rating agencies such as Standard & Poor's Corporation. The ratings indicate the degree of riskiness assigned to the issue. Essentially, the higher the rating (AAA or investment-grade bonds), the more access the company has to investors' capital at a reasonable interest rate. Conversely, the lower the rating (CCC/C or junk bonds), the higher the risk and interest rate to be paid. Since the rating assigned is a function of company performance, this rating can change over the lifespan of the bond issue. Companies will take great care to preserve their high ratings.

Types of Bonds

There are many types of bonds with different features for sale in the marketplace. Some of the more common ones are listed below:

1. **Registered bonds**: Each bond is registered in the investor's name. If the bond is sold, then the certificate is cancelled and a new one is issued.

2. **Coupon or bearer bonds**: The bond is not registered in the investor's name, so whoever holds the bond will receive the interest and face value at maturity.

3. **Term or serial bonds**: Bonds that mature on a single date are term bonds, while those that mature in instalments are serial bonds.

4. **Secured and unsecured bonds**: Secured bonds have security or collateral that was assigned to the issue. For example, mortgage bonds are secured by claims against real estate. If the issuer defaults on payments, the security can be seized through a court order and used to satisfy the amounts owed to the bondholders. Debentures are bonds that are not secured and are often issued by school boards and municipalities.

5. **Callable or convertible bonds**: Callable bonds give the issuer the right to call and retire the bonds before maturity. Convertible bonds allow the holder to convert the bonds into capital such as the common shares in the company. Convertible debt gives rise to some interesting accounting challenges in terms of the embedded debt and equity characteristics for these types of securities. Convertible debt will be discussed in detail in Chapter 14.

13.3.1 Initial and Subsequent Measurement, at Par, at a Discount, and at a Premium

As with notes payable, bonds are initially recognized at their fair value at the time of issuance, which is measured at the present value of their future cash flows. They are subsequently measured at amortized cost. Transaction fees for bonds measured at amortized cost are to be *capitalized*, meaning that the costs will reduce the bond payable amount and be amortized over the life of the bond.

Classification

Bonds are issued as a long-term debt security, which matures in several years, and are classified as long-term payables on the SFP/BS. When a bond issue's maturity date occurs within the next 12 months of the reporting date, or within the business's operating cycle if greater than 12 months, it is classified as a short-term bond payable.

You are encouraged to review the section on time value of money, presented earlier in this chapter, which discussed the present value learning concept.

Bonds Issued at Par

This bond issue is the simplest to account for. If bonds are issued at their face value on their interest payable date with no transaction fees, then the cash proceeds received from the investors will be the initial measurement amount recorded for the bond issue. The interest expense is recorded in the same amount as the cash interest paid, at the face or stated rate, and there is no accrued interest. This means that the effective interest rate (market rate) and the stated rate (face rate) are the same. At maturity, the amount paid to the bondholders is the face value (or par value) amount, which is also the fair value on that date.

To illustrate, on May 1, 2016, Engels Ltd. issued 10-year, 8%, $500,000 par value bonds with interest payable each year on May 1 and November 1. The market rate at the time of issuance is 8% and the company year-end is December 31.

To record the bond issuance on May 1:

General Journal				
Date	Account/Explanation	PR	Debit	Credit
May 1, 2016	Cash		500,000	
	Bond payable.............................			500,000

To record the interest payment on November 1:

	General Journal			
Date	Account/Explanation	PR	Debit	Credit
Nov 1, 2016	Interest expense............................		20,000	
	Cash..			20,000
	(500,000 × 8% × 6 ÷ 12)			

To record the accrued interest on December 31 year-end:

	General Journal			
Date	Account/Explanation	PR	Debit	Credit
Dec 31, 2016	Interest expense............................		6,667	
	Interest payable............................			6,667
	(500,000 × 8% × 2 ÷ 12)			

To record the interest payment on May 1, 2017:

	General Journal			
Date	Account/Explanation	PR	Debit	Credit
May 1, 2017	Interest expense............................		13,333	
	Interest payable............................		6,667	
	Cash..			20,000
	For Interest expense: (500,000 × 8% × 4 ÷ 12)			

Note how the interest payable for the accrued interest recorded at year-end is reversed at the first interest payment the following year, on May 1, 2017.

At maturity, the May 1, 2026, entry would be:

	General Journal			
Date	Account/Explanation	PR	Debit	Credit
May 1, 2026	Bond payable................................		500,000	
	Cash..			500,000

Bonds Issued at a Discount

As explained earlier in this chapter in regards to notes payable, the market rate (effective rate or yield) is not always the same as the stated or face rate. When these two interest rates are different, each one is used to determine certain cash flows required to calculate the present value. The stated or face rate determines the interest payment amount (PMT), while the market or effective rate is used to determine the present value of the bond issuance (I/Y).

To illustrate, on May 1, 2016, Engels Ltd. issued a 10-year, 8%, $500,000 face value bond with interest payable each year on May 1 and November 1. The market rate at the time of issuance is 9% and the company year-end is December 31. In this case the stated rate of 8% is less than the market rate of 9%. This means that the bond issuance is trading at a discount and the fair value, or its present value of the future cash flows, will be less than the face value upon issuance. The present value is calculated as:

20,000	PMT	(where semi-annual interest using the stated or face rate is $500,000 × 8% × 6 ÷ 12)
4.5	I/Y	(where 9% market or effective interest is paid twice per year)
20	N	(where interest is paid twice per year for 10 years)
500,000	FV	(where a single payment of the face value is due in a future year 2026);

Expressed in the following variables string, and using a financial calculator, the present value is calculated:

Present value (PV) = (20,000 PMT, 4.5 I/Y, 20 N, 500,000 FV) = $467,480

	General Journal			
Date	Account/Explanation	PR	Debit	Credit
May 1, 2016	Cash		467,480	
	Bond payable........................			467,480

The stated rate of 8% is less than the market rate of 9%, resulting in a present value less than the face amount of $500,000. This bond issuance is trading at a discount. Since the market rate is greater, the investor would not be willing to purchase bonds paying less interest at the face value. The bond issuer must, therefore, sell these at a discount in order to entice investors to purchase them. The investor pays the reduced price of $467,480. For the seller, the discount amount of $32,520 ($500,000 − 467,480) is then amortized over the life of the bond issuance using one of two possible methods, the same as was explained for long-term notes payable earlier in this chapter. IFRS companies are to amortize discounts and premiums using the effective interest rate method, and ASPE companies can choose between the simpler straight-line method and the effective interest rate method. The total interest expense for either method will be the same.

Assuming the effective interest rate method is used for the example, the interest schedule for the bond issuance is shown below:

	Payment	Interest @ 4.5%	Amortization	Balance
May 1, 2016				467,480
Nov 1, 2016	20,000	21,037	1,037	468,517
May 1, 2017	20,000	21,083	1,083	469,600
Nov 1, 2017	20,000	21,132	1,132	470,732
May 1, 2018	20,000	21,183	1,183	471,915
Nov 1, 2018	20,000	21,236	1,236	473,151
May 1, 2019	20,000	21,292	1,292	474,443
Nov 1, 2019	20,000	21,350	1,350	475,793
May 1, 2020	20,000	21,411	1,411	477,203
Nov 1, 2020	20,000	21,474	1,474	478,677
May 1, 2021	20,000	21,540	1,540	480,218
Nov 1, 2021	20,000	21,610	1,610	481,828
May 1, 2022	20,000	21,682	1,682	483,510
Nov 1, 2022	20,000	21,758	1,758	485,268
May 1, 2023	20,000	21,837	1,837	487,105
Nov 1, 2023	20,000	21,920	1,920	489,025
May 1, 2024	20,000	22,006	2,006	491,031
Nov 1, 2024	20,000	22,096	2,096	493,127
May 1, 2025	20,000	22,191	2,191	495,318
Nov 1, 2025	20,000	22,289	2,289	497,607
May 1, 2026	20,000	22,392	2,392	500,000

Year-end accrued interest is May 1 interest for 2 months:
$21{,}083 \times 2 \div 6 = 7{,}028$
$1{,}083 \times 2 \div 6 = 361$

The effective interest rate method ensures that a consistent interest rate is applied throughout the life of the bonds. Straight-line amortization results in varying interest rates throughout the life of the bonds because of the equal amount of the discount applied at each interest payment date.

Using the information from the schedule, the entries are completed below.

To record the interest payment on November 1:

	General Journal			
Date	Account/Explanation	PR	Debit	Credit
Nov 1, 2016	Interest expense............................		21,037	
	Bond payable............................			1,037
	Cash...................................			20,000
	For Interest expense: (467,480 × 4.5%)			

Recording the accrued interest at the December 31 year-end can be tricky, so preparing the relevant portion of an effective interest schedule will be useful:

72 ■ Long-Term Financial Liabilities

	General Journal			
Date	Account/Explanation	PR	Debit	Credit
Dec 31, 2016	Interest expense............................		7,028	
	Bond payable............................			361
	Interest payable.........................			6,667
	For Interest expense: (21,083 × 2 ÷ 6),			
	For Bond payable: (1,083 × 2 ÷ 6)			

To record the interest payment on May 1, 2017:

	General Journal			
Date	Account/Explanation	PR	Debit	Credit
May 1, 2017	Interest expense............................		14,055	
	Interest payable............................		6,667	
	Bond payable............................			722
	Cash......................................			20,000
	For Interest expense: (21,083 − 7,028)			
	For Bond payable: (1,083 − 361)			

Again, note how the interest payable for accrued interest recorded at year-end is reversed at the first interest payment the following year, on May 1, 2017.

To record the interest payment on November 1, 2017:

	General Journal			
Date	Account/Explanation	PR	Debit	Credit
May 1, 2017	Interest expense............................		21,132	
	Bond payable............................			1,132
	Cash......................................			20,000

At maturity, the May 1, 2026, entry would be:

	General Journal			
Date	Account/Explanation	PR	Debit	Credit
May 1, 2026	Bond payable...............................		500,000	
	Cash......................................			500,000

Bonds – Straight-Line Method

Companies that follow ASPE can choose to use the simpler straight-line interest method. The discount of $32,520 ($500,000 − 467,480) would be amortized on a straight-line basis over the 10 years. The interest was paid on a semi-annual basis in the illustration above, so the amortization of the discount would be $1,626 ($32,520 ÷ 20) on each interest payment date over the 10-year life of the bonds.

The November 1, interest entry would be:

Date	Account/Explanation	PR	Debit	Credit
Nov 1, 2016	Interest expense..............................		21,626	
	Bond payable.............................			1,626
	Cash.......................................			20,000

As stated previously, the interest expense will no longer be a constant rate over the life of the note but the ASPE standard recognizes that privately-held companies will want to apply a simpler method since ownership is usually limited to a small group of shareholders and the shares are not publically traded.

Bonds Issued in Between Interest Payments

If investors purchase bonds on dates falling in between the interest payment dates, then the investor pays an additional interest amount. This is because the bond issuer always pays the full six months interest to the bondholder on the interest payment date because it is the easiest way to administer multiple interest payments to potentially thousands of investors. For example, if an investor purchases a bond four months after the last interest payment, then the issuer will add these additional four months of interest to the purchase price. When the next interest payment date occurs, the issuer pays the full six months interest to the purchaser. The interest amount paid and received by the bond-holder will net to two months. This makes intuitive sense given that the bonds have only been held for two months making interest for two months the correct amount.

For example, on September 1, 2016, an investor purchases $100,000, 10-year, 8% bonds, at par, with interest payable each May 1 and November 1. The market price at the time of issuance was 97. The company year-end is December 31 and it follows ASPE. The amount paid by the investor on September 1, 2016, would be:

Bond face value at market price (100,000 × 0.97)	$97,000
Accrued interest (100,000 × 8% × 4 ÷ 12)	2,667
Total cash paid	$99,667

When the bond issuer pays the full month's interest of $4,000 (100,000 × 8% × 6 ÷ 12), the net interest received by the bondholder will be $1,333 for two months (100,000 × 8% × 2 ÷ 12). Assuming the straight-line (SL) interest rate method is used for the example, a partial interest schedule for the bond issuance is shown below:

	Payment	Interest Expense	Amortization	Balance
May 1, 2016				97,000
Nov 1, 2016	4,000	4,150	150	97,150
May 1, 2017	4,000	4,150	150	97,300
Nov 1, 2017	4,000	4,150	150	97,450

* (discount at SL: 3,000 ÷ 20 = $150 each interest payment date)

To record the bond issuance on September 1:

	General Journal			
Date	Account/Explanation	PR	Debit	Credit
Sep 1, 2016	Cash.............................		99,667	
	Bond payable......................			97,000
	Interest expense..................			2,667

To record the interest payment on November 1:

	General Journal			
Date	Account/Explanation	PR	Debit	Credit
Nov 1, 2016	Interest expense..................		4,150	
	Bond payable......................			150
	Cash..............................			4,000

The December 31 year-end accrued interest entry:

	General Journal			
Date	Account/Explanation	PR	Debit	Credit
Dec 31, 2016	Interest expense..................		1,384	
	Bond payable......................			50
	Interest payable..................			1,334
	For Interest expense: (4,150 × 2 ÷ 6)			
	For Bond payable: (150 × 2 ÷ 6)			
	For Interest payable: (4,000 × 2 ÷ 6)			

To record the interest payment on May 1, 2017:

	General Journal			
Date	Account/Explanation	PR	Debit	Credit
May 1, 2017	Interest expense..................		2,766	
	Interest payable..................		1,334	
	Bond payable......................			100
	Cash..............................			4,000
	For Interest expense: (4,150 − 1,384)			
	For Bond payable (150 − 50)			

To record the interest payment on November 1, 2017:

General Journal				
Date	Account/Explanation	PR	Debit	Credit
May 1, 2017	Interest expense............................		4,150	
	Bond payable............................			150
	Cash.....................................			4,000

At maturity, the May 1, 2026, entry would be:

General Journal				
Date	Account/Explanation	PR	Debit	Credit
May 1, 2026	Bond payable...............................		100,000	
	Cash.....................................			100,000

Bonds Issued at a Premium

If the stated rate is more than the market rate, then the bond trades at a premium. This is because investors are seeking the best interest rate for their investment. If the stated rate is higher, then the bond issuance is more desirable and the investors would be willing to pay more for this investment than for another with a lower stated rate. The accounting for bonds purchased at a premium follows the same method as was illustrated for bonds at a discount. The illustration will be changed slightly to introduce the use of the market spot rate.

To illustrate, on May 1, 2016, Impala Ltd. issued a 10-year, 8%, $500,000 face value bond at a spot rate of 102 (2% above par). Interest is payable each year on May 1 and November 1. The company year-end is December 31 and follows IFRS.

The spot rate is 102, so the amount to be paid is $510,000 (500,000 × 102) and, therefore, represents the fair value or present value of the bond issuance on the purchase date.

The entry for the bond issuance is:

General Journal				
Date	Account/Explanation	PR	Debit	Credit
May 1, 2016	Cash...		510,000	
	Bond payable............................			510,000

However, what effective interest rate would be required to result in a present value of $510,000, a future value of $500,000 payable in 10 years, and a stated or face rate of 8% interest payable semi-annually? As was explained for the long-term notes payable earlier in this chapter, since all the other variables are known, and only the interest rate (I/Y) is unknown, it can be imputed as shown below:

Effective interest rate (I/Y) = (+/- 510,000 PV, 20,000 PMT, 20 N, 500,000 FV)
= 3.8547% semi-annual interest rate or 7.71% per annum

To prove that the 3.85% is the correct semi-annual effective interest rate, the present value is calculated as follows:

20,000 PMT (where semi-annual interest using the stated or face rate is $500,000 × 8% × 6 ÷ 12)
3.8547 I/Y (where market or effective interest is paid twice per year)
20 N (where interest is paid twice a year for 10 years)
500,000 FV (where a single payment of the face value is due in a future year 2026);

Expressed in the following variables string and using a financial calculator, the present value is calculated as follows:

Present value (PV) = (20,000 PMT, 3.8547 I/Y, 20 N, 500,000 FV) = $510,000 (rounded)

	Payment	Interest @ 3.8547%	Amortization	Balance
May 1/16				510,000
Nov 1/16	20,000	19,659	341	509,659
May 1/17	20,000	19,646	354	509,305
Nov 1/17	20,000	19,632	368	508,937

Year-end accrued interest is May 1 interest for 2 months:
19,646 × 2 ÷ 6 = 6,549
354 × 2 ÷ 6 = 118

Using the information from the schedule, the entries are completed below.

To record the interest payment on November 1:

Date	Account/Explanation	PR	Debit	Credit
Nov 1, 2016	Interest expense.............................		19,659	
	Bond payable.................................		341	
	Cash...			20,000

Recording the accrued interest at the December 31 year-end can be tricky, so preparing the relevant portion of an effective interest schedule will be useful:

Date	Account/Explanation	PR	Debit	Credit
Dec 31, 2016	Interest expense.............................		6,549	
	Bond payable.................................		118	
	Interest payable.............................			6,667
	For Interest expense: (19,646 × 2 ÷ 6)			
	For Bond payable: (354 × 2 ÷ 6)			

To record the interest payment on May 1, 2017:

General Journal				
Date	Account/Explanation	PR	Debit	Credit
May 1, 2017	Interest expense............................		13,097	
	Interest payable............................		6,667	
	Bond payable...............................		236	
	Cash......................................			20,000
	For Interest expense: (19,646 − 6,549)			
	For Bond payable: (354 − 118)			

To record the interest payment on November 1, 2017:

General Journal				
Date	Account/Explanation	PR	Debit	Credit
Nov 1, 2017	Interest expense............................		19,632	
	Bond payable...............................		368	
	Cash......................................			20,000

At maturity, the May 1, 2026, entry would be:

General Journal				
Date	Account/Explanation	PR	Debit	Credit
May 1, 2026	Bond payable...............................		500,000	
	Cash......................................			500,000

13.3.2 Repayment Before Maturity Date

In some cases, a company may want to repay a bond issue before its maturity. Examples of such bonds are **callable bonds**, which give the issuer the right to call and retire the bonds before maturity. For example, if market interest rates drop, the issuer will want to take advantage of the lower interest rate. In this case, the reacquisition price paid to extinguish and derecognize the bond issuance will likely be slightly higher than the bond carrying value on that date, and the difference will be recorded by the issuing corporation as a loss on redemption. The company can, then, sell a new bond issuance at the new, lower interest rate.

For example, on January 1, 2016, Angen Ltd. issued bonds with a par value of $500,000 at 99, due in 2026. On January 1, 2020, the entire issue was called at 101 and cancelled. Interest is paid annually and the discount amortized using the straight-line method. The carrying value of the bond on January 1, 2020, would be calculated as follows:

Face value of bond	$500,000
Unamortized discount:	
10 years − 4 years = 6 years	
500,000 × (1 − 0.99) = 5,000 × 6 ÷ 10	(3,000)
Carrying value on call date	$497,000
Re-acquisition price: $500,000 X 101	505,000
Loss on redemption	$ 8,000

Angen Ltd. would make the following entry:

General Journal				
Date	Account/Explanation	PR	Debit	Credit
May 1, 2017	Bonds payable.................................		497,000	
	Loss on redemption of bonds		8,000	
	Cash..			505,000

13.4 Fair Value Option, Defeasance, and Off-Balance Sheet Financing

Notes and Bonds – the Fair Value Option

Long-term debt is usually measured at amortized cost; however there is an alternative called the fair-value option that ASPE allows for all types of financial instruments. If a company chooses to use the fair-value option, then the debt instruments are continually remeasured to their fair value. In the case of IFRS, the fair-value option can be used if it results in more relevant information.

As discussed earlier in this chapter, the higher the credit or solvency risk, the lower the grade assigned by the independent rating agencies. Furthermore, the grade assigned can change for better or for worse, depending on the performance of the company over the life of the debt instrument. In cases where the grade deteriorates because of increasing credit or solvency risk, the effective interest rate must also increase to compensate for the higher risk–causing the fair value of the bond instrument to decrease. A decrease in fair value creates a gain on the credit side of the entry, as shown below:

General Journal				
Date	Account/Explanation	PR	Debit	Credit
	Bond or note payable		xxx	
	Unrealized gain on revaluation (net income)			xxx
	To reduce the payable amount to the lower fair value.			

Reporting a gain in net income at times when credit risk is increasing seems counterintuitive to what one would normally expect when a company's performance is weakening. This is the case, however, for both mandatory ASPE and IFRS standards at the time of writing. However, when IFRS 9 comes into effect on January 1, 2018, any subsequent gain of this nature will be recorded and reported through other comprehensive income (OCI), which will bypass the income statement.

Notes and Bonds – Defeasance and Off-Balance Sheet Financing

Defeasance

If a company wishes to pay off a debt before its maturity date, problems can arise if the debt agreement stipulates early repayment penalties. One way around this issue is for the debtor to deposit sufficient funds into a separate trust account that will generate returns enough to cover the payments owed to the creditor, as outlined in the original agreement. This is called defeasance, and it can be executed in one of two ways. First, as legal defeasance, where the creditor agrees to change the debt obligation from the debtor to the trust. Second, informally as in-substance defeasance, in which case both ASPE and IFRS do not allow the original debt to be derecognized as the company still legally owes the debt.

Off-Balance Sheet and Other Sources of Financing

Company performance is in part measured by its liquidity and solvency position. For this reason, companies are motivated to keep debt off the books. Below are various sources of financing that do not require recording a debt obligation.

- **Operating leases:** Companies can avoid reporting a lease obligation if a lease agreement is written in such a way as to not meet the lease capitalization criteria required by ASPE and IFRS. The lease payments are then recorded as rental expenses in exchange for the use of the asset being leased (leases will be discussed further in a later chapter).

- **Selling receivables and investments:** Companies can obtain funding by selling receivables and other investments to special purpose entities (SPE) in exchange for cash rather than incurring debt. This is known as securitization and is discussed in more detail in the cash and receivables chapter from the previous intermediate accounting text.

- **Parental control of another company:** Companies can obtain access to another company's funds through mergers and acquisitions. Additionally, ASPE gives investee companies the choice to report their investments in other companies using either the equity method or cost, even if control exists. If control in another company is reported only as a single line item asset called "investment" on the SFP/BS, this will obscure any potential significant debt that the investee company may have on their books, which the investor parent company may ultimately be responsible for. Investments are discussed further in the Intercorporate Investments chapter from the previous intermediate accounting text.

It is important to note that adequate disclosures of these arrangements are important for financial statement users.

13.5 Disclosures of Long-Term Debt

Long-term debt that matures within one year is usually reported as a current liability. Similarly, any principal portion of long-term debt due within one year of the reporting date is also to be reported as a current liability. In the absence of a refinancing agreement, any long-term debt that is refinanced is to be reported as a current liability as well. For ASPE, in order to report a long-term debt that is to be refinanced as a long-term debt, the refinancing agreement must be in place prior to the release of the financial statements. Whereas for IFRS, it must be in place prior to the reporting date of the financial statements.

Basic debt disclosures usually include:

- maturity date
- interest rate
- amounts due in each of the next five years
- assets pledged as security
- restrictions by creditors (restrictive covenants)
- call provisions
- conversion details
- information regarding liquidity and solvency risks of the company

Note that the reporting disclosures listed above have been simplified, as the disclosures required by IFRS are, in fact, quite extensive. The disclosures for ASPE are also quite robust but are slightly less extensive than for IFRS.[2]

---

[2] CPA Canada (2016) Part II, Section 3856 and IFRS 7 detail the full disclosure requirements.

13.6 Long-Term Debt Analysis

The chapter on cash and receivables emphasized the importance of maintaining an adequate cash flow and an efficient inventory-to-cash cycle. When debt is incurred, companies are always mindful that the debt, including interest, must be repaid, thereby drawing down on cash flows. For this reason, various liquidity and solvency ratios are constantly monitored by management and investors to ensure company performance is optimal and access to debt financing continue at reasonable interest rates.

Debt can be seen as part of a continuum. Too little debt could mean that companies are not taking advantage of leverage (also known as **gearing**). Too much debt can cause severe shortages in the cash needed to service the debt (pay the interest and principal amounts owing in a timely manner) if it is incurred at a greater rate than the inventory-to-cash cycle can generate cash. Companies in this position can only access additional financial markets at much higher interest rates and are subject to increasingly restrictive debt covenants imposed and monitored by the creditor. Important ratios used in the monitoring process and for restrictive covenants regarding long-term debt include:

- **Debt to equity:** Measures the company's share of debt compared to equity.

    Total debt ÷ Total equity × 100%

    Note: There are also variations of this ratio that only consider long-term debt amounts for the numerator. This occurs when the creditor is concerned with the long-term financial structure of the company.

- **Debt to total assets:** Measures the company's share of assets that are financed by debt.

    Total debt ÷ Total assets × 100%

- **Times interest earned:** Measures the company's ability to cover its interest payments as they come due.

    Income before income taxes and interest expense (IBIT+Interest)÷Interest expense

Below is the unclassified balance sheet for Carmel Corp. as at December 31, 2016:

Carmel Corp.
Balance Sheet
As at December 31, 2016

Cash	$ 84,000	Accounts payable	$ 146,000
Accounts receivable (net)	89,040	Mortgage payable	172,200
Investments – trading	134,400	Common shares	400,000
Buildings (net)	340,200	Retained earnings	297,440
Equipment (net)	168,000		$1,015,640
Land	200,000		
	$1,015,640		

The net income for the year ended December 31, 2016 was broken down as follows:

Revenue	$1,000,000
Gain	2,200
Total revenue	1,002,200
Expenses	
Operating expenses	784,200
Interest expenses	35,000
Depreciation	48,000
Loss	5,000
Income tax	25,000
	897,200
Net income	$ 105,000

$$\text{Debt to equity} = \frac{(\$146,000 + \$172,200)}{(\$400,000 + \$297,440)} \times 100$$

$$= 45.62\%$$

$$\text{Debt to total assets} = \frac{(\$146,000 + \$172,200)}{(\$1,015,640)} \times 100$$

$$= 31.33\%$$

$$\text{Times interest earned} = \frac{(\$105,000 + \$25,000 + \$35,000)}{\$35,000}$$

$$= 4.71 \text{ times}$$

As discussed previously, ratios are difficult to evaluate without something to compare them to, such as previous company trends or industry standards to use as comparative benchmarks. In general terms, if debt to total assets is less than 50%, this would be seen as a reasonable result, meaning that equity has financed greater than 50% of the company's total assets. As well, this shows that the company is profitable and is able to cover its interest expense reasonably.

Companies that are overextended find themselves under increasing pressure to use aggressive accounting policies to stay within the restrictive covenants set by creditors. This can lead to reporting bias. If discovered by the creditor, they can call the loan for immediate repayment, in which case the loan must then be reclassified as a current liability, further worsening the current liability ratios such as the current ratio or acid test ratio. For this reason, it is wise for management to resist the temptation to use such accounting policies.

13.7 IFRS/ASPE Key Differences

Item	ASPE	IFRS
Initial measurement	Fair value as the present value of future cash flows.	Fair value as the present value of future cash flows.
Subsequent measurement	Amortized cost, unless the fair-value option is chosen. Can choose to use either the effective interest rate or straight-line methods to amortize discounts and premiums.	Amortized cost, unless the fair-value option is chosen because it results in more relevant information. The effective interest rate method is the only method allowed to amortize discounts and premiums.
Impairment and troubled debt restructurings	Impairments are recorded by the creditor only. The debtor makes no entry since the amount is still legally owed. Troubled debt restructurings re-measure the new debt using the historic interest rate for comparability. If the difference is less than 10%, the debtor does not record an entry. Creditor records impairment. If the difference is greater than 10%, the debtor recognizes a gain, the old debt is derecognized, and the new debt recognized.	Same as ASPE.

Disclosure	Any principal portion of long-term debt due within one year of the reporting date is to be reported under current liabilities as the current portion of long-term debt. Long-term debt that is refinanced may be classified as long-term provided the refinancing is in place by the time the financial reports are issued.	Any principal portion of long-term debt due within one year of the reporting date is to be reported under current liabilities as the current portion of long-term debt. Long-term debt that is refinanced may be classified as long-term provided the refinancing is in place by the reporting date.

Chapter Summary

LO 1: Describe long-term financial liabilities and their role in accounting and business.

Companies generate cash resources for future business opportunities from three basic sources: (a) internally from its sales, (b) from investors through issuing shares, (c) from borrowing from a creditor. Each source has its advantages and disadvantages. If a company decides to borrow from a creditor then the opportunity to leverage exists. Leveraging occurs when the interest cost of borrowing debt to purchase assets is lower than the return generated by the leveraged assets. However, increasing debt also increases liquidity and solvency risk. Long-term debt is defined as debt with due dates greater than one year. It can be notes payable, such as mortgages, or bonds payable. Both are financial liabilities as they both represent obligations fixed by contract.

LO2: Describe notes payable, and explain how they are classified and how they are initially and subsequently measured and reported.

A note payable is an obligation to pay a specified sum of money in the form of principal and interest through a formal written promissory note or agreement. Long-term notes are initially recorded at their fair value, which is calculated as the present value of the discounted cash flows. Cash flows are characterized by the size and timing of the debt repayment. Repayment can either be a single lump sum of principal and interest at maturity, a series of interest payments with a lump sum payment of principal at maturity, or a series of instalment payments combining both interest and principal over a specified period of time. The variables used to determine the present value of the note are the repayment cash flows, along with the market rate for a note of similar risk, and the timing of the cash flows. The present value of the note is the amount initially recorded as the note payable amount. The term *zero-interest-bearing notes*, or *non-interest-bearing notes*, is a misnomer because they do, in fact, include an interest component: the difference between the borrowed and the repaid amounts.

After issuance, long-term notes payable are subsequently measured at amortized cost. For example, if the note payable is issued at face value, then the present value will be the same as the face value and there will be no premium or discount to amortize. If the stated rate is lower or higher than the market rate, then the present value will be lower or higher and the note will be issued at a discount or at a premium, whichever the case. For IFRS companies, the discount or premium is to be amortized over the life of the note using the effective interest method. For ASPE companies, the choice is between the effective interest method and the straight-line method. For non-interest-bearing notes, the interest rate will usually be the rate that results in the correct interest component amount. The fair value for notes payable in exchange for property, goods, or services is usually determined by the fair value of the good or service given up; however, there can be some issues regarding what constitutes fair value for exchange transactions.

Other issues relating to subsequent measurement of notes payable are accounting for impairment and troubled debt restructurings. If a note subsequently becomes impaired, the creditor will estimate the present value of the impaired cash flow and will write down the note receivable accordingly. The debtor makes no such entry as there is still a legal obligation to fully repay the note. For troubled debt restructurings, there are several calculations and entries for the creditor and the debtor depending on whether there is a settlement of the debt, a modification of terms less than 10%, or a modification of terms for greater than 10%.

LO 3: Describe bonds payable, and explain how they are classified and how they are initially and subsequently measured and reported.

Bond issuance is typically the choice made by companies when the amount of funds needed is significant. Instead of having a single creditor, many bondholders purchase the bonds for investment purposes. A broker or underwriter plays a key role in this process. There are many types of bonds, each with different features that are identified in the bond indenture.

Like long-term notes payable, bonds are classified as long-term debt until they are within one year of their maturity, at which time they are classified as a current liability. They are initially recognized at their fair value, measured by the present value of their future cash flows, and are subsequently measured at amortized cost. Bonds can be issued at par or at either a discount or a premium. The discount or premium is amortized over the life of the bond using the effective interest method. For ASPE companies, straight-line method is also acceptable.

Bond issuers always pay interest according to the bond indenture, which often means payment every six months. For bonds purchased between interest dates, the bondholder will pay an additional sum on the purchase date, which covers the interest since the last interest payment date. When the first six-month interest payment is received, the net amount of the additional monies initially paid out at purchase for accrued interest, and the first interest income actually received, will represent the correct interest income from the date of purchase to the first interest payment received.

If interest rates should drop significantly while a bond issue is outstanding, the bond issuer will be motivated to repay the bondholders before the maturity date and then re-issue the bonds at the lower rate. The slightly higher acquisition price paid to reacquire the bonds will be recorded as a loss on redemption.

LO 4: Define and describe other accounting and valuation issues such as the fair value option, defeasance, and off-balance sheet financing.

ASPE allows for an alternative measure for notes and bonds called the fair-value option. IFRS allows this only if it results in more relevant information or as part of a larger fair-value portfolio. Bond issuers' credit ratings can drop, which will result in a corresponding increase in the interest rate. The resulting decrease in the fair value reduces the bond payable and the offsetting credit is recorded as an unrealized gain. Since these gains are currently reported in the income statement, it seems counter-intuitive for companies whose credit ratings have dropped to report an increase in net income. IFRS 9 will correct this anomaly when it is implemented in 2018.

Companies can be motivated to keep their reported debt at the lowest level legally possible. There are a couple of ways that this can be achieved. First, defeasance involves the debtor paying monies into a separate trust account ahead of time, and the creditor receiving payments directly from that trust. In this way, if done legally, the long-term debt can be removed from the debtor's books. Second, off-balance sheet sources of financing are another way to avoid reporting debt on the balance sheet. An example is operating leases, where the monies paid for the lease are recorded as a rental expense and, therefore, no lease obligation or asset is reported. This will be discussed in further detail in a later chapter about leasing.

LO 5: Explain how long-term debt is disclosed in the financial statements.

There are specific and extensive reporting requirements for long-term debt, including the impact on reporting regarding refinancing agreements. Basic reporting requirements include disclosures of the interest rate, maturity date, security details, restrictive covenants required by creditors, and current portion of long-term debt, to name a few. Since IFRS companies are usually publicly traded, impacting a large number of investors, the reporting requirements are extensive.

LO 6: Identify the different methods used to analyze long-term liabilities; calculate and interpret three specific ratios used to analyze long-term liabilities.

Notes and bonds payable affect the liquidity and solvency of companies since the debt must be repaid at some point. Companies' cash positions must continually be monitored to ensure that there are enough cash reserves to repay maturing debt. Three common ratios that can trigger a further review, if unfavourable, are debt to equity, debt to total assets, and times interest earned. Comparable benchmarks make ratios a useful monitoring tool.

LO 7: Explain the similarities and differences between ASPE and IFRS regarding recognition, measurement, and reporting of long-term payables.

In this case, IFRS and ASPE are quite similar. A difference between them is the choice of amortization method used for bonds and notes that were issued at a discount or premium. ASPE has the added option to amortize the premium or discount using either the straight-line method or the effective method. Additionally, ASPE disclosures are less than those required by IFRS.

References

CPA Canada. (2016). *CPA Canada handbook*. Toronto, ON: CPA Canada.

HSBC. (2013, July). Debt done right. *HSBC Liquid Newsletter*. Retrieved from `http://www.hsbc.com.my/1/PA_ES_Content_Mgmt/content/website/personal/investments/liqui`

d/4491.html

International Accounting Standards (IAS). (2013). *IAS 13—Fair value measurement.* Retrieved from http://www.iasplus.com/en/standards/ifrs/ifrs13

Exercises

EXERCISE 13–1

Evergreen Ltd. is planning to expand its operations and will be looking at various sources of financing to access enough cash to complete the project. At the present time, Evergreen Ltd. has a debt to total assets ratio of 56%, compared to the industry average of 60%.

Required:

a. Identify and explain the three sources of financing available to Evergreen Ltd.

b. Based on the information provided, recommend which would be the best alternative.

EXERCISE 13–2

On January 1, 2016, Vayron Corp. issued a $400,000, three-year, 5%, note at face value to Valleydale Ltd. in exchange for $400,000 cash. The note requires annual interest payments on December 31.

Required: Prepare Vayron Corp.'s journal entries to record:

a. Issuance of the note

b. The December 31 interest payment

c. What would the market interest rate be at the time the note was signed and why?

d. What would the yield be?

e. What is the current portion of the long-term debt, if any? When will this be reported?

EXERCISE 13–3

On January 1, 2016, Compton Corp. issued $500,000, 10-year, 8% bonds that pay interest semi-annually. At the time of issue, the market rate for bonds with similar characteristics and risks was 7%. Compton Corp. follows IFRS.

Required: Prepare Compton Corp.'s journal entries to record:

a. Issuance of the note

b. The June 30 interest payment.

c. The amount of the discount or premium, if any.

Note: Round the percentages to the nearest two decimals and the final answers to the nearest whole number.

EXERCISE 13–4

On January 1, 2016, Termund Co. issued a $120,000, three-year, zero-interest-bearing note to North Lace Ltd. in exchange for $95,260. At the time, the implicit interest rate was 8%. Termund Co. uses the effective interest rate method.

Required: Prepare Termund Co.'s entries for:

a. Issuance of the note

b. Recognition of interest for year-end on December 31, 2016

c. If the implicit rate has not been provided, provide the calculation proof that would determine the implicit rate of 8%.

d. Prepare an amortization table for North Lace Ltd.

Note: Round the percentages to the nearest two decimals and the final answers to the nearest whole number.

EXERCISE 13–5

On January 1, 2016, Odessa Corp. issued an $80,000, four-year, 3% note to Yalta Ltd. in exchange for equipment that normally sells for $74,326. The note requires annual interest payments each December 31. The market rate for a note of similar risk is 5%.

Required: Prepare Odessa Corp.'s entries for:

a. Issuance of the note

b. The first interest payment using the effective interest rate method

c. The first interest payment assuming that Odessa Corp. follows ASPE and has chosen to use the straight-line method for amortization.

Note: Round the percentages to the nearest two decimals and the final answers to the nearest whole number.

EXERCISE 13–6

On January 1, 2016, Edmund Inc. issued a $200,000, five-year, no-interest note to Hillary Ltd. and received $200,000 cash. Included in the terms of the note was an arrangement that Edmund Inc. would sell raw materials to Hillary Ltd. for a discounted price over the five-year period. Edmund Inc. follows IFRS and the market rate at that time was 2.5%.

Required: Prepare Edmund Inc.'s journal entry for the issuance of the note.

Note: Round the percentages to the nearest two decimals and the final answers to the nearest whole number.

EXERCISE 13–7

On January 1, 2016, Melbourne Ltd. signed an instalment note in settlement of an outstanding account payable of $25,000 owed to Yardin Corp. Yardin Corp. is able to earn an 8% return on investments with similar risk. The payment terms determine that the note is to be repaid in three equal cash payments of principal and interest on December 31, 2016, 2017, and 2018.

Required: Calculate the payment amount.

Note: Round the percentages to the nearest two decimals and the final answers to the nearest whole number.

EXERCISE 13–8

On January 1, 2016, Southerly Winds Inc. issued $350,000, 15-year, 5% bonds at face value. The issuance cost from the broker was $25,500 and the difference was paid to Southerly Winds Inc. in cash. The bonds require interest payments annually every December 31. Southerly Winds Inc. follows ASPE and amortizes the bond issue costs using the straight-line method.

Required: Prepare the entries for:

a. The bond issuance

b. The first interest payment and amortization

Note: Round the percentages to the nearest two decimals and the final answers to the nearest whole number.

EXERCISE 13-9

On January 1, 2016, Hobart Services Ltd. issued $200,000 of 7% bonds at 98. Bonds are due January 1, 2021, with interest payable semi-annually on July 1 and January 1.

Required:

a. Prepare all the journal entries relating to the bond for 2016 assuming that Hobart Services Ltd. follows IFRS.

b. Prepare a classified partial statement of financial position as at December 31, 2016.

c. Prepare the entries for 2016 assuming now that Hobart Services Ltd. follows ASPE and uses the straight-line method.

d. Based on the data in part (c), prepare a classified partial balance sheet as at December 31, 2016.

e. Will the total cost of borrowing over the life of the bond, using the effective interest method, be higher, lower, or the same as the total cost of borrowing using the straight-line method?

Note: Round the percentages to the nearest two decimals and the final answers to the nearest whole number.

EXERCISE 13-10

On May 1, 2016, Harper Boyle Construction Ltd. issued $800,000 of 5% bonds. Bonds were dated January 1, 2016, and mature on January 1, 2036, with interest payable each July 1 and January 1. The bonds were issued at 99 plus accrued interest, less brokerage fees of $7,000. Harper Boyle Construction Ltd. follows IFRS and their year-end is December 31.

Required:

Long-Term Financial Liabilities

a. Complete an interest schedule for 2016 to 2018.

b. Prepare all the entries related to the bonds for 2016.

c. Prepare a partial classified statement of financial position as at December 31, 2016 including current liability disclosures, if any. Round the interest rate percentage to the nearest four decimals and the amortization schedule to the nearest whole number.

d. What is the accounting treatment for the brokerage fees of $7,000?

EXERCISE 13–11

On November 1, 2016, Tribecca Ltd., issued $1M of 4%, 15-year bonds, at face value. Interest is payable each December 31. The company has chosen to apply the fair value option as the accounting treatment for the bonds. A risk assessment at December 31, 2017 shows that Tribecca's credit rating has slipped to a lower rating. As a result, the fair value of the bonds on December 31, 2017 is $950,000.

Required:

a. Prepare the journal entries on December 31, 2017, if any, assuming that Tribecca follows ASPE.

b. Prepare the journal entries on December 31, 2017, if any, assuming that Tribecca follows IFRS (IAS 39).

c. What significant issue arises using the fair value method? Round the percentages to the nearest two decimals and the final answers to the nearest whole number.

EXERCISE 13–12

On July 31, 2016, Elmer Fudd Co. retired bonds with a face value of $300,000 at 99. The unamortized discount at that time was $10,150.

Required: Record the entry for the retirement.

Note: Round the percentages to the nearest two decimals and the final answers to the nearest whole number.

EXERCISE 13–13

Kishmir Corp. has a loan that is currently due at December 31, 2016, year-end. This debt is being refinanced by a three-year loan. The refinance documents were signed on January 4, 2017. The financial statements have not yet been issued.

Required:

a. How would the loan be reported in the December 31, 2016, statement of financial position (IFRS)?

b. How would the loan be reported in the December 31, 2016, balance sheet (ASPE)?

EXERCISE 13–14

As at December 31, 2016, Smith and Smith Co. owes $25,000 to First Nearly Trust Co., for a three-year, 8% note due on this date. The note was issued at par. The oil and gas market has dropped significantly, so Smith and Smith Co. is in serious financial trouble due to the drop in sales. First Nearly Trust Co., agrees to some concessions as follows:

- Extend the due date from December 31, 2016, to December 31, 2019.

- Reduce the principal amount owing to $18,000.

- Reduce the interest rate to 6%, payable annually on December 31 at a time when the market rate was 7%.

Required: Prepare the journal entries for the debtor for December 31, 2016, 2017, and 2018. (Note: Round the final answers to the nearest whole number.)

EXERCISE 13–15

On January 1, 2016, Dimor Ltd. purchased a house with a tax assessment value of $590,000 in exchange for an $800,000, zero-interest-bearing note due on January 1, 2022. The house had not been appraised recently, nor did the note have a market value. The bank's interest rate for this type of transaction and risk characteristics was 5.75%. Dimor Ltd. intends to use the entire house as their main office.

Required:

a. What is the carrying value of the note payable on December 31, 2016?

94 Long-Term Financial Liabilities

b. What role, if any, would the tax assessment value of $590,000 play?

EXERCISE 13–16

On January 1, 2016, Seutor Corp. issued an instalment note in exchange for equipment with a list price of $150,000. The note is to be paid in four equal payments of $40,541 of principal and interest each December 31. The market rate that this time is 7% for this type of transaction.

Required:

a. How will the equipment value be established?

b. Prepare the journal entries for 2016 for the note payable.

c. Why would a creditor prefer the instalment note compared to a regular interest-bearing note?

EXERCISE 13–17

On December 31, 2016, Firstly Trust agreed to restructure a $700,000, 8% note, issued at par with Hornblower Corp. The interest is paid annually each December 31. Below are the terms:

- Principal is reduced from $700,000 to $650,000.
- The maturity date is extended from December 31, 2016, to December 31, 2018.
- The interest rate is reduced from 8% to 7%.

On January 1, 2019, Hornblower Corp. pays $650,000 to Firstly Trust.

Required:

For Hornblower Corp.:

a. What entry, if any, would Hornblower Corp. make regarding the loan restructure?

b. What is the interest rate that Hornblower Corp. should use for future periods?

c. Record the interest entry for Hornblower Corp. on December 31, 2017.

d. Record the entry for Hornblower Corp. on January 1, 2019.

For Firstly Trust:

e. Calculate the loss for the debt restructuring and record the entry, if any.

f. Prepare an interest schedule after the debt restructuring.

g. Record the interest entry on December 31, 2017.

h. Record the entry on January 1, 2019.

EXERCISE 13–18

Ulting Ltd. owes Sleazy Finance Co. $150,000 for a 3-year, 10% note, issued at par and due on December 31, 2016. Interest was paid annually each December 31. Ulting Ltd. is now in financial difficulties, so Sleazy Finance Co. agrees to extend the note's maturity date to December 31, 2018, reduce the principal to $130,000, and reduce the interest rate to 9%. The market rate is currently 5%. Both companies follow IFRS.

Required:

a. Prepare all related journal entries for Ulting Ltd. for 2016, 2017, and 2018.

b. Prepare all related journal entries for Sleazy Trust Co. for 2016, 2017, and 2018, assuming that an allowance account was used for this note.

Chapter 14

Complex Financial Instruments

Is Convertible Debt a Viable Financing Option?

Convertible debt is an instrument that can be converted from debt (liability) to equity shares at some point, often due to a triggering event. Creditors can become shareholders by purchasing the equity share offered in the terms of the convertible agreement. Creditors can often purchase these shares at a discount, and this can be a strong motivator for converting the debt to equity.

There are advantages and disadvantages for a company obtaining its financing through convertible debt.

Advantages

Convertible debt can be simpler, cheaper, and faster, since the debt documentation is much shorter and simpler, with fewer terms to negotiate. As a result, legal fees will also likely be less compared to the fees incurred for a small preferred shares offering. The process can be completed within a matter of two weeks compared to several months for other forms of equity financing.

Convertible debt does not require setting a valuation of the company, as is required for other forms of equity financing in order to set the share price in the offering. In the absence of operational history, it is difficult for most new companies to set a valuation. Moreover, company valuations can create a temptation to over-value the company to maximize the share price at that time. Any subsequent issuance of shares would be priced at the lower market price causing discontent for the original shareholders who paid more for the shares due to the initial over-valuation.

Funds received from convertible debt allow companies to keep control, especially if the conversion is from debt to preferred shares with no voting rights. The company control by existing shareholders will become diluted through the alternative of common share offerings to obtain financing.

Disadvantages

Common shares issuances are commonplace and well understood by investors. Convertible debt, on the other hand, is a hybrid instrument with debt and equity features that can be confusing to investors, thus making the instrument harder to sell.

Prior to conversion, convertible debt interest must be paid and the principal amount owed must be reported as a liability, even though it may not be payable until a subsequent triggering event occurs. Since convertible debt is considered debt until conversion, its presence in the balance sheet will negatively impact the liquidity ratios, solvency ratios, and any restrictive covenants currently in force from other creditors.

Assuming that the convertible debt converts to preferred shares, some investors may not like the lack of control compared to investing in common shares. To compensate, companies will often add other attractive features to preferred shares, but investors may still prefer to invest elsewhere rather than give up the rights inherent in common shares.

Other Financial Products

Companies can raise capital by means other than convertible debt. A simple loan is one alternative, but this is often difficult for new companies with higher credit risk to obtain. Preferred shares are an alternative with dividends and preferred rights such as voting rights, but this may cause issues for existing common shareholders. Convertible preferred shares are also an option. These are similar to convertible debt except the loan features such as interest are excluded.

(Source: Scott Legal, 2013)

Chapter 14 Learning Objectives

After completing this chapter, you should be able to:

LO 1: Describe complex financial instruments and their role in accounting and business.

LO 2: Describe the basic differences in the accounting treatments for long-term debt and equity.

LO 3: Describe the two methods acceptable to IFRS and ASPE to separate, classify, measure, and disclose complex financial instruments such as convertible debt and convertible preferred shares.

LO 4: Describe various derivatives such as options, warrants, forwards, and futures.

LO 5: Explain the accounting treatments and reporting requirements for stock options plans.

LO 6: Recall that analyses of complex financial instruments use the same techniques as those used in non-convertible debt and equity instruments.

LO 7: Explain the similarities and differences between ASPE and IFRS regarding recognition, measurement, and reporting of complex financial instruments.

Introduction

This chapter continues on from earlier chapters that examined long-term debt and equity. However, the focus will now be on complex financial instruments, such as convertible bonds and convertible preferred shares, as well as derivatives, such as options and warrants.

Chapter Organization

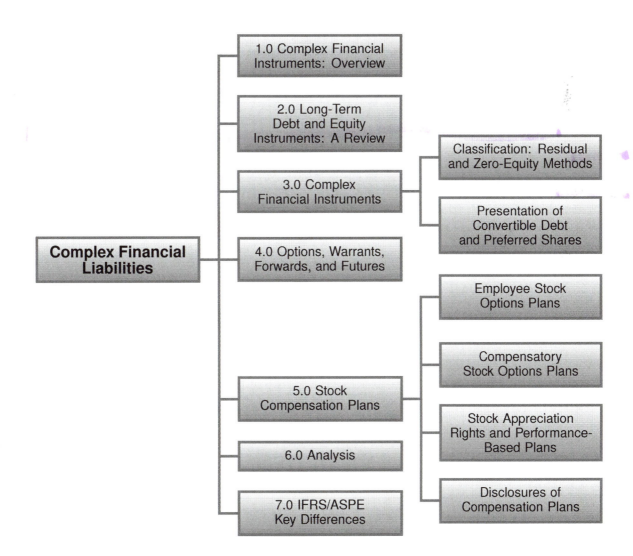

14.1 Complex Financial Instruments: Overview

As stated in the previous chapter regarding long-term debt, most businesses will require financing at various points throughout their lives. For example, new businesses may require start-up cash in order to purchase revenue-generating assets, as they have yet to accumulate cash holdings. Existing companies may want to expand their operations or replenish depleted cash holdings due to a temporary downturn in sales. There are also companies that possess large infrastructures, such as airlines or railways, and require more cash for their capital projects than can be generated from normal operations. These businesses obtain the necessary additional cash through various *financing activities* such as internally generated free cash flow, borrowing from creditors (debt), and issuing capital shares (equity).

The material presented in the previous chapters looked at debt and equity as separate instruments. However, in recent decades financing activities have created hybrid sources of financing where a single instrument can possess characteristics of both debt and equity. Examples of these more complex instruments are convertible debt, convertible preferred shares, and various derivatives such as options and warrants that can be converted into common shares.

Why do companies seek out these alternative financing sources? As the opening story explains, instruments such as convertible debt can often be simpler, cheaper, and faster to obtain – all while maintaining existing control, or at least knowing exactly when the control will change due to the triggering event. Also, these hybrid securities usually include sweeteners, such as conversion to shares at a lower than market price, thereby increasing their attractiveness to investors. Moreover, investors will be more willing to purchase the bonds because they not only provide greater security if secured by company assets, but they also allow investors to participate in the company profits and growth through the option to convert to common shares. Since the conversion feature adds flexibility, and hence increased value, companies can usually obtain convertible debt at cheaper interest rates. However, there is more to the story. Convertible instruments have a significantly different effect on perceptions held by shareholders and the marketplace. For example, if a company issues additional common shares to raise capital, instead of using its own internally generated funds from profits or by borrowing funds (to be repaid by internally generated funds), the market can interpret this negatively, as a sign that the company is unable to obtain debt financing, perhaps due to a poor credit rating. In other words, it sends a signal that the company might not be performing as well as it should. This can lower the market value of the shares, thereby creating a negative climate and causing concern for the shareholders.

If convertible bonds (debt) or convertible preferred shares or warrants (equity) are issued instead, the investment holders will only convert to common shares if conditions are favourable. This sends a positive signal to the market that the company is continuing to do well. As a result, these hybrid instruments become a way to access funding while maintaining a more positive climate, without unduly alarming shareholders and creditors. As such, these hybrid instruments have become widely accepted and commonplace in today's market.

From an accounting standards point of view, the issue becomes: how do you separate, measure, and report the debt and equity attributes of these complex financial instruments throughout their life-cycle of issuance, subsequent measurement, and conversion or retirement?

14.2 Long-Term Debt and Equity Instruments: A Review

Since convertible instruments each possess a combination of debt and equity characteristics, the challenge becomes: how to separate, measure, and report the debt and equity attribute for each type of instrument required by the accounting standards.

For complex financial instruments, once an acceptable method to separate the debt from the equity component is determined, each component will follow its respective accounting standard, as discussed in previous chapters.

It is important to understand the substance of debt and equity instruments so that the classification and amounts reported reflect their true underlying economic substance, rather than simply their legal form. Therefore, a review of debt and equity instruments and their characteristics is presented below:

	Long-Term Liabilities (Debt)	**Equity (Shares)**
Examples	Bonds and long-term notes payable	Preferred and common shares
Maturity	Principal and accrued interest due on various dates identified in the documentation.	Permanent capital unless repurchased by the company.
Secured by and seniority	Usually secured by various company assets. Debt ranks in seniority to shares in terms of windup, bankruptcy, and liquidation.	Unsecured. Shareholders are entitled to whatever assets remain after creditors are paid out. Preferred shares are also senior to common shares.

Advantages and disadvantages	• Interest expense lowers net income and is also tax deductible.	• Dividend payouts have no effect on net income or income taxes.
	• Principal and accrued interest must be repaid on the maturity date unless debt is convertible to shares.	• Dividends payouts are optional and shares are permanent capital held by shareholders unless repurchased by the company.
	• Unpaid principal and interest increase liquidity and solvency risk and could lead to reduced access to other capital.	• Shares balances have no direct effect on liquidity and solvency ratios, but other ratios such as earnings per share are affected.
	• Company does not give up control of company policies.	• Company gives up proportionate share of control for each voting share issued, and existing shareholders' investment holdings become diluted. Market share can also decline in value if a shares issuance is significant.
	• Can use the funds from debt financing to generate profits with higher returns compared to the interest accrued on the debt itself (leveraging).	• Shareholder capital represents company ownership so there is no leveraging opportunity.

The schedule below is a summary of the accounting treatment for long-term liabilities (debt) taken from an earlier chapter:

Financial Liabilities	ASPE	IFRS
Initial measurement	Fair value as the present value of future cash flows.	Fair value as the present value of future cash flows.
Subsequent measurement	Amortized cost unless the fair-value option is chosen. Can choose to use either the effective interest rate or straight-line methods to amortize discounts and premiums.	Amortized cost unless the fair-value option is chosen because it results in more relevant information. The effective interest rate method is the only method allowed to amortize discounts and premiums.
Disclosure	Any principal portion of long-term debt due within one year of the reporting date is to be reported under current liabilities as the current portion of long-term debt. Long-term debt that is refinanced may be classified as long-term provided the refinancing is in place by the time the financial reports are issued.	Any principal portion of long-term debt due within one year of the reporting date is to be reported under current liabilities as the current portion of long-term debt. Long-term debt that is refinanced may be classified as long-term provided the refinancing is in place by the reporting date.

In an earlier chapter we discussed equity—including preferred and common shares. To recap in basic terms, equity shares issuance is accounted for using historical cost, net of any direct costs of the shares issuance such as underwriting costs, accounting and legal fees, and printing costs. Additionally, disclosure includes the number of shares authorized and issued for common and preferred shares. For preferred shares, the per share dividend amount is also disclosed.

14.3 Complex Financial Instruments

Complex financial instruments possess more than one financial component, such as a combination of debt or equity attributes as explained in the introduction. Examples of complex financial instruments are: convertible bonds payable, convertible preferred shares, and options/warrants that attach to shares or bonds. Convertible bonds are usually issued in exchange for cash, which must either be repaid later at maturity (debt attribute) or, alternatively, must be converted into a specific number of common shares at specific points in time (equity attribute). Convertible preferred shares possess both the attributes of preferred shares and common shares if they are converted into a specific number of common shares at specific times. Clearly, these convertible instruments possess more than one debt or equity attribute compared to non-convertible financial instruments.

Convertible debt and convertible preferred shares will be discussed next, and derivative instruments, such as options and warrants, will be discussed briefly towards the end of the chapter.

14.3.1 Convertible Debt and Preferred Shares Classification: Two Methods

The accounting standards require that bonds that are convertible into common shares are to be separated into the value of the bond, without the conversion feature (debt component), and an embedded/attached option to convert the debt into common shares (equity component). Convertible preferred shares are separated into the value of the preferred share, without the conversion feature (shares equity component), and an option to convert preferred shares into common shares (contributed surplus equity component). There are a number of methods that can accomplish the separation of debt from equity components, but IFRS recommends only the residual method, while ASPE allows either the residual method or the zero-equity method.

- The residual method estimates and allocates the fair value of the bond first, without the conversion feature, because debt is usually the more reliably measureable component as compared to equity. As previously discussed in the chapter on long-term debt, the bond valuation basis is the present value of the future cash flows using the market rate of interest for debt instruments with similar attributes and risk. Any residual amount remaining is assigned to the equity component.

- The zero-equity method assigns the full valuation of the transaction to the debt component and a zero-value to the equity component.

Bonds Issued at Par – Residual Method

As an example, on January 1, Willowby Ltd. issues three-year, 8%, convertible bonds with a par value of $250,000 for $256,328 cash. Interest is payable annually on December 31. Each $1,000 bond may be converted into 80 common shares, which are currently trading at $12. Bonds without the conversion feature trade in the market at par.

Using the residual method, the present value of the bonds with the conversion feature is equal to the cash amount received of $256,328. This is compared to the present value of the bonds without the conversion feature or the par value of $250,000 (debt component). The difference between the two values is allocated to the embedded option (equity component).

Face value of the bond	$250,000
Present value of the bond with option feature attached	$256,328
Difference equals option valuation	$ 6,328

The entry to record the issuance of the convertible bond is:

General Journal				
Date	Account/Explanation	PR	Debit	Credit
Jan 1	Cash		256,328	
	Bonds payable (debt component)			250,000
	Contributed surplus – convertible bonds options (equity component)			6,328

At each reporting date, each component would be reported according to their respective standard. For example, bonds would be reported at their amortized cost as a liability and the options at historical cost as contributed surplus in equity. In this case, the bonds were issued at par so there is no premium or discount to amortize, and the bonds payable balance would remain at $250,000 until conversion or maturity.

If the market price of the shares increased to $16, bondholders would be motivated to convert the bonds to shares, even before maturity in three years. This is because each $1,000 would now be worth $1,280 (80 shares × $16). The entry to convert would be:

General Journal				
Date	Account/Explanation	PR	Debit	Credit
Jan 1	Bonds payable............................		250,000	
	Contributed surplus – convertible bonds options..		6,328	
	Common shares.........................			256,328

Note that the carrying values (book values) at the time of conversion were the values used in the conversion entry, hence its name: the **book value method.** This method is required for both IFRS and ASPE when recording bond conversions, and it results in no gain or loss recognized or recorded upon conversion. Any accrued interest that was forfeited at the time of conversion would also be credited to common shares.

Conversely, if the share price did not increase, and the bonds reach maturity without conversion, the amount owing for the bond is payable to the bondholder and the contributed surplus (in some counties referred to as reserves) amount in equity will lapse. The entry for fully amortized bonds at maturity would be:

General Journal				
Date	Account/Explanation	PR	Debit	Credit
Jan 1	Bonds payable.............................		250,000	
	Contributed surplus – convertible bonds options...		6,328	
	Cash.....................................			250,000
	Contributed surplus – expired options....			6,328

Bonds Issued at Par – Zero-Equity Method

For the zero-equity method, the policy choice for ASPE companies, the entry for the bond issuance is straightforward since zero is assigned to the equity component:

General Journal				
Date	Account/Explanation	PR	Debit	Credit
Jan 1	Cash.....................................		250,000	
	Bonds payable (debt component only) ...			250,000

The entry upon conversion would be:

General Journal				
Date	Account/Explanation	PR	Debit	Credit
Jan 1	Bond payable.............................		250,000	
	Common shares.........................			250,000

The entry upon maturity without conversion would be:

General Journal				
Date	Account/Explanation	PR	Debit	Credit
Jan 1	Bond payable.............................		250,000	
	Cash.....................................			250,000

Bonds Issued at a Premium or Discount – Residual Method

On January 1, Jason Inc. issues $300,000, five-year, 7% convertible bonds at 98. Interest is payable annually on December 31. Each $1,000 bond may be converted into 100 common shares, which are currently trading at $9. Bonds without the conversion feature trade in the market at 8%.

Using the residual method, the present value of the bonds at the market-based discounted amount, with the conversion feature, is $294,000. This is compared to the present value of the bonds, without the conversion feature, at the market rate of 8% (debt component). The difference between the two present values is allocated to the option (equity component).

(Face value of the bond $300,000)
Fair market price with conversion feature ($300,000 × 0.98) $294,000
Present value of the bond without the conversion feature at the market
rate of 8%: Interest payment = $300,000 × 7% = $21,000 PMT annually
PV = ($21,000 PMT, 8 I/Y, 5 N, $300,000 FV) $288,022
Difference equals option valuation $ 5,978

The entry to record the issuance of the convertible bond is:

General Journal

Date	Account/Explanation	PR	Debit	Credit
Jan 1	Cash		294,000	
	Bonds payable (debt component)			288,022
	Contributed surplus – convertible bonds options (equity component)			5,978

As in the previous example, bonds would be reported as a long-term liability at their amortized cost and the contributed surplus for the options at historical cost in equity. In this case, the bonds were issued at 98, so the discount amount of $11,978 ($300,000 – $288,022) would be amortized over the five years using the effective method at 8%* for IFRS and ASPE (or the optional straight-line method for ASPE) until conversion or maturity.

*Interest calculation:

PV = (PMT, I/Y, N, FV)
+/- $288,022 PV = $21,000 PMT, I/Y, 5 N, $300,000 FV
I/Y = 8% rounded

The schedule for the effective interest method is shown below:

Jason Inc.
Bond Amortization Schedule
Effective Interest Method

	Cash Payment	Interest Expense @ 8%	Discount Amortization	Carrying Amount
At issuance				$288,022
End of year 1	$21,000	$23,042	$2,042	290,064
End of year 2	21,000	23,205	2,205	292,269
End of year 3	21,000	23,382	2,382	294,650
End of year 4	21,000	23,572	2,572	297,222
End of year 5	21,000	23,778	2,778*	300,000

Conversion date (after End of year 3)

*Some rounding effects are present.

If the market price of shares increased, and all the bonds were converted into shares at the end of three years (prior to maturity), the entry to convert to shares would be:

Date	Account/Explanation	PR	Debit	Credit
Jan 1	Bonds payable (carrying value at amortized cost)		294,650	
	Contributed surplus – convertible bond options (historic cost)		5,978	
	Common shares			300,628

Again, because of the book-value method accounting treatment, the carrying values at the time of conversion were the values used in the conversion entry above with no gain or loss recognized.

Bonds Issued at a Premium or Discount – Zero-Equity Method

With the zero-equity method option for ASPE companies, the entry for the bond issuance is straightforward since zero is assigned to the equity component. The straight-line method is used below to amortize the bond discount (ASPE option).

Date	Account/Explanation	PR	Debit	Credit
Jan 1	Cash		294,000	
	Bonds payable (debt component only)			294,000
	($300,000 × 0.98)			

The entry upon conversion at the end of three years would be:

Date	Account/Explanation	PR	Debit	Credit
Jan 1	Bond payable		297,600*	
	Common shares			297,600

* $300,000 − $294,000 = 6,000 ÷ 5 years = 1,200 discount amortization per year
$1,200 × 3 years = 3,600 + 294,000 = 297,600

The entry when the bonds matured without conversion would also be straightforward, as the bonds would be fully amortized by this time:

	General Journal			
Date	Account/Explanation	PR	Debit	Credit
Jan 1	Bond payable...............................		300,000	
	Cash......................................			300,000

Bonds Retired Prior to Maturity with Incentives

Sometimes a company will want to retire a bonds issue before maturity in order to reduce interest expenses. To facilitate this, any convertible bonds that are repaid prior to maturity will usually include a sweetener, which is added to the repayment proceeds to motivate the bondholders to sell. In this case, both the amounts paid to the bondholders and the sweetener must be allocated between the debt and equity components. Unlike the previous examples with no sweeteners, the additional funds added to the payout as a sweetener will result in a loss and are reported in net income.

For example, on January 1, 2015, Essexive Corp. offers 5-year, 6% convertible bonds with a par value of $1,000. Interest is paid annually on December 31. Each $1,000 bond may be converted into 150 common shares, which are currently trading at $3 per share. Similar bonds without the conversion feature carry an interest rate of 7%. Essexive issues 1,500 bonds at par and allocates the proceeds under the residual method. The entry to record the bond issuance using the residual method would be recorded the same way as par value bonds discussed earlier:

	General Journal			
Date	Account/Explanation	PR	Debit	Credit
Jan 1	Cash.......................................		1,500,000	
	Bonds payable*...........................			1,438,497
	Contributed surplus – convertible bond options......................................			61,503

*PV = ($90,000 PMT, 7 I/Y, 5 N, $1,500,000 FV)
PMT = $1,500,000 × 6% = $90,000 interest payable each December 31

On January 1, 2017, immediately following the interest payment, Essexive Corp. decides to retire the convertible bonds early in order to reduce interest costs. They offer the bondholders $1,600,000 cash, the fair value of the convertible bonds at the time of early retirement, plus a sweetener. The fair value of the debt portion of the payout for the convertible bond is $1,485,000. Because a sweetener is included, the $1,600,000 payout to the bondholders will result in a loss for the company, as shown in the entry below:

General Journal				
Date	Account/Explanation	PR	Debit	Credit
Jan 1	Bond payable (after 2 years)*		1,460,635	
	Contributed surplus – convertible bond options		61,503	
	Loss on redemption of bonds**		24,365	
	Retained earnings, options retired***		53,497	
	Cash			1,600,000

* Carrying value of bonds at the end of two years using the effective interest method = ($90,000 PMT, 7 I/Y, (5 – 2) N, $1,500,000 FV)

** Loss = carrying value of bonds – FV of debt portion allocated from payout amount
    = ($1,460,635 – $1,485,000)
    = $24,365 loss

***Retained earnings, options retired = carrying value of contributed surplus, convertible bond options ($61,503) - FV of equity portion allocated from payout amount ($1,600,000 – $1,485,000 fair value for debt portion)
    = ($61,503 – ($1,600,000 – $1,485,000)) = $53,497

The $24,365 loss is the difference between the carrying value of the bond at the time of early retirement ($1,460,635) and the fair value of the debt component of $1,485,000. The reduction in equity of $53,497 is due to the difference between the carrying value of the contributed surplus, convertible bond options of $61,503, and the fair value of the equity component of $115,000 ($1,600,000 – $1,485,000 debt component).

If the early retirement were in the form of a conversion to common shares, plus an additional cash sweetener of $30,000, instead of a repayment of the debt in cash, the entry using the residual method would be:

General Journal				
Date	Account/Explanation	PR	Debit	Credit
Jan 1	Bond payable (after 2 years)*		1,460,635	
	Contributed surplus – convertible bonds options		61,503	
	Loss on redemption of bonds**		24,365	
	Retained earnings, options retired***		5,635	
	Common shares			1,522,138
	Cash			30,000

* Carrying value of bonds = PV = ($90,000 PMT, 7 I/Y, (5 − 2) N, $1,500,000 FV)

** Loss = carrying value of bonds − FV of debt component
  = ($1,460,635 − $1,485,000)
  = $24,365 loss

*** Reduction in retained earnings (equity) = additional cash of $30,000 −
  loss on redemption of bonds of $24,365

In summary, an early payout, or conversion of convertible bonds, usually requires a sweetener in order to motivate bondholders to accept the deal. This additional cash amount must be allocated between a loss, due to debt component of $24,365, and a reduction in equity, due to a capital transaction cost of $5,635, associated with the convertible capital options retired. The sum of the loss and the reduction to retained earnings should balance with the cash sweetener amount of $30,000. Meaning, other than the addition of the loss ($24,365) and the reduction in retained earnings ($5,635), the accounting treatment for early retirement is basically the same as before (using book values). In other words, the carrying values of the debt ($1,460,635) and equity ($61,503) components are still used to determine the common shares amount ($1,522,138), as was the case in the earlier examples.

14.3.2 Presentation of Convertible Debt and Preferred Shares

At each reporting date, the debt and equity components for convertible instruments would be reported according to their respective standard. Bonds would, therefore, classify the debt component as a long-term liability at amortized cost and the options as contributed surplus in equity at historical cost:

Essexive Corp.
Partial Statement of Financial Position
January 1, 2015

	2015
Long-term liabilities	
Bonds payable, 6% annually, due January 1, 2020	$1,438,497
Shareholders' Equity	
Paid-in capital:	
Contributed surplus, conversion rights	$ 61,503

For convertible preferred shares, reporting as either a liability or equity would depend on the characteristics of the convertible preferred shares. The general rule is that if the company has little control over an obligation to issue common shares in exchange for the preferred shares, or if they have to pay inordinately high dividends upon some threshold being met, then the company must report these preferred shares as a liability because they represent an unavoidable obligation. Moreover, the dividends paid for preferred shares, classified as liabilities, would be reported in net income as an interest expense instead of a reduction to retained earnings, as is the case for preferred shares dividends without liability attributes. An example of convertible preferred shares classified as a liability would be mandatorily redeemable preferred shares, such as preferred shares that must be repurchased if common shares exceed some sort of threshold market price. In this case, it is clear that the company has an obligation over which it has little control. This classification as a liability is a requirement for IFRS companies in all instances. For ASPE companies, the liability classification is used when the likelihood of the obligation arising is high.

14.4 Options, Warrants, Forwards, and Futures

Options, warrants, forwards, and futures are all examples of derivatives. Derivatives are financial instruments whose value is derived from some underlying instrument, object, index, or event. Put another way, a derivative represents a contract arising between two or more parties based upon some underlying instrument, object, index, or event. Its value is determined by fluctuations in the underlying instrument, object, index, or event, and as they have their own value, they can be bought and sold. Reasons for buying or selling are dependent on the need to minimize risk (hedging) or to make a profit (speculation).

A hedge is an investment, such as a futures contract, whose value moves in an offsetting manner to the underlying asset. Hedging is comparable to taking out an insurance policy, for example, when a homeowner in a fire-prone area takes out an insurance policy to protect her from loss in the event of fire. There is a risk/reward trade-off inherent in hedging as it both reduces potential risk and carries an associated cost, such as the fire insurance policy premiums. That said, the majority of homeowners choose to take that predictable loss by paying insurance premiums rather than risk the loss.

Managing foreign exchange rates provides another example of hedging. Fluctuations in foreign exchange rates can be either advantageous or detrimental to businesses depending on whether the exchange rate increases or decreases, and if the business is exporting or importing goods or services. For example, companies buying goods from another country on credit when the domestic currency exchange rate is rising, or selling goods to another country on credit when the foreign country's currency is rising, can reap significant gains. However, the opposite can also occur if the rates are decreasing, causing company profits to plummet. Companies can mitigate these risks by entering into a derivative contract to buy foreign currency at a future date at a specified exchange rate, thereby locking in the purchase price to a known quantity of foreign currency. In this way, a company can manage the risks associated with changes in the foreign exchange rates through hedging.

Speculation regarding derivatives is an effort to make a profit from an unknown outcome. Continuing with the example of foreign currency, if the change in foreign exchange rates favours the speculator, then a profit can be made.

Options, warrants, forwards, and futures are all types of derivatives and each one is summarized below. An in-depth discussion of derivatives is covered in a more advanced accounting course.

Options

Call options contracts give the holder the right to buy an underlying instrument, such as common shares, at a specified price within a specified time frame. The options price is called the exercise, or strike, price and the option must be in the money. That is, the market price must be greater than the exercise price before the holder will consider exercising the options held. This is the most common type of option and employee stock options are a good example.

Put options contracts are the opposite of call options as they give the holder the right to sell common shares at a specified price within a specified time frame. If the market price of the shares should decline, the option holder can still sell their shares at the higher specified price.

Options can be issued either by the company itself, or by another organization and are usually issued independently.

Warrants

Warrants are similar to call options except that they are only issued by the company itself and usually have longer time frames than options. Unlike options, warrants are usually attached to another financial instrument, such as bonds and shares.

Forward Contracts

With forward contracts, both contract parties make a commitment in advance to buy or sell something to each other at a mutually agreed-upon price at a future date. A common example is the purchase or sale of goods in foreign currencies between a supplier and a manufacturer.

Note that once the terms have been agreed upon, and the maturity date occurs, there is no option out of a forward contract. Also, in order for the contract to be acceptable to both parties, the two parties must hold opposite views as to what will happen to the underlying instrument, for example whether a currency exchange rate will increase or decrease. A forward contract can be privately negotiated and, as long as the two parties agree to the terms, price, and future date, then a forward contract is considered to exist between them.

As an example, on November 15, Monnard Inc. agrees to buy $100,000 USD from Oncore Ltd. over the next 90-day period for $108,000 CAD. As nothing is exchanged upon the contract issuance, no accounting entry is required. However, on December 31, the company year-end, the exchange rate has changed and $100,000 USD is now worth only $102,000 CAD. Despite this, Monnard Inc. is still committed to pay the agreed-upon price of $108,000 CAD and, therefore, a loss has occurred. The derivative must be remeasured to fair value at the reporting date and Monnard Inc. must record a loss as follows:

	General Journal			
Date	Account/Explanation	PR	Debit	Credit
Dec 31	Loss on current derivative....................		6,000	
	Foreign currency derivative (liability)			6,000
	($108,000 − $102,000)			

In contrast, Oncore Ltd. will record a corresponding gain and debit a foreign currency derivative asset account.

However, if Monnard Inc. actually purchased the $100,000 USD on December 31, then the entry would include both the remeasurement to fair value loss of $6,000 as well as a credit to cash in a combined entry:

	General Journal			
Date	Account/Explanation	PR	Debit	Credit
Dec 31	Cash (US dollars at the current exchange rate)...		102,000	
	Loss on current derivative....................		6,000	
	Cash (CAD dollars at the contract rate) ..			108,000
	For Loss on current derivative: ($108,000 − $102,000)			

Futures Contracts

These contracts are similar to forwards contracts except that they are highly standardized in terms of price and maturity date so that they may be publicly traded in the stock market. Examples include commodities, such as agricultural products (cattle, corn, wheat), and precious metals (gold, silver). Publicly traded refers to the fact that futures contracts can be used by speculators, rather than used as a hedge against inflation by actual buyers.

14.4. Options, Warrants, Forwards, and Futures

Speculators are looking to make money on a favourable change in the foreign exchange rate, meaning the actual delivery of the commodity rarely ever occurs.

For example, on November 15, instead of a forwards contract, Monnard Inc. bought a futures contract for $1,500 that entitles the company to buy $100,000 USD at a cost of $108,000 CAD on December 15. In this case, $1,500 is paid to obtain the futures contract from the stock market. The entry would be:

General Journal				
Date	Account/Explanation	PR	Debit	Credit
Jan 1	Foreign currency derivative (held for trading)		1,500	
	Cash.................................			1,500

On December 31, company year-end, the exchange rate has changed, and $100,000 USD is worth only $102,000 CAD. This unfavourable drop means that the futures contract value will also drop. If the futures contract now has a negative value of ($1,000), a loss has occurred which Monnard Inc. must record as follows:

General Journal				
Date	Account/Explanation	PR	Debit	Credit
Jan 1	Loss on foreign currency derivative..........		2,500	
	Foreign currency derivative			2,500
	($1,500 − ($1,000))			

If the exchange rate had increased and $100,000 USD were now worth $111,000 CAD, a gain would be recorded as Monnard Inc.'s futures contract had fixed the price at $108,000 CAD. If the fair value of the futures contract increased to $2,000, Monnard Inc.'s entry to record the gain would be:

General Journal				
Date	Account/Explanation	PR	Debit	Credit
Jan 1	Foreign currency derivative..................		500	
	Gain on foreign currency derivative			500
	($2,000 − $1,500)			

As can be seen from the two examples above, derivatives are measured at fair value with the gain or loss reported in net income. There are, however, two exceptions. The first relates to hedging and is beyond the scope of this textbook. The second is with regard to derivatives that relate to a company's own shares which are to be recorded at historic cost. An example would be warrants attached to common shares and employee stock option plans, which will be discussed next.

14.5 Stock Compensation Plans

An employee **stock option** is commonly viewed as a complex call *option* on the common stock of a company, granted by the company to an employee as remuneration or reward. In essence, the belief is that employees holding common shares will be motivated to align themselves with the company's best interests. This is beneficial to the company as it allows them to retain valuable employees long-term in exchange for non-cash forms of compensation or benefits.

The most common stock option plans are employee stock option plans (ESOPs) and compensatory stock option plans (CSOPs), but stock appreciation rights plans (SARs) and other performance criteria based plans are also used in business.

14.5.1 Employee Stock Options Plans

These plans are relatively straightforward. In these plans, the employee is granted the option to purchase shares of the company. This is, therefore, not considered to be a compensation expense as the employee is simply given the opportunity to invest in the company's equity by purchasing shares. By holding company shares, they share in the dividends and capital appreciation of the share in the marketplace the same as any other shareholders.

For example, Besco Ltd. implements an ESOP in which employees can purchase options to buy company shares for $15 per share. The cost of the option is $2 and 20,000 shares are available within this plan. No entry is required at this time because no transactions have occurred yet.

On January 1, employees purchase 12,000 options:

Date	Account/Explanation	PR	Debit	Credit
Jan 1	Cash		24,000	
	Contributed surplus – ESOs			24,000
	(12,000 × $2)			

General Journal

If the market price of the shares later increased to $20 per share, the options will be "in the money," and employees holding these options will be motivated to purchase shares at a share price that is lower than the current share market price. If 8,000 of the 12,000 options were exercised to purchase shares at $15 each, the entry would be:

General Journal				
Date	Account/Explanation	PR	Debit	Credit
Jan 1	Cash		120,000	
	Contributed surplus – ESOs		16,000	
	Common shares			136,000
	For Cash: (8,000 × $15), for Contributed surplus: ((8,000 ÷ 12,000) × $24,000)			

If the remaining options were not used by the end of the exercise period, the entry would be:

General Journal				
Date	Account/Explanation	PR	Debit	Credit
Jan 1	Contributed surplus – ESOs		8,000	
	Contributed surplus – expired ESOs			8,000

14.5.2 Compensatory Stock Options Plans

These plans are compensation based and are usually offered to key executives as part of their remuneration package. The executive is granted the option to purchase shares of the company in lieu of compensation, commencing on the exercise date and throughout the fiscal periods, until the expiry date. By holding company shares, the executives can share in the benefits of ownership, the same as with ESOPs. The difference is that the options are part of their compensation package and are not purchased for cash. Meaning that, as the employment service period is completed, compensation expense is to be allocated and recorded as an expense accrual.

If options are allowed to expire because the service requirement is not met, such as when an employee leaves the company, IFRS requires that this change in estimate be changed prospectively as a change in estimate. In contrast, ASPE gives companies a choice to record the estimate as a change in estimate prospectively or to record forfeitures as they occur.

On August 1, 2015, Silverlights Ltd. granted stock options to its chief executive officer. Details are as follows:

Option to purchase	10,000 common shares
Option price per share	$20
Fair value per common share on grant date	$18
Fair value of options on grant date	$17
Date when options can be exercised	August 1, 2017
Date when options expire	July 31, 2022

On August 1, 2017, 4,000 options were exercised when the fair value of the common shares was $25. Note that the fair value of the options on the grant date has to be determined using an option pricing model, or some other valuation technique, as there is no active market for employee stock options. The remaining stock options were allowed to expire. The company year-end is July 31, follows ASPE, and management chose to account for the expired options as they occurred.

On the August 1, 2015, grant date, no entry is recorded because the service period has only just begun and, as such, no economic event has yet taken place.

On July 31, 2016, year-end date, an adjusting entry to accrue compensation expense for one year of completed service or 50%:

	General Journal			
Date	Account/Explanation	PR	Debit	Credit
Jul 31, 2016	Compensation expense.....................		85,000	
	Contributed surplus – CSOP.............			85,000
	(10,000 × $17 × 50%)			

On July 31, 2017, year-end date, the remaining accrual is completed:

	General Journal			
Date	Account/Explanation	PR	Debit	Credit
Jul 31, 2017	Compensation expense.....................		85,000	
	Contributed surplus – CSOP.............			85,000
	(10,000 × $17 × 50%)			

The total contributed surplus for this plan is now $170,000 ($85,000 year 1 + $85,000 year 2).

On August 1, 2017, exercise date for 4,000 options at the strike price:

	General Journal			
Date	Account/Explanation	PR	Debit	Credit
Aug 1, 2017	Cash...		80,000	
	Contributed surplus – CSOP.............		68,000	
	Common shares...........................			148,000
	For Cash: (4,000 × $20), for Contributed surplus: ((4,000 ÷ 10,000) × $170,000)			

On July 31, 2022, expiry date:

General Journal				
Date	Account/Explanation	PR	Debit	Credit
Jul 31, 2022	Contributed surplus – CSOP................ Contributed surplus – expired stock options....................................... ($170,000 – 68,000)		102,000	102,000

14.5.3 Stock Appreciation Rights and Performance-Based Plans

Stock Appreciation Rights Plans (SARs)

In this plan, employees' entitlement to receive cash-paid compensation is based on an increase in the fair value of a stated number of shares from the pre-existing share price over the exercise period. Note that no shares are actually issued. The share price is tracked and the cash-paid compensation is based on the results of these tracked changes. This plan eliminates the need for employees to actually exercise the options, buy the common shares, and then later sell the common shares, in order to realize the monetary gain. However, the issue is how to best measure the fair value of the shares between the grant date and exercise date. ASPE and IFRS differ in their approach to this valuation, where IFRS requires the use of an options pricing model, while ASPE uses a less complex formula that calculates the difference between the pre-established share price with the market or fair value price on the exercise date for each share granted to the employee. For both standards, the total amount is allocated over the service period and recorded as compensation expense and a corresponding liability.

Performance-Based Plans

Some companies opt to also use other performance criteria, rather than simply the change in share prices. Other ratios, such as growth in sales, earnings per share, and return on assets, may be used as the basis for the compensation payment (which is allocated the same way as SARs, as explained above). Sometimes a performance-based plan will be offered to employees in combination with an options-based plan, and the employee can choose.

14.5.4 Disclosures of Compensation Plans

Some of the main disclosures include:

- Description of the compensation plan, including the numbers and dollar values of the options issued, exercised, forfeited, and expired.

- Description of the assumptions incorporated, and methods used, to determine the fair values.

- Total compensation expense included in net income and its related contributed surplus.

The reporting disclosures listed above are a simplified version of the more extensive disclosures required by the accounting standards. For example, BCE Inc.'s financial statements dedicated a significant number of pages to compensation information contained in Notes 2, 21, and 26.[1] The company also prepared a 61-page compensation discussion and analysis report to supplement the note disclosures. From this example, it is clear that disclosures regarding compensation go far beyond what is normally expected.

14.6 Analysis

Complex financial instruments, including options, would be incorporated into liabilities and equity respectively. Refer to the other chapters on long-term debt and equity for details regarding analysis techniques for debt or equity instruments.

14.7 IFRS/ASPE Key Differences

Item	IFRS	ASPE
Initial measurement – instruments with contingent settlement provisions	Treated as a financial liability.	Treated as a financial liability if the contingency is highly likely.
Measurement of debt and equity components	Residual method: Measure debt component first at net present value of future cash flows. The residual balance to equity.	Policy choice: 1. Residual method 2. Zero-equity method: Equity measured at zero and the balance to liabilities.

---

[1] For information on the extent of disclosures required regarding compensation, refer to BCE (2013) and BCE (2015), notes 2, 21, and 26, starting at page 125.

| CSOP forfeitures | Measure forfeitures upfront as a change in estimate. | Policy choice to measure forfeitures upfront as a change in estimate or later as they occur. |

Chapter Summary

LO 1: Describe complex financial instruments and their role in accounting and business.

Companies obtain cash resources for future business operations and opportunities for internally generated free cash flow from borrowing from a creditor (debt) and from investors through issuing shares. Historically, debt and equity sources were separate instruments. However, in recent decades hybrid (or complex) instruments that include both debt and equity attributes are now available to businesses. Examples include convertible bonds, convertible preferred shares, and various derivatives (such as options and warrants) all of which can be converted into common shares. These instruments are often simpler, cheaper, and quicker to obtain, and they offer greater flexibility and security to investors because of the embedded convertible options to common shares. These complex instruments also have an effect on the perceptions of shareholders and the marketplace. As investors will only convert from the original instrument to common shares if it is favourable to do so, they then send a positive signal to existing shareholders that the company is performing well. The issue from an accounting perspective is how to separate, classify, and value the debt and equity attributes during the instrument's lifecycle of issuance, conversion, and retirement.

LO 2: Describe the basic differences in the accounting treatments for long-term debt and equity.

For complex financial instruments, once an acceptable method to separate the debt from the equity is determined, each component will follow its respective accounting standard as discussed in previous chapters. As such, it is important to understand the basics of debt and equity instruments so that the classification and amounts reported reflect their true underlying economic substance, rather than simply their legal form. For example, equity is measured and reported at historic cost and represents unsecured permanent capital of the company. As a return on their investment, shareholders receive a share of the profits through dividends, which are optional and not subject to income taxes for the company. Long-term debt consists of principal and interest expense, which must be paid when due and is secured by company assets. The debt has a negative effect on company liquidity and solvency ratios, and the interest expense reduces company income taxes. There are differences between IFRS and ASPE regarding amortization of methods and some disclosures of long-term debt.

LO 3: Describe the two methods acceptable to IFRS and ASPE to separate, classify, measure, and disclose complex financial instruments such as convertible debt and convertible preferred shares.

IFRS uses only the residual method for the accounting treatment of convertible debt, such as convertible bonds and preferred shares. This method estimates and allocates the fair value of the most reliable component first, usually the debt component. The residual amount remaining is allocated to the equity component. For the debt component, the valuation is based on the present value of the future cash flows using the prevailing market interest rate at issuance. In contrast, ASPE uses both the residual method and the zero-equity method. The zero-equity method assigns the full value to the debt component and a zero value to the equity component.

These methods are applied at the time of issuance for convertible debt, such as bonds that are issued at par or at a premium or discount. Bonds are subsequently measured at amortized cost. Bonds that are converted to common shares use the book value method to determine the valuations. The book value method uses the carrying values of the debt and contributed surplus at the time of conversion to determine the common shares amount (IFRS and ASPE). Since carrying values are the basis for the conversion, no gains or losses are recorded.

Convertible debt can also be retired prior to maturity, usually with an incentive, also known as a sweetener. This is used to motivate the bondholders to sell the debt back to the company or to convert their bonds into common shares. Both the amounts paid to the bondholders and the sweetener must be allocated between the debt and equity components. Because of the additional proceeds added as an incentive, gains or losses will occur. The sum of the gain or loss from the redemption of the bonds, and the proportionate share of the contributed surplus, must be equal to the additional proceeds paid as a sweetener. Disclosures of convertible debt, or convertible preferred shares, are the same as disclosures of other debt and equity instruments and securities. The determination of the classification, as either a liability or equity, is based on whether or not the company has any control over whether an obligation will arise from these convertible instruments. In cases where there is little or no control over the obligation, the transactions are reported as a liability (IFRS) or if the obligation is only highly likely (ASPE).

LO 4: Describe various derivatives such as options, warrants, forwards, and futures.

Options, warrants, forwards, and futures are all examples of derivatives. They are valued on the basis of the fluctuations in some underlying instrument, object, index, or event. If these derivatives have their own value then they can be bought and sold privately, or through the marketplace. Businesses will buy or sell to minimize risk (hedging) or to make a profit (speculation). An example of hedging can be seen in how companies handle the fluctuations in foreign exchange currency. For example, companies can obtain a derivative contract that locks in the exchange rate in order to manage these fluctuations, thereby hedging their risk. Options are another derivative that gives the options holder the right to purchase or sell common shares in a company at a specified price. The right to purchase common shares at a specified price is called a call option, for example employee stock options; whereas, the right to sell common shares at a specified price is called a put option. In either case, this will only occur if the specified price is favourable compared to the market price. Warrants have characteristics similar to options. Forward and future contracts are typically used to buy and sell any type of commodity, including currencies. In the case of a forward contract, once both parties agree on the terms the contract becomes binding. A futures contract is similar to a forward contract except that it is standardized regarding price and maturity dates, allowing them to be bought and sold in the stock markets. Commodities such as agricultural products and precious metals are examples of futures contracts. Generally, derivatives are subsequently measured at their fair value with a gain or loss reported in net income, except for derivatives that relate to a company's own shares, which are at historic cost.

LO 5: Explain the accounting treatments and reporting requirements for stock options plans.

An employee stock option plan (ESOP) allows employees to purchase shares of the company at a specified price, generally offered as a reward by the company to the employee. As these employees are investing in the company, the proceeds of their shares purchases are recorded to equity. In contrast, a compensatory stock option plan (CSOP) is generally offered to key executives as part of their remuneration package. Their shares entitlement is accrued to compensation expense as earned. Stock appreciation rights (SARs) are an example of compensation based plans where compensation is paid on the basis of the movement of the common shares price, but no actual shares are bought or sold. Performance-based plans use other performance indicators, such as growth in sales, as a basis for compensation. Required disclosures of compensation plans are extensive and include a description of the plan, the assumptions and methods used, and various other data such as the dollar values of the options issued, exercised, forfeited, and expired.

124 • Complex Financial Instruments

LO 6: Recall that analyses of complex financial instruments use the same techniques as those used in non-convertible debt and equity instruments.

LO 7: Explain the similarities and differences between ASPE and IFRS regarding recognition, measurement, and reporting of complex financial instruments.

While IFRS and ASPE are quite similar in this case, differences do remain. For example, regarding the issuance of complex financial instruments, ASPE provides the choice of either the residual method or the zero-equity method, whereas only the residual method is accepted for IFRS. Also, those instruments with contingent liabilities are treated as a liability for IFRS, but are only treated as such with ASPE if the contingency is highly likely. For options forfeitures in a CSOP, ASPE allows a policy choice to measure forfeitures upfront as a change in estimate or later, as they occur; whereas with IFRS, these must be measured upfront.

References

BCE. (2013, March 7). *Extract from the BCE 2013 management proxy circular: Compensation discussion and analysis.* Retrieved from http://www.bce.ca/investors/events-and-presentations/anterior-agm/2013-Compensation-Discussion-Analysis.pdf

BCE. (2015). *Annual report.* Retrieved from http://www.bce.ca/investors/AR-2015/2015-bce-annual-report.pdf

Scott Legal, P. C. (2013, March). *Convertible debt as a financing tool: Friend or foe? Advantages and disadvantages from the perspective of the founder of using convertible debt to raise capital* [blog]. Retrieved from http://legalservicesincorporated.com/convertible-debt-as-a-financing-tool-friend-or-foe-advantages-disadvantages-from-the-perspective-of-the-founder-of-using-convertible-debt-to-raise-capital/

Exercises

EXERCISE 14–1

On January 1, 2015, Largess Ltd. issued 1,000, 4-year, 6% convertible bonds at par of $1,000. Interest is payable each December 31. Each bond is convertible into 100 common shares, and the current fair value of each common share is $7 per share. Similar non-convertible bonds carry an interest rate of 8%.

Required:

a. Calculate the present value of the debt component.

b. Record the bond issuance assuming that Largess Ltd. follows IFRS.

c. Record the bond issuance assuming that Largess Ltd. follows ASPE.

EXERCISE 14–2

Holloway Ltd. issued 600, $1,000 bonds at 102. Each bond was issued with 12 detachable warrants. After issuance, similar bonds were sold at 96, and the warrants had a fair value of $3.

Required:

a. Record the issuance of the bonds and warrants assuming that Holloway Ltd. follows IFRS.

b. Assume now that Holloway Ltd. follows ASPE. Discuss the two alternative methods and record the issuance of the bonds and warrants for each method.

c. What effect does each entry have on the debt to total assets ratio?

EXERCISE 14–3

Snowden Corp. issued 10,000 common shares upon conversion of 8,000 preferred shares. The preferred shares were originally issued at $10 per share and the contributed surplus account for the preferred shares had a balance of $12,000. The common shares were trading at $11.50 per share at the time of the conversion.

Required: Record the conversion of the preferred shares.

EXERCISE 14–4

Rumpled Textures Inc. has $1 million of 7%, convertible bonds outstanding. Each $1,000 bond is convertible into 30 no-par value common shares. The bonds pay interest each

January 31 and July 31. On July 31, 2015, just after the interest payment, the holders of $600,000 worth of these bonds exercised their conversion entitlement. On that date, the following information was determined:

Market price of the bonds	102
Market price of the common shares	$ 26
Carrying value of the common shares	$ 16
Balance in the contributed surplus – convertible bonds	$150,000
Unamortized bond premium	$ 80,000

The remaining bonds were not converted and, at their maturity date, they were retired. The company follows IFRS.

Required:

a. Prepare the journal entry for the bond conversion on July 31, assuming that the company uses the book value method.

b. Prepare the journal entry for the remaining bonds at maturity, if not converted to shares.

c. What risks arise if bondholders choose to wait to convert the bonds?

EXERCISE 14–5

Brownlesh Inc. issued $6 million of par value, 5% bonds at 99, and one detachable warrant was issued with each $100 par value bond. At the time of issuance, the warrants were selling for $5. Brownlesh Inc. follows ASPE.

Required: Prepare the journal entry for the issuance of the instrument for both options allowed by ASPE.

EXERCISE 14–6

Irvin Corp. issued $2 million of par value, 7%, convertible bonds at 98. If the bonds had not been convertible, the fair value at the time of issuance would have been 97. Irvin Corp. follows ASPE.

Required: Prepare the journal entry for the issuance of the instrument for both options allowed by ASPE.

EXERCISE 14-7

On August 1, 2015, Venus Ltd. issued $400,000 of 6%, non-convertible bonds at 102, which are due in ten years. In addition, each $1,000 bond was issued with 10 detachable stock warrants, each of which entitled the bondholder to purchase one of Venus Ltd.'s no-par value common shares for $60. The bonds without the warrants would normally sell at 99. On August 1, 2015, the fair value of Venus Ltd.'s common shares was $50 per share. Venus Ltd. follows IFRS.

Required: Prepare the journal entry for the issuance of the instrument allowed by IFRS.

EXERCISE 14-8

On November 1, 2015, Norfolk Island Ltd. called its 8% convertible bonds for conversion, and $6 million of par value bonds were converted into 600,000 common shares. On this date, there was $350,000 of unamortized bond discount, and the company paid an additional $350,000 cash sweetener to the bondholders. At the time of conversion, the balance in the contributed surplus – convertible bonds account was $125,000, and the bond's fair value without the conversion feature – was $5.95 million. The company follows IFRS and uses the book value method to record the entry for conversion.

Required: Prepare the conversion entry.

EXERCISE 14-9

On September 1, 2015, Carmel Corp. sold 4,500 of its $1,000 face value, ten-year, 8%, non-convertible bonds with detachable warrants at 101 plus accrued interest. Each bond carried two detachable warrants and each warrant was for one common share at the option price of $12 per share. Shortly after issuance, the warrants were selling for $6 each. Assume that no fair value is available for the bonds. Interest is payable on December 1 and June 1. Carmel Corp. follows ASPE.

Required: Prepare the journal entry to record the issuance of the bonds under both options available for ASPE companies.

EXERCISE 14-10

On January 1, 2015, Deliverance Corp. offers five-year, 9% convertible bonds with a par value of $1,000. Interest is calculated every January 1. Each $1,000 bond may be converted into 500 common shares, which are currently trading at $3.50 per share. The effective interest rate on bonds is 10%. Deliverance Corp. issues 1,500 bonds at par and allocates the proceeds under the residual method, using debt first with the remainder of the proceeds allocated to the option.

On January 1, 2017, right after the interest payment, Deliverance Corp. offers an additional cash premium of $10,000 to the bondholders to convert. The bond's fair value at the conversion time is $1,470,000, without the conversion feature. The company follows IFRS.

Required:

a. Record the entry(ies) for the bond issuance.

b. Record the entry(ies) for the bond conversion.

EXERCISE 14–11

On January 1, 2015, Atlantis Corp. offers three-year, 5% convertible bonds with a par value of $1,000. Each $1,000 bond may be converted into 100 common shares, which are currently trading at $5 per share. The effective interest rate on bonds is 8%. Atlantis Corp. issues 1,000 bonds at par and allocates the proceeds under the residual method using debt first with the remainder of the proceeds allocated to the option.

On January 1, 2017, right after the interest payment, Atlantis Corp. decides to retire the convertible debt early and offers the bondholders $1,100,000 cash, which is the fair value of the instrument at the time of early retirement. The fair value of the debt portion of the convertible bonds is $981,462. The company follows IFRS.

Required:

a. Record the entry(ies) for the bond issuance.

b. Record the entry(ies) for the bond retirement.

EXERCISE 14–12

On January 1, 2015, Bronds Inc. entered into a forward contract to purchase $50,000 US for $60,000 CAD in 30 days. On January 15, the present value of the future cash flows of the contract was $25.

Required:

a. Prepare the related entries for January 1, 2015, and January 15, 2015.

b. Assume that the instrument is now a futures contract that is publicly traded on the futures exchange. Bronds Inc. paid a deposit of $20 with the broker. On January 15, the present value of the future cash flows of the contract was $25. Prepare the entries, if any, for January 1, 2015, and January 15, 2015.

EXERCISE 14–13

On January 1, 2015, Twitter Co. granted stock options (CSOP) to its chief executive officer. The details are as follows:

Option to purchase through a stock option plan	10,000 common shares
Options share price	$34 per share
Fair value of shares on grant date	$30 per share
Fair value of options on date of grant	$20 per share
Stock options exercise start date	January 1, 2017
Stock options exercise expiry date	December 31, 2022

On January 1, 2018, 7,000 of the options were exercised when the fair value of the common shares was $45. The remaining stock options were allowed to expire. The chief executive officer remained with the company throughout the period. The company follows ASPE.

Required: Prepare all related journal entries for the stock option plan for:

- January 1, 2015
- December 31, 2015
- December 31, 2016
- January 1, 2018
- December 31, 2022

EXERCISE 14–14

On November 1, 2015, Agencolt Inc. adopted a stock option plan that granted options to employees to purchase 8,000 shares. On January 1, 2016, the options were granted and were exercisable within a two-year period beginning January 1, 2018 (if the employees were still employed by the company at the time of the exercise). The option price was set at $10 per share and the total compensation package was estimated to be worth $200,000, without forfeitures.

On May 1, 2018, 3,000 options were exercised when the market price of Agencolt Inc.'s shares were $15 per share. The remaining options lapsed in 2019 when some of the employees resigned from the company. The company follows IFRS and the initial assumption was that there would be no forfeitures.

Required: (Round final answers to the nearest whole number.)

a. Prepare all related journal entries for the stock option plan for the years ended December 31, 2016, to December 31, 2019, inclusive. Assume that the employees who resigned had fulfilled all their obligations to the employer at the time they purchased any stock options in May of 2018.

b. What is the significance of the $15 per share with regard to the decision to exercise the right to purchase shares?

Chapter 15

Income Taxes

Double Irish with a Dutch Sandwich

In October 2014, readers of business periodicals may have wondered if the headlines were describing the writers' lunch orders. However, the news about the "Double Irish" and the "Dutch Sandwich" dealt with the more complicated issue of multinational tax avoidance. In October 2014, the government of Ireland announced changes to legislation that would effectively phase out the "Double Irish" tax-planning structure favoured by many American technology companies such as Apple, Google, LinkedIn, IBM, Yahoo, and Microsoft. The structure, while perfectly legal, was criticized because it resulted in American corporations paying very little tax on their operations outside of the United States. Some critics have claimed that these types of structures allow multinational companies to avoid paying an equitable share of the tax burden.

The structure required the incorporation of two Irish companies, one of which was considered by Irish law as being resident of an offshore, low-tax jurisdiction (typically countries like Bermuda or the Bahamas). Through a series of arrangements and transactions involving the licensing of intellectual property, the parent company could essentially move profits out of a high-tax jurisdiction to a low-tax jurisdiction. The "Dutch Sandwich" involves the addition of another subsidiary incorporated in the Netherlands, which takes advantage of the European Union (EU) rules that allow tax-free transfers between companies resident in EU countries.

The legislation introduced by the Irish government will eliminate the effectiveness of the structure because new companies registered in Ireland will now also have to be resident in Ireland. Critics have noted, however, that the legislation only applies to newly incorporated companies and that existing companies will have until 2020 to comply with the rules. It was also noted that, at the same time, the Irish government introduced a "knowledge development box," which would essentially allow for a lower tax rate on profits derived from intellectual property. Other critics observed that eliminating the "Double Irish" structure might simply result in EU-based tax havens such as Malta becoming more popular.

Although the effects of the new legislation have yet to be fully realized, the long time-frame allowed in the grandfather clause will likely mean that companies will simply find other ways to minimize their tax payments. The fact that companies invested substantial resources in the planning and development of these tax structures should make it clear that income taxes are a significant issue for company management. Income taxes can be a material expense item on many companies'

> income statements, so the use of these types of tax structures should not be surprising.
>
> (Source: The Economist, 2014)

Chapter 15 Learning Objectives

After completing this chapter, you should be able to:

LO 1: Explain the relationship between taxable profit and accounting profit and calculate current taxes payable.

LO 2: Explain what permanent and temporary differences are and describe the deferred tax effects of those differences.

LO 3: Calculate the deferred tax effects of temporary differences and record the journal entries for current and deferred taxes.

LO 4: Determine the effect of changes in tax rates and calculate current and deferred tax amounts under conditions of changing rates.

LO 5: Analyze the effect of tax losses and determine the appropriate accounting of those losses.

LO 6: Explain the rationale for the annual review of deferred tax assets and describe the effects of this review.

LO 7: Prepare the presentation of income tax amounts on the balance sheet and income statement and explain the disclosure requirements.

LO 8: Explain the key differences between the treatment of income taxes under IFRS and ASPE.

Introduction

The levy of taxes is a well-established method for governments to raise the funds necessary to carry out its various programs and initiatives. There are, of course, always vigorous debates about the appropriate level of taxation and the uses to which the taxation proceeds are put, but it is an inescapable truth that governments require some form of taxation revenue to function. One form of taxation that is commonly used is an *income tax*. Most of us are familiar with the application of personal income tax, as this type of tax is levied on employment and other forms of personal income. Governments also raise funds through assessing income taxes on corporate profits. This practice raises some interesting and complex accounting questions, and it is these questions that will be addressed in this chapter. We will not, however, be examining the processes involved in preparing corporate tax returns or the development of sophisticated tax structures like the one described in the opening vignette, as our focus is on the financial accounting and reporting issues. As well, we will not be looking at other forms of taxation, such as value-added taxes or payroll taxes, as these topics have been discussed in previous chapters.

Chapter Organization

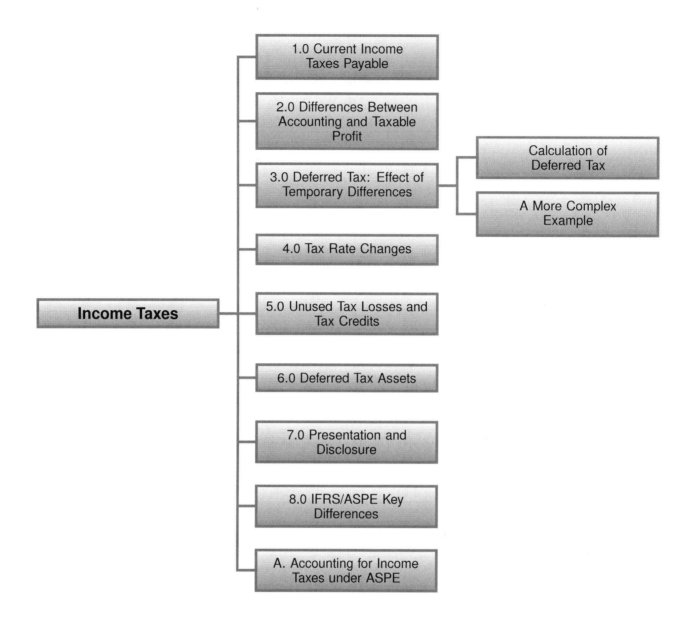

15.1 Current Income Taxes Payable

When a company completes a fiscal year, it will produce a set of financial statements. In most jurisdictions, the financial statements will be the starting point for the income tax calculation. A corporate tax return will usually start with the *net income before taxes* or *accounting profit* taken directly from the company's income statement. This amount will then be subject to a number of adjustments until the final result, the **taxable profit** or **taxable income**, is determined. It is on this taxable profit that the corporate income tax will then be levied.

There are a number of reasons that taxation authorities require adjustments to the accounting profit before levying the tax. As we have seen in previous chapters, there are several areas in accounting standards where significant judgments or estimations are required. As taxation regulations are written into laws, the authorities need to create more certainty in interpretation to enable enforcement. Thus, some types of subjectively determined amounts that are acceptable under IFRS may not be considered appropriate for tax calculation purposes. Another reason is the need for consistency. Although IFRS allows companies the flexibility to choose among different acceptable accounting policies, taxation authorities are more concerned with fairness and transparency, which often requires a higher level of consistency in treatment of certain types of transactions. A third reason is the desire of governments to use the taxation system as a tool to achieve policy goals. For example, if a government wanted to encourage investment in a specific industry sector, it could allow certain tax incentives to those companies that invest in the property, plant, and equipment required for those particular industry activities. These incentives may create a difference in the way accounting profit and taxable profit are calculated.

Regardless of the reasons for the differences, the accountant's objective is to properly record the appropriate income tax expense and outstanding income tax liability at the end of the year. The simplest way to do this is to take the amount of tax owing, as determined on the corporate tax return, and record it. Let's look at an example to see how this would work.

Assume that for financial statement purposes, a company reports revenue from a long-term contract on the basis of services rendered, which results in $30,000 net revenue per year over a two-year period. As well, assume that no cash is received until the end of the second year, and that the taxation authorities tax this revenue at a rate of 20% only when the cash is received. Thus, no tax would be payable in the first year, and $12,000 ($60,000 × 20%) tax would be payable in the second year. If we simply record the tax expense when the taxation authority assesses it, the company's income statement would look like this:

	Year 1	Year 2
Income before tax	$30,000	$30,000
Income tax expense	0	12,000
Net income	$30,000	$18,000

This is clearly not a satisfactory result, as the income tax expense has not been properly matched to the revenue that created it. This approach, sometimes referred to as the **taxes payable method**, is not allowed under IFRS due to this improper matching. It is, however, allowed under ASPE, which will be discussed further in the Appendix.

To properly convey the economic substance of the transactions, the income tax expense should be $6,000 per year, which would result in net income of $24,000 per year. This result would properly show how the reported income is attracting a tax liability, even though the actual levy of the taxes does not occur until year 2. Thus, in year 1, the company has created a *deferred* tax liability that will not need to be paid until year 2. It is these deferred tax amounts that create complications in accounting, and as such, we need to understand their nature in more detail.

15.2 Differences Between Accounting and Taxable Profit

There are a variety of causes of the differences between accounting profit and taxable profit. These can be summarized as follows:

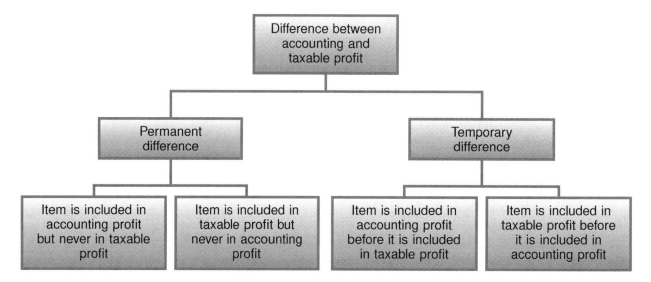

Let's look at each of these situations.

Permanent Differences

These differences arise when an item is included in one type of reporting (accounting or tax) but is permanently excluded from the other type of reporting. Items that are included in the determination of accounting profit but not taxable profit can be both revenue and expense items. An example of a revenue item would be a dividend received from another company that is not taxed in the reporting jurisdiction. Many jurisdictions allow this tax-free flow of inter-corporate dividends. In this case, the dividend would be reported on the company's statement of profit, but would never be taxed. An example of an expense item would be a sports club membership for the company's executive officers. Many businesses consider this type of item to be an appropriate form of promotion and business development, but many tax authorities do not allow this to be deducted when calculating taxable profit. Items that are included in taxable profit but never in accounting profit are less common. These include such items as certain depletion allowances allowed for natural resources and certain types of capital taxes that are not based on income.

The accounting treatment for permanent differences is quite straightforward. Because these items do not affect future periods, there is no effect on future taxes. Thus, the amount is simply included (or excluded) in the determination of current taxable profit and the resulting tax payable is reported as a liability.

Temporary Differences

We can further classify temporary differences as follows:

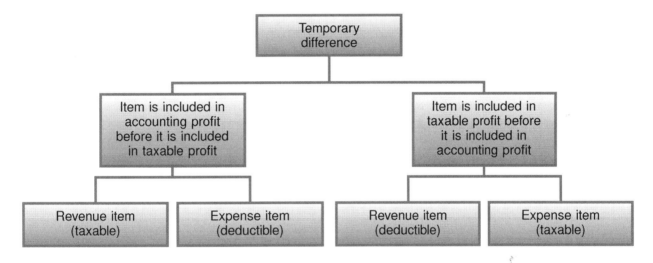

Note that the items are classified as being either **taxable** or **deductible**. This feature refers to the item's effect on *future* tax calculations: taxable temporary differences increase future tax payable while deductible temporary differences decrease future tax payable. For example, a warranty expense to reflect the cost of future repairs may be accrued for accounting purposes, but the appropriate tax law does not allow any deduction in determining taxable profit until the repairs are actually made. In this case, the expense is a deductible temporary difference because it will allow for a deduction against taxable profit in a future period when the repairs actually occur.

The following are some common examples of deductible and taxable temporary differences:

	Revenue Item	**Expense Item**
Taxable	Construction revenue	Capital allowance in excess of depreciation
	Instalment sales	Pension funding in excess of expense
	Unrealized holding gains	Certain prepaid expenses
Deductible	Subscriptions paid in advance	Capital allowance less than depreciation
	Royalties and rent paid in advance	Pension expense in excess of funding
	Sale and leaseback gains	Warranty accruals
		Litigation accruals
		Unrealized holding losses

These examples only represent a sample of the types of items that can result in temporary differences. In determining the tax expense for the year, the accountant must consider the effect on all items for which the accounting treatment and the tax treatment are different. For example, with construction revenue, the company will normally choose the percentage of completion method to recognize revenue for accounting purposes. However, many tax jurisdictions will allow the company to defer the recognition of revenue on a long-term construction contract until the project is completed. This will result in a future taxable amount, as future revenue for tax purposes will be greater since the revenue has already been recognized for accounting purposes.

15.3 Deferred Tax: Effect of Temporary Differences

An important point in understanding the effect of temporary differences on the company's tax expense is the fact that temporary differences reverse themselves. That is, whatever effect the temporary difference has on the current tax expense, it will have an opposite effect in some future period. To determine the amount that will reverse in the future, we first need to consider how the temporary difference is calculated. IAS 12 defines a temporary difference as the "differences between the carrying amount of an asset or liability in the statement of financial position and its tax base" (CPA Canada, 2016, Accounting, IAS 12.5). Note that this definition uses a balance sheet perspective in that it focuses on the balances in the statement of financial position rather than on revenue and expense items recorded in the period. This is consistent with the conceptual framework, which defines revenues and expenses in terms of changes in the net assets of the business. To further understand this definition, we need to consider the item's tax base, which is "the amount attributed to [the] asset or liability for tax purposes" (CPA Canada, 2016, Accounting, IAS 12.5). The tax base of an asset is the amount that will be deductible in future periods against taxable economic benefits when the asset's carrying amount is recovered. If there is no future taxable benefit to be derived from the asset, then the tax base is equal to the carrying amount. The tax base of a liability is its carrying amount, less any amount that will be deductible in future periods with respect to the item. For unearned revenue, the amount that is deductible in the future can be thought of as the amount of revenue that is not taxable.

These definitions can be best understood by looking at a few examples:

- Goods are sold on credit to customers for $6,000, creating an account receivable on the company's records. This asset has a carrying value of $6,000 and tax law requires that the amount to be reported as revenue in the period of the sale. Thus, the amount is fully taxable in the current period and will not be taxable in the future period. Because there is no future taxable benefit derived from this asset, its tax base is $6,000 (i.e., equal to its carrying value) and there is no temporary difference.

- A company reports an accrued liability for warranty costs of $72,000, which is its carrying value. This amount will not be deductible for tax purposes until the costs are actually incurred. The tax base is the carrying value less the amount deductible in future periods ($72,000 − $72,000), or $0. Thus, there is a deductible temporary difference of $72,000.

- A company purchased a piece of equipment for $100,000 several years ago. The current balance of accumulated depreciation is $36,000, thus the carrying value is $64,000. For tax purposes, accelerated capital allowances of $52,000 have been claimed and, therefore, the remaining balance that can be claimed for tax purposes in the future is $48,000. The tax base is $48,000 and there is a taxable temporary difference of $16,000 ($64,000 − $48,000).

- Current liabilities include $21,000 of unearned subscription revenue that was paid in advance and the revenue was taxed in the current period when it was received. The tax base is the carrying value ($21,000) less the amount that is deductible in the future ($21,000, representing the revenue that will not be taxable), or $0. Thus, there is a deductible temporary difference of $21,000 ($21,000 − $0).

- Included in current liabilities are accrued fines and penalties for late payment of taxes in the amount of $8,000. These are not deductible for tax purposes. The tax base is, therefore, $8,000 ($8,000 − $0). There is no difference between the carrying value and the tax base. This is a permanent difference that only affects current taxes, not future taxes.

There are many other examples of temporary and permanent differences. The definitions above should always be applied to determine if a temporary difference exists or not, as this will determine the need to record a deferred tax amount. In some cases, deferred tax balances may result from a situation where there is no asset or liability recorded on the balance sheet. For example, a company may incur a research expense that cannot be capitalized under IFRS. However, the amount may be deductible in a future period against taxable income. In this case, there is no carrying value, as there is no asset, but there is a future deductible amount. This would create a deductible temporary difference.

15.3.1 Calculation of Deferred Tax

Once the temporary and permanent differences have been analyzed, the deferred tax amounts can be calculated and recorded. Let's consider an example where the accounting depreciation and capital allowance for tax purposes are different.

A company purchases an asset on January 1, 2016, for $90,000. For accounting purposes, it will be depreciated straight-line over a three-year useful life with no residual value. For tax purposes, assume that capital allowances can be claimed in the first year equal to 50% of the asset's cost, and in the second and third years equal to 25% of the asset's cost. The carrying values and tax values will, therefore, be calculated as follows:

	Accounting Records			Tax Records		
	2016	2017	2018	2016	2017	2018
Cost	90,000	90,000	90,000	90,000	90,000	90,000
Accumulated depreciation/ Cumulative capital allowance	30,000	60,000	90,000	45,000	67,500	90,000
Carrying amount/tax base	60,000	30,000	0	45,000	22,500	0

The temporary differences are calculated as follows:

  2016: $60,000 − $45,000 = $15,000 taxable temporary difference
  2017: $30,000 − $22,500 = $7,500   taxable temporary difference
  2018: $0 − $0   = nil temporary difference

The company reports net income of $100,000 in 2016, $120,000 in 2017, and $150,000 in 2018 and pays tax at a rate of 20% on its taxable income. Assume that there are no other differences between accounting and taxable income except the depreciation and capital allowances.

Tax payable in each year would be calculated as follows:

15.3. Deferred Tax: Effect of Temporary Differences

	2016	2017	2018
Accounting income	100,000	120,000	150,000
Add non-deductible depreciation	30,000	30,000	30,000
Subtract deductible capital allowance	(45,000)	(22,500)	(22,500)
Taxable income	85,000	127,500	157,500
Tax rate	20%	20%	20%
Tax payable	17,000	25,500	31,500

Note that the tax payable above is the amount of expense that would be recorded if the taxes payable method were used, which is only allowed under ASPE.

The deferred tax each year is calculated as follows:

	2016	2017	2018
Temporary difference	15,000	7,500	0
Tax rate	20%	20%	20%
Deferred tax liability at end of year	3,000	1,500	0
Less previous balance	–	(3,000)	(1,500)
Adjustment required in year	3,000	(1,500)	(1,500)

Note that in 2016, the temporary difference creates a deferred tax liability. This is because the capital allowance claimed is greater than the accounting depreciation, meaning less tax is paid in the current year but more will be paid in future years. In 2017 and 2018, the temporary difference reverses itself.

The company would record the following journal entries each year for the tax amounts:

	General Journal			
Date	Account/Explanation	PR	Debit	Credit
2016	Current tax expense		17,000	
	Income tax payable.			17,000
	Deferred tax expense		3,000	
	Deferred tax liability.			3,000
2017	Current tax expense		25,500	
	Income tax payable.			25,500
	Deferred tax liability		1,500	
	Deferred tax income			1,500
2018	Current tax expense		31,500	
	Income tax payable.			31,500
	Deferred tax liability		1,500	
	Deferred tax income			1,500

The deferred tax income amounts in 2017 and 2018 represent a *negative expense*, or a recovery of the expense that was previously charged in 2016. This represents the tax effect of the reversal of the temporary difference. This type of negative expense may sometimes be referred to as a **deferred tax benefit**.

Excerpts from the company's income statements over the three years will look like this:

	2016	2017	2018
Income before tax	100,000	120,000	150,000
Income taxes:			
Current	(17,000)	(25,500)	(31,500)
Deferred	(3,000)	1,500	1,500
Net income	80,000	96,000	120,000

Note that each year the net income can be calculated as the income before tax multiplied by 1 − tax rate (i.e., 100% − 20% = 80%). The reporting of the deferred tax amount has achieved proper matching by allocating the correct total tax expense to each period, which was the objective of the example examined in section 15.1.

Also note that even though the temporary difference reverses over a period of two years, we have not attempted to account for the time value of money. IAS 12 explicitly prohibits the discounting of future tax amounts, as it views the prediction of temporary difference reversals too complex and impractical. The prohibition of discounting is a way to maintain comparability between companies and acknowledges the trade-off between the costs and benefits of this type of information production.

15.3.2 A More Complex Example

Let's now look at a more complex example involving a deferred tax asset and a permanent difference.

A company that sells computer printers offers a two-year warranty on each model sold. The fair value of the warranty cannot be independently determined, so the company uses the expense approach to determine the provision for the warranty liability. (See the current liabilities chapter for further details of the application of this approach.) In 2016, the total provision determined for future warranty costs was $80,000. The company expects that the actual repair costs will be incurred as follows: $20,000 in 2017 and $60,000 in 2018. No warranty repairs were incurred in 2016 when the sales were made. In the jurisdiction where the company operates, warranty costs are only deductible for tax purposes when they are actually incurred. As well, in 2017 the company received notice of a $5,000 penalty assessed for violation of certain consumer protection laws, and this penalty is not deductible for tax purposes. The company reported accounting income of $320,000 in 2016, $350,000 in 2017, and $390,000 in 2018.

The warranty liability reported in 2016 represents a deductible temporary difference because it results in amounts that will be deductible against future taxable income (i.e., when the warranty repairs are actually incurred). This will result in deferred tax asset originating in 2016 and then reversing in 2017 and 2018. We can analyze this temporary difference as follows:

	Accounting Records			Tax Records		
	2016	2017	2018	2016	2017	2018
Carrying amount, opening	80,000	80,000	60,000	0	0	0
Warranty costs incurred in year	0	20,000	60,000	0	20,000	60,000
Carrying amount, closing	80,000	60,000	0	0	0	0

Note that the calculation of the carrying value for tax purposes, or tax base, follows the general rule described previously for liabilities (i.e., the tax base is the carrying value for accounting purposes less the amount deductible against future taxable income). Thus, the tax base is always nil because the carrying value for accounting purposes always represents the amount deductible against future taxable income.

The temporary differences are calculated as follows:

2016: $80,000 − $0 = $80,000 deductible temporary difference
2017: $60,000 − $0 = $60,000 deductible temporary difference
2018: $0 − $0 = nil temporary difference

The penalty incurred in 2017 represents a permanent difference, as this amount will never be deductible for tax purposes. Thus, this will only affect the current taxes in 2017 and will have no effect on deferred taxes.

If we assume a 20% tax rate, the calculation of tax payable will be as follows:

	2016	2017	2018
Accounting income	320,000	350,000	390,000
Add non-deductible penalty	0	5,000	0
Add non-deductible warranty provision	80,000	0	0
Subtract deductible warranty costs	(0)	(20,000)	(60,000)
Taxable income	400,000	335,000	330,000
Tax rate	20%	20%	20%
Tax payable	80,000	67,000	66,000

The deferred tax each year would be calculated as follows:

	2016	2017	2018
Temporary difference	80,000	60,000	0
Tax rate	20%	20%	20%
Deferred tax asset at end of year	16,000	12,000	0
Less previous balance	–	(16,000)	(12,000)
Adjustment required in year	16,000	(4,000)	(12,000)

The originating temporary difference in 2016 creates a deferred tax asset, which means that more tax is being paid in the current year, but less tax will be paid in future years when the temporary difference reverses itself.

The company will record the following journal entries each year for the tax amounts:

	General Journal			
Date	Account/Explanation	PR	Debit	Credit
2016	Current tax expense		80,000	
	Income tax payable			80,000
	Deferred tax asset		16,000	
	Deferred tax income			16,000
2017	Current tax expense		67,000	
	Income tax payable			67,000
	Deferred tax expense		4,000	
	Deferred tax asset			4,000
2018	Current tax expense		66,000	
	Income tax payable			66,000
	Deferred tax expense		12,000	
	Deferred tax asset			12,000

Excerpts from the company's income statements over the three years will look like this:

	2016	2017	2018
Income before tax	320,000	350,000	390,000
Income taxes:			
Current	(80,000)	(67,000)	(66,000)
Deferred	16,000	(4,000)	(12,000)
Net income	256,000	279,000	312,000

In 2016 and 2018, the total tax expense can be calculated as the income before tax multiplied by the tax rate. Therefore, as previously discussed, proper matching has been achieved. In 2017, the calculation does not reflect this result because of the effect of the permanent difference. The permanent difference creates a difference between tax and accounting income that will not reverse in future periods. Thus, there will be a permanent difference between the nominal and effective tax rate in that year only. We can see this in 2017, where the accounting income multiplied by the nominal tax rate is $70,000 ($350,000 × 20%), but the total tax expense is $71,000 ($67,000 + $4,000). The $1,000 difference is due to the effect of the permanent difference, which results in an effective tax rate of 20.29% ($71,000 ÷ $350,000). Proper matching has still been achieved in this year with respect to the temporary difference, but the permanent difference cannot be matched to a different period.

15.4 Tax Rate Changes

So far our examples have assumed a constant tax rate over the period of temporary difference reversal. However, this may not always be the case, as tax rates and regulations are subject to periodic changes as governments implement new policy directions. IAS 12 requires the deferred tax amounts to be measured at the rate expected to be in effect when the related asset is realized or the liability is settled. The standard further states that the rates should be enacted, or substantively enacted, by the end of the reporting period. **Substantively enacted** means that although the rate may not be formalized into law at the end of the reporting period, it has been publicly announced by the government and is very likely to be subsequently altered through a legislative process. Let's look at an example of how this is applied.

A company reports $30,000 of instalment revenue in 2016 that will be paid in two equal instalments in 2017 and 2018. Additionally, the revenue will be taxed when the payments are actually received. The $30,000 receivable thus creates a taxable temporary difference that reverses over the next two years, and this temporary difference will result in a deferred tax liability. The government has recently announced that tax rates will be implemented as follows: 2016 – 25%, 2017 – 22%, and 2018 – 20%.

The deferred tax liability would be measured as follows:

Total temporary difference arising in 2016	$ 30,000			
Amount reversing in 2017	(15,000)	× 22%	=	$ 3,300
Amount reversing in 2018	(15,000)	× 20%	=	$ 3,000
Total	$ 0			$ 6,300

Thus, on the company's 2016 balance sheet a deferred tax liability of $6,300 would be reported and, on the 2016 income statement, a deferred tax expense of $6,300 would also be reported.

This situation is quite straightforward, as we simply apply the appropriate enacted rate to the amount of the reversing temporary difference each year. However, there can be complications if the reversal can be realized in different ways. For example, many tax jurisdictions apply different tax rates to capital gains and ordinary income. In order to properly determine the deferred tax amount related to an asset, an assumption needs to be made about how the temporary difference will be realized (i.e., will the asset be used or sold during the reversal period?). IAS 12 states that the rate applied should be consistent with the company's intended use of the asset. In other words, two identical assets could result in different deferred tax amounts if one is to be sold and the other is to be used in operations. This difference in treatment reflects the conceptual framework's requirement to convey the economic truth of a transaction, rather than the mere substance.

A more complicated situation arises when tax rates are changed after the deferred tax amount has already been established in previous years. This type of change is treated as a change in estimate and, as such, should be treated prospectively. This means that an adjustment is made in the current period, but no attempt is made to restate prior years. This treatment is considered reasonable as management would not have known about the tax rate change when the deferred tax balance was originally established.

Let's revisit the previous example, with one change. Assume that change in tax rates was not announced until the middle of 2017, and that the 25% rate was already in effect for 2016. At the end of 2016, the company would have recorded a deferred tax liability of $7,500 ($30,000 × 25%).

In 2017 when the rate change is announced, the company needs to recalculate the deferred tax liability and adjust it accordingly. As such, the following journal entry would be required:

	General Journal			
Date	Account/Explanation	PR	Debit	Credit
2017	Deferred tax liability............................		1,200	
	Deferred tax income........................			1,200
	($7,500 − $6,300)			

At the end of the year when the temporary difference partially reverses, the following journal entry would be required:

	General Journal			
Date	Account/Explanation	PR	Debit	Credit
2017	Deferred tax liability............................		3,300	
	Deferred tax income........................			3,300

Thus, in 2017 the company will report a total deferred tax income of $4,500, which represents both the effect of the rate change on the opening temporary difference and the effect of temporary difference reversal during the year. Although this amount may be reported as a single line item on the income statement, IAS 12 does require separate disclosures for the effect of the temporary difference reversal and the effect of the rate change.

15.5 Unused Tax Losses and Tax Credits

A company may, at times, suffer a taxable loss in a given year. Because income tax is based on a percentage of taxable income, this situation results in no tax being payable. However, it does not result in a negative tax (i.e., a refund). Instead, companies are often allowed to apply the taxable loss to other taxation years where taxable profits were earned. Although the tax laws vary by jurisdiction, it is common to allow the loss to be carried back for a certain number of years and carried forward for a certain number of years. In Canada, the current law allows the loss to be carried back 3 years and carried forward 20 years.

When a loss is carried back and applied to previous years' taxable income, the result will be a refund of taxes paid in that year. This will be achieved by filing amended tax returns for the previous year(s) showing the application of the loss, and then requesting a refund of the taxes previously paid. It is important to note that the rate at which the taxes are refunded will be *the rate in effect in the previous year*, not the current tax rate.

Consider the following example. In 2016, a company suffers a taxable loss of $100,000. Taxable incomes reported in the three previous years were as follows:

$$
\begin{array}{ll}
2013 & \$10,000 \\
2014 & 86,000 \\
2015 & 90,000
\end{array}
$$

The tax rates in effect were 30% in 2013, 25% in 2014 and 2015, and 20% in 2016. The loss incurred in 2016 will be carried back and taxes will be recovered as follows:

$$
\begin{array}{lll}
2013 \quad \$10,000 \times 30\% & = & \$ \quad 3,000 \\
2014 \quad \$86,000 \times 25\% & = & 21,500 \\
2015 \quad \$4,000 \times 25\% & = & \underline{1,000} \\
\text{Total refund} & & \$ \quad 25,500
\end{array}
$$

Note that the total amount carried back cannot exceed the amount of the current year loss ($100,000). It is common practice for companies to apply the loss to the oldest tax years first, and then apply remaining amounts to more recent years. However, other patterns of application are also possible, depending on the circumstances of the company and the tax rates in effect each year.

In the above example, the company will record the following journal entry in 2016:

	General Journal			
Date	Account/Explanation	PR	Debit	Credit
2016	Income tax receivable........................		25,500	
	Current tax income			25,500

The company's income statement will be presented as follows:

Loss before tax	(100,000)
Income taxes:	
Current tax income from loss carryback	25,500
Net loss	(74,500)

The income tax receivable will be presented as a current asset on the balance sheet, as it should be recovered within one year. No other accounting entries are required in this case.

A more complicated situation occurs when the amount of the current year tax loss exceeds the taxable income of the previous three years. In this case, a portion of the current tax loss is unused and may be carried forward. When carrying forward a tax loss, the company is expecting to apply it to a future year when taxable income is once again earned. However, this now creates uncertainty, because the company's ability to earn taxable income in the future is not guaranteed. IAS 12 states that a deferred tax asset can be set up to recognize the benefit of the loss carried forward only if it is probable that future taxable profit will be available to utilize the loss. Although the standard does not define **probable**, an accepted interpretation of this term is "more likely than not." IAS 12 indicates that the presence of a loss itself casts some doubt on the company's ability to generate future profits. In assessing the probability of future taxable income, the accountant should consider not only the presence of a current loss, but also other factors such as the existence of temporary differences that will reverse in the future, the persistence and nature of the current loss, and tax planning opportunities that may allow the loss to be used in the future. This is another area where judgment on the part of the accountant is required.

Let's revisit our previous example, with one change. Assume now that the loss in the current year is $300,000 and that all other factors remain the same. In this situation, the company will first apply as much of the loss as possible to the previous three years. This will generate a tax refund calculated as follows:

$$
\begin{aligned}
2013 \quad &\$10,000 \times 30\% = \$\ 3,000 \\
2014 \quad &\$86,000 \times 25\% = 21,500 \\
2015 \quad &\$90,000 \times 25\% = \underline{22,500} \\
\text{Total refund} \quad & \underline{\underline{\$47,000}}
\end{aligned}
$$

The company will make the following journal entry with respect to this loss:

Date	Account/Explanation	PR	Debit	Credit
2016	Income tax receivable...............................		47,000	
	Current tax income			47,000

General Journal

In addition, the company needs to consider the effect of the loss carried forward, which is calculated as $114,000 ($300,000 − $10,000 − $86,000 − $90,000). If, after assessing all the relevant facts and conditions, the company believes it is probable that sufficient future taxable profit will be generated to utilize the loss, a deferred tax asset can be recognized as follows:

Date	Account/Explanation	PR	Debit	Credit
2016	Deferred tax asset.............................		22,800	
	Deferred tax income			22,800

General Journal

The amount is calculated as follows: $114,000 × 20% = $22,800. Note, as with other deferred tax amounts, we are using the rate that we expect to be in effect when the amount is realized. In this case, the current rate of 20% is used, as there is no indication that the rate will change in the future.

The company would report the tax amounts on the 2016 income statement as follows:

Loss before tax	(300,000)
Income taxes:	
Current tax income from loss carryback	47,000
Deferred tax income from loss carryforward	22,800
Net loss	(230,200)

Now, if in 2017 the company earns a profit of $250,000, the loss carryforward can be fully utilized. By doing so, the company could reduce its current tax payable as follows:

Taxable profit reported	$ 250,000
Loss carryforward utilized	(114,000)
Taxable profit, adjusted	136,000
Tax rate	20%
Current tax payable	$ 27,200

The following journal entries would be required in 2017:

General Journal

Date	Account/Explanation	PR	Debit	Credit
2017	Current tax expense		27,200	
	Current tax payable			27,200
	Deferred tax expense		22,800	
	Deferred tax asset			22,800

The company's 2017 income statement is presented as follows:

Income before tax	250,000
Income taxes:	
Current tax expense	(27,200)
Deferred tax expense	(22,800)
Net income	200,000

The deferred tax expense represents the reversal of the benefit realized in 2016, when the loss was initially created. The deferred tax asset would carry a nil balance at the end of the 2017.

Returning to 2016, if the company had determined that it was not probable that it would be able to generate future taxable profits to utilize the loss, then no deferred tax asset would be recorded in that year. In a subsequent year, if profits were actually generated, then the current tax expense for that year would simply be reduced by the effect of the loss carryforward. In our example above, only the current tax entries would be recorded, and the deferred tax recognition and reversal entries would not be recorded. Although this treatment would mean presentation of a single, reduced current tax amount in the year that the loss is utilized, disclosure must be made of the components of this reduced tax, that is, the current tax otherwise calculated less the effect of the loss carryforward.

15.6 Deferred Tax Assets

As we have seen, deferred tax assets are created when there are loss carryforwards or deductible temporary differences. Consistent with the conceptual framework, IAS 12 only allows recognition of these assets when their future realization is probable. However, as discussed previously, there can be a fair degree of uncertainty in making this determination. As a result of this uncertainty, IAS 12 requires a review of any deferred tax assets at the end of every reporting period. If the initial recognition assessment has changed, and it is no longer probable that part or all of the deferred tax asset will be realized, then the carrying value of the asset should be reduced and charged against profit as part of the deferred tax expense.

The opposite situation, however, can also occur. If a deferred tax asset was not recognized in a previous period because the future realization was not probable, and conditions in the current year have changed to the point that future realization is now probable, then the deferred tax asset can be established and the income can be reported on the income statement. Although this may create unusual effects on the company's income statement, the recognition or non-recognition of deferred tax assets is consistent with the conceptual framework's balance sheet approach to financial reporting.

15.7 Presentation and Disclosure

Income tax expense can be a significant portion of a company's profit. As such, there are a number of specific presentation and disclosure requirements for income taxes. The requirements include:

- Tax expense (income) from ordinary activities
- Tax expense (income) from discontinued operations
- Tax amounts charged directly to equity and other comprehensive income
- Major components of tax expense (income), including:
  - Deferred tax related to the origination and reversal of temporary differences
  - Deferred tax related to changes in tax rates
  - Current tax amounts related to prior period taxes
  - The benefit arising from the utilization or recognition of previously unrecognized tax losses
  - Amounts of deferred tax asset write-downs
- Details of unrecognized deferred tax assets
- Details of temporary differences and the amount of related deferred tax recognized on the balance sheet

- Reconciliation between the statutory tax rate and the effective tax rate actually realized

There are also specific requirements in IAS 12 and IAS 1 regarding the balance sheet presentation of tax amounts such as: (a) current taxes payable (receivable) should be presented as a current liability (asset); (b) any deferred tax amounts should be presented as non-current assets or liabilities; and (c) current tax assets and liabilities can only offset each other if the company has the legal right to offset them and intends to settle them with a net payment (receipt). This last situation would usually occur when a single taxation authority that allows offset assesses the taxes. A similar prohibition exists against offsetting for deferred taxes, although there is a further condition that allows for offsetting of deferred taxes originated by different entities within a group structure that will experience reversals of temporary differences in a similar fashion or are allowed to offset current tax amounts. In this case, the deferred taxes must still relate to the same taxation authority.

15.8 IFRS/ASPE Key Differences

IFRS	ASPE
Terminology: accounting and taxable profit, deferred taxes, tax base, and tax income.	Terminology: accounting and taxable income, future income taxes, tax basis, and tax benefit.
Deferred tax asset is recognized when the future realization is considered probable. No valuation allowance is used.	Future tax asset can be recognized for the full amount of the effect of the temporary difference, with an offsetting valuation allowance used to reflect the possibility that future realization is not "more likely than not."
Deferred tax balances are classified as non-current.	Classification of future tax amounts will depend on the classification of the underlying asset or liability. If there is no underlying asset or liability, classification will be determined by the expected reversal of the temporary differences.
More disclosures.	Fewer disclosures.
Companies can only apply the deferred tax approach.	Companies can choose between the taxes payable method and the future income taxes method. The future income taxes method is similar to the deferred tax approach, although some of the terminology is slightly different.

15.9 Appendix A: Accounting for Income Taxes under ASPE

Under ASPE, a company has two choices of how to account for its income taxes: the taxes payable method or the future income taxes method. The taxes payable method, described previously, simply reports the balance of current taxes payable or receivable, and no attempt is made to account for the effect of temporary differences. If a loss is carried back, then the amount of the expected tax receivable can be recorded, however no amount is considered with respect to the loss carried forward. Although this method can result in a mismatched income tax expense, many small businesses choose it because of its simplicity, as the amount of tax calculated on the tax return needs to be recorded and nothing else. However, the company is still required to disclose a reconciliation of the statutory tax rate to the effective tax rate and the amount of unused tax losses carried forward. This simplified method is an example of how the cost versus benefit constraint is applied to financial reporting standards.

If a company chooses the future income taxes method, it will follow procedures very similar to what has been described in this chapter. Although the term **future income taxes** is used instead of deferred taxes, the concepts are essentially the same. There are other minor differences in terminology, as well, such as the use of income instead of profit for both accounting and tax purposes, the use of tax basis instead of tax base, and the use of tax benefit instead of tax income. Another difference in terminology is present in the evaluation of future tax assets. ASPE only allows a future tax asset to be recorded if its future realization is "more likely than not." Although this term is not defined, it is generally interpreted in the same way as "probable" in IFRS.

Another significant difference between the two standards deals with the treatment of future tax assets. The initial calculation and measurement is similar under both standards, however ASPE allows the use of a valuation allowance. This is essentially a contra-account that reduces the future tax asset to a net amount that is "more likely than not" to be realized. This means that the full amount of the future tax asset can be recorded and offset by an amount believed to represent the risk that future income will not be sufficient to realize the asset. Although, conceptually, this is different from the IFRS approach of only recognizing an asset if its realization is "probable," the net effect of the two methods remains the same. That is, the "more likely than not" criteria used in ASPE to determine the valuation allowance will generally produce the same result as the "probable" criteria used by IFRS to determine the asset value.

Additionally, a difference exists between the two standards in the presentation of future tax amounts. IFRS simply states that all deferred tax balances should be disclosed as non-current items on the balance sheet. In ASPE, however, the classification of future tax balances is more complicated as the classification of a future tax balance depends on the classification of the underlying asset or liability. For example, if the temporary difference relates to the difference between depreciation taken for tax and accounting purposes, then the future tax balance would be classified as non-current since the underlying asset (property, plant, and equipment) is reported as non-current. If the temporary difference relates to a difference in the treatment of warranty costs, then the future tax balance would likely be classified as current because the underlying liability (warranty liability) is classified as current. This rule can create a situation where a temporary difference may result in the future tax balance being classified as both current and non-current. This could happen if the underlying asset was an installment receivable that required payments in the next year and in subsequent years. If the future tax amount resulted from a temporary difference that did not arise from a balance sheet amount, such as research costs, then the classification would be based on the expected reversal of the temporary difference. Again, this could result in a split classification of the amount.

Chapter Summary

LO 1: Explain the relationship between taxable profit and accounting profit and calculate current taxes payable.

Tax authorities apply certain rules in the calculation of taxable profit that differ from accounting rules. Taxable profit will, therefore, not always equal accounting profit. It is common to use accounting profit as the starting point for the calculation of taxable profit, and once taxable profit is determined, the appropriate tax rate is applied to calculate current taxes payable.

LO 2: Explain what permanent and temporary differences are and describe the deferred tax effects of those differences.

A temporary difference occurs when an income or expense item is recognized in a different reporting period for tax purposes than for accounting purposes. This is not the same as a permanent difference, which is an item that is included in one type of reporting (tax or accounting) but never the other. Permanent differences affect current taxes but have no effect on future taxes. Temporary differences, on the other hand, will have an effect on future accounting periods when the temporary difference reverses. Temporary differences can be either taxable (i.e., they increase the future tax payable) or deductible (i.e., they decrease the future tax payable).

LO 3: Calculate the deferred tax effects of temporary differences and record the journal entries for current and deferred taxes.

When a temporary difference is identified, the deferred tax asset or liability is calculated by multiplying the amount of the difference by the tax rate expected to be in effect when the difference reverses. Current taxes are recorded as a debit to current tax expense and a credit to current taxes payable. The deferred tax expense or income for the year will be determined by comparing the current year's deferred tax asset/liability balance to the previous year's deferred tax asset/liability balance. Deferred taxes will create either a debit to deferred tax asset or a credit to deferred tax liability. A deferred tax asset will create a credit on the income statement described as deferred tax income, while a deferred tax liability will result in a debit on the income statement described as deferred tax expense.

LO 4: Determine the effect of changes in tax rates and calculate current and deferred tax amounts under conditions of changing rates.

Current taxes should always be calculated at the rate currently in effect. Deferred taxes are calculated at the rate expected to be in effect when the temporary difference reverses. This will be based on the rates in effect or substantively enacted at the reporting date. If a future tax rate changes after the deferred tax amount has already been recorded, then the deferred tax amount must be adjusted for the effect of the rate change. This adjustment is prospective and, thus, prior periods are not adjusted. The effect of the rate change needs to be disclosed separately from the other components of deferred tax expense.

LO 5: Analyze the effect of tax losses and determine the appropriate accounting of those losses.

Current tax losses can often be carried back or carried forward and applied against taxable profits for other years. When losses are carried back, a receivable and a tax income amount will be established based on the rates in effect in the previous years. When losses are carried forward, a determination must be made whether the future realization of these losses is probable or not. If it is not probable, then no amount is recorded until such time as the benefit of the loss is actually realized, resulting in no deferred tax asset being carried on the balance sheet. If it is, in fact, probable, then a deferred tax asset and deferred tax income amount is recognized based on the rate expected to be in effect when the loss is utilized. In the future year when the loss is utilized, the deferred tax asset is eliminated and a deferred tax expense is recorded.

LO 6: Explain the rationale for the annual review of deferred tax assets and describe the effects of this review.

A fair degree of uncertainty exists around the future benefits that can be derived from tax losses. The benefit of a tax loss can only be realized if there is sufficient taxable profit, or reversals of taxable temporary differences, in the future. Although the criteria for recognition may be met in one accounting period, circumstances can change in a later period, creating doubt about the amount that can be realized. As such, a review of deferred tax assets is required at every reporting period to determine if the recognition criteria still holds true. If it doesn't, then the deferred tax asset needs to be partially or fully derecognized and an expense recorded. If a previously unrecorded tax loss now meets the probability criteria, then the benefit and asset will be recorded in the current year.

LO 7: Prepare the presentation of income tax amounts on the balance sheet and income statement and explain the disclosure requirements.

Current taxes payable should be disclosed as a current liability, and deferred tax assets or liabilities should be disclosed as non-current items. Note that different rules apply under ASPE. The components of deferred tax should be disclosed as well as a description of temporary differences. Unrecognized tax losses should be disclosed as well as the effect of tax rate changes, and a reconciliation of the statutory and effective tax rates needs to be disclosed as well.

LO 8: Explain the key differences between the treatment of income taxes under IFRS and ASPE.

Under IFRS, companies can only use the deferred tax approach, whereas under ASPE, companies can choose either the taxes payable method or the future income taxes method. Under IFRS, a deferred tax asset can only be recognized if future realization is probable, while under ASPE, the realization must be more likely than not. As well, ASPE allows the use of a valuation allowance. Under IFRS, all deferred tax balances are classified as non-current, whereas under ASPE, the classification will depend on the underlying, asset, liability, or temporary difference. There are differences in disclosure requirements and terminology as well.

References

CPA Canada. (2016). *CPA handbook*. Toronto, ON: CPA Canada.

The Economist. (2014, October 18). *Death of the double Irish: The Irish government plans to alter one of its more controversial tax policies*. Retrieved from `http://www.economist.com/news/finance-and-economics/21625876-irish-government-plans-alter-one-its-more-controversial-tax`

Exercises

EXERCISE 15–1

For each of the items listed below, identify whether the item is a taxable temporary difference, a deductible temporary difference, or a permanent difference.

Item	Taxable Temporary Difference	Deductible Temporary Difference	Permanent Difference
A property owner collects rent in advance. The amounts are taxed when they are received.			
Depreciation claimed for tax purposes exceeds depreciation charged for accounting purposes.			
Dividends received from an investment in another company are reported as income, but are not taxable.			
A provision for future warranty costs is recorded but is not deductible for tax purposes until the expenditure is actually incurred.			
Membership dues at a golf club are reported as a promotion expense but are not deductible for tax purposes.			
Construction revenue is reported using the percentage of completion method but is not taxed until the project is finished.			

The present value of the costs for the future site remediation of an oil-drilling property has been capitalized as part of the asset's carrying value. This will increase the amount of depreciation claimed over the life of the asset. These costs are not deductible for tax purposes until they are actually incurred.			
A revaluation surplus (accumulated other comprehensive income) is reported for assets accounted for under the revaluation model. The gains will not be taxed until the respective assets are sold.			
Included in current assets is a prepaid expense that is fully deductible for tax purposes when paid.			
A penalty is paid for the late filing of the company's income tax return. This penalty is not deductible for tax purposes.			

EXERCISE 15–2

A company reports an accounting profit of $350,000. Included in the profit is $100,000 of proceeds from a life insurance policy for one of the key executives who passed away during the year. These proceeds are not taxable. As well, the company charged accounting depreciation that was $20,000 greater than the capital allowances claimed for tax purposes.

Required: Calculate the amount of taxes payable and the income tax expense for the year. The current tax rate is 20%.

EXERCISE 15–3

In 2016, Pryderi Inc. completed its first year of operations and reports a net profit of $3,500,000, which included revenue from construction and other projects. During the year, the company started a large construction project that it expected would take two years to complete. The company uses the percentage of completion method for accounting purposes and reported a profit from this project of $900,000. All other projects were completed during the year. For tax purposes, the company reports profits on construction projects only when the project is finished. Also, the company reported the following with respect to its property, plant, and equipment:

Total cost	$6,800,000
Accumulated depreciation	1,200,000
Tax base	4,500,000

Note: The currently enacted corporate tax rate is 30%.

Required:

a. Calculate the year-end balances for deferred taxes and current taxes payable.

b. Prepare the journal entries to record the taxes for 2016.

c. Prepare the income statement presentation of the tax amounts.

EXERCISE 15–4

Refer to the facts presented in the Exercise 15–3. In 2017, Pryderi Inc. completed the construction project that it began in 2016 and reported a further profit from the project of $600,000. The total amount of profit earned on the project is taxable in 2017. The company also completed other projects during the year and reported a net profit of $3,700,000. At the end of 2017, the company reported the following with respect to its property, plant, and equipment:

Total cost	$6,800,000
Accumulated depreciation	2,600,000
Tax base	3,500,000

Note: The tax rate has remained unchanged at 30%.

Required:

a. Calculate the year-end balances for deferred taxes and current taxes payable.

b. Prepare the journal entries to record taxes for 2017.

c. Prepare the income statement presentation of the tax amounts.

EXERCISE 15–5

Corin Ltd. began operations in 2016 and reported a deferred tax liability balance of $17,500 at the end of that year. This balance resulted from the difference between the amount of depreciation charged for accounting purposes and the capital allowances claimed for tax purposes. The carrying amount of the asset in the company's accounting records on December 31, 2016, was $320,000. The tax rate of 25% has not changed for several years and is not expected to change in the future. Also, by the end of December 2016, all current taxes had been paid.

In 2017, the company reported the following:

- Accounting profit for the year was $416,000.

- The company began offering a one-year warranty to its customers in 2017. A warranty provision was established, resulting in a reported expense of $73,000. Actual warranty costs incurred during the year were $17,000. For tax purposes, warranty costs can only be deducted when actually paid.

- In 2017, entertainment costs of $28,000 were paid and expensed. For tax purposes, only 25% of these amounts can be claimed.

- In 2017, the company expensed depreciation of $50,000 and claimed capital allowances for tax purposes of $58,000. There were no sales or disposals of property, plant, and equipment during the year.

Required:

a. Calculate the balances of deferred taxes and current taxes payable for the year ended December 31, 2017.

b. Prepare the journal entries to record the current and deferred taxes for 2017.

c. Prepare the income statement presentation of the income tax amounts for 2017.

d. Prepare the balance sheet presentation of the current and deferred tax balances on December 31, 2017.

EXERCISE 15–6

Adken Enterprises reported the following accounting and taxable profits:

	Accounting Profit	Taxable Profit	Tax Rate
2016	$110,000	$ 85,000	20%
2017	242,000	196,000	23%
2018	261,000	285,000	23%

Note: Included in the accounting profit is $10,000 dividend income each year that is never taxable. Also, the remainder of the difference between accounting and taxable profits relates to a temporary difference, and there were no deferred taxes reported prior to 2016. The tax rate change in 2017 was not enacted until 2017.

Required:

a. Calculate the current and deferred tax expense for 2016 to 2018.

b. Calculate the amount of the deferred tax balance reported on the balance sheet for each of the three years.

c. Prepare the disclosure of the income tax expense amounts in 2017, the year of the rate change.

EXERCISE 15-7

Refer to the information in Exercise 15-6.

Required: Repeat the requirements of the previous question, assuming that the rate change for 2017 was enacted in 2016. That is, the rate in effect for 2016 was 20%, but the legislation changing the rate for 2017 had already been passed by the end of 2016.

EXERCISE 15-8

Baden Ltd. reported the following taxable profits (losses):

	Taxable Profit (Loss)	Tax Rate
2016	$ 10,000	25%
2017	55,000	20%
2018	(112,000)	20%
2019	21,000	18%

Note: There are no temporary or permanent differences to account for. The management of the company believes that it is probable that future taxable profits will be available to utilize any tax losses carried forward. However, the company carries losses back whenever possible. Also, tax rate changes are not enacted until the year of the change.

Required:

a. Prepare journal entries to record the tax amounts for each year.

b. Repeat part (a) assuming that management does not believe it is probable that future taxable profits will be available to utilize tax losses carried forward.

EXERCISE 15–9

Genaro Publishing Ltd. is a publisher of a wide range of consumer magazines. The company reported the following on its December 31, 2016, balance sheet:

Income tax receivable	$16,250
Deferred tax asset	38,400

The deferred tax asset relates to two temporary differences: subscription revenue and depreciation. The company receives subscription payments in advance on the magazines it publishes, the amounts are taxed immediately when they are received, but are reported as revenue as they are earned over the subscription period. On December 31, 2016, the balance in the unearned revenue account was $247,000 and it was expected to be earned as follows:

2017	$95,000
2018	80,000
2019	72,000

The company's printing equipment is currently being depreciated on a straight-line basis and the carrying amount of the equipment on December 31, 2016, was $357,000. For tax purposes, the equipment is depreciated using the declining balance method and the tax base on December 31, 2016, was $238,000. A single taxation authority assesses the company, and payments/receipts are settled on a net basis. The income tax receivable resulted from a taxable loss suffered in 2016 that was fully carried back to previous taxation years. The tax rate enacted on December 31, 2016, was 30%.

In 2017, the company reported the following:

Accounting profit	$750,000
Tax refund received	16,250
Depreciation expense	59,000
Capital allowance claimed for tax purposes	46,000
New subscriptions received in the year, unearned at year-end	68,000
Fines paid due to contamination of a factory site, not deductible for tax purposes	12,000
Dividends received from an investment that are not taxable	7,500

Required:

a. Calculate the current and deferred tax expense for 2017.

b. Prepare the journal entries for the tax amounts in 2017.

c. Prepare the income statement presentation of the tax amounts for 2017.

d. Prepare the balance sheet presentation of the tax amounts, with comparatives, as on December 31, 2017.

EXERCISE 15–10

Zucharras Ltd. began operations in 2016. The following information is available regarding its years ended December 31 ($ amounts in '000s):

	2016	2017	2018	2019	2020
Accounting profit (loss) reported	150	60	(440)	(80)	350
Depreciation expense	20	20	20	20	20
Capital allowance claimed for tax purposes	35	30	0	0	25
Enacted tax rate	25%	30%	35%	35%	30%

The depreciation relates to a single asset that was purchased early in 2016 for $200,000, and there were no other asset purchases or sales during the five years. The tax rates were enacted in each year and the changes were not known prior to the year to which they apply. In 2018, management carried back the loss to the fullest extent possible and estimated that there was an 80% probability that future taxable profits would be available to use the remaining loss carried forward. In 2019, management revised this estimate to a 10% probability, and in 2020, management utilized the maximum possible amount of the loss carried forward. In all years, management estimated that future reversals of temporary differences would be available to utilize the benefits of any deferred tax assets other than the losses carried forward.

Required:

a. Calculate the balance of the deferred tax liability or asset and related adjustment required for the temporary difference related to depreciation at the end of each year.

b. Calculate the current tax payable for each year.

c. Calculate the balance of the deferred tax asset related to the loss carried forward at the end of each the years 2018 to 2020.

d. Calculate the current, deferred, and total tax expense for each year.

EXERCISE 15-11

(from Appendix) Sammon Inc. reports under ASPE and has chosen to use the future income taxes method. It has reported the following regarding its income taxes:

Accounting income for year ended December 31, 2016	$150,000
Depreciation charged in 2016	12,000
Capital allowances deducted for tax purposes in 2016	16,000
Carrying amount of plant assets on January 1, 2016	120,000
Tax basis of plant assets on January 1, 2016	135,000
Unearned rent revenue on December 31, 2016*	96,000
Percentage of completion revenue in 2016**	90,000

* Note: The rent revenue collected in advance represents an amount prepaid by a tenant for the next two years. Rent is earned at the rate of $4,000 per month, is collected on December 31, 2016, and is taxable when collected.

** Note: The company commenced a single construction contract during the year. The contract revenue has been reported using the percentage of completion method, but the completed contract method is used for tax purposes. The company expects the project to be completed in 2017.

Also, there are no other temporary or permanent differences aside from those identified above. The current tax rate is 30%, which has been in effect for several years.

Required:

a. Calculate the current and future tax expenses for the year ended December 31, 2016.

b. Prepare the balance sheet presentation of the tax amounts on December 31, 2016.

c. Repeat parts (a) and (b) assuming that the company uses the taxes payable method instead.

Chapter 16

Pensions and Other Employment Benefits

Golden Years for Bombardier Employees?

In previous generations, employees yearned for a stable job where they could work until retirement. The dream included a reasonable pension that allowed retirees the chance to enjoy a comfortable life. However, changes in demographics and economics have altered the retirement landscape. These changes not only affect the employees but also the companies for which they worked. Bombardier Inc., a Canadian manufacturer of aircraft and rail transportation systems, provides an example of the effects of these changes.

At the end of December 2014, Bombardier reported a net loss of $1.2 billion USD. Contributing to this loss was a net pension expense of $400 million, an amount that represents over 70% of the company's loss before tax and interest. But this expense only tells part of the story. Bombardier also reported pension plan assets of $8.8 billion and a pension plan obligation of $10.9 billion, leaving an unfunded obligation of approximately $2.1 billion. This unfunded obligation had increased by over $500 million from the previous year, but still represented an improvement over the company's highest unfunded obligation of $2.9 billion, reported in 2011.

Pension obligations represent the present value of future payments to be paid to retired employees. These payments are often based on the employees' highest salary during their employment and usually continue until the employees' death. Because of this, the actual amount paid out in the future can only be estimated, and this is done using an actuary. Actuaries are professionals trained in statistical sciences who use existing data and assumptions to make these predictions. With improvements in medical technologies, people are living longer than they once did, and actuarial calculations of the pension obligation reflect this. As well, investment returns on pension plan assets suffered during the 2008 financial crisis and resulting recession. Increased pension obligations and reduced returns have increased the unfunded amount of pensions for many companies, including Bombardier.

A further complicating factor is the rate used to discount the obligation. In Bombardier's case, a 1% drop in the discount rate used in 2014 resulted in an increase in the pension obligation of over $1.4 billion. This was offset, in part, by improved asset values, but this discount rate provides an example of a factor that management cannot control.

Many companies carry similar unfunded pension liabilities on their balance sheets and it is becoming increasingly challenging for managers to deal with this problem. A drastic way to address the growing liability is to stop admitting new members to the pension plan. Bombardier did this in 2013, and other companies have taken similar steps. This may limit the scale of the problem, but the managers still need to find ways to fund a liability whose amount changes in response to unpredictable factors. The managers also need to deal with the more subtle and complex problem of managing employee expectations when those employees receive differing levels of benefits. This, in fact, may prove to be a bigger challenge than finding the funds to maintain existing plans.

(Source: Bombardier, 2015)

Chapter 16 Learning Objectives

After completing this chapter, you should be able to:

LO 1: Describe the nature of a pension plan and identify the key issues in accounting for a pension plan.

LO 2: Define and contrast *defined contribution pension plans* and *defined benefit pension plans*.

LO 3: Prepare the accounting entries for a defined contribution pension plan.

LO 4: Describe the various estimations required and elements included in the accounting for defined benefit pension plans, and evaluate the effects of these estimations on the accounting for these plans.

  LO 4.1: Calculate pension expense for a defined benefit pension plan and prepare the accounting entries for the plan.

  LO 4.2: Describe the accounting treatment of net defined benefit assets.

LO 5: Discuss the challenges in accounting for other post-employment benefits.

LO 6: Describe the accounting treatment for other employment benefits.

LO 7: Identify the presentation and disclosure requirements for defined benefit pension plans.

LO 8: Identify differences in the accounting treatment of post-employment benefits between ASPE and IFRS.

Introduction

Changing demographic patterns have recently thrust pension plans into the headlines. Many mature economies are experiencing low or non-existent growth combined with an aging population. A combination of declining birthrates and improvements in health care is shifting the overall composition of certain populations to people of retirement age. This shift creates a challenge for both public and private pension plans, many of which were established when expectations about life after retirement were quite different. As pension plans are put under increased pressure, it becomes even more important for stakeholders to have a clear understanding of the financial status of the plans and the risks they face as sponsors of the plans. This chapter will examine the accounting issues surrounding private (non-government) pension plans, as well as the treatment of other employment benefits offered by employers. This chapter only deals with the accounting issues of the employer providing the employment and post-employment benefits. The accounting for the pension plan and other benefit plans themselves (i.e., the accounting performed by the trustee of the pension plan assets) is described in IAS 26 and is not covered in this chapter.

Chapter Organization

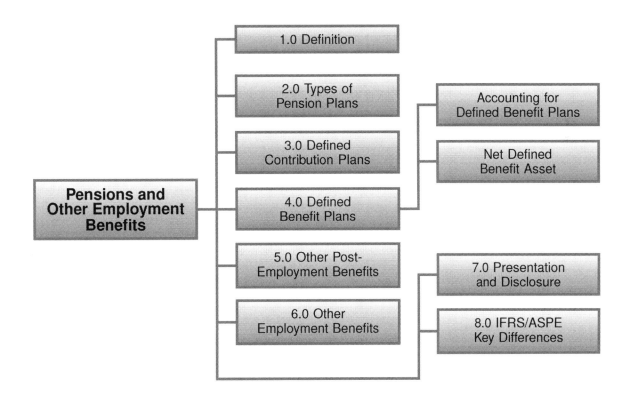

16.1 Definition

The term pension plans is not specifically used in IAS 19 (CPA Canada, 2016). Instead it refers to "post-employment benefit plans," which are simply arrangements by which employers offer benefits to employees after the completion of their employment. However, as the term **pension plan** is widely used and understood, this chapter will use it to distinguish such plans from other types of post-employment benefits.

A key element in the definition of employee benefits in IAS 19 is that the benefits are payable in exchange for service by the employee. This is generally how most employees understand the concept of a pension plan: each year of employment entitles the employee to a future payment that will be received after the employee retires from the job. The pension plan is designed to encourage a sense of loyalty in the employee by providing a benefit that cannot be realized until the employee has spent often many years in the job. The plan also provides a sense of security to the employee, which is provided in exchange for the employee's service to the company. From an accounting perspective, the important questions are: Who pays for the plan? How will the plan's activities be measured? How will the plan be reported?

16.2 Types of Pension Plans

There are two general forms that pension plans can take: they can be defined contribution plans or defined benefit plans. A **defined contribution plan** refers to a plan where the employer pays a fixed contribution into a fund and has no further legal or constructive obligation to provide additional funds should the plan not have sufficient resources to pay the required benefits in the future. A **defined benefit plan** is simply any other post-employment benefit plan that does not meet this definition. Under a defined benefit plan, the employer does hold a legal or constructive obligation to provide additional funds to the plan if the resources are not sufficient to pay the required benefits. Accounting for defined contribution plans is quite straightforward, whereas accounting for defined benefit plans is more complicated. We will examine both types of plans.

16.3 Defined Contribution Plans

With this type of plan, the amount the employer contributes is defined by the contract or relationship the employer has negotiated with its employees. This means that the employer has agreed to fund the plan at a specified amount, usually calculated as a fixed amount or as some percentage of the employee's pay. However, the employer has not agreed to provide any specific amount of pension income to the employee once he or she retires. The amount of pension income available to the employee will depend on how the pension plan assets have performed over the years. The pension plan assets are usually delivered to an independent trustee who will be given the task, and legal right, to invest the assets on behalf of the employees, and this trust is legally separate from the employer. While the trustee will prudently invest the assets in order to provide pension payments to the employees when they retire, there is no guarantee of how much retirement income an individual employee will receive as these funds are subject to investment risk. With a defined contribution plan, the employee bears all of the investment risk, as the employer has only agreed to contribute a specified amount to the plan.

Because the employer bears no investment risk, and no obligation for future pension payments, the accounting for the employer is quite simple. The amount the employer has agreed to pay on behalf of the employees is simply recorded as an expense every year, usually described as a pension or post-employment benefit expense. A liability would only be recorded if the company had not remitted the required funds to the pension plan trustee by the end of the fiscal year. It is also possible that an asset could be recorded if the employer had remitted more funds to the trustee than were required by the agreement with the employees. If either a liability or asset exists at the end of the fiscal period, it would likely be classified as current, as it would normally be expected that the amount would be settled within one year. However, there can be situations where future contributions may be required for current service under a defined contribution plan, such as a deferred contribution required under the terms of a collective agreement negotiated with an employee union. In this case, the future contributions would need to be discounted using the same interest rate as would be applied to a defined benefit plan.

16.4 Defined Benefit Plans

Defined benefit plans are the opposite of defined contribution plans. With a defined benefit plan, the amount of pension income the employee will receive upon retirement is defined either as a pre-determined amount or by calculation using a prescribed formula. Because the ultimate payment from the plan is defined, the risks of the plan now fall upon the employer. If the plan fails to retain sufficient assets to pay out the defined pension benefits, the employer is required to make up the difference through additional contributions. As noted in the example of Bombardier, this amount can be significant.

An important concept of defined benefit plans is that of **vesting**. Vesting refers to the principle that employees are entitled to receive certain benefits even if they cease to be employed by the company. Non-vested benefits are those that are lost once the employee ceases to provide service to the employer. With pension plans, there is usually a minimum term of service that is required before the pension benefits will vest.

Because the employer is responsible for the defined benefit that the pension plan will ultimately pay out, the accounting becomes more complicated. This is because the existence of the defined benefit creates a liability to the company. The liability represents the present value of future cash flows related to the payment of pensions to retired employees. Offsetting this liability are the assets held by the trustee in the pension plan.

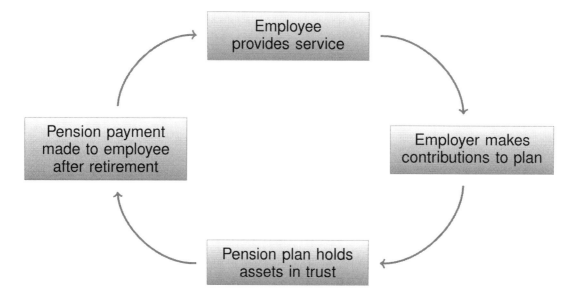

Although it is fairly easy to determine the fair value of the assets held by the trustee, it is not as simple to determine the present value of future pension payments. A number of assumptions and estimates are required to make this determination, including:

- When will the employee retire?
- How long will the employee live after retirement?
- What level of salary will the pension payments be based on?
- What return will be earned on the plan assets in the future?
- What discount rate is appropriate for the present value calculation?

Accountants generally don't have the specialized knowledge or expertise to make these kinds of estimates. However, a particular group of professionals called **actuaries** can help with this process. Actuaries are trained in statistical sciences and they understand how to use existing data to make these kinds of determinations. Because pension payments are often made far in the future, and are based on unknowable factors such as an employee's lifespan, there is the potential for estimation error. As such, an accountant will often review the work of the actuary to ensure it is appropriate for financial reporting purposes. Although IAS 19 does not require the use of actuaries, it is unlikely that an accountant would have sufficient technical knowledge to carry out these calculations on his or her own, except in the case of the most basic pension plan arrangements.

So what exactly does the actuary measure? The main focus of the actuary's work is called the **defined benefit obligation (DBO)**. This represents the present value of all future pension payments for current employees, based on their expected salaries at the time they retire. This calculation takes into account all service provided by the employees up to the reporting date, but it does not include future service. However, a key assumption is that the pension plan will continue to operate and employees will continue to work until their expected retirement date. This calculation requires estimations regarding employee turnover, inflation, and other factors affecting future salaries, such as expected retirement dates and mortality. Note that this calculation also includes estimates related to unvested benefits, as it is expected that the benefits will vest to the employees in the normal course of their employment.

The balance of the defined benefit obligation will be affected by a number of factors each year:

- Current service cost
- Interest on the obligation
- Benefits paid to retirees
- Past service costs and plan amendments
- Actuarial gains and losses

Current service cost is an essential element to the pension obligation. It represents the present value of future benefits required to be paid to current employees, based on the service they have provided in the current accounting period. This amount is estimated by the actuary, taking into account the formula for calculating the pension entitlement, the expected number of years until retirement, and other actuarial factors. The amount is calculated using the **projected unit credit method**, which allocates the ultimate pension benefit payable in roughly equal proportions over the employee's working life. This present value technique, thus, will take into account the effect of future salary increases on the current service obligation.

The **interest cost on the obligation** is a basic concept that reflects the time value of money. Because the payments to retirees will be made in the future, the obligation must be discounted to its present value. As time passes, interest must be accrued on the obligation during each accounting period, increasing the obligation's carrying value each period until it reaches the ultimate amount payable to the employee on the date of retirement. Although the correct accounting treatment requires calculation of the interest cost based on actual transactions in the plan during the year, a simplifying assumption we will make is that transactions occur at the end of the year. This means that, unless otherwise stated, we will assume that the interest cost is based on the opening balance of the DBO.

The third essential element in the calculation of the DBO is the value of *benefits paid to retirees*. As these benefits are paid, the obligation is reduced because the company is fulfilling its obligation to its employees under the plan. These payments will reduce the outstanding present value otherwise calculated.

Sometimes a pension plan may be amended or additional pension entitlements granted. This could occur, for example, when a company first commences a new pension plan and wants to grant entitlement to long-serving employees for their service prior to the start of the plan. Or, with an existing plan, the company may want to grant additional pension entitlements to certain groups of employees, such as those who have joined the company through a merger. It is also possible that a company could reduce future pension benefits payable to employees, such as through a renegotiation of collective agreements with unions resulting from reorganization or other type of financial distress. Whatever the reason, the change in the future benefits resulting from *past service costs* must be adjusted and reflected in the DBO.

The last element of the DBO is perhaps the most difficult to determine. Actuaries, as noted before, are trained in analyzing and using various types of data to make their predictions and calculations of the DBO. However, predicting the future is imprecise and sometimes the actuary will need to change the projected amounts based on new calculations. These new calculations could result from observations of actual patterns that are different from what was previously predicted, or from completely new data that changes the existing assumptions. For example, if during the year there was a significant turnover of employees and the new group is significantly younger than the previous group, the calculation of the DBO would change. Similarly, if new scientific data were released showing that, on average, people are now living longer due to improved health-care services, the DBO would have to be adjusted. Changes in actuarial assumptions are a normal part of the process of estimating the DBO, resulting in *actuarial gains or losses* during the period.

Aside from the DBO, the other major element of the pension plan is the assets the pension plan holds in trust for the employees. The assets are typically held in a separate entity from the company and are usually legally restricted in a way that prevents their conversion for use in settlement of other non-pension liabilities of the company. The plan assets will usually be held in low-risk investments such as high-quality debt and equity securities, stable real estate properties, cash and other cash equivalents. The goal of the plan is to earn a reasonable return without taking too much risk. However, even a prudent investment strategy can be mismanaged, as discovered by pension fund managers after the 2008 financial crisis, who found that some of the double and triple-A securities they had invested in were not as sound as first believed.

There are three determinants of the value of the pension plan assets:

- Contributions by the employer, and in some cases, the employee
- The actual return on the assets
- Benefits paid to retirees

Contributions are payments made by the employer to the plan based on agreed upon amounts. This would typically be an amount determined by the actuary and is often based on a percentage of employee salaries. In some cases, the employees will also contribute their own money to the plan. This is referred to as a **contributory plan**. The amount the employee contributes will often be based on tax legislation in the relevant jurisdiction.

The return on the plan's assets consists of various types of investment returns, such as interest, dividends, and gains and losses on the disposal of plan assets (less any administration fees charged by the pension plan manager). Additionally, IAS 19 requires the plan's assets to be valued at their fair values, meaning that unrealized gains and losses will also be included in the final balance. Because certain investment markets can be volatile, the actual return earned on the assets from year to year can vary significantly. However, most plan managers will attempt to diversify their portfolios and apply prudent investment strategies to minimize this risk.

As noted previously, actual pension benefits paid to retirees reduce the obligation of the plan. However, they also reduce the assets in the plan.

16.4.1 Accounting for Defined Benefit Plans

Although there are a number of complex elements that comprise defined benefit pension plans, the accounting concern of the company reporting under IFRS is simpler. On the sponsoring company's accounting records, only four relevant accounts need to be considered: the pension expense that will be recorded each year, the net defined benefit asset or liability that will appear on the balance sheet, the cash that is contributed to the plan, and the company's other comprehensive income (OCI). We will examine how each of these accounts is affected by the pension plan transactions.

It is important to note that the pension plan assets and obligation are not recorded anywhere on the sponsoring company's financial statements, as these are held by the trustee in the pension plan. Changes in the pension plan's obligation and assets are, however, accounted for indirectly on the sponsoring company's financial statements. This is done in the following manner:

- Current and past service costs are reported in net income.
- Net interest is reported in net income.
- Gains and losses from remeasurements of the net asset or liability are reported in other comprehensive income.
- Cash contributions to the plan reduce the company's liability.

This treatment will result in a net defined benefit expense being reported on the income statement (an adjustment to OCI) and an amount, the net defined benefit liability, being reported on the balance sheet equal to the net difference between the DBO and the fair value of the plan assets. One important point to note in the accounting treatment is the manner in which interest is recorded. Interest on the DBO should be calculated using an appropriate interest rate, which IAS 19 suggests should be a market-based interest rate that is comparable to the current yield on high-quality debt instruments, such as corporate bonds. The rate used would normally be the rate present at the end of the reporting period. A further requirement of IAS 19 is that the interest rate used to discount the DBO should also be used to calculate the return on the plan assets. In other words, the interest cost is calculated only on the *net* balance of the obligation. The result of using the same interest rate for determining the return on plan assets is that there will likely be a difference between the calculated amount and the actual return on the assets. This difference is accounted for in OCI, much in the same manner as remeasurement gains or losses resulting from changes in actuarial assumptions.

The accounting treatment for pensions under ASPE is slightly different. These differences will be explained in 16.9 Appendix A.

The accounting treatment under IFRS is best illustrated with an example. Consider the following facts: Ballard Ltd. initiated a defined benefit pension plan in 2010. On January 1, 2015, the balance of the DBO as determined by an actuary was $535,000, and the fair value of the plan assets was $500,000.

The following information relates to the three-year period 2015 to 2017:

	2015	2016	2017
Current service cost for the year	$57,000	$65,000	$76,000
Interest rate on corporate bonds	8%	8%	9%
Actual earnings on plan assets	43,000	35,000	70,000
Employer contributions	50,000	55,000	60,000
Benefits paid to retirees	20,000	23,000	25,000
Actuarial gain due to change in assumptions	–	16,000	–
Cost of past service benefits granted on January 1, 2017	–	–	62,000

An easy way to understand the accounting for pension plan transactions is to use a worksheet. The worksheet can help organize the relevant data and provides reconciliation between the company's records and the amounts held in the pension plan. The worksheet format that we will use is comprised of two parts. The left-hand portion represents the amounts held in the pension plan. These are not accounted for directly in the company's records. The right-hand side of the worksheet represents the company's accounting records. The data on this side can be used to directly generate the journal entries required and also provides a way to compare the company's records to those of the pension plan. In our worksheet we will use Debit (DR) and Credit (CR) notations even though the company does not directly record all parts of the worksheet. The use of DR and CR will help us understand how to reconcile the pension plan and company records.

Let's start with the worksheet for 2015:

	Pension Plan		Company Accounting Records			
	DBO	Plan Assets	Net Defined Benefit Balance	Cash	Annual Pension Expense	OCI
Opening balance	535,000 CR	500,000 DR	35,000 CR			
Service cost	57,000 CR				57,000 DR	
Interest: DBO[1]	42,800 CR				42,800 DR	
Interest: assets[2]		40,000 DR			40,000 CR	
Contribution		50,000 DR		50,000 CR		
Benefits paid	20,000 DR	20,000 CR				
Remeasurement gain: assets[3]		3,000 DR				3,000 CR
Journal entry			6,800 CR	50,000 CR	59,800 DR	3,000 CR
Closing balance	614,800 CR	573,000 DR	41,800 CR			

1. Interest on DBO = $535,000 \times 8\% = $42,800
2. Interest on assets = $500,000 \times 8\% = $40,000
3. Remeasurement gain = $43,000 (actual earnings) − $40,000 (calculated above) = $3,000

There are a few key points to note from the worksheet:

- The net defined benefit balance at the start of the year represents the amount the company would report on its balance sheet. It also represents the difference between the opening balances of the DBO and the plan assets.

- The interest on the DBO and the plan assets is calculated by simply taking the appropriate interest rate and multiplying it by the opening balance of each item. This calculation has assumed that all pension transactions occur at the end of the year. In practice, pension transactions may occur throughout the year. In that case, interest would need to be calculated on the weighted-average balance in each account.

- Benefits paid to retirees do not affect the company's accounting records, as these transactions occur between the pension plan and the retirees directly.

- The remeasurement gain represents the difference between the interest calculated on the plan asset balance and the actual return earned by those assets during the year. This gain is taken directly to other comprehensive income.

From this worksheet, the company would make the following journal entry:

	General Journal			
Date	Account/Explanation	PR	Debit	Credit
	Pension expense............................		59,800	
	Other comprehensive income............			3,000
	Net defined benefit liability...............			56,800
	Net defined benefit liability...................		50,000	
	Cash.....................................			50,000

The result of this journal entry is a credit of $6,800 to the net defined benefit liability that is reported on the company's balance sheet. This agrees with the calculation on the worksheet. In practice, the part of the journal entry reflecting the cash contributions by the company would be recorded throughout the year as the company remits pension payments to the plan. On the company's balance sheet, a net defined benefit liability of $41,800 would be disclosed. This would usually be disclosed as a non-current liability, as it is not normal for a pension liability to be settled within the next year. This balance also represents the net **underfunding** of the plan at the end of the year. This means that the pension plan does not have sufficient assets to settle the future expected liability for pension payments. In the short term this is not really a problem, as the pension plan payments will occur over a period of many years and it is possible to correct an underfunded plan over time. However, if a pension plan remains chronically underfunded, this may result in problems making payments to retirees. With a defined benefit plan, the sponsoring company will ultimately be responsible for making up this difference, although employees may also be asked to contribute if the plan is contributory. The plan could also be **overfunded**, which would mean that the fair value of the plan assets exceeds the DBO. This excess amount belongs to the sponsoring company, although legal requirements may prevent the company from withdrawing the amount from the plan. Usually, the excess would be recovered through a reduction of future contributions.

The company would also disclose a pension expense of $59,800 on the income statement and a $3,000 credit to other comprehensive income. There are further disclosure requirements, which are detailed later in this chapter.

Let's now look at the 2016 transactions:

	Pension Plan		Company Accounting Records			
	DBO	Plan Assets	Net Defined Benefit Balance	Cash	Annual Pension Expense	OCI
Opening balance	614,800 CR	573,000 DR	41,800 CR			
Service cost	65,000 CR				65,000 DR	
Interest: DBO[1]	49,184 CR				49,184 DR	
Interest: assets[2]		45,840 DR			45,840 CR	
Contribution		55,000 DR		55,000 CR		
Benefits paid	23,000 DR	23,000 CR				
Remeasurement loss: assets[3]		10,840 CR				10,840 DR
Remeasurement gain: DBO	16,000 DR					16,000 CR
Journal entry			8,184 CR	55,000 CR	68,344 DR	5,160 CR
Closing balance	689,984 CR	640,000 DR	49,984 CR			

1. Interest on DBO = $614,800 \times 8\% = \$49,184$
2. Interest on assets = $573,000 \times 8\% = \$45,840$
3. Remeasurement loss = $35,000 (actual earnings) − $45,840 (calculated above) = ($10,840)

The process used is the same as was applied in 2015. However, note one additional difference in 2016: the actuary revised some of the actuarial assumptions. This could result from new data regarding life expectancy, changes in assumptions about expected period of service of employees, changes in assumptions about future wage levels, and several other factors. The change in the assumptions has resulted in an actuarial gain, which means the present value of the future pension payments (and thus, also the DBO) has been reduced. This reduction to the DBO has been recorded as a credit to other comprehensive income and does not directly affect the pension expense recorded. In this example, we have assumed that the change in assumptions occurred at the end of the year. If the change occurred at some other time during the year, the interest calculation would need to be adjusted to reflect weighted average DBO balance throughout the year.

As before, the company will make the following journal entry:

	General Journal			
Date	Account/Explanation	PR	Debit	Credit
	Pension expense............................		68,344	
	Other comprehensive income............			5,160
	Net defined benefit liability...............			63,184
	Net defined benefit liability.................		55,000	
	Cash.....................................			55,000

As a result of this journal entry, the company will now report a net defined benefit liability of $49,984 on the balance sheet, representing a net underfunded position.

In 2017, the pension worksheet looks like this:

	Pension Plan		Company Accounting Records			
	DBO	Plan Assets	Net Defined Benefit Balance	Cash	Annual Pension Expense	OCI
Opening balance	689,984 CR	640,000 DR	49,984 CR			
Past service	62,000 CR				62,000 DR	
Service cost	76,000 CR				76,000 DR	
Interest: DBO^1	67,679 CR				67,679 DR	
Interest: assets^2		57,600 DR			57,600 CR	
Contribution		60,000 DR		60,000 CR		
Benefits paid	25,000 DR	25,000 CR				
Remeasurement gain: assets^3		12,400 DR				12,400 CR
Journal entry			75,679 CR	60,000 CR	148,079 DR	12,400 CR
Closing balance	870,663 CR	745,000 DR	125,663 CR			

1. Interest on DBO = ($689,984 + $62,000) × 9% = $67,679
2. Interest on assets = $640,000 × 9% = $57,600
3. Remeasurement gain = $70,000 (actual earnings) − $57,600 (calculated above) = $12,400

Note that the cost of additional pension benefits granted to employees based on their past service has been immediately expensed. This amount represents the increase in the DBO calculated by the actuary as a result of giving the employees these benefits. The granting of these entitlements is treated as a new event, so it would not be appropriate to adjust prior periods for the additional amount. It would also be inappropriate to capitalize this amount as the employee service that has generated the benefit has already occurred (i.e., there is no future benefit to the company). The result is a significantly larger pension expense in the current year. The company will also report a significantly higher liability, $125,663, on its balance sheet.

The company will make the following journal entry in 2017:

	General Journal			
Date	Account/Explanation	PR	Debit	Credit
	Pension expense............................		148,079	
	Other Comprehensive Income			12,400
	Net defined benefit liability			135,679
	Net defined benefit liability		60,000	
	Cash			60,000

16.4.2 Net Defined Benefit Asset

In our examples, the net defined benefit balance was always in a credit position, meaning the plan was underfunded. However, a plan can be overfunded as well, meaning the fair value of the assets held in the plan exceeds the actuarially determined present value of the DBO. This doesn't create any particular accounting problem, as the amount would simply be reported as an asset on the sponsoring company's balance sheet. However, IAS 19 requires that the balance of an overfunded plan be reported at the lesser of:

- The amount of the surplus (the overfunding in the plan)
- The asset ceiling

The **asset ceiling** is defined as the present value of "future economic benefits available to the entity in the form of a reduction in future contributions or a cash refund, either directly to the entity or indirectly to another plan in deficit" (CPA Canada, 2016, IAS 19.65.c). The present value would be determined using the same interest rate as was used in the pension expense calculations. This provision ensures that the net asset reported under the plan does not exceed the present value of the amount that is reasonably expected to be recovered from the overfunded plan.

16.5 Other Post-Employment Benefits

In addition to pension plans, employers will often provide other types of post-employment benefits to their employees. While there are many other benefits that employers may offer to encourage long service by employees, the most common is additional health care coverage. As IAS 19 requires other post-employment benefits to be accounted for in essentially the same manner as pension plans, this can create some measurement challenges because the use of these benefits is less predictable than a regular monthly pension payment. Health care costs will be incurred when the retired employee becomes ill, and the required amounts to be paid are widely variable. However, despite these measurement challenges, the amounts must still be estimated and accounted for in order to provide a true and fair representation of the company's financial position.

16.6 Other Employment Benefits

Employers also offer many incentives and benefits to their employees while they are still employed. Some benefits, such as vacation time, may be required by law while other benefits, such as paid sabbaticals, may not be. When determining the accounting treatment for these types of benefits, it is important to understand whether the benefits vest or not. When employment benefits vest with service, they should be accounted for in a similar manner to pension plans (i.e., the amount of the future payment should be estimated and accrued). In the case of short-term benefits, such as annual vacations, the amount is not usually discounted. These types of benefits were covered in more detail in Chapter 12: Current Liabilities. For long-term employment benefits, such as paid sabbaticals, the treatment is also similar to that of pension plans, except that remeasurement gains and losses are accounted for in net income, and not in other comprehensive income.

For employment benefits that do not vest, the accounting treatment is simpler. An example of a benefit that does not vest is a monthly sick leave allowance. An employee may be allowed a certain number of sick days every month, but these do not accumulate if they are not used. In this case, an expense is recorded when the benefit is actually used by the employee, but no accrual is made for any unused amounts. This type of benefit was covered in more detail in Chapter 12.

16.7 Presentation and Disclosure

The complexities and estimations involved in pension plans have resulted in fairly significant disclosure requirements. Pension plans can create a significant liability to companies, so it is important that financial statement readers have a good understanding of the timing and risks related to future pension plan payments. Below is a summary of the presentation and disclosure requirements of IAS 19.

Balance Sheet

The standard doesn't specify whether the net defined benefit liability or asset should be disclosed as current or non-current. In the absence of specific guidance, reasonable judgment would suggest that these balances should usually be disclosed as non-current. This is because it is normally unlikely that the entire amount of a pension plan obligation would be settled within the next fiscal year, as the payments will be made for many years in the future.

IAS 19 does not allow the netting of a defined benefit asset and a defined benefit liability when the company has more than one pension plan, except in limited circumstances. This is because the assets of each plan are usually protected by legislation in such a way that they cannot be used to settle other obligations. Multiple plans may be presented as a single line item if they are all assets or all liabilities. However, further details will be required in the note disclosures to identify the risks of each plan.

Comprehensive Income Statement

IAS 19 does not specify how the annual pension cost should be reported on the income statement. Although a company could disclose the various components that make up the pension expense separately, it is common practice to simply include a single line item described as pension expense or similar. This amount, however, may be split between various functions consistent with reporting of other employee expenses. Remeasurement gains and losses included in other comprehensive income should be identified as such.

Note Disclosures

The three main disclosure categories identified in IAS 19 are:

- Explanations of the characteristics and risks of the plans
- Explanations of amounts in the financial statements
- Descriptions of how the defined benefit plans will affect the amount, timing, and uncertainty of future cash flow

Although these categories appear fairly simple, IAS provides a significant amount of guidance on how to meet these disclosure objectives. Some of the requirements include:

- The nature of the benefits payable under the plan
- Details of the regulatory environment under which the plan operates
- Disaggregation of financial statement amounts where risk profiles differ
- Reconciliations of opening and closing balances of plan assets and the DBO
- Disaggregation of plan assets where the risks and investment types differ
- Details of significant actuarial assumptions
- A sensitivity analysis showing the effect of changes in the actuarial assumptions
- Information about the timing of future maturities of the plan obligation

There are many other specific disclosure requirements in IAS 19 designed to help the reader understand the possible effects of these plans on future cash flow.

16.8 IFRS/ASPE Key Differences

IFRS	ASPE
Remeasurement gains and losses on the DBO and the plan assets are reported as part of other comprehensive income.	Remeasurement gains and losses are reported as part of current pension expense.
The projected unit credit method is used to determine the amount of the DBO.	A company can choose to use the actuarial valuation used for funding purposes, or an actuarial valuation prepared specifically for accounting purposes. If the second option is chosen, then either the accumulated benefit method or projected benefit method can be used. (NOTE: a detailed discussion of different actuarial techniques is beyond the scope of this text. All of these techniques represent variations of a present value calculation.)
Net defined benefit asset positions should be reported at the lesser of the actual surplus or the asset ceiling amount.	Net defined benefit asset positions should be reported using a valuation allowance
The interest rate used for discounting should be the rate on high-quality debt investments with similar maturity patterns.	The interest rate used for discounting should be the rate on high-quality debt investments with similar maturity patterns or the rate imputed by the determination of immediate settlement amount, if available.
Provides limited guidance on defined contribution plans.	Provides more detailed guidance, including how to determine the discounted amount of future payments for current services and how to treat interest on unallocated surpluses on converted plans.
Actuarial valuations required with sufficient frequency.	Actuarial valuations required every three years, or sooner, if circumstances change.
Requires detailed disclosures.	Requires simpler disclosures.

16.9 Appendix A: Accounting for Post-Employment Benefits Under ASPE

Prior to 2014, there were some significant differences between ASPE and IFRS with respect to pension plan accounting. The former ASPE standard allowed the use of a technique referred to as the **deferral and amortization approach**. This technique allowed the costs of past service amendments, and other actuarial gains and losses, to be deferred and recognized in expense over time. This approach was eliminated when Section 3462[1] of the ASPE standards was issued. Section 3462 is effective for all year-ends commencing on January 1, 2014, or later, and it is this standard that we will examine in this appendix.

The approach to accounting for pensions under ASPE 3462 is similar to that of IAS 19, but there are some differences in definitions and procedures. For example, one of the key differences is that ASPE allows for two different methods of valuing the DBO. The company may choose to use the actuarial valuation that has been prepared for the purposes of determining the funding levels for the plan, or the company may choose to use a separately prepared actuarial valuation for accounting purposes. It is possible that certain actuarial assumptions, and other factors, may differ between these two valuations. If the company chooses to use a valuation prepared specifically for accounting purposes, then it must choose between two approaches used for valuation of the DBO. The company may choose to use either the accumulated benefit method or the projected benefit method. The **accumulated benefit method** essentially calculates the present value of future pension payments for vested and non-vested employees using their current salary levels. Whereas, the **projected benefit method** performs this calculation using future expected salaries. Generally, the projected benefit method will result in a larger DBO. Whichever method the company chooses, it must apply the policy consistently to all of its pension plans. A detailed discussion of the different types of actuarial valuations is beyond the scope of this text. They all represent variations of a present value calculation that will normally be provided by the actuary.

Another key difference between ASPE 3462 and IAS 19 is that any remeasurement gains or losses due to changes in actuarial assumptions, or differences between the actual return on plan assets and the calculated return based on the appropriate interest rate, are charged directly to the pension expense for the year, rather than being captured by other comprehensive income.

Let's consider our previous example using the facts presented for Ballard Ltd. in 2016:

---

[1] CPA Canada (2016), Part II – Accounting, Section 3462.

	Pension Plan		Company Accounting Records		
	DBO	Plan Assets	Net Defined Benefit Balance	Cash	Annual Pension Expense
Opening balance	614,800 CR	573,000 DR	41,800 CR		
Service cost	65,000 CR				65,000 DR
Interest: DBO	49,184 CR				49,184 DR
Interest: assets		45,840 DR			45,840 CR
Contribution		55,000 DR		55,000 CR	
Benefits paid	23,000 DR	23,000 CR			
Remeasurement loss: assets		10,840 CR			10,840 DR
Remeasurement gain: DBO	16,000 DR				16,000 CR
Journal entry			8,184 CR	55,000 CR	63,184 DR
Closing balance	689,984 CR	640,000 DR	49,984 CR		

Note that the remeasurement gain due to changes in actuarial assumptions, and the remeasurement loss due to the deficiency in the actual return on plan assets, are both included in pension expense for the year, rather than in other comprehensive income. This treatment will result in the following journal entry in 2016:

General Journal				
Date	Account/Explanation	PR	Debit	Credit
	Pension expense.................................		63,184	
	Net defined benefit liability...............			63,184
	Net defined benefit liability...................		55,000	
	Cash..			55,000

The absence of other comprehensive income in the adjustment means that current net income will be more volatile for companies reporting under ASPE. However, under Section 3462, companies are required to disclose the effects of any remeasurements separately, so readers will be able to clearly see the effects of these items on net income.

Another difference between Section 3462 and IAS 19 is in the treatment of net defined benefit assets. While IAS 19 requires the amount be reported at the lesser of the surplus amount or the asset ceiling, Section 3462 instead requires the use of a valuation allowance. The valuation allowance essentially represents the amount of the surplus that will not be recoverable through future reductions in contributions or withdrawals. The net effect of this approach is essentially the same as IAS 19, but Section 3462 provides more detailed guidance on how to calculate the amounts recoverable from the plan in the future.

Section 3462 also provides a choice of interest to use for discounting purposes. The first option is the same as IAS 19 (i.e., the rate on high-quality debt instruments), but the second option allowed is the imputed interest that would be determined if the plan were to be settled. This option, however, should only be used in cases where the option of immediate settlement, such as through the purchase of an annuity contract from an insurance company, is actually available.

The treatment of defined contribution plans under Section 3462 is essentially the same as IAS 19, although Section 3462 provides a more detailed description on how to determine when future payments for current services are to be discounted. Additionally, Section 3462 discusses how to treat unallocated plan surpluses that could arise when a defined benefit plan is converted to a defined contribution plan. Interest on these surpluses would be deducted from the pension expense otherwise determined.

Section 3462 requires that an actuarial valuation of the plan be carried out at least every three years, and more frequently if there have been any significant changes in the plan. IAS 19 does not specify the frequency of actuarial valuations, but suggests that they be carried out with sufficient frequency as to ensure there are no material errors in the reported balance.

Chapter Summary

LO 1: Describe the nature of a pension plan and identify the key issues in accounting for a pension plan.

A pension plan is an arrangement by which employers offer benefits to employees after the completion of their employment. Employees earn pension benefits over the course of their employment with the company. These benefits can take many forms, but pension plans usually involve post-employment payments made to the retired employee on a periodic basis. The key accounting issues are: Who pays for the plan? How will the plan's activities be measured? How will the plan be reported?

LO 2: Define and contrast *defined contribution pension plans* and *defined benefit pension plans*.

A defined contribution pension plan is one in which the employer has agreed to contribute a specified amount on behalf of an employee, but has not guaranteed the amount of retirement income the employee will receive. In contrast, a defined benefit pension plan does specify the amount of income the employee will receive upon retirement. Under both types of plans, it is the employers' responsibility to make sufficient contributions to the plans as per the agreements made with their employees. The key accounting difference between the two plans is that a defined benefit pension plan creates a liability for the employer to cover any shortfall of funding, based on the present value of future expected payments, to ensure the agreed upon amount of retirement income is available to the employee. A defined contribution pension plan, on the other hand, only creates a liability to the extent that the company is required to make the agreed upon contributions to the plan. The employer is not responsible for the performance of a defined contribution pension plan, but is indirectly responsible for the performance of a defined benefit pension plan.

LO 3: Prepare the accounting entries for a defined contribution pension plan.

The employer records an expense every year for the amount of contributions they are required to make. They will also record a liability if the contributions are unpaid at the end of the year. However, as there is no guarantee of future retirement income, the company does not record any liability beyond the amount of contributions required.

LO 4: Describe the various estimations required and elements included in the accounting for defined benefit pension plans, and evaluate the effects of these estimations on the accounting for these plans.

The determination of the DBO requires estimation of several amounts. The expected date of the employee's retirement and the expected duration of pension payments (i.e., the amount of time between the employee's retirement and death) need to be estimated. As well, the amount of the expected pension payment will need to be predicted, as this amount may be based on future salary levels. The interest rate used to discount the obligation should be based on the yields on high-quality debt instruments, but there may be subjectivity in determining which instruments to choose. Most accountants don't have the required training to make these kinds of estimations, so they will likely have to rely on the work of an expert called an actuary. Because the estimates can change every year based on new information and assumptions, it is possible that the accounting for the pension plan may create some volatility in reported earnings, including comprehensive income.

LO 4.1: Calculate pension expense for a defined benefit pension plan and prepare the accounting entries for the plan.

The pension expense includes the cost of current service provided by employees, the net interest on the scheme, and changes due to past service adjustments and other amendments. The net interest represents the difference between interest calculated on the DBO and the interest expected to be earned on the plan assets. Both calculations use the same interest rate—the yield available on high-quality debt instruments. The pension expense should be allocated to the various components of net income in the same fashion as the underlying compensation costs.

The DBO is increased by the current service cost, the cost of any past service benefits granted during the year, and interest calculated on the balance. The DBO will be decreased by any pension payments made during the year and may be increased or decreased by any remeasurements caused by changes in actuarial assumptions. The pension plan assets will be increased by actual returns earned on the assets and contributions made by the employer. The pension plan assets will be decreased by any pension payments made during the year.

Several issues are involved in the determination of the net asset or liability to be reported on the balance sheet. First, the amount of the DBO is based on future events for which complex actuarial calculations are required. Second, the fair value of the pension plan assets must be determined. For many assets, this is quite straightforward, but if the pension plan holds real estate or other assets not actively traded, expert consultations may be required. Once the amounts are determined, the net pension liability (asset) can be determined and reported on the balance sheet, usually as a non-current item. Other changes in value, such as changes in actuarial assumptions used to determine the DBO or differences between the expected and actual return on plan assets, are recorded as part of other comprehensive income.

LO 4.2: Describe the accounting treatment of net defined benefit assets.

A net defined benefit asset represents a situation in which the plan assets exceed the DBO. This means that the plan is overfunded. The amount of overfunding should be reported as an asset, but only to the extent that it doesn't exceed the asset ceiling, that is, the present value of the future benefits available to the plan sponsor, either through reduced contributions or cash refunds.

LO 5: Discuss the challenges in accounting for other post-employment benefits.

Other post-employment benefits, such as supplementary health coverage, are treated in a similar fashion as pension plans for accounting purposes. However, challenges can arise in estimating the future payable amounts and the amount of the obligation. Future payments for health care coverage can be very unpredictable in both the timing and the amount. A greater degree of estimation risk may exist for these kinds of benefits as compared to pension plans.

LO 6: Describe the accounting treatment for other employment benefits.

Other kinds of employment benefits may include paid vacations, sabbaticals, or sick leave. For these kinds of benefits, it is important to understand whether they vest or not. Benefits that vest, such as paid vacations, must be accrued and recorded by the company. However, these benefits are not normally discounted, and any remeasurement gains or losses that occur are recorded directly in net income instead of other comprehensive income. For benefits that do not vest, an expense is recorded when the benefit is used, but no amounts are accrued.

LO 7: Identify the presentation and disclosure requirements for defined benefit pension plans.

Accrued net defined benefit amounts are normally recorded as non-current liabilities or assets. When the company sponsors multiple pension plans, they are generally not netted on the balance sheet. Pension expense can be shown as a single item on the income statement or it can be split into component parts. Remeasurement amounts recorded in other comprehensive income should be disclosed separately. There are extensive note disclosure requirements for pension plans to help the readers understand the risks of these plans and potential effects on future cash flow.

LO 8: Identify differences in the accounting treatment of post-employment benefits between ASPE and IFRS.

The treatment under ASPE is similar to the treatment under IFRS, but there are some differences. Under APSE, remeasurement amounts are reported directly in net income, rather than in other comprehensive income. Also, companies have a choice in the method used to measure the DBO and in the interest rate chosen to discount the obligation. If a net defined benefit asset is reported, ASPE requires the use of a valuation allowance. ASPE provides more detailed guidance on how to calculate some of the amounts required to determine the DBO, but less detailed guidance on disclosure requirements. They also require actuarial valuations every three years, whereas IFRS only requirements them with sufficient frequency.

References

Bombardier. (2015). *2014 financial report*. Retrieved from `http://ir.bombardier.com/modules/misc/documents/66/00/27/88/14/Bombardier-Financial-Report-2014-en2.pdf`

CPA Canada. (2016). *CPA Canada handbook*. Toronto, ON: CPA Canada.

Exercises

EXERCISE 16–1

Identify each statement below regarding pension plans, as being true for either defined contribution plans (DC) or defined benefit plans (DB):

	DC or DB
The employer has no obligation to the fund beyond the required payment	
Accounting for this type of plan is more complicated	
The employer bears the investment risk with this type of plan	
A liability is only recorded when the required payment is not made by year-end	
Accounting for this type of plan will likely require the use of actuarial specialists	

EXERCISE 16–2

On January 1, 2017, Trelayne Industries Inc. established a defined contribution plan for its employees. The plan requires the employees to contribute 4% of their gross pay to the plan, with Trelayne Industries Inc. contributing an additional 6% of the gross pay. In 2017, employees covered by the pension plan earned total gross salaries of $10,500,000. Employees are paid monthly, and the contributions to the pension plan are made on the 10th of the month following the month worked. All required contributions in 2017 were paid to the pension plan, except for the December payroll, which was not remitted until January 10, 2018. Assume employees' pay is earned equally throughout the year.

Required:

a. Prepare a summary journal entry for Trelayne Industries Inc.'s pension plan transactions for 2017.

b. What is the amount of pension expense that the company will report in 2017?

c. What is the amount of pension liability that the company will report on December 31, 2017?

EXERCISE 16–3

With respect to its pension plan, Renaldi Ltd. reported a net defined benefit balance of $750,000 CR on January 1, 2018, and $832,000 CR on December 31, 2018. During 2018, the company contributed $57,000 to the pension plan. The company reports under IFRS.

Required:

a. Assuming there were no remeasurement gains or losses in 2018, determine the pension expense that would be reported for the year.

b. Repeat part (a), assuming that the company experienced a remeasurement loss of $12,000 with respect to plan assets.

EXERCISE 16–4

Mackaby Inc.'s defined benefit pension plan reported a current service cost of $1,600,000 in the current year. As well, the expected return on the plan assets using a market-based interest rate was $900,000, while the actual return earned on the assets was $870,000. The interest calculated on the DBO was $936,000. There were no remeasurement gains or losses related to the DBO during the year.

Required: Calculate the pension expense for the year.

EXERCISE 16–5

Franck Ltd. initiated a defined benefit pension plan for its employees in 2007. On January 1, 2016, the plan showed a DBO balance of $6,300,000 and plan assets of $5,950,000. In 2016, the company reported a current service cost of $575,000. The current interest rate on high-quality corporate bonds is 7%. During the year, the pension plan assets earned a return of $437,000. In 2016, the company contributed $682,000 to the plan, and the plan paid out pension benefits of $186,000.

Required:

a. Complete the pension worksheet for 2016.

b. Prepare the journal entry required to report the pension transactions in 2016.

c. What is the net defined benefit balance reported on the balance sheet on December 31, 2016, and how would it be classified?

EXERCISE 16–6

The following information regarding Mirocek Inc.'s defined benefit pension plan is available:

DBO: January 1, 2017	$4,400,000
Plan assets: January 1, 2017	$4,550,000
Current service cost for 2017	$ 565,000
Interest rate on high-quality corporate bonds	$ 8%
Actual return on plan assets in 2017	$ 312,000
Remeasurement loss due to changes in actuarial assumptions on the DBO	$ 176,000
Contributions made by the company to the plan in 2017	$ 422,000
Payments made by the plan to retirees in 2017	$ 166,000

Required:

a. Complete the pension worksheet for 2017.

b. Prepare the journal entry required to report the pension transactions in 2017.

c. Prepare the balance sheet excerpt showing how the pension amounts would be disclosed at 31 December 2017.

EXERCISE 16–7

Morant Ltd. initiated a defined benefit pension plan for its employees on January 1, 2015. The plan trustee has provided the following information:

	2015	2016	2017
Fair value of plan assets on December 31	$350,000	$610,000	?
DBO on December 31	$362,000	?	?
Remeasurement loss (gain) re: DBO	$(27,000)	0	$ 42,000
Remeasurement loss (gain) re: plan assets	?	?	$ 15,000
Contributions by Morant Ltd.	$348,000	$301,000	$265,000

There were no balances in the plan when it was initiated on January 1, 2015. The appropriate interest rate for this plan was 7% in 2015 and 2016, and 8% in 2017. The current service cost was $389,000 in 2015, $395,000 in 2016, and $410,000 in 2017. The plan paid no benefits in 2015, but paid $50,000 in 2016 and $54,000 in 2017. Assume that all cash payments into and out of the plan were made on December 31 of each year.

Required:

a. Complete the pension worksheets for the years 2015 to 2017.

b. Prepare the journal entries required for the years 2015 to 2017.

c. Prepare the balance sheet presentation of the relevant pension accounts for each year-end from 2015 to 2017, and identify if the pension plan is overfunded or underfunded.

EXERCISE 16–8

Weitz Inc. has provided a post-employment supplemental health care plan for its employees for many years. On January 1, 2016, the company granted past service credits with an actuarially determined value of $215,000 to a group of employees. The balance of the health benefit obligation on January 1, 2016, immediately prior to the granting of the past service credit, was $6,246,000. The appropriate discount rate during 2016 was 9%. The fair value of the plan assets on January 1, 2016 was $6,871,000. During the year, the current service cost was $510,000 and contributions to the plan were $430,000. Health benefits paid out to retired employees by the plan during 2016 totalled $850,000. Assume all cash transfers in and out of the plan occurred at the end of the year and that there were no other remeasurement gains or losses.

Required:

a. Determine the post-employment supplemental health expense for the year ending December 31, 2016.

b. Determine the net amount of the liability or asset for this plan to be reported on December 31, 2016.

EXERCISE 16–9

Repeat the requirements of Exercise 16–5, assuming the company reports under ASPE.

EXERCISE 16–10

Repeat the requirements of Exercise 16–6, assuming the company reports under ASPE.

Chapter 17

Leases

Leasing Versus Buying Equipment: Which is the Best Choice?

The short answer to this question is "it depends." The question of leasing versus buying has always been a sticking point for business management decisions because equipment is often a high-priced item and can require the firm to pay out a lot of cash. The following are some of the advantages and disadvantages of leasing equipment.

Leasing Advantages

- **Low up-front costs and predictable payments over the lease term.** Leasing allows for a minimal initial cash payment and regular, predicable payments and interest rate over the life of the lease, making cash flow management easier. This is a significant consideration for new companies with a lot of competing cash flow needs, or existing companies expanding their business market share or product lines.

- **Protects against obsolescence.** Non-current assets such as equipment are the base from which a company generates its revenue and profits. For this reason, these assets should be monitored and kept as efficient and productive as possible. That said, many businesses treat owned equipment as a permanent fixture and often do not plan for major repairs or eventual replacement. As a result when that time comes, there may not be enough cash set aside to address these *repair or replace* requirements adequately. Old equipment often gets stretched to the limit and beyond, increasing production downtime and negatively impacting revenue and profits. Often the additional costs to operate and repair old and outdated equipment outweighs any interest costs incurred for leasing new equipment that would maximize efficient production costs, generating more revenue and profits.

- **New technology improves productivity.** The lower entry cash requirements and the option to dispose of the equipment at the end of the lease term enable businesses to employ the most advanced technology within their industry sector. This gives them an edge over their competitors in terms of better productivity, more competitive pricing, and potentially employing fewer people. Leasing also enables businesses more flexibility so they can change equipment more quickly in response to changing environments and customer needs.

- **Tax benefits.** Operating leases are recorded as an operating expense, so they are tax deductible. They are therefore not reported as a liability on the balance sheet (referred to as **off-balance sheet financing**). This means that operating leases will not usually negatively affect the company's liquidity and solvency ratios or significantly impact any restrictive covenants from other creditors.

Leasing Disadvantages

- **Higher ownership costs.** Leased equipment is generally new, which tends to depreciate the most in the early years.

- **No accumulated equity.** Depending on the type of lease, businesses will never have title or ownership, so there is no equity to accumulate.

- **Lease payments always exist.** If a business is seasonal, there may be slow cycles throughout the year where the equipment is idle. Under a lease agreement, cash payments continue, which could put a strain on a business going through a slow cycle or downturn. Also, with leasing agreements, negotiations are necessary, and businesses are then tied to the specific lease term.

- **Scheduled maintenance and repair costs.** Many leasing agreements include a structured repair and maintenance schedule that must be followed by the lessee. With equipment ownership, the business can make its own decisions about when maintenance is required.

(Source: Landscape Managing Network, 2010)

Chapter 17 Learning Objectives

After completing this chapter, you should be able to:

LO 1: Describe leases and their role in accounting and business.

LO 2: Describe the criteria used for ASPE and IFRS to classify a lease as a capital/finance lease.

LO 3: Prepare the accounting entries of a capitalized lease for both the lessee and lessor.

LO 4: Prepare the accounting entries of a capitalized sale and leaseback transaction.

LO 5: Explain how leases are disclosed in the financial statements.

LO 6: Explain the similarities and differences between ASPE and IFRS regarding capitalization criteria, interest rates, and disclosures.

Introduction

This chapter will focus on the basics of leasing agreements. Leases can be classified as either an operating lease, similar to a simple rental agreement, or a finance/capital (IFRS/ASPE) lease, where the leased item is classified as an asset with a corresponding liability (even if the legal title has not transferred to the lessee). The accounting standards focus on the economic substance rather than on the legal form. Leases will be discussed in terms of their use in business, their recognition, measurement, reporting and analysis. Leases will also be discussed and illustrated from both the viewpoint of the company leasing from another party (lessee), and the company leasing to another party (lessor).

Chapter Organization

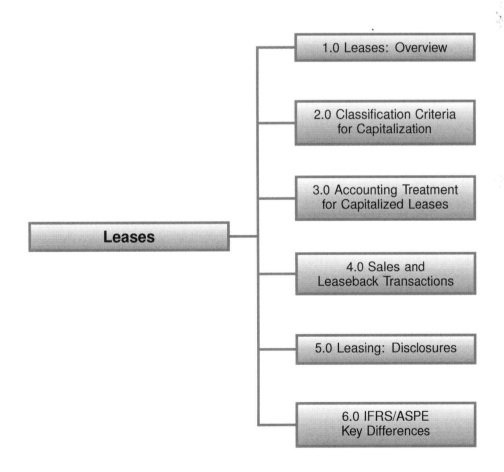

17.1 Leases: Overview

Businesses often need to update their existing equipment or business space, or perhaps acquire entirely new equipment or accommodation as they expand their operations. The opening story describes the pros and cons of leasing assets versus buying them. As demonstrated, the answer isn't straightforward and requires an analysis of the business on a case-by-case basis in order to determine whether buying or leasing is the best option. This chapter will focus on a business's decision to lease equipment and the accounting treatment that is required as a result.

Leasing is simply defined as the temporary right to use an asset for a specified period of time in exchange for cash payments or other consideration. This definition is broad and includes common transactions, such as leasing an apartment from a landlord or leasing a car from a dealership. In the case of a private individual, these types of leases are generally treated as rental agreements and a rental expense. In the case of businesses entering into leasing agreements, such as renting office space or equipment, the accounting treatment is more complex. It depends on the economic substance of the transaction and how closely the transaction meets certain prescribed criteria set out in the ASPE and IFRS accounting standards. In some cases, an operating lease is used, which is a simple rental agreement where payments made are recorded to rental expense. In other cases, it will be classified as a capital lease where the business would report the leased asset in the balance sheet, along with an associated lease obligation as a liability. The main focus of this chapter will be the difference between the classification of a lease as an operating lease or a capital (ASPE)/finance (IFRS) lease and the accounting treatment that follows.

17.2 Classification Criteria for Capitalization

For all businesses to comply with the accounting standards, lease agreements must be classified as either an operating lease or as a capital (ASPE)/finance (IFRS) lease. Each accounting standard has set its own criteria to determine the classification and is based on who substantively bears the risks and rewards of ownership.

Lessee Classification

Below is a recap of the criteria needed for the lessee classification for a capital/finance lease:

17.2. Classification Criteria for Capitalization

ASPE	IFRS
The criteria are much more prescriptive than with IFRS.	More professional judgment is needed since the criteria below are qualitative and do not include numeric thresholds.
The ASPE criteria requires the lessee to classify the lease as a capital lease if *any one or more* of the following criteria is met:	*Any one or more* of the criteria below supports the classification as a finance lease:
1. There is either a transfer of ownership or a bargain purchase option (BPO) included in the lease agreement. If a BPO exists, it is assumed that the lessee will exercise the right to purchase the asset at the BPO price because this price is significantly lower than the asset's fair value at that time.	1. Same as ASPE.
2. The lease term, which includes any bargain renewal option, covers most of the leased asset's economic life. It is assumed that the lessee will exercise the right to extend the agreement at the bargain renewal price because this price is significantly lower than market at that time. The threshold calculation is: Lease term must be at least 75% of the asset's estimated economic or useful life.	2. The lease term will make up the major part of the estimated useful life of the lease asset. If a bargain renewal option was included in the lease agreement, it is assumed that the lessee will exercise the right to extend the agreement at the bargain renewal price because this price is significantly lower than market at that time.

3. The lessor will recover substantially all of the leased asset's fair value as well as realizing a return on the investment. The lessee is in substance purchasing the asset. The threshold calculation is the present value of the sum of: • the lease payments (excluding any executory, maintenance, or contingent costs paid by the lessee that are included in the lease payment); • a *guaranteed* residual value; or • a bargain purchase option that is equal to 90% or more of the fair value of the leased asset. This sum is referred to as the **minimum lease payment**.[1] The interest rate used in the present value calculation is *the lower of* the lessor's implicit rate if known, or the lessee's incremental borrowing rate.	3. The lessor will recover substantially all of the leased asset's fair value as well as realizing a return on the investment. The lessee is, in substance, purchasing the asset. This is substantiated if the present value of the minimum lease payment* is substantially all of the fair value of the leased asset. The interest rate used for the present value calculation is the *lessor's implicit rate*, unless it cannot be reasonably determined, in which case the lessee's incremental borrowing rate will be used instead.
4.	4. The leased assets are so specialized that they will only benefit the lessee without major modifications.
5.	5. The lessee reimburses the lessor for any losses if the lessee cancels the lease.

For points 2 and 3 above, note that even though the leased asset's title has not legally transferred to the lessee, the risks and rewards of ownership have been substantially transferred to the lessee, hence the accounting treatment to capitalize the lease. This is an example of a case in which the economic substance, rather than the legal form, dictates the accounting treatment.

Note: For both standards, the leased asset valuation amount cannot exceed its fair value at that date.

---

[1] The lessee's *minimum lease payments* are essentially all the payments that the lessee is required to make over the lease term, which includes any guaranteed residual value and any BPO or bargain renewal option, but excludes any executory, maintenance, or contingent costs that are included in the lease payment. A contingent cost might be additional lease payments required to be paid that are based on subsequent events, such as if the lessee's sales exceed a certain threshold amount during the lease term.

Lessor Classification

For the lessor classification as a capital lease, ASPE requires any one of the three ASPE criteria for the lessee above to be met, plus two additional criteria:

1. Collectability of the lease payments is reasonably predictable.

2. There are no important uncertainties about costs that have not yet been incurred by the lessor.

If the above two additional criteria are not met, it would not be appropriate for the lessor to remove the leased asset from its accounting records. On the rare occasions where this is the case, it would require special accounting treatment, which is beyond the scope of this textbook.

Further analysis is required to determine if the lease is a sales-type lease, indicated by the existence of a profit, or is a direct-financing lease, where no sales and cost of goods sold are involved (which is usually the case when lessors are finance companies or banks and not manufacturers or dealers).

For the lessor classification to be a capital lease, IFRS indicators include the five IFRS qualitative criteria above. Professional judgment is applied to these to determine if classification as a finance lease is appropriate. Usually, if any one of the first three qualitative criteria above is met then it is likely to be classified as a finance lease. Similar to ASPE, if the lessor is a dealer or manufacturer the accounting treatment will likely require sales and cost of goods sold, whereas for a finance company or bank the entries will be recorded to a lease receivable with interest earned on the receivable.

If the lease is deemed to be a capital/finance lease then the lessee records the leased asset and the corresponding lease obligation as though it was a purchase subject to depreciation with payments and interest on an instalment loan. The lessor derecognizes the leased asset by removing it from its leased assets inventory and records a receivable amount equal to the sum of the lease payments, the residual value, or the bargain purchase option. The lessor must also record the lease as either a sale, if the present value of the lease is greater than the cost of goods sold (a profit), or as a financing arrangement (no profit). This will be illustrated shortly.

Special Items

Indirect costs. Indirect costs arise if the lessor is not a manufacturer or dealer. Any initial direct costs of negotiating and arranging the lease are included in the investment amount to be recovered when calculating the lease payment. Recall that the lease payment is determined by the lessor to recover all costs.

Economic life versus lease term. The economic life of an asset is usually longer than the lease term. Depreciation of a leased asset by the lessee for a capitalized lease is based on whether or not the title of the leased asset transfers to the lessee. If the legal title remains with the lessor, and the leased equipment is returned to the lessor at the end of the lease term, then the depreciation period of the leased asset will be the lease term. If the legal title to the leased asset transfers to the lessee at the end of the lease term, or there is a bargain purchase or bargain renewal option, it is assumed that the lessee will exercise this option since the price of either a BPO or a bargain renewal option is significantly lower than the market price at that time. For this reason, a leased asset under these circumstances will be depreciated over its economic or useful life instead of over the lease term. This makes intuitive sense, given that the lessee intends to continue to use the asset beyond the lease term.

Interest rates. As previously stated, the *lessor's implicit interest rate* is to be used in the present value calculation since it is usually the more realistic rate for IFRS. Alternatively, the lessee's incremental borrowing rate is used if the lessee does not know the lessor's implicit rate. ASPE advocates the lower of either the lessor's implicit rate (if known) or the lessee's incremental borrowing rate. This is to ensure that an artificially high interest rate is not used. Recall from previous chapters regarding long-term debt that the higher the interest rate, the lower the present value of the debt obligation. In leasing terms, using an unrealistically high interest rate could reduce the present value of the lease to below the capitalization threshold criterion (90% for ASPE, and "substantially all" for IFRS), thus avoiding a capitalization classification with its requirement to report a lease asset and obligation. Once an interest rate is selected, the accrued interest for the lessee and interest income for the lessor are calculated using the effective interest method as discussed in the long-term debt chapter.

Executory costs. Lease payments often include leased asset use costs that the lessor has paid and wants to recoup from the lessee, such as insurance, maintenance, licenses, or tax costs. These **executory costs** are to be excluded when calculating the present value of the lease and separately recorded as an expense, as they don't arise from the acquisition of the leased asset, but rather from its use. For example, if the lease payment of $14,000 included $2,000 for insurance of the leased asset, the lessee's journal entry would be:

General Journal				
Date	Account/Explanation	PR	Debit	Credit
	Insurance expense...........................		2,000	
	Obligations under lease.....................		12,000	
	Cash..			14,000
	To record the lease payment.			

Operating Lease. If the criteria identified above for either ASPE or IFRS are not met, then the lease would be treated as an operating lease and the subsequent entries are straightforward. For example, if the lessee pays $12,000 per year, and the lease is classified as an operating lease, then the entries are as follows:

For lessee:

General Journal				
Date	Account/Explanation	PR	Debit	Credit
	Rent expense...............................		12,000	
	Cash......................................			12,000

For lessor:

General Journal				
Date	Account/Explanation	PR	Debit	Credit
	Cash..		12,000	
	Rental revenue...........................			12,000

Note: No entries are made by the lessee to classify a leased asset or to recognize a lease obligation. No obligation means that the lessee can use the leased asset exclusively without any impact on its liquidity, coverage, or debt ratios. Classification as an operating lease in this instance is an example of *off-balance sheet financing*. The avoidance of reporting debt can motivate manufacturers and lessee businesses to play with the numbers in order to stay under the ASPE capitalization criteria, enabling management to classify the lease as an operating lease and avoid reporting an additional liability for the lease obligation. This allows a business to report operations in the best light, even though from an economic standpoint the results reported to shareholders and creditors do not reflect the economic reality. Whereas, since IFRS considers the substance of the transaction rather than simply using hard thresholds, it may be more difficult under IFRS for management to manipulate the numbers.

17.3 Accounting Treatment for Capitalized Leases

Example 1: Sales-type lease for the lessor

The accounting treatment is best explained using a numeric example. On January 1, 2016, Tweenix Corp. (lessee) entered into an agreement to lease a piece of landscaping equipment from Morganette Ltd. (lessor). The lease details are below:

Non-cancellable lease term	8 years
Lease bargain renewal option or a bargain purchase option	None – equipment reverts back to lessor
Residual value (not guaranteed by lessee)	$36,000
Annual lease payment due each January 1 (annuity due)	Lessor to determine
Equipment cost to lessor	$666,000
Equipment estimated economic life	9 years
Equipment fair value on January 1, 2016	$864,000
Lessor has set the following implicit rate of return, which is known to lessee	7%
Lessee incremental borrowing rate	8%

Other information:

- Both companies' year-ends are December 31 and both follow ASPE.

- Collectability of the lease payments is reasonably predictable and there are no important uncertainties about costs that have not yet been incurred by the lessor.

- The lessee depreciates all equipment on a straight-line basis.

Accounting Treatment – Summary of the Steps

1. Lease terms determined by the lessor include the lease payment amount, the length of the lease, the interest (discount) rate, the bargain purchase option or bargain renewal option (if any), and the residual value as either guaranteed or unguaranteed by the lessee. These terms may be subject to some negotiation between the lessee and lessor but the lease payment amount is calculated from the lessor's point of view.

For both the lessee and lessor:

2. Once the lease terms are known, analysis and classification of the lease as either an operating or capital (ASPE)/finance (IFRS) lease is required.

3. Record initial entry(ies) to recognize and valuate the lease.

4. Record lease payment entry(ies) throughout the reporting periods over the lease term.

5. Record adjusting entries, if any, at each reporting date over the lease term.

6. Report the results. Typically, it will be the balance sheet for the lessee and the income statement for the lessor.

7. Record the final entry at the end of the lease term.

Each of the steps above is now considered and journal entry accounts and amounts determined.

Applying the Steps:

Step 1. Lease terms determined by the lessor include the lease payment amount, the length of the lease, the interest (discount) rate, the bargain purchase option or bargain renewal option (if any), and the residual value whether guaranteed or unguaranteed by the lessee:

In this case, the lessor wants to get a return of 7% on the investment. Other negotiated details between the lessor and lessee result in a lease term of eight years, no bargain purchase or bargain renewal options, and the lease will revert back to lessor at the end of the lease term. The lessee does not guarantee the residual value of the equipment at the end of the lease term in this case. The equipment originally cost $666,000 and has a current fair value of $864,000. On this basis, the lessor must now calculate the lease payment amount that the lessee will pay at the beginning of each year. For this reason, the payment calculation using present values and a financial calculator will be for an annuity due (AD). This simply means that, in this example, the lease payment is to be made at the beginning of each year instead of at the end. The annuity due concept was discussed in further detail in the chapter on long-term debt under present values and timelines.

The lessor must also calculate the lease payment amount on a present value basis. The data that the lessor must use to calculate the lease payment amount is the 7% expected rate of return (I/Y), the $864,000 current fair value as the present value (PV) of the equipment, the eight years duration of the arrangement (N), and the $36,000 unguaranteed residual value (FV) that the lessor hopes to receive by reselling the used equipment in the marketplace at the end of the lease term.

Note that when calculating the lease payment, it does not matter if the residual value is guaranteed or not guaranteed by the lessee because the residual value represents a cash flow in, no matter the source. Recall that the lease payment calculation is from the lessor's point of view. However, whether the residual value is guaranteed or not by the lessee does matter for the lessee present value calculation of the minimum lease payments as shown below in step 2. In the meantime, the present value calculation, using a financial calculator, for an annuity due is:

$$PV = (PMT/AD, I/Y, N, FV)$$

or

$$PMT/AD = (+/- PV, I/Y, N, FV)$$
$$PMT/AD = (+/- 864{,}000 \text{ PV}, 7 \text{ I/Y}, 8 \text{ N}, 36{,}000 \text{ FV})$$
$$PMT/AD = \$131{,}947.0162$$

or $\underline{\$131{,}947}$ due at the beginning of each year (annuity due)

The lease payment will be $131,947 per year for eight years in order for the lessor to recoup the asset's fair value of $864,000, earn a 7% return, and recoup a residual value of $36,000 from the marketplace at the end of eight years. The unguaranteed residual value that the lessor expects to receive once the leased asset is sold in the marketplace at the end of the lease term causes the lease payment amount for the lessee to be reduced. Had there been no residual value, the lessee's lease payment amount would be the higher amount of $135,226 (+/- 864,000 PV, 7 I/Y, 8 N, 0 FV).

Valuation of the lessee's lease obligation, and the corresponding leased asset, is based on calculating the present value of the estimated net cash flows, same as was done for other long-term debt in a previous chapter. In the case of leasing, these estimated net cash flows are referred to as the minimum lease payments from the lessee's point of view. This will be included below in step 2. The important thing to remember is that the valuation of the lessee's asset and associated obligation must be the lower of the present value of the minimum lease payments and the fair value of the leased asset at the time of the lease agreement.

Step 2. Analysis and classification of the lease as an operating or capital lease:

The terms of the lease agreement are now set, and it is time to determine whether the lease is to be classified as an operating or capital lease by both parties. Since these companies follow ASPE, this will be the criterion used.

Lessee Analysis

At least one of the four criteria below must be met in order for the lease to be classified as capital, otherwise it will be classified as operating. Below, highlighted in red, are the results of the analysis for this example:

- Does ownership title pass? No, title remains with the lessor.

- Is there a BPO or a bargain renewal option? No
- Is the lease term at least 75% of the asset's estimated economic or useful life? Yes, capitalize leased asset.

  8 years ÷ 9 years = 89% which is greater than 75%

Note: At this point, as one of the criteria has been met, the capitalization of the lease is now applicable, but the lessee analysis will continue for illustrative purposes.

- Is the present value of the minimum lease payment (net cash flows) at least 90% of the fair value of the leased asset? Yes, as calculated below.

$$
\begin{aligned}
\text{The lease cash flows} = \ & \$131{,}947 \text{ lease payment} \\
& + \$0 \text{ guaranteed residual value} \\
& + \$0 \text{ BPO} \\
& - \$0 \text{ executory costs paid by lessee included in} \\
& \quad \text{the } \$131{,}947 \text{ lease payment}
\end{aligned}
$$

Discounted at the lowest of either the lessor's implicit rate (7%) or the lessee's incremental borrowing rate (8%).

Present value calculation:

$$PV = (PMT/AD, I/Y, N, FV)$$
$$PV = (131{,}947 \text{ PMT/AD}, 7 \text{ I/Y}, 8 \text{ N}, 0 \text{ FV*})$$

*As residual value is not guaranteed by the lessee, it is not included in the lessee's present value calculation.

Using a financial calculator, the present value of the leased asset is calculated as:

$$PV = \$843{,}047.5687 \text{ or } \underline{\$843{,}048} \text{ rounded}$$

If the fair value of the leased asset is $864,000, then the present value of the net cash flows is 97.575% and is, therefore, greater than the threshold criterion of 90%. The leased asset and the associated lease obligation will, then, be the amount of the present value of the lessee's minimum lease payments of $843,048.

Note: Had the present value yielded a higher amount, the maximum valuation for the lease asset and obligation would be the fair value amount of $864,000.

For the lessee, the analysis reveals that this lease meets two of the criteria for capitalization. Since only one criterion needs to be met, the lessee will classify this lease as a capital lease.

Lessor Analysis

The criteria above are also used to determine if the lease is to be a capital/finance lease for the lessor, plus two additional criteria:

- Collectability of the lease payments is reasonably predictable. Yes

- There are no important uncertainties about the un-reimbursable costs yet to be incurred by the lessor. Yes

The lessor must now determine if the lease is to be treated as a sales-type lease or a direct-financing lease under ASPE (note that with IFRS, the lease is either a manufacturer/dealer lease or a finance lease). In this case, the fair value of the lease of $864,000 exceeds the lessor's cost of $666,000, meaning that a profit exists that classifies it as a sales-type lease treatment. If the lessor were not a manufacturer or dealer, such as if the lessor was a finance company, then the lease would be treated as a direct-financing lease.

To summarize the analyses above, if the lease meets the criteria for capitalization for the lessee, it will also be classified as a capital lease for the lessor, unless there are collectability issues or uncertainties about un-reimbursable costs as identified above. Once the capitalization of the lease classification is determined for both the lessee and the lessor, further analysis is necessary to determine if the lease is to be treated as either a sales-type or direct-financing lease (ASPE) for the lessor.

As a capital lease, the lessee records the leased asset and the corresponding lease obligation based on the lower of the present value of the minimum lease payments or the leased asset's fair value at that time. The payments made to the lessor are recorded as a reduction in the lease obligation. At year-end, the leased asset is depreciated, and accrued interest expense of the leased obligation is recorded.

As a sales-type lease, the lessor recorded the lease receivable, the sales revenue, and the unearned interest income that will be realized over the lease term. The leased asset is transferred from the leased assets inventory to cost of goods sold. Any lease payments received are recorded as a reduction of the lease receivable. At year-end, the interest earned for the year is reclassified from unearned interest income to earned interest income.

Steps 3, 4, and 5:

The entries for both the lessee and lessor are recorded below:

For lessee:

\multicolumn{5}{c}{General Journal}				
Date	Account/Explanation	PR	Debit	Credit
Jan 1	Equipment under lease (asset)*............ Obligations under lease (liability)......... To record the lease arrangement on January 1.		843,048	843,048
Jan 1	Obligations under lease..................... Cash..................................... To record the lease payment on January 1.		131,947	131,947
Dec 31	Depreciation expense**..................... Accumulated depreciation, leased equipment.. To record year-end adjusting entry for depreciation.		105,381	105,381
Dec 31	Interest expense***........................ Interest payable.......................... To record year-end adjusting entry for accrued interest.		49,777	49,777

* PV = (131,947 PMT/AD, 7 I/Y, 8 N, 0 FV)
** 843,048 lease asset amount divided by 8 years lease term if SL depreciation policy is used.
*** $843,048 lease obligation − $131,947 lease payment) × 7% for 1 year

For lessor:

	General Journal			
Date	Account/Explanation	PR	Debit	Credit
Jan 1	Lease receivable*............................		1,091,576	
	Cost of goods sold**........................		645,048	
	Sales revenue***............................			843,048
	Inventory.......................................			666,000
	Unearned interest income****.............			227,576
	To record the lease arrangement on January 1.			
Jan 1	Cash...		131,947	
	Lease receivable............................			131,947
	To record the lease payment on January 1.			
Dec 31	Unearned interest income†..................		51,244	
	Interest Income.............................			51,244
	To record year-end adjusting entry for interest earned for 1 year.			

* 131,947 lease payment × 8 years + 36,000 residual value

Since the residual value is *not guaranteed* by the lessee, its present value is excluded from both COGS and sales as shown below:

** $666,000 cost − 20,952 present value of residual value

PV = (7 I/Y, 8 N, 36,000 FV) = 20,952

*** $864,000 fair value − 20,952 present value of residual

**** $1,091,576 lease receivable − 864,000 fair value

† $864,000 fair value − 131,947 lease payment) × 7% for 1 year

Step 6. Report the results:

Lessee – Balance Sheet as at December 31, 2016		Lessor – Income Statement for the year ended December 31, 2016	
Property, plant, and equipment			
Equipment under lease	$ 843,048	Sales revenue	843,048
Accumulated depreciation	(105,381)	Cost of goods sold	645,048
	737,667	Gross profit	198,000
Current liabilities		**Other revenue**	
Interest payable	$ 49,777	Interest income	51,244
Current portion of lease obligation*	82,170		
Long-term liabilities			
Lease obligation (note X)**	628,931		

* ($131,947 − ($843,048 − $131,947) × 7%) = $82,170 principal portion due in one year

** ($843,048 − $131,947 − $82,170) = $628,931 long-term portion

Step 7. Record the final entry at the end of the lease term:

At the end of the lease term, the leased asset is returned to the lessor. The lessee's accounting records will show that the leased asset will now be fully depreciated and the lease obligation will have a zero balance owing. Assuming that the residual value of $36,000 is equal to the fair value at that time, the final entries for the lessee and lessor at the end of the lease term would be:

For lessee:

	General Journal			
Date	Account/Explanation	PR	Debit	Credit
Jan 1/23	Accumulated depreciation, leased equipment		843,048	
	Equipment under lease..................			843,048

For lessor:

	General Journal			
Date	Account/Explanation	PR	Debit	Credit
Jan 1/23	Leased inventory (or equipment for disposal)		36,000	
	Lease receivable........................			36,000

If the lessor is able to receive the full amount of the unguaranteed residual value from the marketplace, then the entry would be:

For lessor:

	General Journal			
Date	Account/Explanation	PR	Debit	Credit
Jan 1/23	Cash..		36,000	
	Leased inventory (or equipment for disposal)..			36,000

The example above is for a lease where the lessee has not guaranteed the residual value. If the lessee guaranteed the residual value, the entries would be as follows (shown in red):

For lessee:

\multicolumn{5}{c	}{General Journal}
Date	Account/Explanation	PR	Debit	Credit
Jan 1	Equipment under lease (asset)*............		864,000	
	Obligations under lease (liability).........			864,000
	To record the lease arrangement on January 1.			
Jan 1	Obligations under lease....................		131,947	
	Cash.....................................			131,947
	To record the lease payment on January 1.			
Dec 31	Depreciation expense**....................		103,500	
	Accumulated depreciation, leased equipment......................................			103,500
	To record year-end adjusting entry for depreciation.			
Dec 31	Interest expense***.......................		51,244	
	Interest payable..........................			51,244
	To record year-end adjusting entry for accrued interest.			

* PV = (131,947 PMT/AD, 7 I/Y, 8 N, 36,000 FV)

** 864,000 lease asset amount minus the guaranteed residual value of 36,000 divided by an 8-year lease term

*** ($864,000 lease obligation − $131,947 lease payment) × 7% for 1 year

For lessor:

\multicolumn{5}{c	}{General Journal}
Date	Account/Explanation	PR	Debit	Credit
Jan 1	Lease receivable*.........................		1,091,576	
	Cost of goods sold........................		666,000	
	Sales revenue............................			864,000
	Inventory.................................			666,000
	Unearned interest income**..............			227,576
	To record the lease arrangement on January 1.			
Jan 1	Cash......................................		131,947	
	Lease receivable.........................			131,947
	To record the lease payment on January 1.			
Dec 31	Unearned interest income***..............		51,244	
	Interest Income...........................			51,244
	To record year-end adjusting entry for interest earned for 1 year.			

* 131,947 lease payment × 8 years + 36,000 residual value

Since the residual value is guaranteed by the lessee, its present value is included in both COGS and sales as shown below:

** $1,091,576 lease receivable − 864,000 fair value
*** ($864,000 fair value − 131,947 lease payment) × 7% for 1 year

At the end of the lease, the leased asset is returned to the lessor. The lessor is able to sell the asset for $30,000, so the lessee now owes the lessor $6,000 for the unrecovered portion of the guaranteed residual value of $36,000. The lessee's lease amortization schedule using the effective interest method would be:

Lessee Lease Amortization Schedule
Annuity Due, Guaranteed Residual Value

Year	Payment	Interest @ 7%	Principal	Balance
2016				864,000
2016	131,947			732,053
2017	131,947	51,244	80,703	651,350
2018	131,947	45,594	86,353	564,997
2019	131,947	39,550	92,397	472,600
2020	131,947	33,082	98,865	373,735
2021	131,947	26,161	105,786	267,949
2022	131,947	18,756	113,191	154,759
2023	131,947	10,833	121,114	33,645
2023	36,000	2,355	33,645	0

The entries for the lessee and lessor at the end of the lease term would be:

For lessee:

	General Journal			
Date	Account/Explanation	PR	Debit	Credit
Jan 1, 2024	Accumulated depreciation, leased equipment		828,000	
	Loss on lease...............................		6,000	
	Interest payable............................		2,355	
	Obligation under lease.....................		33,645	
	Equipment under lease.................			864,000
	Cash.....................................			6,000
	For Accumulated depreciation: ($864,000 − 36,000)			

For lessor:

	General Journal			
Date	Account/Explanation	PR	Debit	Credit
Jan 1/24	Cash..		6,000	
	Leased inventory (or equipment for disposal)		30,000	
	Lease receivable.......................			36,000

Note the differences in the journal entries for the non-guaranteed residual value compared to the guaranteed residual value highlighted in red.

What if the lessor included a bargain purchase option (BPO) that is clearly less than its fair value at the end of the lease? In that case, it is assumed that the lessee will exercise the right to purchase the leased asset at the end of the lease term for the BPO price. The leased asset will no longer revert back to the lessor and the residual value will apply now to the lessee and not to the lessor. Since title to the asset will transfer to the lessee, the asset will be depreciated over its economic life instead of the lease term.

For simplicity, the fair value of $864,000 will remain the same. The lease payment amount calculated by the lessor will be adjusted to include a BPO of $20,000 in place of the residual value:

$$\text{PMT/AD} = (+/- 864{,}000 \text{ PV}, 7 \text{ I/Y}, 8 \text{ N}, 20{,}000 \text{ FV})$$
$$= \underline{\underline{\$133{,}404}} \text{ due at the beginning of each year (annuity due)}$$

The lease payment must, therefore, be $133,404 per year for eight years in order for the lessor to recoup the asset's fair value of $864,000, earn a 7% return, and receive a bargain payment option from the lessee of $20,000 at the end of eight years.

The entries assuming a BPO of $20,000 are shown below. Assume for purposes of depreciation that the asset will have a residual value of $31,500 at the end of its useful life.

For lessee:

\multicolumn{5}{c}{General Journal}
Date	Account/Explanation	PR	Debit	Credit
Jan 1	Equipment under lease (asset)*............ Obligations under lease (liability)......... To record the lease arrangement on January 1.		864,000	864,000
Jan 1	Obligations under lease.................... Cash..................................... To record the lease payment on January 1.		133,404	133,404
Dec 31	Depreciation expense**.................... Accumulated depreciation, leased equipment.................................... To record year-end adjusting entry for depreciation.		92,500	92,500
Dec 31	Interest expense***........................ Interest payable.......................... To record year-end adjusting entry for accrued interest.		51,142	51,142

* PV = (133,404 PMT/AD, 7 I/Y, 8 N, 20,000 FV)
** (864,000 lease asset amount minus a residual value of 31,500) divided by 9 years economic life
*** ($864,000 lease obligation − $133,404 lease payment) × 7% for 1 year

For lessor:

Date	Account/Explanation	PR	Debit	Credit
Jan 1	Lease receivable*............................		1,087,232	
	Cost of goods sold...........................		666,000	
	Sales revenue.............................			864,000
	Inventory..................................			666,000
	Unearned interest income**..............			223,232
	To record the lease arrangement on January 1.			
Jan 1	Cash...		133,404	
	Lease receivable..........................			133,404
	To record the lease payment on January 1.			
Dec 31	Unearned interest income***...............		51,142	
	Interest Income...........................			51,142
	To record year-end adjusting entry for interest earned for 1 year.			

* 133,404 lease payment × 8 years + 20,000 BPO
** $1,087,232 lease receivable − 864,000 fair value
*** ($864,000 fair value − 133,404 lease payment) × 7% for 1 year

Note that the lessee's depreciation decreases significantly with the existence of a BPO and with changing the depreciation period to the asset's economic life instead of the lease term (highlighted above in red).

The lessee's lease amortization schedule would be:

Lessee Lease Amortization Schedule
Annuity Due, Bargain Purchase Option

Year	Payment	Interest @ 7%	Principal	Balance
2016				864,000
2016	133,404			730,596
2017	133,404	51,142	82,262	648,334
2018	133,404	45,383	88,021	560,313
2019	133,404	39,222	94,182	466,131
2020	133,404	32,629	100,775	365,356
2021	133,404	25,575	107,829	257,527
2022	131,947	18,027	115,377	142,150
2023	133,404	9,950	123,454	18,696
2023	20,000	1,304	18,696	0

The entries for the lessee and lessor at the end of the lease term would be:

For lessee:

	General Journal			
Date	Account/Explanation	PR	Debit	Credit
Jan 1, 2024	Interest payable.............................		1,304	
	Obligation under lease......................		18,696	
	Cash..			20,000

For lessor:

	General Journal			
Date	Account/Explanation	PR	Debit	Credit
Jan 1, 2024	Cash..		20,000	
	Lease receivable...........................			20,000

Example 2: Direct-financing lease for the lessor

On May 31, 2016, Visuel Ltd. (lessee) leases its equipment from First Finance Corporation (lessor). The lease has the following terms:

Non-cancellable lease term	5 years
Lease bargain renewal option or a bargain purchase option	None – equipment reverts back to lessor
Residual value (guaranteed by lessee)	$19,652
Annual lease payment due each May 31 (annuity due)	$41,400
Equipment estimated economic life	6 years
Equipment fair value on May 31, 2016	$203,600
Lessor has set the following implicit rate of return, which is known to lessee	5%
Lessee incremental borrowing rate	6%

Other information:

- Both companies' year-ends are December 31 and both follow ASPE.
- Collectability of the lease payments is reasonably predictable and there are no important uncertainties about costs that have not yet been incurred by the lessor.
- The lessee depreciates all equipment on a straight-line basis.

Applying the Steps:

Step 1. Lease terms determined by the lessor include the lease payment amount, the length of the lease, the interest (discount) rate, the bargain purchase option or bargain renewal option, if any, and the residual value as either guaranteed or unguaranteed by the lessee. These terms may be subject to some negotiation between the lessee and lessor:

In this case, the lease payment of $41,400 is already calculated. All other terms are known.

Step 2. Analysis and classification of the lease as an operating or capital lease:

The terms of the lease agreement are set, and it is time to determine whether the lease is to be classified as an operating or capital lease by both parties. Since these companies follow ASPE, these will be the criteria used.

Lessee Analysis

At least one of the four criteria below must be met in order for the lease to be classified as a capital lease, otherwise it will be classified as an operating lease:

- Does ownership title pass? No, title remains with the lessor.
- Is there a BPO or a bargain renewal option? No.
- Is the lease term at least 75% of the asset's estimated economic or useful life? Yes, capitalize leased asset.

  5 years ÷ 6 years = 83% which is greater than 75%

Note: At this point, since at least one of the above criteria has been met, the capitalization of the lease is now applicable. However, the lessee analysis will continue for illustrative purposes.

- Is the present value of the minimum lease payment (net cash flows) at least 90% of the fair value of the leased asset? Yes, as calculated below.

  Present value calculation:

  PV = (41,400 PMT/AD, 5 I/Y*, 5 N, 19,652 FV**)

  * Recall that the ASPE standards state that the lower of the two interest rates is to be used since both are known to the lessee. In this case, 5% is the lower of the two interest rates.

** Residual value is guaranteed by the lessee, so it is included in the lessee's present value calculation.

Using a financial calculator, the present value of the leased asset is calculated as:

$$PV = \underline{\$203,600} \text{ rounded}$$

If the fair value of the leased asset is $203,600, then the present value of the net cash flows is 100% and is, therefore, greater than the threshold of 90%.

For the lessee, this analysis reveals that the lease meets two of the criteria for capitalization. Since only one criterion needs to be met, this lease can be classified as a capital lease by the lessee.

Lessor Analysis

The lease will be a capital lease to the lessor provided that:

- Collectability of the lease payments is reasonably predictable. Yes
- There are no important uncertainties about the un-reimbursable costs yet to be incurred by the lessor. Yes

To determine type of lease, as the cost to the lessor is the same as the fair value (i.e., there is no profit), and as First Finance Corporation is not a manufacturer or dealer, the lease is classified as a direct-financing lease for the lessor.

To summarize, if the lease meets the criteria for capitalization for the lessee, it will also be classified as a capital transaction for the lessor, since there are no collectability issues or uncertainties about un-reimbursable costs.

Further analysis determines that this is to be treated as a direct-financing lease under ASPE (IFRS: finance lease).

As a direct-financing capital lease, the lessor removes the leased asset from the leased asset account and records the lease as receivable. The difference is recorded to un-earned interest income, which will be earned over the lease term. Any lease payments received are recorded as a reduction of the lease receivable. At year-end, the portion of the interest earned for the current fiscal year is reclassified from unearned interest income to earned interest income.

These entries are recorded below.

Steps 3, 4, and 5:

For lessee:

	General Journal			
Date	Account/Explanation	PR	Debit	Credit

May 31	Equipment under lease (asset)*............
	    Obligations under lease (liability).........
	    To record the lease arrangement on May 31.
			203,600	203,600

May 31	Obligations under lease....................
	    Cash......................................
	    To record the lease payment on May 31.
			41,400	41,400

Dec 31	Depreciation expense**.....................
	    Accumulated depreciation, leased equipment...............................
	    To record year-end adjusting entry for depreciation.
			21,461	21,461

Dec 31	Interest expense***.........................
	    Interest payable..........................
	    To record year-end adjusting entry for accrued interest for 7/12 months.
			4,731	4,731

* PV = (41,400 PMT/AD, 5 I/Y, 5 N, 19,652 FV)

** ($203,600 lease asset amount minus the guaranteed residual value of $19,652) divided by 5 years lease term for 7/12 months

*** ($203,600 lease obligation − 41,400 lease payment) × 5% for 7/12 months

For lessor:

	General Journal			
Date	Account/Explanation	PR	Debit	Credit

May 31	Lease receivable*...........................
	    Equipment acquired for lease............
	    Unearned interest revenue**.............
	    To record the lease arrangement on May 31.
			226,652	203,600
				23,052

May 31	Cash..
	    Lease receivable........................
	    To record the lease payment on May 31.
			41,400	41,400

Dec 31	Unearned interest revenue***...............
	    Interest revenue.........................
	    To record year-end adjusting entry for interest earned for 7/12 months.
			4,731	4,731

* 41,400 lease payment × 5 years + 19,652 residual value

** 226,652 lease receivable − $203,600 fair value
*** ($203,600 fair value − 41,400 lease payment) × 5% for 7/12 months

Step 6. Report the results:

Lessee – Balance Sheet as at December 31, 2016			Lessor – Income Statement for the year ended December 31, 2016	
Property, plant, and equipment				
Equipment under lease		$203,600	Interest revenue	$4,731
Accumulated depreciation		(21,461)		
		182,139		
Current liabilities				
Interest payable		$ 4,731		
Current portion of lease obligation*		33,290		
Long-term liabilities				
Lease obligation (note X)**		128,910		

* 41,400 − (203,600 − 41,400) × 5%
** 203,600 − 41,400 − 33,290

Step 7. Record the final entry at the end of the lease term:

At the end of the lease, the leased asset is returned to the lessor. As the lessor is able to sell the asset for $15,000, the lessee now owes the lessor $4,652 for the unrecovered portion of the guaranteed residual value. The lease amortization schedule using the effective interest method would be:

Lessee Lease Amortization Schedule
Annuity Due, Guaranteed Residual Value

Year	Payment	Interest @ 5%	Principal	Balance
2016				203,600
2016	41,400			162,200
2017	41,400	8,110	33,290	128,910
2018	41,400	6,446	34,955	93,956
2019	41,400	4,698	36,702	57,253
2020	41,400	2,863	38,537	18,716
2020	19,652	936	18,716	0

The entries for the lessee and lessor at the end of the lease term would be:

For lessee:

General Journal				
Date	Account/Explanation	PR	Debit	Credit
May 31, 2020	Accumulated depreciation, leased equipment		183,948	
	Loss on lease...............................		4,652	
	Interest payable............................		936	
	Obligation under lease.....................		18,716	
	Equipment under lease..................			203,600
	Cash			4,652
	For Accumulated depreciation: ($203,600 − 19,652 residual value)			

For lessor:

General Journal				
Date	Account/Explanation	PR	Debit	Credit
May 31, 2020	Cash		4,652	
	Leased inventory (or equipment for disposal)		15,000	
	Lease receivable			19,652

17.4 Sales and Leaseback Transactions

This occurs when a seller sells an asset and then, immediately after, leases the asset back from the buyer. The seller becomes the lessee, and the buyer becomes the lessor. This is common in situations where the seller/lessee needs to generate cash. They can obtain the cash they need through the sale of the asset, but, as they need to continue using it, they lease it back right away. This represents a bundled transaction (sale/lease) between two parties. Typically, gains on sale and leaseback transactions that are classified as a finance lease are to be deferred and amortized. For a finance lease, the amortization of the deferred gain/loss uses the same basis as the depreciation policy of the lessee.

For example, on January 1, Langmeyer Ltd. owns an office building, which it sells to Bagel Ltd. for $20 million, which is the fair value on that date. It is then immediately leased back to Langmeyer Ltd. for a 25-year term, which is equal to the office's remaining useful life. At the time of the sale, the asset had a cost of $5 million and accumulated depreciation of $4 million. The purchaser/lessor wants to obtain an 8% return on the lease, so the lease payments would be:

PMT/AD = (+/− PV, I/Y, N, FV)

PMT/AD = (+/− 20,000,000 PV, 8 I/Y, 25 N, 0 FV)

PMT/AD = $1,734,792 due at the beginning of each year (annuity due)

Since the lease term is 25 years, which is equal to the remaining useful life of the asset, it meets the criteria necessary to be classified as a finance lease for the lessee. Collectability is assured, and there are no important uncertainties for the lessor, making it a finance lease for the lessor as well. The year-end for both companies is December 31, and both follow IFRS.

The first entry for this transaction will be for the sale, where the removal of the asset and its related accumulated depreciation is recorded along with a deferred gain/loss. For the buyer, it is simply a purchase of an asset for cash. The remaining entries will be for the lease agreement, as previously illustrated earlier in this chapter. The only change is that, for the lessee, there will be an additional entry for the amortization of a portion of the deferred gain.

For seller/lessee:

Date	Account/Explanation	PR	Debit	Credit
Jan 1	Cash...		20,000,000	
	Accumulated depreciation, office building....		4,000,000	
	Office building.............................			5,000,000
	Deferred gain on sale – leaseback.......			19,000,000
	To record the sale of the asset and removal from the accounting records.			
Jan 1	Building under lease (asset)................		20,000,000	
	Obligations under lease (liability).........			20,000,000
	To record the lease asset and obligation.			
Jan 1	Obligations under lease.....................		1,734,792	
	Cash..			1,734,792
	To record the lease payment on January 1.			
Dec 31	Depreciation expense........................		800,000	
	Accumulated depreciation, leased equipment...			800,000
	To record year-end adjusting entry for depreciation. ($20,000,000 ÷ 25)			
Dec 31	Interest expense..............................		1,461,217	
	Interest payable...........................			1,461,217
	To record year-end adjusting entry for accrued interest. ($20,000,000 – 1,734,792 × 8%)			
Dec 31	Deferred gain on sale – leaseback..........		760,000	
	Depreciation expense.....................			760,000
	To record year-end adjusting entry for amortized deferred gain for the year. ($19,000,000 ÷ 25)			

For buyer/lessor:

	General Journal			
Date	Account/Explanation	PR	Debit	Credit
Jan 1	Office building acquired for lease............		20,000,000	
	Cash.....................................			20,000,000
	To record the purchase of the asset for cash.			
Jan 1	Lease receivable............................		43,369,800	
	Office building acquired for lease.........			20,000,000
	Unearned interest revenue...............			23,369,800
	To record the lease receivable.			
	For Lease receivable:			
	(1,734,792 lease payment × 25 years)			
Jan 1	Cash.......................................		1,734,792	
	Lease receivable			1,734,792
	To record the lease payment on January 1.			
Dec 31	Unearned interest revenue...................		1,461,217	
	Interest revenue			1,461,217
	To record year-end adjusting entry for interest earned.			
	($20,000,000 − 1,734,792 × 8%)			

Recall that the amortization for the deferred gain used the same basis (25 years) as the depreciation policy of the company. Also, note that the realized gain of $760,000 is credited to depreciation expense as a reduction to this operating expense.

17.5 Leasing: Disclosures

As leases tend to be long-term commitments, it is important to disclose information about the leased asset, lease obligation, and leased receivables. Below is a summary of some of the main IFRS disclosures. Note that ASPE disclosures are similar but more simplified.

Operating Leases: Disclosures are basically the same as those required for any assets, liabilities, and financial instruments.		Finance Leases: Disclosures are basically the same as those required for any assets, liabilities, and financial instruments.	
Lessee	Lessor	Lessee	Lessor
A description of any significant leases, including contingent amounts, renewal options, purchase options, and any restrictions to company operations and activities.	Same	A description of any significant leases, including contingent amounts, renewal options, purchase options, and any restrictions to company operations and activities.	Same
Minimum lease payments within the next fiscal year, between the second and fifth future years (inclusive), and after the fifth future year. (Note: For ASPE, the aggregate lease payments for the next 5 years are to be reported.)	Same	Minimum lease payments within the next fiscal year, between the second and fifth future years (inclusive), and after the fifth future year. (Note: for ASPE, the aggregate lease payments for the next 5 years are to be reported.)	Same
		The net carrying amount of each class of leased asset.	The allowance of uncollectible amounts relating to lease receivables.
		A reconciliation between the undiscounted total future minimum lease payments and their present value at each reporting date. This will report how much interest cost is included in the minimum lease payments.	A reconciliation between the gross lease receivable and their present value at each reporting date. This will report how much interest revenue is included in the minimum lease payments.
		Lease obligation is to be separated into current and long-term liability portions.	Lease receivable is to be separated into current and long-term portions.

17.6 IFRS/ASPE Key Differences

Item	ASPE	IFRS
Lessee – capitalization criteria	The criteria are much more prescriptive using numerical thresholds. Refer to details in section 17.2. A lease can be classified as an operating or a capital lease for the lessee.	More professional judgment is needed since the criteria are qualitative and do not include numeric thresholds. A lease can be classified as an operating or a finance lease for the lessee.
Lessor – capitalization criteria	The same criteria are used as for the lessee, but two more criteria must be met to be capitalized by the lessor. Any capitalized leases are further broken down into either a sales-type lease or a direct-financing lease, depending on whether a profit exists.	The same as ASPE except capitalized leases for the lessor are classified as a finance lease, with manufacturer/dealer leases being further distinguished from other finance leases.
Lessee's interest rate	Use the lower of the lessee's incremental borrowing rate or the lessor's implicit rate of return.	Use the implicit rate, if known, otherwise use the incremental borrowing rate.
Disclosure	Similar to the disclosures required for other assets, liabilities, or financial instruments.	Additional disclosures are required as noted above under disclosures.

Chapter Summary

LO 1: Describe leases and their role in accounting and business.

A lease is one method of financing the use of an asset. For example, when businesses want to update their equipment or expand their operations, they might lease rather than buy. A lease will provide the company with a temporary right to use an asset, over a specified period of time, in exchange for some other consideration, usually cash. Leases can be classified as either an operating lease or capitalized as a capital/finance lease, depending on whether the transaction meets the ASPE or IFRS criteria, which look at the economic substance of a lease rather than its legal form. An operating lease is recorded to rental expense for the lessee, and recorded to rental income for the lessor. A capitalized lease is recorded to an asset and a related obligation for the lessee, and to lease receivable as either a sale or as a financing agreement similar to an instalment loan.

LO 2: Describe the criteria used for ASPE and IFRS to classify a lease as a capital/finance lease.

While ASPE criteria are more prescriptive and contain numerical thresholds, IFRS criteria are more qualitative and require more professional judgment. For ASPE, three criteria are required in order for capitalization classification for the lessee to occur. If any one of the following are met, then classification as a capital lease is required. First, if legal ownership passes, or substantively passes, through the existence of a bargain purchase option or bargain renewal option. Second, if the lease term is at least 75% of the asset's estimated economic or useful life. Third, if the present value of the minimum lease payments is equal to 90% or more of the fair value of the asset at that time. In the case of the lessor, the same three criteria are considered, plus two additional criteria involving collectability of lease payments and no uncertainties regarding lessor costs. If any one of the three criteria and both of the additional criteria are met, then the lessor is required to classify the lease as a capital lease. Additional analysis is required to determine if the capital lease for the lessor is a sales-type lease, where there is a profit, or a direct-financing lease for banks or finance companies.

In the case of IFRS, the lessee analysis uses the same three criteria as was stated for ASPE, but without the numeric thresholds. Furthermore, there are two additional indicators, involving specialized equipment and reimbursements of losses to the lessor, that could sway the classification in favour of a finance lease. If the lessor is a dealer or manufacturer, then the entries will include sales and cost of goods sold, otherwise the lease will be treated as a financing lease if the lessor is a bank or financing company.

If the lease does not meet the criteria for capitalization, then it is treated as an operating lease with lease payments recorded as rent expense for the lessee and rent revenue for the lessor.

LO 3: Prepare the accounting entries of a capitalized lease for both the lessee and lessor.

The accounting treatment for capitalized leases follows certain steps. These steps dictate the types and timing of the entries throughout the lease term for both the lessee and lessor. If the lease is capitalized, the lessee records a leased asset and a related lease obligation, including lease payments, depreciation, and accrued interest on the debt. The lessor removes the asset from their inventory and records either a sale or a financing lease. Additionally, lease payments reduce the amount of the lessor's lease receivable and interest is earned over the lease term. The effective interest method is applied to calculate the interest component of the lease obligation. Special items, such as economic life versus the lease term, and the lessor's implicit interest rate versus the lessee's incremental borrowing rate, can affect some of the lessee and lessor accounting entries. This chapter presents several examples from the perspectives of the lessee and the lessor, including unguaranteed and guaranteed residual values, a bargain purchase option, and a direct-finance lease.

LO 4: Prepare the accounting entries of a capitalized sale and leaseback transaction.

Another form of financing involves a sale and a leaseback. This is when a seller sells an asset and then immediately leases it back from the buyer. The seller becomes the lessee and the buyer becomes the lessor. Since this transaction is actually a bundled sale/lease transaction, care must be taken to ensure that both parties do not try to manipulate the numbers unrealistically. For this reason, capitalized sale and leaseback transactions typically defer and amortize the gains/losses, usually on the same basis as the depreciation policy.

LO 5: Explain how leases are disclosed in the financial statements.

As leases are usually long-term commitments, disclosures must be in-depth enough to provide shareholders and creditors with adequate information to assess liquidity and solvency. The disclosures for ASPE and IFRS are similar, although IFRS also requires additional disclosures for various classes of leases and reconciliations that assist financial statement readers to assess the amount of interest cost included in the minimum lease payments. As is the case with other long-term financial instruments, both the lease obligation and the lease receivable are separated into current and long-term balances in the balance sheet/SFP.

LO 6: Explain the similarities and differences between ASPE and IFRS regarding capitalization criteria, interest rates, and disclosures.

ASPE capitalization criteria contain numeric thresholds, making it much more prescriptive than IFRS. As IFRS does not have the numeric thresholds, professional judgment is needed to determine if capitalization is required. For the lessor, both ASPE and IFRS have similar accounting treatments for either a lease that includes a profit element (sales and cost of goods sold), or as a finance lease, with an interest component only. In some cases, the interest rate used when calculating the present value of the minimum lease payments can differ between ASPE and IFRS. While the disclosures for ASPE and IFRS are similar, IFRS does require some additional disclosures to be made.

References

Landscape Managing Network (LMN). (2010, November 10). *The great equipment debate part I: Leasing vs. buying*. Retrieved from `http://www.golmn.com/the-great-equipment-debate-part-i-leasing-vs-buying/`

Exercises

EXERCISE 17–1

Below is information about a lease agreement signed by Oakland Ltd. (lessee) and Hartford Corp. (lessor). Both follow ASPE.

Type of lease	non-cancellable
Lease date	July 1, 2016
Annual lease payment amount in advance	$25,100
Bargain purchase option at the end of the lease term	$3,000
Lease term	6 years
Estimated economic life of the leased asset	10 years
Residual value after 10 years	$1,500
Lessor's cost	$90,000
Leased asset fair value, July 1, 2016	$130,000
Executory costs	paid directly by lessee
Lessee's incremental borrowing rate	8%
Lessor's implicit rate (known to lessee)	7%

Collectability of lease payments	no uncertainties
Costs not yet incurred by the lessor	no uncertainties
Year-end for lessee and lessor	December 31

Required:

a. Analyze and classify the lease for both the lessee and lessor using data to support the classification.

b. Calculate the gross and net investment amount as at July 1, 2016, for the lessor.

c. Prepare a lease amortization schedule for the lessee and lessor over the term of the lease.

d. Record the journal entries for 2016 and 2017 for the lessee.

e. Record the journal entries for 2016 and 2017 for the lessor.

f. Explain the differences, if any, to both the lessee and lessor if they followed IFRS.

g. How might the depreciation differ had the lease included a guaranteed residual instead of a bargain purchase option?

EXERCISE 17–2

On January 1, 2016, Mercy Ltd. (lessee) signed an 8-year, non-cancellable lease agreement to lease a highly specialized landscaping machine from Bergess Corp. (lessor). The agreement is non-renewable and requires a cash payment of $46,754 each January 1, commencing in 2016. The yearly cash payment includes $2,000 of executory costs related to insurance on the machine. At the end of the lease term, the machine reverts to the lessor. The machine has an estimated economic life of 10 years and an unguaranteed residual value of $10,000. The fair value of the machine on January 1, 2016, was $270,000. Mercy Ltd. follows IFRS and its year-end is December 31. Mercy Ltd. also uses the straight-line method for depreciation, and its incremental borrowing rate is 9% per year. Bergess Corp.'s rate, implicit in the lease, is not known to Mercy Ltd.

Required:

a. Analyze and classify the lease for the lessee and the lessor.

b. Prepare an amortization schedule for the term of the lease to be used by Mercy Ltd.

c. Prepare all related journal entries for 2016 and 2017 for Mercy Ltd.

d. Prepare Mercy Ltd.'s balance sheet and required disclosures for the lease for the fiscal year ending December 31, 2017.

EXERCISE 17–3

On January 1, 2016, Cappic Ltd. signed an 8-year, non-cancellable lease agreement to lease a highly specialized landscaping machine from Jedii Corp. The agreement is non-renewable and requires the payment of $50,397 every January 1, starting in 2016. The yearly rental payment includes $2,500 of executory costs related to a maintenance contract on the machine, and at the end of the lease term, the machine reverts to the lessor. The machine has an estimated economic life of 12 years, with an unguaranteed residual value of $22,000. Cappic Ltd. uses the straight-line method for depreciation, and the fair value of the machine on January 1, 2016, was $300,000. Cappic Ltd. follows IFRS and its year-end is June 30. Additionally, its incremental borrowing rate is 8% per year. Jedii Corp.'s implicit rate is 9%, which is known to Cappic Ltd.

Required: Prepare all related journal entries for 2016 and 2017 for the lessee.

EXERCISE 17–4

On January 1, 2016, Oberton Ltd. entered into an agreement to lease a truck from Black Ltd. The details of the agreement are as follows:

Carrying value of asset for Black Ltd.	$ 18,000
Fair value of truck	$ 18,000
Economic life of truck	6 years
Lease term	4 year
Rental payments, annually, starting January 1, 2016	$ 4,333
Executory costs included in each rental payment for insurance	$ 20
Incremental borrowing rate for Oberton Ltd.	6%
Lessor's effective interest rate	8%
Guaranteed residual value	$ 3,500

Additional information:

1. There are no uncertainties regarding lease payments or additional un-reimbursable costs.

2. At the end of the lease term, Black Ltd. sold the truck to a third party for $3,200, which was the truck's fair value on January 1, 2020. Oberton Ltd. paid Black Ltd.

the difference between the guaranteed residual value of $3,500 and the proceeds obtained on the resale.

3. Oberton Ltd. knows the interest rate that is implicit in the lease.

4. Oberton Ltd. knows the amount of executory costs included in the minimum lease payments.

5. Oberton Ltd. uses straight-line depreciation for its assets.

6. Both Oberton Ltd. and Black Ltd. use IFRS and their year-ends are both December 31.

Required:

a. Discuss the nature of this lease for both Oberton Ltd. (the lessee) and Black Ltd. (the lessor).

b. Prove the effective interest rate of 8% using a financial calculator.

c. Prepare a lease amortization schedule for the full term of the lease.

d. Prepare all related journal entries for Oberton Ltd. over the period from January 1, 2016, to January 1, 2017, including any year-end adjusting journal entries. Assume that Oberton Ltd. does not use reversing entries.

e. Prepare Oberton Ltd.'s partial classified statement of financial position at December 31, 2016, along with relevant note disclosures and the income statement for the fiscal year ending December 31, 2016.

f. Prepare the journal entry for Oberton Ltd.'s payment on January 1, 2020, to Black Ltd. to settle the guaranteed residual value deficiency. Assume that the year-end depreciation has been already recorded but that no accruals for interest have been recorded as yet during 2019.

g. Prepare all relevant journal entries that Black Ltd. would record from January 1 to December 31, 2016.

h. Prepare a partial income statement for Black Ltd. for the year ended December 31, 2016.

EXERCISE 17-5

Helmac Ltd. manufactures equipment and leased it to Tolmin Ltd. for a period of ten years beginning on January 1, 2016. The equipment has an estimated economic life of twelve years. The equipment's normal selling price is $299,122, and its unguaranteed residual value at the end of the lease term is estimated to be $25,000. Tolmin Ltd. will pay annual payments of $35,000 at the beginning of each year, as well as all maintenance and insurance costs over the lease term. The cost to manufacture the equipment was $100,000. Helmac Ltd. also incurred $10,000 in closing lease costs. Helmac Ltd. has determined that there is no uncertainty with regard to the collectability of the lease payments or additional costs. The lessee's incremental borrowing rate is 6% and the lessor's effective interest rate is 5%, which is known to the lessee. Both Helmac Ltd. and Tolmin Ltd. follow ASPE.

Required:

a. Discuss the nature of this lease in relation to the lessor.

b. Prepare all of the lessor's journal entries for the first year of the lease, assuming the lessor's fiscal year-end is five months into the lease. Reversing entries are not used.

c. How would the initial entry to record the lease change if $25,000 residual value was guaranteed by the lessee?

d. Assume now that the lease term is for 12 years. How much would Helmac Ltd. charge the lessee annually for a 12-year lease, assuming that the sales price and interest rate remains unchanged, but that the residual value was $40,000 and unguaranteed by the lessee?

EXERCISE 17-6

On January 1, 2016, Kimble Ltd. sells specialty equipment to Quick Finance Corp. for $432,000 and immediately leases the equipment back from them. Other relevant information is as follows:

1. The equipment has a fair value of $432,000 on January 1, 2016, and an estimated economic life of 10 years, with no residual value.

2. The equipment's carrying value on Kimble Ltd.'s books on January 1, 2016, is $385,000.

3. The term of the non-cancellable lease is 10 years and the title (legal title for ownership) will transfer to Kimble Ltd. at the end of the lease due to its specialty.

4. The lease agreement requires equal payments of $61,507 at the end of each year.

5. The incremental borrowing rate of Kimble Ltd. is 8%. The effective interest rate for Quick Finance Corp. is set to return 7% and is known by Kimble Ltd.

6. Kimble Ltd. pays executory costs of $7,200 per year directly to appropriate third parties.

7. Both Kimble Ltd. and Quick Finance Corp. use ASPE. No uncertainties exist regarding future unrecoverable costs and collectability is reasonably certain.

Required:

a. Demonstrate how this lease meets the criteria for classification as a capitalized lease.

b. Prepare the journal entries for both the lessee and the lessor for 2016 to reflect the sale and leaseback agreement.

Chapter 18

Shareholders' Equity

Google This!

On April 2, 2014, Google Inc. paid its shareholders a share dividend, an event that was later described as the "1,998 for 1,000 stock split." For every 1,000 shares that were held prior to the split, an additional 998 shares were issued. This essentially doubled the number of outstanding shares and caused the share price to fall to approximately half of its pre-split price, which had been hovering above $1,000 per share. This technique is called a stock split and is commonly used by companies to lower a share price when it starts rising to levels that are unaffordable for the average investor.

Although Google's share price certainly justified a stock split, the unique structure of this split suggests other motivations as well. Prior to the split, Google Inc. had two classes of shares: Class A, which carried one vote each and were publicly traded, and Class B, which carried ten votes each and were not publicly traded (held mostly by the company's founders, Larry Page and Sergey Brin). Because of the super-voting rights of their Class B shares, the founders were able to maintain control of the company. However, as many Class A shares were issued over the years to acquire new businesses or to reward employee performance, the founders' share of the ownership became diluted.

When the split occurred, in 2014, Google took the unusual step of creating a new class of shares, Class C, to distribute to existing Class A shareholders. However, the new Class C shares did not carry any voting rights. The Class A shareholders immediately objected to this arrangement, as they felt that these new shares would not be as valuable as the existing shares because they lacked voting rights. The company argued that, because the founders already controlled the majority of the shares, the voting rights of the Class A shares were of no significant value. In response, the shareholders launched a class action lawsuit, which was eventually settled when the company agreed to pay compensation to the existing Class A shareholders if, after one year, the Class C shares were trading at a discount of more than 1%, as compared to the Class A shares. On April 3, 2015, the Class A shares were trading at $542.08 per share and the Class C shares were trading at $535.76, a difference of 1.2%. Apparently, the market did attach some value to minority voting rights. Google agreed to pay an "adjustment payment" of $522 million to Class A shareholders in May 2015.

As demonstrated in this example, the rights of shareholders can create complicated legal issues. The right to vote and the right to receive dividends are the two essential elements that shareholders have in order to protect their investment. Proper and detailed disclosure in the shareholders' equity section of the balance sheet can help shareholders better understand their relationship with the company and the risks that they face.

(Sources: Alphabet Investor Relations, 2015; Liedtke, 2014)

Chapter 18 Learning Objectives

After completing this chapter, you should be able to:

LO 1: Describe the different forms of equity and identify the key features that are important for accounting purposes.

LO 2: Explain and apply accounting standards for different types of share issues.

LO 3: Explain and apply accounting standards for different situations that can occur when shares are reacquired.

LO 4: Describe the accounting treatments for different types of dividends and calculate divided allocations when preferred shares exist.

LO 5: Describe the presentation and disclosure requirements for shareholders' equity accounts.

LO 6: Identify differences in the accounting treatment of shareholders' equity between IFRS and ASPE.

Introduction

The *Conceptual Framework* provides a deceptively simple definition for equity: "the residual interest in the assets of the entity after deducting all its liabilities" (CPA Canada, 2016, Part I, The Conceptual Framework for Financial Reporting, 4.4 (c)). This definition confirms the most elementary principle in accounting, which is embodied in the accounting equation: Assets = Liabilities + Equity. This apparent conceptual simplicity is further confirmed by the fact that IFRS does not actually contain a separate handbook section devoted to shareholders' equity. However, despite this lack of structured guidance, we should not define equity as a simple concept that doesn't require much attention. On the contrary, there are a number of ways in which the accounting, presentation, and disclosure of equity transactions can be quite complex. Although equity is the residual interest of the business's owners, it is not simply a plug figure used to balance the accounting equation. In this chapter, we will discuss some of the complexities in accounting for equity transactions and we will look at the presentation and disclosure requirements for what can be legally complicated instruments.

Chapter Organization

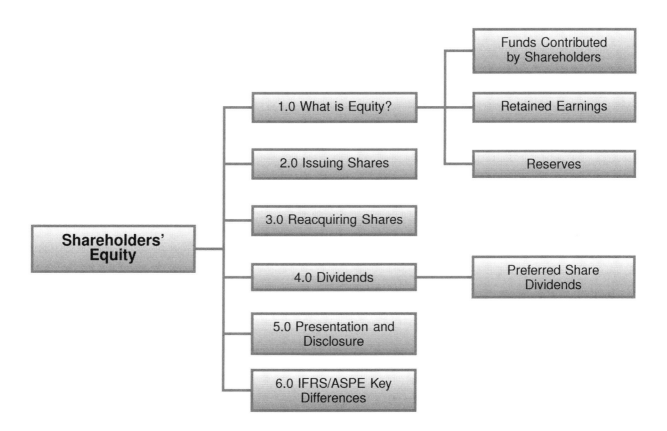

18.1 What is Equity?

Despite the simple definition initially provided, the *Conceptual Framework* does expand on the concept of equity by explaining that funds contributed by shareholders, retained earnings, and other reserves may require separate disclosures. The reasons given for a more detailed disclosure include the objective of providing information about legal restrictions on the distribution of equity that may be useful to investors for decision-making purposes, and the need to disclose the different legal rights that may attach to the various types of equity interests. The *Conceptual Framework* also notes that although, by definition, equity is affected by the measurement of assets and liabilities, the amount of equity reported would only coincidentally be equal to the current market value of a company. This is an important point, as it highlights one of the limitations of financial reporting: that financial statements by themselves cannot tell an investor what a company is worth.

The components of equity will vary from business to business and will be affected by the type of legal structure adopted by the business. This chapter will focus on the accounting used in the most common type of business organization – the corporation. Accounting and disclosure for other types of entities, such as proprietorships and partnerships, will be different. However, the same basic principles apply to those types of entities as well.

Let's now look at the various components of equity, using the classification from the *Conceptual Framework*: funds contributed by shareholders, retained earnings, and reserves.

18.1.1 Funds Contributed by Shareholders

The funds contributed by shareholders are often the initial capital used to start a business. These funds are often referred to as contributed capital. In a corporate structure, contributed capital will take the form of shares, which can be classified into several different types. Shares, themselves, are legal instruments that provide certain rights to the holder and indicate a residual interest in the corporation's assets. When a company is created, its incorporating documents will specify the maximum number of shares that can be issued. In some cases, this amount, referred to as **authorized shares**, may be specified as unlimited, meaning the company can issue as many shares as it wants. From an accounting perspective, the number of authorized shares is not relevant but the number of issued shares is. **Issued shares** are shares that have been issued to shareholders, usually in exchange for money, services, or other assets. Sometimes, a company may repurchase its own shares and keep them in *treasury*, in which case the number of issued shares will be greater than the number of outstanding shares (those shares held by parties outside of the company). In some jurisdictions, shares can be issued with a **par value**. This is the stated value of the share and will be directly indicated on the share certificate. Where par value shares exist, the actual issue price may differ from the par value. Amounts received by the corporation in excess of the par value represent another form of contributed capital. This amount will be reported separately from the par value of the shares and is often described as either **contributed surplus** or **share premium**. Note that many jurisdictions do not allow par value shares, meaning the issue price would simply be reported as the share capital amount. Shares can be stratified into different classes, based on the different rights and characteristics. We will discuss some of these different characteristics below.

Common Shares

Common shares, also referred to as **ordinary shares**, represent the final residual interest in a company's assets after all other claims, including other equity interests, have been satisfied. In some companies, these are the only types of shares issued. These shares represent the greatest level of risk to an investor should the company fail, as all other claims against the company's assets would need to be paid first. On the other hand, these shares also represent potentially the greatest rewards, as all the profits not otherwise allocated to debt and equity holders would belong to the common shareholders. All companies must have at least one class of common shares, although they are not always described this way. If a company issues more than one class of shares, and the other classes have additional rights over the common shares, then those classes are not common shares. Rather, they would be described as preferred shares.

Preferred Shares

Preferred shares, also known as **preference shares**, have special rights and privileges that give them priority over the common shares. These special privileges are often included to make the shares more attractive to investors. As well, the special rights can allow for complex ownership structures where certain groups or individuals want to maintain a degree of control. Because the preferred shares have special rights over the common shares, they are not considered a residual interest. In the event of a business's liquidation, the preferred shareholders would rank ahead of the common shareholders in the priority of payment, but they would still be subordinated to the debt holders.

Preferred shares have many different features that can be combined in multiple configurations to provide many classes of shares for investors to choose from. However, to gain these special features, preferred shareholders often give up certain rights as well, most commonly, the right to vote on the company's management. In many corporate structures, only the common shareholders have the right to vote for the board of directors, even though there may be several classes of shares. It is also important to note that the classes of shares may not always be described as common or preferred in the incorporation documents. The accountant must always be careful to closely examine the economic substance of the share features, and not just rely on the descriptions used by the company.

Let's now look at some of the features of preferred shares.

- **Fixed Dividend**: Preferred shares often have a fixed dividend amount, usually expressed as a numerical amount per share or sometimes as a percentage of the par value of the share. For example, a preferred share could be entitled to a dividend of 5% of the par value, or $5 per share. These dividends would be equivalent if the share were issued at, or had a par value of, $100. Although the dividend amount is stated, this does not guarantee that the preferred shareholder will receive the dividend in any given year. Dividends must always be declared by the board of directors, and the directors have the discretion not to pay a dividend. However, when dividends are declared the holders of the preferred shares must be paid their stated dividends first before any distributions can be made to the common shareholders.

- **Cumulative Dividend**: If the directors do not declare a dividend in a current year, the holders of cumulative preferred shares would be entitled to payment of the dividend in a future year. For this type of share, undeclared dividends will accumulate at the stated rate for each year and must all be paid before any dividends can be paid to the common shareholders. These unpaid dividends do not represent a liability until the directors declare a dividend. Preferred shares can also specify a **non-cumulative** dividend, which means any undeclared dividends in a given year are simply lost and are not required to be paid in future years.

- **Participating Dividend**: When a preferred share is described as participating, it retains the right to receive not only the stated amount of dividends, but also additional dividends based on certain criteria. A typical participation calculation would involve first determining the fixed dividend on the preferred shares, and then allocating a similar proportion to the common shares. Then, additional dividends beyond these two amounts would be shared between the preferred and common shares on a pro-rata basis. There are other, more complex, ways in which participation can be calculated. The specific features of the preferred share would need to be examined to determine the method of calculation. The participation feature can make a preferred share more attractive to investors, as it provides the stability of the fixed dividend, plus the ability to receive further dividends if the company is successful.

- **Redemption**: A preferred share may be described as being redeemable. This means the company has the right to *call* the shares and repurchase them at a specified price during a specified time period. When the shares are redeemed, any dividends in arrears must be paid.

- **Retraction**: This feature is attractive to shareholders, as it allows them the right to require the company to repurchase the shares at a set price. Usually, time limits are set for the retraction period.

- **Convertibility**: Some preferred shares retain the right to be converted into common shares. The holder may choose to do this if the company has been successful and if common dividends exceed the amount that can be earned by the fixed, preferred dividend. The amount of common shares that can be obtained on conversion will be specified as a ratio, such as two common shares for each preferred share held.

Any or all of these features can be attached to classes of preferred shares. Many companies will report multiple share classes, each with different features. In some cases, the features included in a preferred share may suggest that its economic substance is more akin to debt rather than equity. These types of shares should be classified as liabilities, and their dividends would be classified as financing costs on the income statement. Shares with these features are discussed further in Chapter 14: Complex Financial Instruments.

18.1.2 Retained Earnings

The retained earnings account is a separate category of equity that represents the cumulative amount of profit earned by the company since its inception, less the cumulative amount of dividends declared. Sometimes, either as a management choice or as a legal requirement, certain portions of the retained earnings are set aside or **appropriated**. Appropriations of retained earnings are created to ensure that dividends are not paid from these balances, and these appropriations need to be reported separately. When the retained earnings account falls into a negative (debit) balance, it is usually referred to as a deficit, or retained losses. Retained earnings are sometimes subject to other types of accounting adjustments, such as accounting policy changes and error corrections, which are discussed in other chapters.

18.1.3 Reserves

The term **reserves** can refer to a number of different accounts. The previously noted appropriations of retained earnings are normally described as reserves. Another type of reserve is **accumulated other comprehensive income** (AOCI). As discussed in other chapters, comprehensive income results from recognition of income or expense items that are not included in the calculation of net income. There are only a few items that fall into this category, the most common of which are gains resulting from the application of the revaluation method for property, plant, and equipment, and intangibles; remeasurements of defined benefit plans; and gains resulting from remeasurement of available-for-sale financial instruments. These transactions create reserves that must be reported separately on the balance sheet. However, they may not always be described as accumulated other comprehensive income. For example, the term **revaluation surplus** is often used instead. Regardless of the name, the reserves must clearly identify the source of the surplus, and separate reserves are required for each type of item.

18.2 Issuing Shares

When a company is first incorporated, it will be authorized to issue a certain number of shares. This authorization does not, in and of itself, create any accounting transaction that needs to be recorded. However, after the shares are authorized they can be issued, which creates an accounting transaction. We will look at several examples of different types of share issuances.

Shares Issued for Cash

This is the simplest scenario: shares will be issued to the holder in exchange for a cash payment. For example, if 10,000 common shares are issued at a price of $10 each, the journal entry would be:

\multicolumn{5}{c}{General Journal}				
Date	Account/Explanation	PR	Debit	Credit
	Cash		100,000	
	Common shares			100,000

Note: Each class of shares should be recorded in a different account, as the disclosure of the amounts of different classes of shares is required. Also, when brokerage houses, agents, lawyers, and other professionals are involved in issuing the shares, any fees or commissions charged by these parties should be directly deducted from the share capital amount.

Par Value Shares Issued for Cash

In the example above, the net amount of cash received simply becomes the stated capital amount of the shares. In some jurisdictions, shares are authorized with a par value, which is a value that will be directly stated on the share certificate. However, as market conditions will dictate the actual issue price of the shares, it is possible that an amount greater than the par value will be received when the shares are issued. The excess amount over the par value still represents contributed capital, but it must be recorded separately. If, for example, 5,000 shares with a par value of $2 per share are issued for $8, the journal entry would be:

\multicolumn{5}{c}{General Journal}				
Date	Account/Explanation	PR	Debit	Credit
	Cash		40,000	
	Common shares			10,000
	Contributed surplus			30,000

The contributed surplus amount will be reported as part of the contributed capital on the balance sheet. This account is sometimes described as *share premium* or *additional paid-in capital*.

Subscribed Shares

Sometimes a company may offer shares on a subscription basis, allowing the holder to pay for the shares in a series of payments. The accounting for these types of transactions will depend on local legislation, the terms of the subscription contract, and corporate policy. We will look at a few different examples of these types of transactions.

Scenario 1

A company offers to issue its shares in blocks of 20 at a price $60 per share. The contract requires a 25% down payment with the remaining 75% payable in six months, and 100 individuals accept the offer. Local legislation does not allow shares to be issued until they are fully paid. The following journal entries are required:

	General Journal			
Date	Account/Explanation	PR	Debit	Credit
When shares are first subscribed	Cash .... Share subscription receivable .... Common shares subscribed .... For Cash: (100 × 20 × $60 × 25%) For Share subscription: (100 × 20 × $60 × 75%)		30,000 90,000	120,000

The share subscription receivable conceptually does not represent a receivable in the conventional sense, as it represents a capital and not an income transaction. As such, the most appropriate treatment would be to show it as a contra-equity account. However, some argue that because it does represent a future benefit to the company, it should be reported as an asset. Both presentations can be found in practice. The common shares subscribed account should be shown as part of the contributed capital section, but it should be segregated from the issued share capital.

In six months' time, the following journal entry is required:

	General Journal			
Date	Account/Explanation	PR	Debit	Credit
When shares are paid	Cash .... Share subscription receivable............ Common shares subscribed .... Common shares........................		90,000 120,000	90,000 120,000

Note: If a dividend is declared between the subscription date and the final payment date, the treatment of that dividend will depend on local legislation. Although it is likely that the shares will not be eligible for dividends, as they have not yet been issued, some jurisdictions allow the distribution of a pro-rata dividend based on the amount of cash received to date. In our example, the subscribers would be eligible for 25% of the regular dividend amount declared. Similarly, if a shareholders' meeting is held during this interim period, the subscribers may be eligible for a pro-rata share of votes at the meeting.

Scenario 2

Let's assume the same set of facts as Scenario 1, except that 10 of the subscribers default on their final payments. At the time of the initial subscription, the journal entry will be identical to the one used in Scenario 1. However, at the time of final payment, the journal entry will depend on local legislation, the subscription contract, and corporate policy. If we assume that legislation requires a refund of the initial deposit to the defaulting subscribers, then the journal entry would look like this:

	General Journal			
Date	Account/Explanation	PR	Debit	Credit
When 90% of the shares are paid	Cash		81,000	
	Share subscription receivable			90,000
	Common shares subscribed		120,000	
	Common shares			108,000
	Accounts payable			3,000
	For Cash: (90 × 20 × $60 × 75%)			
	For Common shares: ($120,000 × 90%)			
	For Accounts payable: ($30,000 × 10%)			

Scenario 3

Let's assume the same set of facts as Scenario 2, except that local legislation allows shares to be issued to defaulting subscribers pro-rata, based on the amounts of their deposits. The journal entry on issuance would look like this:

	General Journal			
Date	Account/Explanation	PR	Debit	Credit
When 90% of the shares are paid	Cash		81,000	
	Share subscription receivable			90,000
	Common shares subscribed		120,000	
	Common shares			111,000
	For Cash: (90 × 20 × $60 × 75%)			
	For Common shares: (($120,000 × 90%) + (10 × 20 × $60 × 25%))			

In some cases, the company may charge a fee to the defaulting subscribers, which would be allocated to contributed surplus, rather than to common share capital.

Scenario 4

Let's assume the same set of facts as Scenario 2, except that local legislation allows the company to keep the defaulting subscribers' deposits. In this case, the following journal entry is recorded at issuance:

General Journal				
Date	Account/Explanation	PR	Debit	Credit
When 90% of the shares are paid	Cash		81,000	
	Share subscription receivable			90,000
	Common shares subscribed		120,000	
	Common shares			108,000
	Contributed surplus			3,000
	For Cash: (90 × 20 × $60 × 75%)			
	For Common shares: ($120,000 × 90%)			
	For Contributed surplus: ($30,000 × 10%)			

Shares Issued for Goods or Services

Sometimes a company may issue shares in exchange for assets other than cash, or in exchange for services provided. These situations may occur when a company is in the start-up phase of its life cycle and wishes to preserve scarce cash resources. In these cases, the shares should be recorded at the fair value of the asset acquired or service received. Note that this treatment is different than the treatment of non-monetary exchanges of assets, where the fair value of the asset given up is normally used as the transaction amount. This difference results because fair values of assets or services are usually more reliable than fair values of shares. In the rare circumstance that the fair values of the assets or services cannot be determined, the fair value of the shares issued should then be used. This value is obviously easier to determine for a publicly traded company. In all cases, non-monetary exchanges for shares will involve the exercise of good judgment on the part of the accountant.

A company may also issue its shares in exchange for shares of another company. This type of business combination is an advanced financial accounting concept that is not covered in this text.

18.3 Reacquiring Shares

Companies will sometimes buy back their own shares, often done to try to stabilize their share price or improve certain financial ratios, such as earnings per share. A share may also be repurchased as a way to return excess cash to shareholders without having to pay a dividend. Additionally, there may also be certain strategic benefits in repurchasing shares. Whatever the reason, the result is the same: the shares are no longer outstanding. After repurchase, the shares may continue to be held by the company as issued shares, which are referred to as **treasury shares**, or they may be cancelled. If they are held as treasury shares, they may be resold at a later date to new shareholders. However, if the shares are cancelled, then they must be completely removed from the accounting records. Note that some jurisdictions do not allow treasury shares, meaning that any repurchased shares must be immediately cancelled. We will examine the reacquisition of shares for both cancellation and non-cancellation situations below.

Shares Repurchased and Cancelled

The IFRS does not provide any specific guidance on how to account for the repurchase of shares. However, ASPE does provide a set of steps to apply when shares are either repurchased or cancelled. These procedures contemplate two possible situations:

a. The shares' acquisition cost is greater than, or equal to, the assigned value.

   In this situation, the acquisition cost is allocated in the following sequence:

   - First to share capital in an amount equal to the par, stated, or assigned value
   - Any excess to contributed surplus, to the extent that the balance of contributed surplus was created by a previous cancellation of the same class of shares
   - Any further excess to contributed surplus in an amount equal to the pro-rata share of the contributed surplus that arose from transactions, other than those above, in the same class of shares (for example, a share premium from a previous issue of par value shares)
   - Any remaining excess to retained earnings.

b. The shares acquisition cost is less than, or equal to, the assigned value.

   In this situation, the acquisition cost is allocated in the following sequence:

   - First to share capital in an amount equal to the par, stated, or assigned value
   - Any excess to contributed surplus (CPA Canada, 2016, Accounting, ASPE 3240.11 and 3240.13).

In part (b), the balance is included as an increase to contributed surplus because it wouldn't be appropriate to report income from a share capital transaction. Also, note that where the shares are not par value shares, the assigned value indicated above is calculated as the weighted average cost of the shares at the transaction date.

The following illustration demonstrates the above rules:

On January 1, 2016, a company had 100,000, no-par value common shares outstanding that were issued for total proceeds of $1,060,000. There was no contributed surplus associated with these shares on that date. On March 1, 2016, the company repurchased and cancelled 8,000 of these shares at a cost of $8 per share. The journal entry would be:

18.3. Reacquiring Shares

	General Journal			
Date	Account/Explanation	PR	Debit	Credit
Mar 1	Common shares............................		84,800	
	Cash......................................			64,000
	Contributed surplus.......................			20,800

Note: The common shares are eliminated at their average cost.
($1,060,000 ÷ 100,000) = $10.60 per share; $10.60 per share × 8,000 shares = $84,800
The contributed surplus is calculated as ($10.60 − $8.00) × 8,000 shares = $20,800

On October 1, 2016, the company repurchased and cancelled a further 11,000 shares at a cost of $14 per share. The journal entry would be:

	General Journal			
Date	Account/Explanation	PR	Debit	Credit
Oct 1	Common shares............................		116,600	
	Contributed surplus.......................		20,800	
	Retained earnings.........................		16,600	
	Cash......................................			154,000

The common shares are again eliminated at their new average cost: ($975,200 ÷ 92,000) = $10.60. The previous contributed surplus is fully utilized, with an additional excess amount being charged to retained earnings.

In some jurisdictions, such as the United Kingdom, there may be additional legal restrictions that influence the accounting for share repurchases and cancellations. For example, on a share repurchase a company may be required to reallocate part of the retained earnings balance to a capital redemption reserve. This is done to provide a level of protection to the company's creditors, as the capital redemption reserve is generally not available for use in subsequent dividend payments.

Shares Repurchased and Not Cancelled

When a company repurchases its own shares, but doesn't cancel them, the returned shares are referred to as *treasury shares*. These shares are essentially held by the company to be issued at a later date. ASPE indicates a preference for what is known as the single-transaction method, which considers the repurchase, and subsequent re-issuance of the shares, as a single transaction. In this case, treasury shares held at the balance sheet date that have not yet been re-issued or cancelled are reported as a deduction from the total shareholders' equity. They cannot be considered an asset as the company is merely holding shares of itself. When the treasury shares are first acquired, the journal entry would simply require a debit to the treasury shares account and a credit to cash. If the shares are subsequently re-issued, then the treasury shares account will be credited and cash will be debited. Any difference will be allocated to contributed surplus or retained earnings in a process that is essentially the inverse of the cancellation journal entries shown previously. If the shares are subsequently cancelled, rather than being reissued, then cancellation procedures outlined previously are followed.

18.4 Dividends

Cash Dividends

For investors, receiving dividends represents one of the essential motivations for holding shares. Although many established companies may have a policy of paying regular and predictable dividends, shareholders understand that there is no automatic right to dividends. The payment of dividends is decided by the board of directors and is based on several relevant criteria. First, the dividend must be legal. The rules for dividends vary by jurisdiction, but essentially the company must have sufficient *distributable profits* to pay the dividend. Some jurisdictions have complex methods of calculating this amount, but it can often be approximated using the balance in the retained earnings account. The purpose of limiting the dividends is to ensure that the company is not left in a position where it cannot pay its liabilities. Directors need to be aware of the legal requirements for dividend payments, as the payment of an illegal dividend could result in personal liability to the director if the company cannot, subsequently, pay its creditors. Second, the company must have sufficient cash to pay the dividend. Cash flow planning is important to the management of a business, and although the company may have sufficient retained earnings to declare a dividend, it may not have the cash readily available. Remember that the retained earnings balance does not equal cash, as companies will invest in many different types of assets. Third, the dividend must fit with the company's strategic priorities. A company that is able to pay dividends may choose not to in order to preserve cash for various future uses, such as reinvestment in capital assets, funding strategic acquisitions, entrance into new markets, funding share buybacks, and committing to research and development. As well, a company may not want to pay the maximum dividend it is legally entitled to because it does not want to create unrealistic expectations among shareholders for future dividends.

Once the directors have decided to declare a dividend, three significant dates need to be considered. First, the **date of declaration** is the date the board of directors meets to approve the dividend payment. This will be formally documented as a directors' resolution, and it is on this date that a liability is created, for both legal and accounting purposes. Second, in the directors' resolution, the **date of record** will be specified, which is the date on which a list of the shareholders who will receive dividends is compiled. Obviously, between the date of declaration and the date of record, shares will trade at a price based on the understanding that whoever holds the shares on the date of record is eligible for the dividend. Note, for many public stock exchanges, an **ex-dividend date** may also be relevant. This is a date several days before the date of record, which allows a period of time for share transactions to be processed. Third, sometime after the date of record is the **date of payment**. It is on this day that dividend payments are distributed to the shareholders of record.

Consider the following example. A company with 500,000 outstanding common shares declares a dividend of $0.75 per share on January 20. The resolution indicates a record date of January 31 and a payment date of February 15. The following journal entries would be made on each date:

Declaration date:

	General Journal			
Date	Account/Explanation	PR	Debit	Credit
Jan 20	Dividends declared (retained earnings)......		375,000	
	Dividends payable........................			375,000
	Dividends are calculated as 500,000 × $0.75 = $375,000			

Note: The debit can either be made to a temporary account called Dividends declared, which will be closed to retained earnings at year-end, or it can be made directly to retained earnings.

Date of record:

	General Journal			
Date	Account/Explanation	PR	Debit	Credit
Jan 31	No entry required............................			

No entry is made here, as the date of record does not represent an accounting event.

Date of payment:

	General Journal			
Date	Account/Explanation	PR	Debit	Credit
Feb 15	Dividends payable...........................		375,000	
	Cash.......................................			375,000

Note: The dividends can be expressed as a per share amount, or they may be described as a percentage of the share's par value. Also, no dividends are paid on treasury shares as the company cannot pay itself.

Property Dividends

In certain instances, a company may choose to pay a dividend with assets other than cash. This could include shares of other companies held as investments, property, plant and equipment, inventory, or any other asset held. These types of transactions are rare for three obvious reasons: 1) the asset must be equally divisible among all holders of a particular class of shares, 2) the fair value of the asset needs to be determined, and 3) the asset must be able to be physically distributed to the shareholders. When the company can overcome these restrictions, the property dividend will be recorded in a manner similar to the journal entries previously identified. There will be an additional step, however, in that the asset must first be revalued to its fair value before the dividend is distributed. This will usually result in a gain or loss being recorded, which is appropriate as the asset is being disposed of to settle a liability.

Share Dividends

One way that a company can distribute a dividend to shareholders without depleting its cash resources is to pay a share (stock) dividend. This dividend distributes additional shares of the company to the shareholders proportional to their current holdings. For example, if a company declares a 5% share dividend, a shareholder who currently holds 100 shares would receive an additional five shares. Although there may be some complicated jurisdictional legal requirements regarding share dividends, the general principle is that they should be recorded at the fair value of the shares issued.

Consider the following example. A company currently has 100,000 shares outstanding that are trading at $5.25 per share. The company decides to declare a 5% share dividend, which means an additional 5,000 shares will be issued to existing shareholders (100,000 × 5%). Immediately prior to the dividend declaration, the implied value of the company is $525,000 (100,000 × $5.25). Because a share dividend does not have any effect on the assets or liabilities of the company, we would expect the total value of the company to remain the same after the dividend. However, we would expect the market price per share to drop to $5.00 per share ($525,000 ÷ 105,000), as the value is now spread among more shares.

The journal entries to record this transaction, assuming the share price drops to $5 as expected, would be as follows:

Declaration date:

General Journal				
Date	Account/Explanation	PR	Debit	Credit
	Dividends declared (retained earnings)......		25,000	
	Share dividends distributable			25,000

Payment date:

General Journal				
Date	Account/Explanation	PR	Debit	Credit
	Share dividends distributable..............		25,000	
	Common shares.......................			25,000

Note: The fair value we use to determine the amount is the post-dividend (sometimes referred to as ex-dividend) value of $5.00 per share × 5,000 shares = $25,000. Also, if the company's year-end were to fall between the declaration date and the payment date, then the share dividends distributable balance would be reported in the equity section of the balance sheet, as it does not represent a liability like a cash dividend payable.

Declaring a share dividend causes part of the company's retained earnings to become capitalized as contributed capital (common shares). By doing so, the company has removed this portion of retained earnings from the pool of distributable earnings that can be later used to pay cash dividends.

Share Splits

Share splits, also known as stock splits, scrip issues, or bonus issues, are similar to share dividends except they have a different accounting treatment. Generally, the motivation for a share split is to reduce the market price of the share. For example, if the share price has risen to a point where it is no longer affordable, this makes it difficult for the company to sell shares to the public. A share split will be expressed as a proportion, such as a 2-for-1 split. This means that for every share held an additional share will be issued. Thus, after the 2-for-1 split, the number of outstanding shares will be twice the previous number. This will normally have the effect of reducing the market price of the share by half, so that the total market capitalization remains unchanged.

Because there is no change in the economic resources or position of the company, no journal entry is required to record a share split. However, a memorandum entry should be made, noting the new number of shares. This will be important in the future for the purposes of calculating dividend payments and earnings per share amounts.

In some cases, it may be difficult to distinguish between a share split and a large share dividend. For example, the effects of a 100% share dividend and a 2-for-1 share split are essentially the same. As IFRS does not provide any specific guidance on this issue, professional judgment and consideration of the relevant legal framework will be required in determining how to record large share dividends.

A company may also engage in a reverse share split, sometimes referred to as a share consolidation. This will reduce the number of outstanding shares by a certain proportion. This type of transaction is usually motivated by the need to increase the market price of a share.

18.4.1 Preferred Share Dividends

As noted previously, a feature of preferred shares is that they often receive preferential treatment when dividends are declared. We will now look at some examples of how dividends are calculated when preferred shares are outstanding.

Assume a company has two classes of shares: 1) common shares, of which 100,000 are outstanding with a carrying amount of $480,000, and 2) preferred shares with a fixed dividend of $2 per share, of which 20,000 are outstanding with a carrying amount of $320,000. In the current year, the company has declared total dividends of $120,000. Dividends will be allocated to each class of shares as follows:

a. Preferred shares are non-cumulative and non-participating:

Calculation	Preferred	Common	Total
Current year: 20,000 shares × $2	$ 40,000		$ 40,000
Balance of dividends ($120,000 − $40,000)	-	$ 80,000	80,000
	$ 40,000	$ 80,000	$120,000

b. Preferred shares are cumulative and non-participating, and dividends were not paid last year:

Calculation	Preferred	Common	Total
Arrears: 20,000 shares × $2	$ 40,000		$ 40,000
Current year: 20,000 shares × $2	40,000		40,000
Balance of dividends ($120,000 − $80,000)	-	$ 40,000	40,000
	$ 80,000	$ 40,000	$120,000

c. Preferred shares are cumulative and non-participating, and dividends were not paid for the last two years:

Calculation	Preferred	Common	Total
Arrears: 20,000 shares × $2 × 2 years	$ 80,000		$ 80,000
Current year: 20,000 shares × $2	40,000		40,000
Balance of dividends ($120,000 − $120,000)	-	-	-
	$ 120,000	-	$120,000

d. Preferred shares are non-cumulative and fully participating:

Calculation	Preferred	Common	Total
Current year basic dividend	$ 40,000	$ 60,000	$100,000
Current year participating dividend	8,000	12,000	20,000
	$ 48,000	$ 72,000	$120,000

Note: The basic preferred dividend is calculated as before. Then, a like amount is allocated to the common shares. The preferred dividend can be expressed as a percentage: $40,000 ÷ $320,000 = 12.5%. Therefore, the common shares are also allocated a basic dividend of (12.5% × $480,000) = $60,000. This leaves a remaining dividend of $20,000, which is available for participation. The participation is allocated on a pro-rata basis as follows:

Carrying amounts of each class:

Preferred	$320,000	40%
Common	480,000	60%
Total	$800,000	100%

The participating dividend is therefore:

Preferred	$20,000 × 40%	=	$ 8,000
Common	$20,000 × 60%	=	$12,000

If the preferred shares were cumulative and fully participating, the process followed is the same as above, except the dividends available for participation must be reduced by any preferred dividends in arrears, as these must be paid first before any dividends can be paid to common shareholders.

The pro-rata allocation of the participating dividend, shown above, is one way to determine the rate of participation. However, if a company's articles of incorporation specify other methods of participation for different classes of shares, then these calculations must be applied instead.

18.5 Presentation and Disclosure

Previously, we have examined the statement of changes of equity, which is one of the required financial statements under IFRS. Recall that this statement is usually presented in a worksheet format and can contain substantial detail of the various classes of equity accounts. Consider, for example, this excerpt from the 2014 financial statements of a multinational energy company:

Group statement of changes in equity
($ million)

	Share capital and reserves	Treasury shares	Foreign currency translation reserves	Fair value reserves	Profit and loss account	Total controlling interests	Non-controlling interests	Total equity
Balance 1 January 2016	40,567	(15,978)	3,111	(525)	108,421	135,596	1,259	136,855
Profit for the year					4,257	4,257	226	4,483
Other comprehensive income			(6,264)	(197)	2,699	(3,762)	(21)	(3,783)
Total comprehensive income			(6,264)	(197)	6,956	495	205	700
Dividends					(3,655)	(3,655)	(166)	(3,821)
Repurchases of ordinary shares					(3,187)	(3,187)		(3,187)
Share-based payments, net of tax	241	268			(297)	212		212
Share of equity-accounted entities' changes in equity, net of tax					67	67		67
Transactions involving non-controlling interests							112	112
Balance 31 December 2016	40,808	(15,710)	(3,153)	(722)	108,305	129,528	1,410	130,938

Note that a number of contributed capital accounts are included, such as the share capital and the capital reserves, along with a deduction for treasury shares. Other reserve accounts with specific purposes, such as fair value reserves (i.e., accumulated other comprehensive income), are also identified and segregated based on their purpose. The company also separately identifies an account for retained earnings, using the title Profit and Loss account. IAS 1: 106 specifies the disclosure requirements of the statement of changes in equity. Key disclosures include total comprehensive income for the period, a reconciliation of the opening and closing balances of each component of equity, including changes due to other comprehensive income and profit or loss, dividends, transactions with owners, and changes due to retrospective adjustments due to error corrections or accounting policy changes. As long as the meaning and purpose of the accounts are clear, companies may use terminology that is not precisely the same as suggested in the *Conceptual Framework*. Additionally, companies may choose to provide subtotals for certain types of account categories, such as contributed capital or reserves. Contributed capital represents amounts contributed by shareholders, including share capital, share premiums, and contributed surplus balances related to share transactions.

In addition to the statement of changes in equity, the financial statements of this energy company contain a further five pages of explanatory notes, which provide more details of the equity accounts. Some of these details include a breakdown of the features and rights of different classes of share capital, a reconciliation of the six reserve accounts, and details of treasury share transactions. IAS 1 specifically requires the following disclosures either in the statement of changes in equity or in the notes:

a. For each class of share capital:

   i. The number of shares authorized
   ii. The number of shares issued and fully paid, and issued but not fully paid
   iii. Par value per share, or that the shares have no par value
   iv. A reconciliation of the number of shares outstanding at the beginning and at the end of the period
   v. The rights, preferences, and restrictions attaching to that class including restrictions on the distribution of dividends and the repayment of capital
   vi. Shares in the entity held by the entity or by its subsidiaries or associates and
   vii. Shares reserved for issue under options and contracts for the sale of shares, including terms and amounts

b. A description of the nature and purpose of each reserve within equity (CPA Canada, 2016, Accounting, IAS 1: 79).

Disclosure must also be made of the amount of dividends declared during the year, both in total and per share. Paragraphs 134 to 138 of IAS 1 also contain detailed requirements of information to be disclosed regarding the company's objectives, policies, and processes for managing capital.

The substantial disclosure requirements for equity accounts result from the need to serve one of the primary user groups of financial statements: the investors. When investing in a company, one needs a clear understanding of how capital is structured, the various rights and restrictions of different equity categories, and the impact of dividend payments. The need for this type of information, combined with the complex legal nature of equity instruments, creates substantial disclosure requirements that the professional accountant needs to be aware of when drafting financial statements.

18.6 IFRS/ASPE Key Differences

IFRS	ASPE
No specific guidance for treasury shares.	Treasury shares can be accounted for as either a single transaction or as two transactions, although ASPE expresses a preference for the single-transaction method.
No specific guidance for reacquisition of shares.	Guidance provided that shows the order in which proceeds paid should be applied (share capital, contributed surplus, retained earnings).
Accumulated other comprehensive income is included as a component of equity, usually disclosed as part the balance of reserves.	There is no concept of other comprehensive income in ASPE.
Balances and transactions for all equity accounts are presented in the statement of changes in equity.	The retained earnings statement presents changes in retained earnings, while other equity transactions are usually presented in the notes.
Disclosure of the objectives, polices, processes for managing capital are required.	No such disclosures are required.

Chapter Summary

LO 1: Describe the different forms of equity and identify the key features that are important for accounting purposes.

Equity represents the residual interest in a business held by the owners, or the difference between assets and liabilities. Equity can take the form of funds contributed by shareholders (common and preferred shares and contributed surplus), retained earnings, and other reserves. Preferred shares will have legal features that give them preference when dividends are distributed, and may have other features that will affect their classification as a liability or equity. Retained earnings represent the accumulated profits of a business, less any dividend distributions made. Reserves can take a number of forms, but are often the result of retained earnings appropriations or the application of several accounting standards that result in remeasurements that lead to revaluation surpluses.

LO 2: Explain and apply accounting standards for different types of share issues.

When shares are issued for cash, the par value (or full amount of proceeds if there is no par value) is credited to common share capital. The balance of proceeds in excess of the par value is credited to contributed surplus. When shares are issued by subscription, a receivable is created and an interim share capital account (shares subscribed) is created, as unpaid shares normally cannot be issued. The interim share account is eliminated when the final payment is received and shares are actually issued. If a subscriber defaults, the accounting treatment will depend on legal requirements, the subscription contract, and corporate policy. When shares are issued in exchange for goods or services, the shares should be recorded at the fair value of the goods or services received.

LO 3: Explain and apply accounting standards for different situations that can occur when shares are reacquired.

When shares are reacquired, they may either be cancelled or retained as treasury shares. When they are cancelled, the proceeds paid should first be allocated to share capital at the average issue cost, then to contributed surplus that relates to the class of shares, and finally to retained earnings, if necessary. When shares are retained as treasury shares, the amount of the proceeds is a debit to a treasury share account until the shares are either reissued or cancelled. The treasury share account is reported as a contra-equity amount.

LO 4: Describe the accounting treatments for different types of dividends and calculate divided allocations when preferred shares exist.

Dividends represent distributions of earnings to shareholders and may take several forms. The most common form is dividends paid in cash. When dividends are declared, a journal entry is required to establish the liability. No journal entry is required on the date of record, but a journal entry will be required to record the actual payment of dividends. Property dividends require the asset being distributed to be revalued to its fair value immediately prior to the distribution. Share dividends should be reported at the share's fair value immediately after the distribution (ex-dividend amount). Share dividends essentially capitalize part of the company's retained earnings and remove them from future dividend distributions. Share splits do not require any journal entries, and are usually motivated by a desire to lower the company's share price. When preferred shares are outstanding, the declared dividends must first be allocated to the preferred shares, based on the stated rate and the cumulative and participating features that may be present in those shares.

LO 5: Describe the presentation and disclosure requirements for shareholders' equity accounts.

IFRS requires presentation of a statement of changes in equity that details the opening and closing balances of all equity accounts, along with details of changes during the year. As well, significant disclosures of the legal requirements and features of different classes of shares are required, along with descriptions of the purposes of the different reserve accounts. Dividends declared during the year must also be disclosed, along with a discussion of the company's capital management activities.

LO 6: Identify differences in the accounting treatment of shareholders' equity between IFRS and ASPE.

ASPE provides specific guidance for treasury shares and the reacquisition of shares, whereas IFRS does not. Accumulated other comprehensive income is a category of equity that exists in IFRS but not ASPE. A statement of changes in equity is required by IFRS, but ASPE usually presents a retained earnings statement and note disclosures. Capital management disclosures are required under IFRS but not ASPE.

References

Alphabet Investor Relations. (2015, April 23). *Google Inc. announces first quarter 2015 results*. Retrieved from `https://abc.xyz/investor/news/earnings/2015/Q1_google_earnings/`

CPA Canada. (2016). *CPA Canada handbook.* Toronto, ON: CPA Canada.

Liedtke, M. (2014, April 23). Here's why Google Inc. is about to split its shares for the first time in its history. *Financial Post.* Retrieved from `http://business.financialpost.com/fp-tech-desk/google-inc-stock-split?__lsa=8b87-2a81`

Exercises

EXERCISE 18-1

Identify if the following transactions will increase (I), decrease (D), or have no effect (NE) on retained earnings:

Transaction	Effect
Issuance of common shares	
Share split	
A revaluation of surplus resulting from a remeasurement of an available-for-sale asset	
Declaration of a cash dividend	
Net income earned during the year	
Declaration of a share dividend	
Payment of a cash dividend	
Issuance of preferred shares	
Reacquisition of common shares	
Appropriation of retained earnings for a reserve	
A cumulative, preferred dividend that is unpaid at the end of the year	

EXERCISE 18-2

Lainez Ltd. was incorporated on January 1, 2016. During its first year of operations, the following share transactions occurred:

January 1:   Issued 20,000 common shares for cash at a price of $15 per share.

February 1: Issued 500 common shares to settle an invoice from the law firm that handled the incorporation of the company. The invoice amount was $9,000.

March 15:   Issued 10,000 preferred shares for cash at a price of $50 per share.

April 30:   Issued 2,500 common shares in exchange for a piece of specialized manufacturing equipment. The carrying value of the equipment on the seller's books was $40,000, but the asking price was $55,000. An independent engineering report estimated the value in use for this equipment at $50,000.

June 15:   Issued 5,000 common shares for cash at a price of $25 per share.

Required: Prepare the journal entries for the share transactions.

EXERCISE 18–3

Papini Inc. decides to issue its common shares on a subscription basis. Each share can be purchased for $15 per share, with a deposit of $5 per share due at the time of subscription, and the remaining $10 per share due after three months. A total of 100,000 shares was subscribed at the time of the initial offering.

Required:

a. Prepare the journal entries to record the initial subscription and the receipt of the deposits.

b. Prepare the journal entries to record the collection of the balance owed and the issuance of the shares, assuming all subscribers complete the transaction.

c. Repeat part (b) assuming that 10% of the subscribers default on the final payment and the company refunds the deposits.

d. Repeat part (b) assuming that 10% of the subscribers default on the final payment and the company keeps the deposits.

e. Repeat part (b) assuming that 10% of the subscribers default on the final payment and the company issues pro-rata shares to the defaulting subscribers.

EXERCISE 18-4

Pinera Ltd. reacquired 5,000 of its no-par common shares at a price of $11 per share. It subsequently resold the shares at $16 per share.

Required: Using the single-transaction method, record the above treasury share transactions.

EXERCISE 18-5

On January 1, 2016, Alarcon Inc. issued 20,000, $5 par value shares at $17 each. On June 30, 2016, 10,000 of the shares were reacquired at $19 each and subsequently cancelled.

Required: Prepare the journal entries to record the issuance and reacquisition of the above shares.

EXERCISE 18-6

Tanizaki Enterprises Ltd. reported the following share transactions during 2016, its first year of operations:

   January 15: Issued 150,000 no-par common shares at $25 each.

   March 30: Reacquired and cancelled 10,000 shares at $20 each.

   July 31: Issued 20,000 shares at $22 each.

   October 31: Reacquired and cancelled 15,000 shares at $29 each.

Required: Prepare the journal entries to record the above transactions.

EXERCISE 18-7

On January 1, 2017, Belloc Limited, a toy manufacturer, had outstanding share capital of 100,000 common shares. During 2017, the following dividend transactions occurred:

May 5: A 10% share dividend was declared and distributed. On this date, the ex-dividend price was $25 per share.

May 15: A cash dividend of $0.80 per share was declared for shareholders of record on May 20, to be distributed on May 25.

May 25: The cash dividend was distributed.

May 27: In order to reduce some excess inventory levels, the company declared a property dividend. Each share was to receive eight units of the Atomic Accountant action figure. Due to declining sales levels, the inventory carrying amount had previously been written down to its estimated realizable value of $0.75 per unit. The record date for this dividend was May 30, and the distribution date was May 31.

May 31: The property dividend was distributed.

Required: Prepare all the journal entries necessary to record the above dividend transactions.

EXERCISE 18–8

Ayme Inc. had the following share capital outstanding on January 1, 2017:

Class A common shares, unlimited authorized, 250,000 issued	$8,000,000
Class B preferred shares, $100 par value, $3 dividend, 100,000 authorized, 50,000 issued	5,000,000

At the end of 2017, the company declared total dividends of $1,200,000. No dividends had been paid in either 2015 or 2016.

Required:

Determine the amount of dividends paid to each class of share under each of the following independent conditions:

a. The Class B preferred shares are non-cumulative and non-participating.

b. The Class B preferred shares are cumulative and non-participating.

c. The Class B preferred shares are cumulative and fully participating.

EXERCISE 18-9

You have been asked to provide advice to the board of directors of Denevi Ltd., a publicly traded company. The company's shares are currently trading at $12 per share, and the board is considering whether to issue a 50% share dividend or a 3-for-2 share split, which means that for every two shares held, an additional share will be issued. The company currently has 5,000,000 common shares outstanding at a total carrying amount of $12,500,000 and retained earnings of $42,000,000. There are no other equity accounts reported.

Required:

a. Calculate the price the shares are expected to trade at after each of the proposed transactions.

b. Determine the balances to be reported in the shareholders' equity section after each of the proposed transactions.

c. Provide a recommendation to the board of directors as to which action they should take.

EXERCISE 18-10

Ocampo Inc. reported the following amounts in the shareholders' equity section of its December 31, 2016, balance sheet:

Preferred shares, $2 dividend, 10,000 shares authorized, 4,500 issued	$225,000
Common shares, 100,000 shares authorized, 35,000 issued	280,000
Contributed surplus	7,000
Retained earnings	590,000
Accumulated other comprehensive income	115,000

The contributed surplus arose from past reacquisitions of common shares.

During 2017, the following transactions occurred in the order listed below:

i. Issued 5,000 common shares at $9 per share.

ii. Reacquired 10,000 of the outstanding common shares for $14 per share and cancelled them.

iii. Declared a 10% share dividend on the outstanding common shares. The ex-dividend price of the shares was $16.

iv. Issued the share dividend.

v. Exchanged 1,000 preferred shares for a piece of vacant land. The land's fair value, as determined by a qualified appraiser, was $19,000 and the shares were actively traded on this day for $21 per share.

vi. Declared and paid the preferred share dividend and a $1 per share dividend on the common shares.

Required:

a. Prepare the journal entries to record the 2017 equity transactions.

b. Prepare the Statement of Changes in Shareholders' Equity for the year ended December 31, 2017. Net income for the year was $120,000 and other comprehensive income resulting from a revaluation of property, plant, and equipment was $23,000.

EXERCISE 18–11

Manguel Merchandising Ltd. reported the following amounts in the shareholders' equity section of its December 31, 2015, balance sheet:

Preferred shares, $1 cumulative dividend, 100,000 shares authorized, 75,000 issued	$1,875,000
Common shares, unlimited shares authorized, 250,000 issued, 210,000 outstanding	3,800,000
Contributed surplus	58,000
Treasury shares (40,000 common shares)	(440,000)
Retained earnings	4,260,000
Total shareholders' equity	$9,553,000

The contributed surplus arose from past reacquisitions of common shares. On December 31, 2015, two years of preferred dividends were in arrears, that is, preferred dividends were not paid in 2014 or 2015.

The following transactions occurred in 2016:

i. January 15: 10,000 of the shares held in treasury were resold at a price of $13 per share.

ii. February 28: 50,000 common shares were reacquired and immediately cancelled for total cash proceeds of $705,000.

iii. June 30: 25,000 preferred shares were reacquired and immediately cancelled at a price of $31 per share.

iv. December 31: A 5% share dividend was declared and distributed on the common shares. The ex-dividend price of the share was $17. Preferred dividends were also declared and paid in cash, as they needed to be declared before the common share dividend could be declared.

Required: Prepare the journal entries to record 2016 equity transactions.

Chapter 19

Earnings per Share

Facebook and Twitter: Same Industry, But Two Different Stories

Facebook and Twitter reported very different earnings performance in Q2 of 2015. Facebook stocks increased by nearly 30% in the previous year while Twitter struggled. Twitter's stock had lost more than 7% from 2014 and more than 33% from its high in April, 2015. Since both are social media companies, why such a difference?

Twitter was in transition while it searched for a new CEO, resulting in a company operating without a leader or a strategic plan. Moreover, plans to make the software app more user-friendly had been delayed. Some increases in earnings per share were anticipated by the market, but this was overshadowed by the key performance metric of growth for this industry, the Average Monthly Active Users (MAUs), which fell short of analysts' expectations.

Facebook on the other hand had 4.7 times Twitter's user base and had been increasing its earnings per share by giant leaps, making this company the eighth largest company in America by the market. Growth is expected to continue, even if at a slower rate typical of companies that reach giant-size proportions. Moreover, Bank of America has added Facebook to its list of top investment ideas due to the firm's improved advertising targeting through Instagram, its video campaigns, and its growth of new software platforms such as Messenger. Facebook has also leveraged its investments in ramping up sharing instant news articles and following public figures campaigns (areas that were once dominated by Twitter). Both developments have resulted in increased followers and have been very successful.

Time will tell if Twitter can make up for its lost market position.

(Source: Boorstin, 2015)

Chapter 19 Learning Objectives

After completing this chapter, you should be able to:

LO 1: Describe earnings per share (EPS) and their role in accounting and business.

LO 2: Describe basic and diluted earnings per share in terms of an overview.

    LO 2.1: Calculate basic earnings per share.

    LO 2.2: Calculate diluted earnings per share and report the final results.

LO 3: Describe the issues that can affect both basic and diluted earnings per share.

LO 4: Calculate basic and diluted earnings per share in terms of a comprehensive illustration.

LO 5: Identify and explain how earnings per share and price-earnings ratio are used to analyze company performance from an investor perspective.

LO 6: Explain the difference between ASPE and IFRS regarding earnings per share.

Introduction

This chapter will focus on the basics of calculating, reporting, and interpreting earnings per share (EPS) as an important shareholder and potential investor evaluation metric. The chapter will discuss two primary types of EPS, namely basic and diluted earnings per share.

Chapter Organization

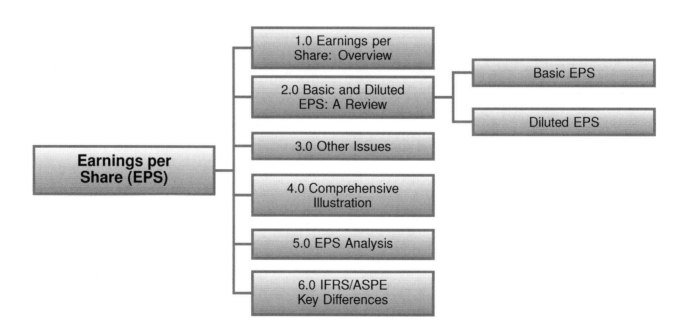

19.1 Earnings per Share: Overview

Just how important are earnings per share? Before that question can be answered, it is important to understand what this metric is. Earnings are simply a company's net income or net profit. As every company has a different number of shares owned by its shareholders, comparing only their earnings figures is like comparing apples to oranges. It does not indicate how much income each company earned for each of its common shareholders. So, earnings per share (EPS) becomes a *per share* way of describing net income, making EPS a good metric for shareholders and potential investors.

Earnings season is the stock market's equivalent to a school report card. It happens four times per year in many countries where publicly traded companies report their financial results. Although it is important to remember that investors look at all financial information, EPS is the most important number released during an earnings season and it attracts the most attention and media coverage. Before earnings reports come out, stock market analysts issue earnings estimates in terms of what they think earnings will be. Research firms then compile these forecasts into a consensus earnings estimate. When a company is able to beat this estimate, it is called an **earnings surprise**, and the stock market price usually moves higher. Conversely, if a company releases earnings below these estimates, it is said to *disappoint*, and the market price for the stock typically moves lower. It is difficult to guess how a stock will move during an earnings season as it is based on expectations, which supports the efficient market hypothesis. Shareholders and potential investors care about EPS because it ultimately drives stock prices.

Sometimes a company with a sky-rocketing stock price might not be making the earnings to support the rise, but the rising price means that investors are hoping – the expectation factor – that the company will be profitable in the future. But, there are no guarantees that the company will fulfill investors' current expectations.

When a company is making net income and has a positive EPS, it has two options. First, it can retain its net income to improve its products and develop new ones. Second, it can either pay a dividend as a return on investment, or offer a share buyback at a higher price. In the first instance, management reinvests profits in the hope of making more profits. In the second instance, the investor receives a more immediate return on investment via the dividend and capital appreciation of the share market price. Typically, smaller companies attempt to create shareholder value by reinvesting profits, while more mature companies pay out dividends. Neither method is necessarily better, but both rely on the same idea: in the long run, earnings provide a return on shareholders' investments, and EPS is the metric used to determine the magnitude of this return.

To summarize, earnings means profit, and is often evaluated in terms of earnings per share. Existing and potential shareholders and analysts use EPS to evaluate a company's performance, to predict future earnings, and to estimate the value of a company's shares.

In terms of the stock market, EPS is the most important indicator of a company's financial health. Earnings reports are released quarterly and are followed very closely by the stock market, news media, and company shareholders. It is little wonder that EPS has become such a deeply entrenched metric to evaluate company performance for common shareholders and potential investors (Investopedia, n.d.).

19.2 Basic and Diluted Earnings per Share: A Review

Basic earnings per share (EPS) is simply:

$$\text{Basic EPS} = \frac{\text{Net income available to common shareholders}}{\text{Weighted average number of common shares outstanding}}$$

In other words, **basic EPS** is an indicator of how much of a publicly traded company's earnings are attributable to each common, or ordinary, share issued.

If a company's capital is composed of common shares and preferred shares or debt that has no conversion rights, then this is referred to as a company with a **simple capital structure**. Capital structures that include securities that have conversion rights such as convertible preferred shares, convertible bonds payable, and stock options are known as companies with **complex capital structures**. Complex capital structures for publicly traded companies require another indicator to be calculated and reported, which is called **diluted EPS**. Dilution occurs when additional common shares are issued without a proportionate increase in the level of earnings or resources that generate those earnings. For example, shares issued for cash will increase both the number of shares and the resources (cash as an asset) so they are not dilutive. Shares issued to holders of convertible securities increases the number of shares and not necessarily with a corresponding increase in company resources. They are, therefore, potentially dilutive. Diluted EPS is often referred to as a worst-case scenario measurement, where the effect on earnings per share is measured assuming that all potential additional common shares for convertible securities, options, and warrants have *already* been issued since the beginning of the year.

In terms of reporting requirements, ASPE companies are not required to report EPS statistics, which makes intuitive sense given that these companies are privately owned and the stockholder base is often closely held and not often bought or sold. On the other hand, an IFRS company that is publicly traded is required to disclose basic EPS and diluted EPS on the face of its income statement. Moreover, if a company reports discontinued operations, EPS disclosures must also further break down EPS into income from continuing operations, discontinued operations, and net income. An example of basic and diluted EPS with discontinued operations is shown below:

Earnings per share	Basic	Diluted
Income from continuing operations	$ 1.25	$ 1.10
Loss from discontinued operations, net of tax*	(0.15)	(0.08)
Net income	$ 1.10	$ 1.02

* EPS for discontinued operations disclosures is a required disclosure, but it may be included in the notes to financial statements.

Recall the importance of being able to differentiate between what earnings from ongoing, or continuing, operations from those that will not continue into the future. This was discussed in the chapter regarding the statement of net Income.

The components of the basic EPS numerator and denominator are discussed next.

19.2.1 Basic Earnings per Share

Numerator: Net Income Available to Common Shareholders

Two things to keep in mind with regard to determining the net income numerator amount:

1. Net income is relevant to this calculation but other comprehensive income (OCI) is not. OCI includes items such as unrealized gains or losses for securities that management does not intend to actively trade, hence these types of gains and losses are not deemed to be part of the company's current period performance.

2. If preferred shares exist, then net income (or loss) available to common shareholders must be adjusted by the preferred shares dividends. This is because preferred shares rank in seniority over common shares with regard to dividends, therefore, if necessary, a portion of net income has to be set aside to cover these dividends. The adjustment amount to deduct from net income will differ if the preferred shares are cumulative or non-cumulative:

    - If cumulative, deduct the dividend amount from net income according to the preferred share's **entitlement**, which is the stated dividend rate regardless of whether or not they were declared or paid. If dividends are in arrears, only the current year's dividend is to be deducted from net income since the EPS figures reported in previous years already included the dividend for that year.
    - If non-cumulative, deduct the dividend amount from net income only if it has been declared, regardless of their stated dividend rate or if they were paid or not. Non-cumulative preferred shares are only entitled to a dividend if the board of directors declares one. The amount of the dividend declared can be based

on their stated dividend rate or it can be less. There are no dividends in arrears for non-cumulative preferred shares in cases where the board does not declare one.

For example, Ogdell Co. has a net income of $350,000 and has two classes of preferred shares as follows:

- Class A: $3 cumulative preferred shares. Authorized 20,000; issued and outstanding, 10,000 shares.

- Class B: $4 non-cumulative preferred shares. Authorized 30,000; issued and outstanding, 15,000 shares.

- No dividends have been declared or paid in the current year. The income available to common shareholders would be calculated as follows:

Income Available to Common Shareholders

Net income (loss)		$350,000
Less:		
Class A: $3, cumulative, preferred shares (issued 10,000 shares × stated rate of $3)	(30,000)	Dividend entitlement
Class B: $4, non-cumulative, preferred shares (no dividend declared)	–	Dividend declared
Income available to common shareholders		$320,000

Assume now that Ogdell Co. has a net loss of $125,000 and that the Class A preferred shares have dividends in arrears from the previous year of $15,000. In the current year, the board of directors declared a total dividend to both classes of preferred shareholders of $50,000. The income available to common shareholders would be calculated as follows:

Income Available to Common Shareholders

Net income (loss)		($125,000)
Plus:		
Class A: $3, cumulative, preferred shares (issued 10,000 shares × stated rate of $3)	(30,000)	Dividend entitlement
Class B: $4, non-cumulative, preferred shares ($50,000 – 15,000 arrears – 30,000)	(5,000)*	Dividend declared
Net income (loss) available to common shareholders		($160,000)

* The total dividend of $50,000 declared will first be applied to the Class A preferred shares dividends in arrears of $15,000 and next to the Class A current year dividends of $30,000, leaving a declared dividend for the Class B, non-cumulative shares of $5,000.

Denominator: Weighted Average Number of Common Shares Outstanding (WACS)

Two types of events can affect the WACS calculation:

1. If common shares have been issued or purchased for consideration, that is, cash in exchange for assets or other consideration, the average must be weighted by the number of months these have been outstanding during the current fiscal year.

2. If stock dividends or stock splits (or reverse stock splits) occur, then the number of shares outstanding must be restated on a retroactive basis as though the stock dividend or split had occurred at the beginning of the year. (These may also be referred to as share dividends and share splits.) The shares issued before the stock dividend or split will now be restated on the same basis as shares issued after the stock dividend or split. If the stock dividend or split occurs after the year-end, but before the financial statements are issued, the WACS are to be restated for the year just ended. Additionally, any previous year's EPS included in the comparative financial statements are also to be restated. The restatement ensures that the EPS is prepared on a consistent basis over the reporting period to enhance comparability and minimize potential manipulation of the EPS amounts because of performance benchmarks or restrictive debt covenants.

To ensure that the WACS are calculated correctly, there are three steps in the preparation of the WACS schedule:

- **Step 1:** Record the opening balance of shares outstanding and each subsequent event, date, description, and number of shares for the current reporting period. An event is when the outstanding number of shares changes, such as when shares are issued or repurchased for either cash, as stock dividends, or for stock splits. Complete the total shares outstanding for each row. If shares are issued on December 31, 2015, they are ignored for the purposes of calculating the WACS because they have not been outstanding during the year.

- **Step 2:** For stock dividends or stock splits, apply the required retroactive restatement factor(s) from the event date when it initially occurs, and backwards to the beginning of the fiscal year.

- **Step 3:** For each event, complete the duration between events under the date column and complete the corresponding fraction of the year column accordingly. Multiply the shares outstanding times the retroactive restatement factor(s) times the fraction of the year for each event. Sum the amounts to determine the WACS total amount.

Continuing with our example for Ogdell Co., assume that the company had 130,000 common shares outstanding on January 1, 2015. The following events occurred during the year:

- On February 1, 2015, an additional 20,000 shares were issued.
- On May 1, 2015, the company repurchased 1,000 shares.
- On July 1, 2015, the company declared and issued a 10% stock dividend.
- On September 1, 2015, the company issued another 15,000 shares.
- On November 1, 2015, the company declared and issued a two-for-one stock split.

Step 1: Record the opening balance of shares outstanding and each subsequent event, date, description, and number of shares for the current reporting period. An event is where the outstanding number of shares changes such as when shares are issued or repurchased for either cash, as stock dividends or for stock splits. Complete the total shares outstanding for each row. If shares are issued on December 31, 2015, they are ignored for the purposes of calculating the WACS because they have not been outstanding during the year.

Event	Date	Description	Shares Outstanding	Retroactive Restatement Factor(s)	Fraction of the Year	Total Shares Outstanding ×Factor ×Fraction of the Year
1	January 1	Opening balance	130,000			
2	February 1	Issued shares	20,000			
			150,000			
3	May 1	Repurchased shares	(1,000)			
			149,000			
4	July 1	10% stock dividend	×1.1			
			163,900			
5	September 1	Issued shares	15,000			
			178,900			
6	November 1	2-for-1 stock split	×2			
			357,800			

Step 2: For stock dividends or stock splits, apply the required retroactive restatement factor(s) from the event date it initially occurs and backwards to the beginning of the fiscal year.

19.2. Basic and Diluted Earnings per Share: A Review

Event	Date	Description	Shares Outstanding	Retroactive Restatement Factor(s)	Fraction of the Year	Total Shares Outstanding × Factor × Fraction of the Year
1	January 1	Opening balance	130,000	1.1 × 2		
2	February 1	Issued shares	20,000			
			150,000	1.1 × 2		
3	May 1	Repurchased shares	(1,000)			
			149,000	1.1 × 2		
4	July 1	10% stock dividend	× 1.1			
			163,900	2		
5	September 1	Issued shares	15,000			
			178,900	2		
6	November 1	2-for-1 stock split	× 2			
			357,800			

Step 3: For each event, complete the duration between events under the date column and complete the corresponding fraction of the year column accordingly. Multiply the shares outstanding times the retroactive restatement factor(s) times the fraction of the year for each event. Sum the amounts to determine the WACS amount.

Event	Date	Description	Shares Outstanding	Retroactive Restatement Factor(s)	Fraction of the Year	Total Shares Outstanding × Factor × Fraction of the Year
1	January 1	Opening balance	130,000	1.1 × 2	1/12	23,833*
	Jan 1 – Feb 1					
2	February 1	Issued shares	20,000			
	Feb 1 – May 1		150,000	1.1 × 2	3/12	82,500
3	May 1	Repurchased shares	(1,000)			
	May 1 – Jul 1		149,000	1.1 × 2	2/12	54,633
4	July 1	10% stock dividend	× 1.1			
	Jul 1 – Sep 1		163,900	2	2/12	54,633
5	September 1	Issued shares	15,000			
	Sep 1 – Nov 1		178,900	2	2/12	59,633
6	November 1	2-for-1 stock split	× 2			
	Nov 1 – Dec 31		357,800		2/12	59,633
					12/12	334,865

* 130,000 × 1.1 × 2 × (1 ÷ 12) = 23,833

Note: Under the fraction of year column the total should always sum to 12/12. Going back to the earlier calculation regarding income available to common shareholders, Ogdell

Co.'s net income was $350,000, and the company had two classes of preferred shares as follows:

- Class A: $3 cumulative preferred shares, authorized 20,000, issued and outstanding, 10,000 shares.
- Class B: $4 non-cumulative preferred shares, authorized 30,000, issued and outstanding, 15,000 shares.
- No dividends have been declared or paid in the current year. The income available to common shareholders was calculated earlier to be $320,000 ($350,000 − $30,000 preferred dividends).

The numerator and denominator are now both calculated, so the basic earnings per share calculation can now be completed as follows:

$$\text{Basic EPS} = \frac{\text{Net income available to common shareholders}}{\text{Weighted average number of common shares outstanding}}$$

$$\text{Basic EPS} = \frac{\$320{,}000}{334{,}865} = \$0.9556 \text{ or } \$0.96 \text{ rounded per share}$$

If Ogdell Co. also had a discontinued operations loss of $20,000 net of tax, the basic EPS would be calculated as follows:

	Income	WACS	Basic EPS
Net Income (from continuing operations available to common shareholders)	$320,000	334,865	$ 0.9556
Loss from discontinued operations net of tax*	(20,000)	334,865	(0.0597)
Net income available to common shareholders	$300,000	334,865	$ 0.8959

* Discontinued operations: ($20,000 ÷ 334,865) = ($0.0597)

The reporting disclosures for basic earnings per share are shown below:

Earnings per share:	
Income from continuing operations	$ 0.96
Loss from discontinued operations, net of tax*	(0.06)
Net income	$ 0.90

* EPS for discontinued operations disclosures may be included in the notes to financial statements.

19.2.2 Diluted Earnings per Share

As previously stated, any publicly traded company with a complex capital structure is to also disclose diluted EPS, separated into continuing operations and non-continuing operations, similar to basic EPS illustrated above. This indicator assumes that all dilutive securities are converted to common shares, which give shareholders a worst-case scenario of the lowest possible EPS with regard to company performance. The dilutive calculation also assumes that, since the conversion to common shares has fully taken place, the convertible securities themselves will be extinguished and the company will no longer be obligated to pay interest or dividends on the original security. In other words, the dilutive calculation will affect both the income available to shareholders (numerator) and the weighted average number of common shares outstanding (denominator) in the original equation:

$$\text{Diluted EPS} = \frac{\text{Net income available to common shareholder} + \text{adjustments from dilutive securities that are ranked from most dilutive to least dilutive}}{\text{Weighted average number of common shares outstanding} + \text{adjustments from dilutive securities that are ranked from most dilutive to least dilutive}}$$

Below are three steps that, if followed carefully, will make the diluted EPS calculation easier:

Step 1: Identify all potentially dilutive securities. These can be convertible bonds or convertible preferred shares, both exchangeable into common shares or stock options and warrants that entitle the holder to buy common shares at a specified price. The conversion feature details will be itemized in the documentation for each convertible security and will include information regarding the conversion timeframe, the rate of conversion to common shares, and the specified price to purchase common shares, if applicable.

Step 2: Calculate the individual effect of each potentially dilutive security and rank them from most to least dilutive. Some of these securities will only affect the number of shares (denominator) such as stock options, warrants, and contingent commitments for shares, while others such as convertible bonds and convertible preferred shares will affect both the income available to common shareholders (numerator) and number of shares (denominator).

Step 3: Complete a diluted EPS schedule and report the results, starting with the basic EPS numerator and denominator amounts. Transfer the numerator and denominator amounts from the individual effects calculated in Step 2 above for each convertible security identified as dilutive, in ranked order, and calculate a diluted EPS subtotal after each. Remove any securities whose subtotal indicates that an increase in diluted EPS has occurred. Complete the EPS disclosures resulting from the analyses.

Diluted EPS Example

Using the steps outlined above, and continuing with the example for Ogdell Co., the basic EPS before discontinued operations is:

	Income	WACS	Basic EPS
Income from continuing operations available to common shareholders	$320,000	334,865	$0.9556

Step 1: Identify and calculate the individual effects for all potentially dilutive options, warrants, and other contingent commitments.

Stock options allow the option holder either to buy shares (**call options**) or sell shares (**put options**) for a specified price (**exercise price**) within a time limit as defined by the option document. If the options are **in the money** (i.e., the specified price compared to the current market price will result in a benefit to the holder), and the holder proceeds to exercise the options, then the company is obligated to sell (write) or to buy (purchase) the shares as set out in the options agreement. Conversely, if the options are not in the money, then the option holder will not exercise them and the options will eventually expire. Therefore, it follows that only options that are in the money will be dilutive as they are the only ones that will be exercised.

For example, if the option holder purchased call options that entitles her or him to purchase common shares for $30 each, at a time when the current market price for the shares has risen to $36 each, it is likely that the option holder will exercise the right to purchase as the shares are considered to be in the money. Issuing more shares to the option holder increases the total number of shares issued (denominator); as such, the options must be included in the diluted EPS calculations. However, as the effect on net income from the exercise of options is not easy to estimate, the **treasury stock method** is chosen to calculate the dilutive effect of options and warrants, which limits the calculation to the number of shares denominator value. It also assumes that the company would use the monies received from the option holders to repurchase common shares from the market and then retire them. This would lessen the dilutive impact on EPS. Put another way, shares would be issued to the holders and the resulting proceeds would be used to repurchase its own shares from the market. Since the exercise price is less than the current market price, more shares would be issued than could be repurchased from the market. This difference is the additional number of shares to be included in the diluted EPS calculation using the treasury stock method.

For example, Ogdell Co. has (call) options outstanding that entitle the option holder to purchase 1,000 common shares for an exercise, or strike, price of $30 per share. The company has performed well lately, and the average market price per share has risen to $50.[1] Option holders will benefit from purchasing the shares for $30, so these options are considered to be in the money and are dilutive under the treasury stock method. The difference between the 1,000 shares issued to the option holders and the number of shares that the company could repurchase with the proceeds, given a market price of $50, is as follows:

Treasury Stock Method		
Proceeds received from exercise of options (1,000 shares × $30 per share = $30,000)	1,000	shares
Proceeds used to purchase common shares from the market ($30,000 ÷ $50 market price per share)	(600)	shares
Incremental shares issued	400	shares

If Ogdell has (put) options outstanding that entitle the option holder to sell 1,000 common shares back to the company at an exercise price of $40 per share, when the current average market price is $35, then these would also be considered in the money and dilutive. In this case, the **reverse treasury stock method** would be used, which assumes that the company would issue enough shares for cash in the market at the beginning of the year to cover their obligation to buy back the put options. As option holders will benefit from selling the shares at $40 each, the options are considered in the money and dilutive under the reverse treasury stock method. The proceeds required by the company to meet their obligations to the option holders would be $40,000 (1,000 × $40). If the current market price is currently $35 per share, the company would have to ensure that it issued an additional 1,143 shares ($40,000 ÷ $35) at the beginning of the year in order to have enough proceeds available to meet their obligation to buy back the 1,000 shares from the option holders. The difference between the 1,143 shares issued for cash at the beginning of the year and the subsequent buy-back of 1,000 shares from the options holders, or 143 shares, would be included in the diluted EPS calculation in the same way as is shown for the (call) options illustrated above.

Contingently issuable shares can also be considered dilutive if they meet the criteria at any point during the reporting period. For example, if shares are issuable to key executive

---

[1]IAS 33.45 (CPA Canada, 2016) states that the average market price is to be used in the following manner: "For the purpose of calculating diluted earnings per share, an entity shall assume the exercise of dilutive options and warrants of the entity. The assumed proceeds from these instruments shall be regarded as having been received from the issue of ordinary shares at the average market price of ordinary shares during the period. The difference between the number of ordinary shares issued and the number of ordinary shares that would have been issued at the average market price of ordinary shares during the period shall be treated as an issue of ordinary shares for no consideration" (CPA Canada, 2016, Accounting, IAS 33.45).

when earnings reach a certain level, and this level had already been achieved by the beginning of the reporting period, then the diluted earnings per share calculation would include these contingent shares in the denominator since the beginning of the reporting period. If Ogdell Co. had agreed to issue 50 shares to any division manager who was able to increase their respective divisional earnings by 10% in the current year, and three such managers did in fact achieve the 10% increase, then the diluted EPS calculation would include 150 (50 × 3 managers) additional shares.

The incremental shares for the options and the contingently issuable shares will be included in the diluted EPS schedule as denominator values as shown below:

Diluted EPS Calculation Schedule

	Income (numerator)	# of shares (denominator)	EPS
Basic EPS	$320,000	334,865	$0.9556
Call options:			
Shares issued @ $30 per share		1,000	
Shares repurchased (1,000 × $30) ÷ $50		(600)	
	-	400	
Contingently issuable shares:			
(3 managers × 50 shares)		150	
	-	150	
Put options:			
Shares issued ($40,000 ÷ $35)		1,143	
Share repurchased (1,000 @ $40)		(1,000)	
	-	143	
Diluted EPS	$320,000	335,558	$0.9536

As seen above, the net additional 693 shares (400 + 143 + 150) have resulted in a diluted EPS of $0.95, or $0.01 less per share than the basic EPS of $0.96 (rounded). The dilutive effect of the options and contingently issuable shares makes sense as only the number of shares has increased with no effect on the income numerator. Mathematically, an increasing denominator with an unchanged numerator will be the most dilutive and will be listed first in the diluted EPS calculation, which is illustrated later in Step 3.

Step 2: Calculate the individual effect of each potentially dilutive convertible security and rank them from most to least dilutive.

Convertible debts, such as bonds and cumulative preferred shares that are convertible into common shares, are potentially dilutive convertible securities. Unlike options, both of these securities will affect not only the number of shares but also the net income. For example, if bonds are converted into common shares, then the number of shares will increase (denominator), and the interest expense saved due to the conversion of the debt to common shares will increase the amount of income available to common shareholders (numerator).

If cumulative preferred shares are converted to common shares, then the number of shares will increase (denominator) and the dividends for the preferred shares saved, due to the conversion to common shares, will increase the income available to the common shareholders (numerator). Again, the assumption is that these outstanding convertible securities would have converted to common shares since the beginning of the period, using the *if-converted method*. For both types of securities, the income (numerator) and number of shares (denominator) are affected, but are they dilutive? Two steps are needed to determine this:

a. First, calculate the individual EPS effect on income (numerator) and number of shares (denominator) for each type of convertible security. If the individual EPS effect is less than the basic EPS calculated earlier, then it is dilutive. If the individual EPS effect is more than the basic EPS, then it is anti-dilutive and can be excluded from the subsequent calculations.

b. Second, rank the dilutive securities from most to least dilutive and complete the diluted EPS calculation as shown in the example below.

For example, Ogdell Co. has the following convertible debt and equity securities:

Bonds payable, 3.2% annually, 20-year amortization, due 2035,
  issued at par, each $1,000 bond is convertible into 30 common shares   400,000

Bonds payable, 2.5% annually, 15-year amortization, due 2030,
  issued at par, each $1,000 bond is convertible into 23 common shares   300,000

Class A: $3 cumulative, convertible, preferred shares; authorized, 20,000
  issued and outstanding, 10,000 shares, each share is convertible
  into three common shares   800,000

Ogdell Co.'s income tax rate is 27%. Preferred dividends were not declared in the current year.

Solution:

Calculate the individual EPS effect on income (numerator) and number of shares (denominator) for each type of convertible security and compare each to the basic EPS amount. If the individual EPS effect for each security is *less than* the basic EPS, it is dilutive. If the individual EPS is *more than* the basic EPS, it is anti-dilutive and can be excluded from the subsequent calculations.

Individual Effects Calculations

	Income (numerator)	# of shares (denominator)	EPS	
Basic EPS	$320,000	334,865	$0.9556	
Individual effects:				
3.2%, convertible bond:				
Interest savings ($400,000 × 3.2% × 73%) net of tax	9,344			#1 most dilutive
Shares issued ($400,000 ÷ $1,000 × 30)		12,000	0.7787	
		0.7787 is less than 0.96		dilutive
2.5%, convertible bond:				
Interest savings ($300,000 × 2.5% × 73%) net of tax	5,475			#2 most dilutive
Shares issued ($300,000 ÷ $1,000 × 23)		6,900	0.7935	
		0.7935 is less than 0.96		dilutive
$3, convertible preferred shares:				
~~Dividend savings (10,000 × $3)~~	~~30,000~~			exclude
~~Shares issued (10,000 × 3)~~		~~30,000~~	~~1.00~~	
		1.00 is more than 0.96		anti-dilutive

For the 3.2% convertible bonds, the calculation above assumes that interest will no longer be paid if the bond is converted to common shares. The effect of the interest expense savings on net income would be:

$$\$400,000 \times 3.2\% \text{ per annum} \times (1 - 0.27) = \$9,344 \text{ after-tax increase to net income}$$

The increase in common shares if converted would be:

$$\$400,000 \div \$1,000 \times 30 \text{ shares} = 12,000 \text{ additional shares}$$

The individual EPS effect compared to basic EPS would be:

$9,344 ÷ 12,000 shares = $0.7787 compared to basic EPS of $0.9556 and is, therefore, dilutive. This security will be included in the overall diluted EPS calculation illustrated in Step 3 below.

The same calculation is done for the 2.5% convertible bonds. The individual EPS effect is $0.7935, which is less than the basic EPS of $0.9556, and is, therefore, dilutive.

For the convertible preferred shares, the calculation above assumes that the dividends will no longer be paid if the preferred shares are converted into common shares. The effect of the dividends saved will increase the net income available to common shareholders because that portion of net income no longer has to be set aside, as done in the basic EPS calculation illustrated earlier. Below is the calculation of the individual effects of the preferred shares using the if-converted method:

10,000 shares × $3 dividends = $30,000 dividend savings, resulting in additional income available to common shareholders. Note that there is no tax effect on dividends.

The increase in common shares if converted would be:

$$10,000 \times 3 \text{ shares} = 30,000 \text{ additional shares}$$

The individual EPS effect compared to basic EPS would be:

$30,000 ÷ 30,000 shares = $1.00 which is more than the basic EPS of $0.9556 and is, therefore, anti-dilutive. This security will be excluded from the diluted EPS calculation illustrated in Step 3 below.

Both convertible bonds are dilutive and are ranked from most to lease dilutive as follows:

3.2% bonds $0.7787   #2, ranked most dilutive after options and contingent shares

2.5% bonds $0.7935   #3, ranked next most dilutive after options and contingent shares

Step 3: Consolidating the results – complete a diluted EPS schedule and report the results.

Starting with basic EPS, input all of the dilutive securities in ranked order starting with options, warrants, and contingently issuable securities (which are the most dilutive). Subtotal the diluted EPS calculation for each type of security to ensure that each continues to be dilutive when included in the overall diluted EPS calculation. Any securities that are no longer contributing to the dilutive EPS are removed, and the remaining securities are considered to be dilutive. This process is shown in the dilutive EPS schedule below:

Individual Effects Calculations			
	Income (numerator)	# of shares (denominator)	Diluted EPS
Basic EPS	$320,000	334,865	$0.9556
Call options:			
Shares issued @ $30 per share		1,000	
Shares repurchased (1,000 × $30) ÷ $50		(600)	
	–	400	
Contingently issuable shares:			
(3 managers × 50 shares)		150	
Put options:			
Shares issued ($40,000 ÷ $35)		1,143	
Share repurchased (1,000 @ $40)		(1,000)	
	–	143	
Subtotal	$320,000	335,558	$0.9536
Convertible bond:			
3.2%, convertible bond:			
Interest savings ($400,000 × 3.2% × 73%) net of tax	9,344		
Shares issued ($400,000 ÷ $1,000 × 30)		12,000	
Subtotal	$329,344	347,558	$0.9476
2.5%, convertible bond:			
Interest savings ($300,000 × 2.5% × 73%) net of tax	5,475		
Shares issued ($300,000 ÷ $1,000 × 23)		6,900	
Subtotal	$334,819	354,458	$0.9446

Rank #1 most dilutive

Rank #2 most dilutive

Rank #3 most dilutive

Note that the dilutive EPS starts at $0.9536 as a result of the options and contingently issuable shares. It then decreases to $0.9476 for the next most dilutive 3.2% convertible bonds, and finally it decreases once more to $0.9446 for the third-ranked 2.5% convertible bond. This means that each of the securities continues to contribute to the dilutive EPS and should be kept in the schedule. As previously stated, and important to remember, if any of the securities cause the diluted EPS subtotal to increase, then it must be removed from the calculation as it is no longer dilutive.

Carrying out these steps in the correct sequence is critical in order to ensure that the securities reported as dilutive continue to have a dilutive effect throughout the entire diluted EPS calculation.

The final diluted EPS amounts are disclosed on the face of the income statement and rounded to the nearest two decimals:

Earnings per share:	Basic	Diluted
Income from continuing operations	$ 0.96	$ 0.94
Loss from discontinued operations, net of tax*	(0.06)	(0.06)
Net income	$ 0.90	$ 0.88

* Basic – Discontinued operations: ($20,000 net of tax loss ÷ 334,865 basic EPS shares) = ($0.06)
   Diluted – Discontinued operations: ($20,000 net of tax loss ÷ 354,458 diluted EPS shares) = ($0.06)

Companies can choose to disclose EPS – discontinued operations in the notes to the financial statements.

19.3 Other Issues

Convertible securities and other dilutive instruments are not always outstanding throughout the entire current reporting period. They can also be issued or converted during the current reporting period. These transactions can affect both basic and diluted EPS. Below are some different examples of convertible securities and other issues that can have an impact on the calculations for basic EPS or diluted EPS.

Type of Security and Description of Transaction	Effect on EPS
Convertible security or option is issued during the reporting period.	Basic EPS: If the security is preferred shares, then the dividend entitlement (cumulative) or dividend declared (non-cumulative) will be subtracted from net income. Diluted EPS: Income and shares effects are prorated to reflect the duration from the issuance date of the convertible security to the end of the reporting period.
Convertible security or option is converted to common shares during the reporting period.	Basic EPS: The common shares issued will be included in the WACS calculation from the date of conversion to the end of the reporting period. Diluted EPS: Income and shares effects are prorated from the date that the security was converted backwards to the beginning of the reporting period. The shares issued for the actual conversion are already included in the basic EPS calculation.

286 ■ Earnings per Share

Convertible security or option is either redeemed or its conversion rights expire during the reporting period.	Basic EPS: There is no effect regarding the redemption or expiration of conversion rights. Diluted EPS: If dilutive, the income and shares effects are prorated to reflect the duration from the beginning of the reporting period to the redemption or expiry date. For options, the shares effect would be prorated for any period during the current reporting period that they were in the money.
Convertible security has more than one conversion point in time.	Diluted EPS will be included in the diluted EPS calculation using the most dilutive alternative.
Convertible security cannot be converted until some future point in time.	Diluted EPS will be included in the diluted EPS calculations, if dilutive.
Convertible debt such as bonds issued at a discount or premium.	Diluted EPS will use the effective interest method to determine the income effect regarding the income expense saved.
Options that are repurchased from option holders by the company (of its own shares).	Diluted EPS will be excluded from the diluted EPS because the company would not purchase the options if it were not favourable for them to do so.
A company with a net loss from continuing operations.	Diluted EPS will be equal to basic EPS because the individual income and shares effects for the diluted calculations will result in a reduction in the net loss from continuing operations and will, hence, be anti-dilutive.

19.4 Comprehensive Illustration

Yondif Ltd. is a publicly traded corporation that follows IFRS. It has a complex capital structure with convertible debt and equity securities. Below is selected information about long-term debt and equity instruments as at December 31, 2015:

Long-term debt:	
7% bonds, at face value, due April 1, 2028	$780,000
10-year, 8% convertible bonds, at face value (Each $1,000 bond is convertible into 50 Class A Common shares, commencing August 1, 2015)	350,000
Share capital:	
$8, convertible, cumulative, preferred shares; each preferred share is convertible into 1 Class A common share, issued and outstanding, 12,500 shares	250,000
Class A common shares, issued and outstanding, 122,500 shares	2,450,000
Options:	
1,000 employee stock options, issued on December 31, 2012, each exchangeable for 1 Class A common shares at a price of $18 per share any time prior to December 31, 2018. 500 executive stock options, issued on December 31, 2012, each exchangeable for 1 Class A common share as follows:	

$20 per share prior to January 1, 2016 $25 per share from January 1, 2016 to December 31, 2016 $27 per share from January 1, 2017 to December 31, 2018 Options expire on January 1, 2019	
Contingent shares:	
The company has an agreement with each of its five divisional managers to issue 500 Class A common shares on January 1, 2017, if the manager's respective division before-tax earnings for 2015 increases by more than 10% compared to the 2014 year-end reported before-tax earnings. To date, divisional earnings for three managers have met and surpassed the 10% increase.	

Additional information:

1. Earnings (net income) for the year ended December 31, 2015, were $690,000. Included were discontinued operations of $210,000 loss, net of tax. Income tax rate was 20%.

2. The average market price for Class A common shares was $21.

3. Dividends were paid on the preferred shares annually and no dividends were in arrears.

4. On July 1, 2015, a 10% stock dividend was declared and issued to the Class A common shareholders. At the beginning of the year, the total number of common shares outstanding was 100,000.

5. On June 1, 2015, ten-year, 8% bonds, were issued at par for $600,000. Each $1,000 bond is convertible into 50 Class A common shares commencing August 1, 2015. Using the residual value method, the liability component's present value of cash flows for interest and principal at a market rate of 9% for non-convertible bonds was $561,494. The equity component was for the remainder of $38,506.

6. On August 1, 2015, $250,000 of the 8% convertible bonds were converted.

Basic Earnings per Share Calculation:

Step 1: Record the opening balance of shares outstanding and each subsequent event, date, description, and number of shares for the current reporting. An event is where the outstanding number of shares changes.

Step 2: For stock dividends or stock splits, apply the required retroactive restatement factor(s) from the event point where it initially occurs and backwards to the beginning of the fiscal year.

Step 3: For each event, complete the duration between events under the date column and complete the corresponding fraction of the year column accordingly. Multiply the shares outstanding times the retroactive restatement factor(s) times the fraction of the year for each event. Sum the amounts to determine the WACS amount.

Event	Date	Description	Shares Outstanding	Retroactive Restatement Factor(s)	Fraction of the Year	Total Shares Outstanding ×Factor ×Fraction of the Year
1	January 1	Opening balance	100,000	1.1	6/12	55,000
	Jan 1 – Jul 1					
2	July 1	10% stock dividend	×1.1			
	Jul 1 – Aug 1		110,000		1/12	9,167
3	August 1	12,500 shares issued				
	Aug 1 –	($250,000 ÷ 1,000)				
	Dec 31	×50 shares	12,500			
			122,500		5/12	51,042
	Total WACS				12/12	115,209

	Income	WACS	Basic EPS
Net income from continuing operations ($690,000 + $210,000 discontinued operations)	900,000		
Less preferred dividends (12,500 × $8)	(100,000)		
Net income available to common shareholders	800,000	115,209	$6.94

Note that income from continuing operations of $900,000, as shown above, was not given in the question data. The amount must be derived by working backwards from the net income amount of $690,000, after discontinued operations and net of tax, for $210,000. If the discontinued operations had been stated in before-tax dollars, an additional calculation would be required to determine the net of tax amount, which is the amount deducted from income from continuing operations to arrive at net income. There were no shares issued in 2015 due to contingent shares. However, the contingent shares disclosed by the company may be dilutive, which will be tested in the diluted EPS calculations in the next section.

Diluted Earnings per Share Calculation:

Step 1: Identify and calculate the individual effects for all potentially dilutive options, warrants, and other contingent commitments.

	Income (Numerator)	Number of Shares (Denominator)	Individual EPS Effect
Basic EPS (from continuing operations)	$800,000	115,209	$6.94
Options:			
Employee stock options:			
Shares issued @ $18 per share		1,000	
Shares repurchased (1,000 × $18) ÷ $21		(857)	
		143	
Executive stock options:			
Shares issued @ $20 per share		500	
Shares repurchased (500 × $20) ÷ $21		(476)	
		24	
Contingent shares:			
500 shares × 3 divisional managers		1,500	
Subtotal	$800,000	116,876	$6.84

The employee stock options have an exercise price of $18 per share, compared to the average market price of $21 per share. The options are in the money because the exercise price is less than the average market price and option holders will be motivated to exercise the options and purchase the common shares. As discussed previously, if the options were not in the money, then they would be excluded from the dilutive calculation.

The executive stock options are in the money at the exercise price of $20 per share, so these will be included in the diluted EPS calculation as shown above.

Also, a portion of the contingently issuable shares is to be included in the dilutive calculation because three of the managers have already met the 10% increase.

Together, the options and contingently issuable shares are ranked number one, as the most dilutive securities as a group.

Step 2: Calculate the individual effect of each potentially dilutive convertible security and rank them from most to least dilutive.

	Income (Numerator)	Number of Shares (Denominator)	Individual EPS Effect	
Basic EPS (from continuing operations)	$800,000	115,209	$6.94	
Individual effects:				
Preferred shares (per share)	$8	1	$8.00	Not dilutive
8% bonds - actual conversion on Aug 1 Interest saved ($250,000 ÷ $600,000) × $561,494 × 9% × (1 − 0.2) × 2 ÷ 12 June 1 to August 1	2,807			
Additional shares ($250,000 ÷ $1,000) × 50 × 2 ÷ 12		2,083	$1.35	Dilutive
Remainder of the convertible 8% bonds Interest saved ($350,000 ÷ $600,000) × $561,494 × 9% × (1 − 0.2) × (7 ÷ 12) June 1 to December 31	13,757			
Additional shares ($350,000 ÷ $1,000) × 50 shares × (7 ÷ 12)		10,208	$1.35	Dilutive

Note that the 7% bond is not convertible, so it is not dilutive. Also, a portion of the 8% convertible bonds was actually converted on August 1. Note that the basic EPS included the 12,500 converted shares from August 1 to December 31, or for the five months remaining after conversion. The diluted calculation for the interest saved and the additional shares calculates the effect from the August 1 conversion date backwards to the June 1 purchase date, or for two months. The remainder of the 8% convertible bonds is calculated backwards from the purchase date of June 1 to year-end, since they have not been converted.

Ranking the securities above from most to least dilutive results in the 8% converted bonds being ranked as the second most dilutive after options and contingently issuable shares. The preferred shares are not dilutive at an individual EPS amount of $8.00 per share, compared to the basic EPS of $6.94.

Step 3: Consolidating the results – complete a diluted EPS schedule and report the results.

	Income (Numerator)	Number of Shares (Denominator)	Individual EPS Effect
Basic EPS (from continuing operations)	$800,000	115,209	$6.94
Options:			
Employee stock options:			
Shares issued @ $18 per share		1,000	
Shares repurchased (1,000 × $18) × $21		(857)	
		143	
Executive stock options:			
Shares issued @ $20 per share		500	
Shares repurchased (500 × $20) ÷ $21		(476)	
		24	
Contingent shares:			
500 shares × 3 divisional managers		1,500	
Subtotal	$800,000	116,876	$6.84
8% bonds converted August 1	2,807		
Additional shares		2,083	
Subtotal	802,807	118,959	6.75
8% bonds - remaining	13,757		
Additional shares		10,208	
Diluted EPS	$816,564	129,167	$6.32

The dilutive securities are input into the schedule in ranked order from most to least dilutive. A subtotal diluted EPS is calculated between each entry to ensure that each security continues to contribute to the dilutive EPS. If any of the securities caused the diluted EPS subtotal to increase, then it must be removed from the calculation, as it is no longer dilutive.

The final diluted EPS amounts are to be disclosed on the face of the income statement and rounded to the nearest two decimals. However, as stated previously, companies can choose to disclose the EPS for discontinued operations in the notes to the financial statements. Below is an example of the disclosure on the face of the income statement:

Earnings per share:	Basic	Diluted
Income from continuing operations	$ 6.94	$ 6.32
Loss from discontinued operations, net of tax*	(1.82)	(1.63)
Net income	$ 5.12	$ 4.69

* Basic – Discontinued operations: ($210,000 net of tax loss ÷ 115,209 basic EPS shares) = ($1.82)
  Diluted – Discontinued operations: ($210,000 net of tax loss ÷ 129,167 diluted EPS shares) = ($1.63)

Restatement of EPS

Examples of when EPS is to be retrospectively restated include when a prior period error is discovered, when there is a change in accounting policy (voluntarily or in response to a change in accounting standard), when a stock dividend/split is declared, or when a subsequent event occurs. Subsequent events can occur after the fiscal year, but before the financial statement have been issued. Examples include an issuance, conversion or redemption of convertible securities, options or warrants, or a stock dividend or split declared after the fiscal year but before the financial statements have been issued. Restatements require extensive disclosures, which are discussed in a later chapter.

19.5 Earnings per Share Analysis

Basic EPS is an indicator that uses historic financial data, such as net income, and an average based on actual shares outstanding from the reporting period just ended. Over time, EPS trends can help shareholders and potential investors to determine if performance is on an upward or a downward swing. These trends can assist in forecasting future performance based on what happened historically.

Diluted EPS is an indicator that is forward-looking. It quantifies the impact that exercising options, and potentially convertible securities, will have on current earnings available to common shareholders.

Price-earnings ratio (P/E) is an important measure of company's performance. It measures how investors evaluate a company's future performance and is calculated as:

$$\text{Price-earnings ratio} = \frac{\text{Market price per share}}{\text{Earnings per share}}$$

If the market price for ABC Ltd. as at December 31, 2013, and 2014, was $43.29 and $45.86, respectively. Using the EPS of $2.98 from the company's financial statements, the price-earnings ratios, using the market prices as high and low figures, are calculated as follows:

$$\text{Low: } \frac{\$43.29}{\$2.98} = 14.5 \qquad \text{High: } \frac{\$45.86}{\$2.98} = 15.39$$

The P/E ratio indicates the dollar amount an investor can expect to invest in a company in order to receive one dollar of that company's earnings. This is why the P/E is sometimes referred to as the **multiple**, because it shows how much investors are willing to pay per dollar of earnings. Using the figures from the calculations above, if a company was currently trading at a multiple (P/E) of between 14.5 and 15.4, the interpretation is that an investor would be willing to pay between $14 and $15 for $1 of current earnings.

In general, a high P/E ratio suggests that investors are expecting higher earnings growth in the future compared to companies with a lower P/E. It could also mean that the company is currently overvalued by the market, which may lead to a market correction of the stock price in the future. Conversely, a low P/E ratio can indicate that a company may currently be undervalued.

Like any other ratios or analytical tools, basic and diluted EPS and the price-earnings ratio are not meaningful unless compared with something else, such as a company's historical trend. Also, EPS based on income from continuing operations is a more relevant performance indicator and forecasting tool than EPS on net income, which may include discontinued operations.

EPS as a single measure obscures important information about the company's selection of accounting policies, estimates, and valuations. As illustrated in the diluted EPS calculation above, the calculations for EPS are complex and can be manipulated like any other analytical tool. For this reason, EPS should be only one assessment tool of many that would comprise an informed analysis of a company's performance and overall health.

19.6 IFRS/ASPE Key Differences

Item	ASPE	IFRS IAS 33
Reporting requirement for basic and diluted earnings per share.	Not required	Publicly traded companies are to present basic and diluted earnings per share. Privately held companies choosing to follow IFRS are not required to report earnings per share unless they are in the process of going public.

Chapter Summary

LO 1: Describe earnings per share (EPS) and their role in accounting and business.

Earnings per share measure how much income individual companies earn for each of its common shareholders. EPS is a per share method of describing net income (earnings), making EPS a good metric for investors. EPS is also a key metric used by stock market analysts to measure if the reported EPS is higher or lower than the analysts' forecasted EPS. This movement affects the market price per share for this stock. Management can reinvest profits in hopes of making more profits or they can pay a dividend or a share buy-back to the investors as a way to provide a return on the shareholders' investment. EPS is the metric used to determine the magnitude of this return.

LO 2: Describe basic and diluted earnings per share in terms of an overview.

Basic EPS is a ratio that is calculated as net income available to common shareholders after preferred shares dividends, if applicable, divided by the weighted average number of common shares outstanding. A simple capital structure means that there are no debt or equity securities convertible into common shares. If there are, the company is said to have a complex capital structure. Diluted EPS is a worst-case scenario measurement where the effect on earnings per share is measured assuming that all potential additional common shares for convertible securities and options have already been issued. Publicly traded companies must report earnings per share while companies that follow ASPE, or companies that follow IFRS but are not publicly traded, do not. If the publicly traded company has a complex capital structure, then they must report both basic and diluted EPS on the face of the income statement. EPS must also be broken down further to report EPS, discontinued operations, net of tax, if applicable.

LO 2.1: Calculate basic earnings per share.

To calculate basic EPS, net income available to common shareholders after preferred shares dividends is calculated for the numerator, and a weighted average number of common shares outstanding is calculated for the denominator. For the numerator, only net income, and not OCI, is relevant. The preferred shares dividends amount is subtracted from net income to determine the income available to common shareholders. The cumulative preferred shares dividend amount is based on dividend entitlement while the non-cumulative preferred shares dividends amount is based on dividend declared in the current reporting period. For the denominator, the weighted average common shares outstanding (WACS) is affected by common shares issued or repurchased as well as any stock dividends and stock splits, both of which are restated retroactively back to the beginning of the year. All these are further prorated by the number of months that they have been outstanding during the year. There are three steps that, if followed, will simplify this calculation.

LO 2.2: Calculate diluted earnings per share and report the final results.

Diluted EPS starts with the basic EPS numerator, denominator, and ratio. There are four steps that, if followed, will simplify this calculation. In basic terms, options, warrants, and contingent shares use the treasury stock method to determine their respective denominator amounts. For convertible securities such as convertible bonds and convertible preferred shares, the if-converted method is used to determine both the income effect (numerator) and the shares effect (denominator). All dilutive securities are, at this point, ranked from most to least dilutive and the diluted EPS is calculated using a subtotal between each security to ensure that each one continues to contribute a dilutive factor. Any that do not are removed.

The final results of the basic and diluted EPS from continuing operations, discontinued operations, and net income are disclosed. Basic and diluted EPS from continuing operations and net income must be disclosed on the face of the income statement while EPS for discontinued operations can be disclosed in the notes to the financial statements.

LO 3: Describe the issues that can affect both basic and diluted earnings per share.

There are several issues with regard to EPS. For example, convertible securities, options, and warrants can be issued, converted, redeemed, or can expire during the reporting period. Convertible securities can also have more than one conversion point, or may not be convertible until sometime in the future. Also, convertible bonds can be issued at a discount or at a premium, options can be repurchased from shareholders, or a company may experience a net loss. All these factors may affect basic and diluted EPS.

LO 4: Calculate basic and diluted earnings per share in terms of a comprehensive illustration.

A comprehensive step-by-step illustration is presented which applies the concepts as summarized above.

LO 5: Identify and explain how earnings per share and price-earnings ratio are used to analyze company performance from an investor perspective.

Basic EPS uses historical data in order to be useful and relevant while diluted EPS is more forward-looking and quantifies the impact that exercising options and potentially convertible securities has on current earnings available to common shareholders. Price-earnings ratio is a percentage-based measure of company performance and is an indicator of the share price that an investor can expect to pay to invest in the company. Ratios must be comparable to something, such as historical trends or industry standards, in order to be meaningful. As EPS is expressed as a single ratio figure it can obscure important information about a company's selection of accounting policies, estimates, and valuations. Like any other ratio, EPS can be subject to manipulation and, therefore, should only be one of a more comprehensive set of ratios and other types of analysis techniques used to evaluate company performance.

LO 6: Explain the difference between ASPE and IFRS regarding earnings per share.

ASPE companies and non-publicly traded IFRS companies are not required to report EPS figures. However, publicly traded companies must report basic EPS and diluted EPS, if applicable.

References

Boorstin, J. (2015, July 27). *Facebook vs. Twitter: A tale of two very different social stocks*. CNBC. Retrieved from http://www.cnbc.com/2015/07/27/facebook-vs-twitter-a-tale-of-two-very-different-social-stocks.html

CPA Canada. (2016). *CPA Canada handbook*. Toronto, ON: CPA Canada.

Investopedia. (n.d.). *Everything investors need to know about earnings*. Retrieved from http://www.investopedia.com/articles/basics/03/052303.asp

Exercises

EXERCISE 19–1

Everest Corp. had 100,000 common shares outstanding on December 31, 2015. During 2016 the company:

- issued 6,000 shares on March 1
- retired 2,000 shares on July 1
- distributed a 15% stock dividend on October 1
- issued 10,000 shares on December 1

For 2016, the company reported net income of $310,000 after a loss from discontinued operations, before tax, of $35,000. The tax rate is 25%. The company also issued a 2-for-1 stock split on February 1, 2017. The company issued its 2016 financial statements on February 28, 2017.

Required:

a. Calculate earnings per share for 2016.

b. Explain why Everest Corp.'s reporting of EPS is useful to company shareholders.

c. Explain the effect that a stock dividend or split has on the price-earnings ratio.

EXERCISE 19–2

Mame Ltd. had 475,000 common shares outstanding on January 1, 2016. During 2016 the company:

- issued 25,000 common shares on May 1
- declared and distributed a 10% stock dividend on July 1
- repurchased 15,000 of its own shares on October 1

Required:

a. Calculate the WACS outstanding as at December 31, 2016.

b. Assume that the company had a 1-for-5 reverse stock split instead of the 10% stock dividend on July 1. Calculate the WACS as at December 31, 2016.

EXERCISE 19–3

Calvert Corp. had 500,000 common shares outstanding on January 1, 2016. During 2016 the company:

- issued 180,000 common shares on February 1
- declared and distributed a 10% stock dividend on March 1
- repurchased 200,000 of its own shares and retired them on May 1
- issued a 3-for-1 stock split on June 1
- issued 60,000 common shares on October 1

The company's year-end is December 31.

Required:

a. Calculate the WACS outstanding as at December 31, 2016.

b. Assume that the company had net income of $3,500,000 during 2016. In addition, it had 100,000 of 8%, $100 par, non-convertible, non-cumulative preferred shares outstanding the entire year. No dividend was declared or paid for the preferred shares in 2016. Calculate EPS using the WACS from part (a).

c. Assume now that the preferred shares were cumulative. Calculate EPS for 2016.

d. Assume the data from part (b), except that net income included a loss from discontinued operations, net of tax, of $432,000. Calculate EPS for 2016.

e. Why does the basic EPS denominator use the weighted average number of shares instead of just the ending balance of shares?

EXERCISE 19–4

Switzer Ltd. reported net income of $385,000 for the year ended December 31, 2015, and had 700,000 common shares outstanding throughout the fiscal year. On July 1, 2015, the company issued 3-year, 4% convertible bonds at par for $800,000. Each $1,000 bond is convertible into 100 common shares. Using the residual value method, the liability component's present value of cash flows for interest and principal at a market rate 6%

for non-convertible bonds was $757,232. The equity component was for the remainder of $42,768. Switzer Ltd.'s tax rate is 25%.

Required:

a. Calculate the 2015 earnings per share and complete the required disclosures, if any.

b. Calculate the earnings per share with required disclosures, assuming that net income was $280,000 in 2015.

EXERCISE 19-5

Below is data for Hurrington Inc.:

Net income	$4,500,000
$6, cumulative preferred shares, issued and outstanding 40,000 shares	4,000,000 $4,000,000
Common shares activity for 2016:	
Common shares, January 1, 2016	550,000
Mar 1 – issued	50,000
Jun 1 – repurchased	100,000
Aug 1 – 2-for-1 stock split	

Additional information:

All dividends were paid and no dividends were in arrears as at December 31, 2016. Year-end is December 31.

Required:

a. Calculate EPS for 2016.

b. Assume that dividends on preferred shares were two years in arrears, and that dividends were not declared or paid in 2016. Calculate the EPS for 2016.

c. Assume that preferred shares are non-cumulative and all dividends paid are up to date. Calculate the EPS for 2016.

d. Assume that preferred shares are non-cumulative and dividends were not paid in 2016. Calculate the EPS for 2016.

e. Discuss the effect that a stock split would have on the company's market price per share.

f. Discuss why the weighted average number of common shares must be adjusted for stock dividends and stock splits.

EXERCISE 19–6

Somos Novios Co. reported net income of $350,000 in 2016 and had 200,000 common shares outstanding throughout the year. Also outstanding throughout the year were 45,000 options for option holders to purchase common shares at $10 per share at any time. The average market price for the common shares during 2016 was $11 per share.

Required:

a. What type of capital structure does Somos Novios Co. have and why? What would be the required EPS disclosures for this company?

b. Calculate EPS for 2016, including the required disclosures.

c. Assume that the average market price for the common shares during 2016 was $9. Calculate EPS for 2016, including the required disclosures.

EXERCISE 19–7

Diamante Inc. purchased 20,000 call options during the year. The options give the company the right to buy back its own common shares for $10 each. The average market price was $13 per share.

Required:

a. Calculate the incremental shares outstanding for Diamante Inc.

b. Assume, instead, that Diamante Inc. wrote 20,000 put options that allow the option holder to sell common shares back to the company for $14 per share. Market price per share is $13. Calculate the incremental shares outstanding for Diamante Inc. How would the answer change if the exercise price was $12 instead of $14?

c. Assume that Diamante Inc. purchased 20,000 put options that allow the company to sell its own common shares for $11 each. Market price per share is $13. How should the options be treated when calculating diluted EPS?

EXERCISE 19-8

Etnik Ltd. reported net income for the year ended December 31, 2016, of $400,000 and there were 60,000 common shares outstanding during the entire year. Etnik also has two securities outstanding during 2016:

- 4%, convertible bonds, purchased at par for $800,000. Each $1,000 bond is convertible into 25 common shares.

- $20, cumulative, convertible $100 par value preferred shares; each preferred share is convertible into 10 common shares. Total paid: $50,000.

Both convertible securities were issued in 2012 and there were no conversions during 2016. Using the residual value method, the liability component's present value of cash flows for interest and principal at a market rate 5% for non-convertible bonds was $97,277. The equity component was for the remainder of $2,723. Etnik Ltd.'s tax rate is 24%.

Required:

a. Calculate EPS, including required disclosures, for 2016.

b. Assume that Etnik Ltd. also reported a discontinued operations gain before tax of $20,000. Calculate EPS, including required disclosures for 2016.

EXERCISE 19-9

Renato Inc. has the following information available as at December 31, 2016:

Net income	$350,000
Average market price of common shares during 2016 (adjusted for the stock dividend)	$ 18
Income tax rate for 2016	25%
6%, convertible bonds, issued at par on May 1, 2016, convertible into a total of 8,000 common shares	$ 80,000
Stock options for 10,000 shares, exercisable at the option price of $16 (adjusted for the stock dividend)	
$2, cumulative convertible preferred shares, 1,000 shares, convertible in 2018 into a total of 10,000 common shares (adjusted for the stock dividend)	

Common shares transactions for 2016:

January 1	Common shares outstanding	70,000
March 1	Issuance of common shares	30,000
June 1	10% stock dividend	10,000
November 1	Repurchase of common shares	(20,000)

Additional information:

Options and preferred shares were outstanding throughout all of 2016.

Required:

Calculate and disclose earnings per share for 2016. No dividends were in arrears and preferred dividends were paid in 2016. For simplicity, assume that the number of shares for the convertible bonds have already been adjusted for the stock dividend and ignore the requirement to record the debt and equity components of the bonds separately.

Chapter 20

Statement of Cash Flows

The Importance of Cash Flow – For Better, For Worse, For Richer, For Poorer...

A business is a lot like a marriage. It takes work to make it succeed. One of the keys to business success is managing and maintaining adequate cash flows. In the field of financial management, there is an old saying that *revenue is vanity, profits are sanity, but cash is king.* In other words, a firm's revenues and profits may look spectacular, but this does not guarantee there will be cash in the bank. Without cash, a business cannot pay its bills and it will ultimately not survive.

Let's take a look at the distinctions between revenue and profits, and cash, using a numeric example for a new business:

Income Statement		Cash Flows	
Revenue*	$1,000,000	Revenue (cash received)	$ 400,000
Cost of goods sold**	(500,000)	Cost of goods sold (paid in cash)	(300,000)
Gross profit	500,000	Net cash	100,000
Operating expenses***	200,000	Operating expenses (paid in cash)	90,000
Net income/net profit	$ 300,000	Net cash	$ 10,000

* Sales of $400,000 were paid in cash
** Purchases of $300,000 were paid in cash
*** Operating expenses of $90,000 were cash paid

Revenue is reported in the income statement as $1 million which is a sizeable amount, but only $400,000 was cash paid by customers. (The rest is reported as accounts receivable.) Gross profit is reported in the income statement as $500,000. This is also a respectable number, but only $100,000 translates into a positive cash flow, because some of the inventory purchases were paid in cash. (The rest of the inventory is reported as accounts payable.) The company must still pay some of its operating expenses, leaving only $10,000 cash in the bank.

When investors and creditors review the income statement, they will see $1 million in revenue with gross profits of one-half million or 50%, and a respectable net income of $300,000 or 30% of revenue. They could conclude that this looks pretty good for the first year of operations and incorrectly assume that the company now has $300,000 available to spend.

> However, lurking deeper in the financial statements is the cash position of the company–the amount of cash left over from this operating cycle. Sadly, there is only $10,000 cash in the bank, so the company cannot even pay its remaining accounts payable in the short term. So, how can management keep track of its cash?
>
> The statement of cash flows is the definitive financial statement to bridge the gaps between revenues and profits, and cash. Therefore, it is vital to understand the statement of cash flows.

Chapter 20 Learning Objectives

After completing this chapter, you should be able to:

LO 1: Describe the statement of cash flows (SCF) in accounting and business.

LO 2: Explain the purpose of the statement of cash flows and the two methods used.

LO 3: Describe the statement of cash flows using the *direct method* and explain the difference in format from the *indirect method*.

LO 4: Describe how the results from the statement of cash flows are interpreted.

LO 5: Describe the required disclosures for the statement of cash flows.

LO 6: Describe the types of analysis techniques used for the statement of cash flows.

LO 7: Review and understand a comprehensive example of an indirect and direct statement of cash flows that includes complex transactions from intermediate accounting courses.

LO 8: Discuss specific items that affect the statement of cash flows.

LO 9: Summarize the differences between ASPE and IFRS regarding reporting and disclosure requirements of the statement of cash flows.

Introduction

The statement of cash flows is a critical financial report used to assess a company's financial status and its current cash position, as uniquely demonstrated in the opening story about revenue and profits versus cash. As cash is generally viewed by many as the most critical asset to success, this chapter will focus on how to correctly prepare and interpret the statement of cash flows.

Chapter Organization

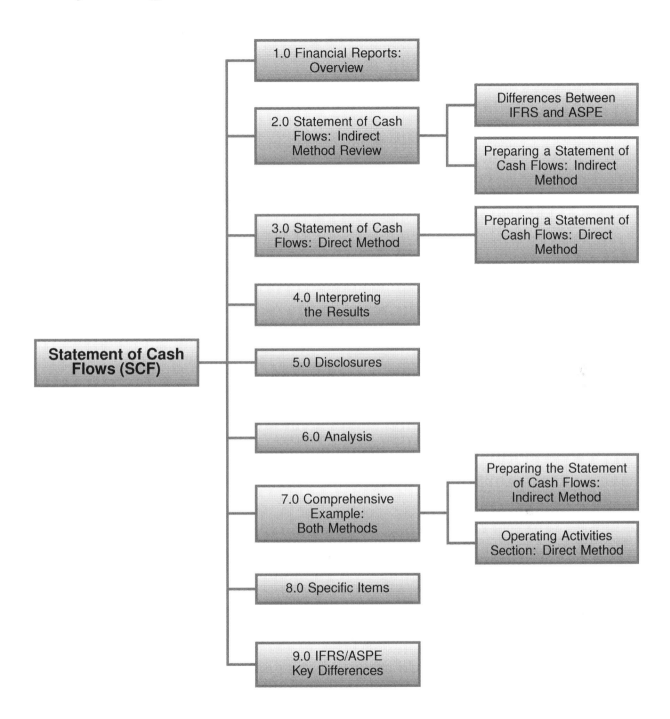

20.1 Financial Reports: Overview

As discussed in previous chapters, shareholders, potential investors, and creditors use published financial statements to assess a company's overall financial health. Recall how the five core financial statements link together into a cohesive network of financial information. One of these links is the match between the ending cash balance reported in the statement of cash flows (SCF) and the ending cash balance in the statement of financial position (IFRS), or balance sheet (ASPE).

For example, below is the statement of cash flows for the year ended December 31, 2015, and the statement of financial position (SFP) for Wellbourn Services Ltd. at December 31, 2015.

Wellbourn Services Ltd.
Statement of Financial Position
December 31, 2015

Assets		Liabilities	
Current assets		Current liabilities	
Cash	$135,500	Accounts payable	$ 77,500
Accounts receivable (net)	225,000	Accrued liabilities	225,000
Inventory	130,000	Total current liabilities	302,500
Total current assets	490,500	Bonds payable	160,000
Investments	100,000	Total liabilities	462,500
Property, plant, and equipment (net)	246,000	Equity	
Intangible assets	15,000	Share capital	210,000
Total assets	$851,500	Contributed surplus	25,000
		Retained earnings	105,500
		Accum. Other Comp. Income(AOCI)	48,500
		Total equity	389,000
		Liabilities and equity	$851,500

Wellbourn Services Ltd.
Statement of Cash Flows
For the year ended December 31, 2015

Cash flows from operating activities		
Cash received from sales	$ 50,000	
Cash paid for goods and services	(25,000)	
Cash paid to or on behalf of employees	(51,200)	
Net cash flows from operating activities		(26,200)
Cash flows from investing activities		
Purchase of equipment	(25,000)	
Net cash flows from investing activities		(25,000)
Cash flows from financing activities		
Dividends paid	(50,000)	
Issued bonds	160,000	
Net cash flows from financing activities		110,000
Net increase in cash		58,800
Cash balance, January 1		76,700
Cash balance, December 31		$135,500

Note how Wellbourn's ending cash balance of $135,500, from the statement of cash flows for the year ended December 31, matches the ending cash balance in the SFP on that date. This is a critical relationship between these two financial statements. The SFP provides information about a company's resources (assets) *at a specific point in time*, and whether these resources are financed mainly by debt (current and long-term liabilities) or equity (shareholders' equity). The statement of cash flows identifies how the company utilized its cash inflows and outflows *over the reporting period* and, ultimately, ends with its current cash and cash equivalents position at the statement of financial position date.

As well, since the statement of cash flows is prepared on a cash basis, it excludes non-cash accruals like depreciation and interest, making the statement of cash flows harder to manipulate than the other financial statements.

Since the statement of cash flows separates cash flows into those resulting from ongoing operating activities versus investing and financing activities, investors and creditors can quickly see where the main sources of cash originate. If cash inflows are originating mainly from operating activities, then this provides insight into a company's ability to generate sufficient cash to maintain its operations, pay its debts, and make new investments without the need for external financing. If cash sources originate more from investing activities, then this means that the company is likely selling off some of its assets to cover its obligations. This may be appropriate if these assets are idle and are no longer generating profit; otherwise it may suggest a downward spiral resulting in plummeting profits. If cash sources are originating mainly from financing activities, then the company is likely sourcing more cash from debt or from issuing shares (equity). Higher debt means that more cash reserves are needed to make the principal and interest payments. Higher equity means more shares issued and more dividends to be paid out, not to mention the dilution of existing shareholders investments. Either scenario is cause for concern for both shareholders and creditors.

Even if the majority of cash inflows are mainly from operating activities, if there is a large difference between net income and the total cash inflows from operating activities then that is a warning sign that shareholders and creditors should be digging deeper. This is because a company's quality of earnings, and hence its reliability, relates to how closely reported net income corresponds to net cash flows. For example, if reported net income is consistently close to, or less than, net cash operating activities, the company's earnings are considered to be high quality and, therefore, reliable. Conversely, if reported net income is significantly more than net cash flows from operating activities, then reported net income is not matched by a corresponding increase in cash, creating a need to investigate the cause. After reviewing the statement of cash flows and the balance sheet, the bottom line is: if debt is high and cash balances are low, the greater the risk of business failure.

This chapter will explain how to prepare the statement of cash flows using either the direct or indirect method, and how to interpret the results.

20.2 Statement of Cash Flows: Indirect Method Review

The statement of cash flows using the indirect method has been discussed in most introductory accounting courses. Since the statement of cash flows can be challenging, a review of the basic concepts is presented below.

20.2. Statement of Cash Flows: Indirect Method Review

The purpose of the statement of cash flows is to provide a means "to assess the enterprise's capacity to generate cash and cash equivalents, and to enable users to compare cash flows of different entities" (CPA Canada, 2016, Accounting, Part II, Section 1540.01 and IAS 7.4). This statement is an integral part of the financial statements for three reasons. First, this statement helps readers to understand where these cash flows in (out) originated from during the current year. This helps management, shareholders, and creditors to assess a company's liquidity, solvency, and financial flexibility. Second, these historic cash flows in (out) can be used to predict future company performance. Third, the statement of cash flows can shed light on a company's quality of earnings and if there may be a disconnect between reported earnings and net cash flows from operating activities, as explained earlier.

Two methods are used to prepare a statement of cash flows, namely the indirect method and the direct method. The indirect method was discussed in previous accounting courses and will be reviewed again in this chapter. The direct method introduced in this chapter may be new for many students. Both methods organize the reported cash flows into three activities: operating, investing, and financing. As discussed next, the difference between the two methods occurs only in the first section for operating activities.

The indirect method reports cash flows from operating activities into categories such as:

- Net income/loss is reported.
- A series of adjustments to net income/loss for non-cash items are reported in the income statement.
- Changes in each non-cash working capital account. The current portion of long-term debt, including lease obligations and dividends payable, are not considered to be working capital accounts. They are included with their respective account to which they relate. For example, the current portion of long-term debt or lease is included with its related long-term liability account. Dividends payable is included with its related retained earnings account.

The direct method reports cash flows from operating activities into categories based on the nature of the cash flows, such as:

- cash received for sales
- cash paid for goods and services
- cash paid to or on behalf of employees
- cash received and paid for interest
- cash received and paid for dividends

- cash paid for income taxes

The statement of cash flows above for Wellbourn Services Ltd. is an example of a statement using the direct method. Note that the operating section line items using the direct method are based on the nature of the cash flows, whereas the indirect method line items are based on their connections with the income statement and working capital accounts.

There are some similarities between the two methods. For instance, the net cash flows from operating activities is the same for both methods, and the investing and financing activities are identical for both methods as well.

Below is an example of the format using the indirect method. Note the connections to the other financial statements.

20.2. Statement of Cash Flows: Indirect Method Review

XYZ Company Ltd.
Statement of Cash Flows
For the year ended December 31, 2015

		Linkage to other financial statements:
Cash flows from operating activities		
Net income (loss)	$$$ or ($$$)	
Non-cash items (adjusted from net income)		
Depreciation, depletion and amortization expenses	+ $$$	
Losses (gains) from sale of non-current tangible assets	$$$ or ($$$)	line items from the income statement
Deferred income tax expense	+ $$$	
Impairment losses from inventory or receivables	+ $$$	
Investment income from investment in associate	($$$)	
Unrealized foreign exchange losses (gains)	$$$ or ($$$)	
Cash in (out) from operating working capital		
Decrease (increase) in trading investments	$$$ or ($$$)	
Decrease (increase) in accounts receivable	$$$ or ($$$)	
Decrease (increase) in notes receivable	$$$ or ($$$)	
Decrease (increase) in inventory	$$$ or ($$$)	
Decrease (increase) in prepaid expenses	$$$ or ($$$)	changes in current assets and current liabilities from the balance sheet
Decrease (increase) in accounts payable	$$$ or ($$$)	
Decrease (increase) in interest payable	$$$ or ($$$)	
Decrease (increase) in other liabilities	$$$ or ($$$)	
Decrease (increase) in income taxes payable	$$$ or ($$$)	
Decrease (increase) in unearned revenue	$$$ or ($$$)	
Net cash from operating activities	$$$ or ($$$)	
Cash flows from investing activities		
Sales proceeds or (purchase) of non-current investments	$$$ or ($$$)	
Sales proceeds or (purchase) of property, plant, and equipment	$$$ or ($$$)	changes in non-current assets accounts
Sales proceeds or (purchase) of intangible assets	$$$ or ($$$)	
Net cash from investing activities	$$$ or ($$$)	
Cash flows from financing activities		
Additions to or (repayment) of long-term debt	$$$ or ($$$)	changes in non-current liabilities and equity accounts (share capital and dividends)
Proceeds from shares issuance	$$$ or ($$$)	
Dividends paid	($$$)	
Net cash from financing activities	$$$ or ($$$)	
Net increase (decrease) in cash and cash equivalents	$$$ or ($$$)	← sum of the 3 sections above
Cash and cash equivalents, January 1	$$$	reconciles the net change with opening and closing cash and cash equivalent balances from the balance sheet
Cash and cash equivalents, December 31	$$$	

20.2.1 Differences Between IFRS and ASPE

There are differences in some of the reporting items between IFRS and ASPE. For example, ASPE has mandatory disclosures as follows:

- cash dividends received and interest received or paid if reported in net income – operating section
- interest or cash dividends debited to retained earnings – financing section
- Cash paid income taxes are often reported separately but it is not a reporting requirement.

For IFRS, there are policy choices that, once made, should be applied consistently:

- interest received – choice of operating or investing section
- interest paid – choice of operating or financing section
- dividends received – choice of operating or investing section
- dividends paid – choice of operating or financing section
- cash paid income taxes – separately reported

For simplicity, this chapter will use the following norms for both IFRS and ASPE:

- interest received – operating section
- interest paid – operating section
- dividends received – operating section
- dividends paid – financing section
- income taxes paid – separately reported

As illustrated above, when using the indirect method, the sum of the non-cash adjustments to net income and changes to non-cash working capital accounts result in the total cash flows in (out) from operating activities. The other two activities for investing and financing follow. Any non-cash transactions occurring in the investing or financing sections are not reported in a statement of cash flows. Instead, they are disclosed separately in the notes to the financial statements. Examples of non-cash transactions would be an exchange of property, plant, or equipment for common shares, or the conversion of convertible bonds payable to common shares and stock dividends. If the transaction is a mix of cash and non-cash, the cash-related portion of the transaction is reported in the statement of cash flows with a note in financial statements detailing the non-cash and cash elements. The final section of the statement reconciles the net change in cash flows of the three activities, with the opening and closing cash and cash equivalents balances taken from the balance sheet.

20.2.2 Preparing a Statement of Cash Flows: Indirect Method

Presented below is the balance sheet and income statement for Watson Ltd.

Watson Ltd.
Balance Sheet
as at December 31, 2015

	2015	2014
Assets		
Current assets		
Cash	$ 307,500	$ 250,000
Investments (Held for trading at fair value)	12,000	10,000
Accounts receivable (net)	249,510	165,000
Notes receivable	18,450	22,000
Inventory (at lower of FIFO cost and NRV)	708,970	650,000
Prepaid insurance expenses	18,450	15,000
Total current assets	1,314,880	1,112,000
Long term investments (Held to maturity at cost)	30,750	0
Property, plant, and equipment		
Land	92,250	92,250
Building (net)	232,000	325,000
	324,250	417,250
Intangible assets (net)	110,700	125,000
Total assets	$1,780,580	$1,654,250
Liabilities and Shareholders' Equity		
Current liabilities		
Accounts payable	$ 221,000	$ 78,000
Accrued interest payable	24,600	33,000
Income taxes payable	54,120	60,000
Unearned revenue	25,000	225,000
Current portion of long-term notes payable	60,000	45,000
Total current liabilities	384,720	441,000
Long-term notes payable (due June 30, 2020)	246,000	280,000
Total liabilities	630,720	721,000
Shareholders' equity		
Paid in capital		
Preferred, ($2, cumulative, participating – authorized issued and outstanding, 15,000 shares)	184,500	184,500
Common (authorized, 400,000 shares; issued and outstanding (O/S) 250,000 shares for 2015); (2014: 200,000 shares issued and O/S)	862,500	680,300
Contributed surplus	18,450	18,450
	1,065,450	883,250
Retained earnings	84,410	50,000
	1,149,860	933,250
Total liabilities and shareholders' equity	$1,780,580	$1,654,250

Watson Ltd.
Income Statement
For the year ended December 31, 2015

Sales	$3,500,000
Cost of goods sold	2,100,000
Gross profit	1,400,000
Operating expenses	
Salaries and benefits expense	800,000
Depreciation expense	43,000
Travel and entertainment expense	134,000
Advertising expense	35,000
Freight-out expenses	50,000
Supplies and postage expense	12,000
Telephone and internet expense	125,000
Legal and professional expenses	48,000
Insurance expense	50,000
	1,297,000
Income from operations	103,000
Other revenue and expenses	
Dividend income	3,000
Interest income from investments	2,000
Gain from sale of building	5,000
Interest expense	(3,000)
	7,000
Income from continuing operations before income tax	110,000
Income tax expense	33,000
Net income	$ 77,000

Additional information:

- The trading investment does not meet the criteria to be classified as a cash equivalent (see section 20.8 Specific Items for a discussion on cash equivalents) and no purchases or sales took place in the current year.

- An examination of the intangible assets sub-ledger revealed that a patent had been sold in the current year. The intangible assets have an indefinite life.

- No long-term investments were sold during the year.

- No buildings or patents were purchased during the year.

- There were no other additions to the long-term note payable during the year.

- Common shares were sold for cash. No other share transactions occurred during the year.

- Cash dividends were declared and paid.
- The note receivable maturity date is January 31, 2016, and was for a sale.

The statement of cash flows is the most complex statement to prepare. This is because preparation of the entries requires analysis of multiple accounts. Moreover, the transactions resulting in cash inflows are to be differentiated from the transactions resulting in cash outflows for each account. Preparing a statement of cash flows is made much easier if specific sequential steps are followed. Below is a summary of those steps.

- Complete the statement headings.

- Operating activities section – record the net income/(loss).

- Adjust out any non-cash line items reported in the income statement to remove them from the statement of cash flows. Examples of these are depreciation, amortization, and most gains or losses such as gains/losses from the sale of assets, gain/loss from redemption of debt, impairment losses, and fair value changes reported in net income.

- Record the description and change amount for each non-cash working capital account (current assets and current liabilities) except for the current portion of long-term debt line item since it is not a working capital account. Subtotal the operating activities section.

- Investment activities section – using T-accounts or other techniques, determine the change for each non-current (long-term) asset account. Analyze and determine the reason for the change(s). Record the reason and change amount(s) as cash inflows or outflows.

- Financing activities section – add back to long-term debt any current portion identified in the SFP/BS for both years, if any. Using T-accounts, or other techniques, determine the change for each non-current (long-term) liability and equity account. Analyze and determine the reason for the change(s). Record the reason and change amount(s) as cash inflows or outflows. One anomaly occurs with pension benefit liability. This liability is non-current, but it is not a financing activity as its nature is to benefit employees. For this reason, any change in funding for the pension liability, even though classified as non-current, is to be reported in operating activities.

- Subtotal the three sections. Record the opening and closing cash, including cash equivalents, if any. Reconcile the opening balance plus the subtotal from the three sections to the closing balance to ensure that the accounts balance correctly.

- Complete any required disclosures.

Here is a summary of the steps above, labelled with a key word or phrase for you to remember:

1. **Headings**
2. **Record net income/(loss)**
3. **Adjust out non-cash items**
4. **Current assets and current liabilities changes**
5. **Non-current asset accounts changes**
6. **Non-current liabilities and equity accounts changes**
7. **Subtotal and reconcile**
8. **Disclosures**

Applying the Steps:

Step 1. Headings:

Watson Ltd.
Statement of Cash Flows
For the year ended December 31, 2015

Cash flows from operating activities
   Net income (loss)
   Non-cash items (adjusted from net income):

Net cash from operating activities
Cash flows from investing activities

Net cash from investing activities
Cash flows from financing activities

Net cash from financing activities
Net increase (decrease) in cash
Cash, January 1
Cash, December 31

Step 2. Record net income/(loss):

As illustrated in step 3 below.

Step 3. Adjustments:

Watson Ltd.
Income Statement
For the year ended December 31, 2015

Sales	$3,500,000
Cost of goods sold	2,100,000
Gross profit	1,400,000
Operating expenses	
Salaries and benefits expense	800,000
Depreciation expense	43,000
Travel and entertainment expense	134,000
Advertising expense	35,000
Freight-out expenses	50,000
Supplies and postage expense	12,000
Telephone and internet expense	125,000
Legal and professional expenses	48,000
Insurance expense	50,000
	1,297,000
Income from operations	103,000
Other revenue and expenses	
Dividend income	3,000
Interest income from investments	2,000
Gain from sale of building	5,000
Interest expense	(3,000)
	7,000
Income from continuing operations before income tax	110,000
Income tax expense	33,000
Net income	$ 77,000

Watson Ltd.
Statement of Cash Flows
For the year ended December 31, 2015

Cash flows from operating activities	
Net income (loss)	$77,000
Non-cash items (adjusted from net income):	
Depreciation expense	43,000
Gain from sale of building	(5,000)

Enter the amount of the net income/(loss) as the first amount in the operating activities section. Next, review the income statement and select all the non-cash items. Look for items such as depreciation, depletion, amortization, and gains or losses (such as with the sale or disposal of assets). In this case, there are two non-cash items to adjust from net income. Record them as adjustments to net income in the statement of cash flows.

Step 4. Current assets and liabilities:

Calculate and record the change between the opening and closing balances for each non-cash working capital account as shown below (with the exception of the current portion of long-term notes payable, which is netted with its respective long-term notes payable account) as shown below:

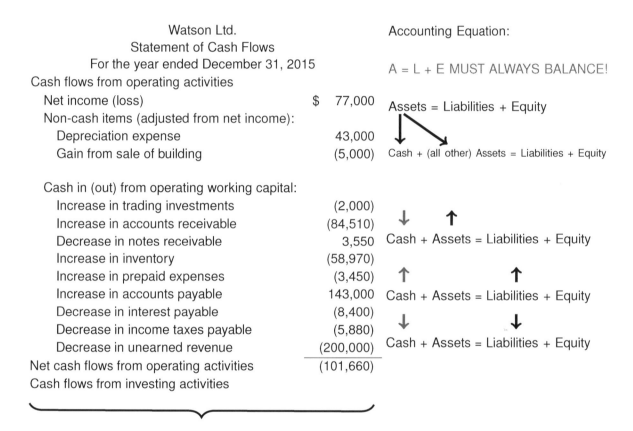

Cash inflows to the company are reported as positive numbers while cash outflows are reported as negative numbers using brackets. How does one determine if the amount is a positive or a negative number? A simple tool is to use the accounting equation to determine whether cash is increasing as a positive number or decreasing as a negative number. Recall the accounting equation:

$$\text{Assets} = \text{Liabilities} + \text{Equity}$$

This must always remain in balance. This equation can be applied when analyzing the various accounts to record the changes. For example, accounts receivable has increased from $165,000 to $249,510 for a total increase of $84,510. Using the accounting equation, this can be expressed as:

$$A = L + E$$

Expanding the equation a bit:

Cash + accounts receivable + all other assets = Liabilities + Equity

If accounts receivable INCREASES by $84,510, then this can be expressed as a black up-arrow above the account in the equation:

$$\uparrow$$
Cash + accounts receivable + all other assets = Liabilities + Equity

Holding everything in the equation constant, except for cash, if accounts receivable IN-CREASES, then the effect on the cash account must have a corresponding DECREASE in order to keep the equation balanced:

$$\downarrow \quad\quad \uparrow$$
Cash + accounts receivable + all other assets = Liabilities + Equity

If cash DECREASES, then it is a cash outflow and the number must be negative with brackets as shown in the statement above.

Conversely, when analyzing liability or equity accounts, the same technique can be used. For example, an increase in account payable (liability) of $143,000 will affect the equation as follows:

$$\uparrow$$
Cash + all other assets = Liabilities + Equity

Again, holding everything else constant except for cash, if accounts payable INCREASES as shown by the black up-arrow above, then cash must also INCREASE by a corresponding amount in order to keep the equation in balance.

$$\uparrow \quad\quad \uparrow$$
Cash + all other assets = Liabilities + Equity

If cash INCREASES, then it is a cash inflow and the number will be positive with no brackets as shown in the statement above.

Step 5. Non-current asset changes:

The next section to complete is the investing activities section. The analysis of all of the non-current assets accounts must also take into account whether there have been any current year purchases, disposals, or adjustments as part of the analysis. The use of T-accounts for this type of analysis provides a useful visual tool to help understand whether the changes that occurred in the account are cash inflows or outflows, as shown below.

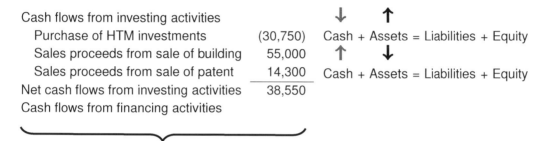

There are four non-current asset accounts: long-term investments, land, buildings, and intangible assets. The land account had no change, as there were no purchases or sales of land. Analyzing the investment account results in the following cash flows:

```
         Long-term investment
         —   |
         ??  |       = purchase of investment
         30,750 |
```

Additional information in note #3 above stated that there were no sales of long-term investments during the year, the entry would have been for a purchase:

	General Journal			
Date	Account/Explanation	PR	Debit	Credit
	Investment (HTM)............................		30,750	
	Cash			30,750

Cash paid for the investment was therefore $30,750.

Analysis of the buildings account is a bit more complex because of the effects of the contra account for accumulated depreciation. In this case, the buildings account, and its contra account, must be merged together since the SFP/BS reports only the net carrying amount. Analyzing the buildings account results in the following cash flows:

```
         Building (net of accum. depr.)
              325,000
                            43,000    current year accum. Depr.
                            50,000    = X sale of building
              232,000
```

Additional information note # 4 states that no buildings were purchased so the balancing amount of $50,000 must be for a sale of a building.

Since there was a gain from the sale of buildings, the entry would have been:

	General Journal			
Date	Account/Explanation	PR	Debit	Credit
	Cash.........................		55,000	
	Gain on sale of building..............			5,000
	Buildings (net).......................			50,000

Cash proceeds were therefore $55,000.

The sale of the patent is straightforward since there were no other sales, purchases, or amortization in the current year (as stated in steps 2 and 4).

Step 6. Non-current liabilities and equity changes:

Net cash flows from investing activities	38,550
Cash flows from financing activities	
Repayment of long-term note	(19,000)
Proceeds from shares issuance	182,200
Dividends paid	(42,590)
Net cash flows from financing activities	120,610

↑   ↑
Cash + Assets = Liabilities + Equity
↓   ↓
Cash + Assets = Liabilities + Equity

There are five long-term liability and equity accounts: long-term notes payable, preferred shares, common shares, contributed surplus, and retained earnings. The preferred shares and contributed surplus accounts had no changes to report. Note that just because an account balance has no change during the year, this does not necessarily mean that there were no transactions. For example, old shares could be retired and new shares issued for the same face value. These transactions would need to be reported in the cash flow statement, even though the net change in the account is zero.

Analyzing the long-term notes payable account results in the following cash flows:

Long-term note payable		
325,000		the sum of both the current and long-term amounts
	19,000 X = repayment	
306,000		the sum of both the current and long-term amounts

Since there were no other transactions stated in the additional information note # 5 above, the entry would have been:

General Journal				
Date	Account/Explanation	PR	Debit	Credit
	LT note payable............................		19,000	
	Cash			19,000

Cash paid was therefore $19,000.

Note how the current portion of long-term debt has been included in the analysis of the long-term note payable. The current portion line item is a reporting requirement relating to the principal amount owing one year after the reporting date. As it is not actually a working capital account, it is omitted from the operating section and included with its corresponding long-term liability account in the financing activities. For example, the opening balance of $325,000 above is the sum of the current portion ($45,000) plus the long-term portion ($280,000). Similarly, the ending balance of $306,000 is the sum of the current portion ($60,000) plus the long-term portion ($246,000).

The common shares and retained earnings accounts are straightforward and the analysis of each is shown below.

Common shares	
680,300	
182,200	X = share issuance
862,500	

Since there were no other transactions stated in the additional information note #6 above, the entry would have been:

	General Journal			
Date	Account/Explanation	PR	Debit	Credit
	Cash		182,200	
	Common shares			182,200

Cash received was therefore $182,200.

```
           Retained earnings
                      |  50,000
                      |  77,000      net income
           X = 42,590 |              dividends paid
                      |  84,410
```

The additional information note #7 stated that cash dividends were declared and paid, so the entry would have been:

	General Journal			
Date	Account/Explanation	PR	Debit	Credit
	Retained earnings		42,590	
	Cash			42,590

Cash paid was therefore $42,590.

Step 7. Subtotal and reconcile:

The three activities total a net increase in cash of $57,500. When added to the opening cash balance of $250,000, the resulting total of $307,500 is equal to the ending cash balance for the year ending December 31, 2015. This can be seen in the completed statement of cash flows following step 8.

Step 8. Required disclosures:

The statement of cash flows using the indirect method must separately disclose the cash flows for:

- Interest paid

- Interest received

- Dividends received (dividends paid are reported in the financing section)

- Cash paid income taxes

- Non-cash transactions that may have occurred in the current year.

If not too lengthy, these items can be disclosed in the notes or at the bottom of the statement. The cash received for dividend income and interest income was taken directly from the income statement since no accrual accounts exist on the balance sheet for these items. Cash paid for interest charges and income taxes are calculated on the basis of an analysis of their respective liability accounts from the balance sheet and expense accounts from the income statement.

Below is the completed statement of cash flows using the indirect method with required disclosures for Watson Ltd., for the year ending December 31, 2015:

Watson Ltd.
Statement of Cash Flows
For the year ended December 31, 2015

Cash flows from operating activities		
Net income (loss)		$ 77,000
Non-cash items (adjusted from net income):		
Depreciation expense		43,000
Gain from sale of building		(5,000)
Cash in (out) from operating working capital:		
Increase in trading investments	(2,000)	
Increase in accounts receivable	(84,510)	
Decrease in notes receivable	3,550	
Increase in inventory	(58,970)	
Increase in prepaid expenses	(3,450)	
Increase in accounts payable	143,000	
Decrease in interest payable	(8,400)	
Decrease in income taxes payable	(5,880)	
Decrease in unearned revenue	(200,000)	
Net cash flows from operating activities		(101,660)
Cash flows from investing activities		
Purchase of HTM investments	(30,750)	
Sales proceeds from sale of building	55,000	
Sales proceeds from sale of patent	14,300	
Net cash flows from investing activities		38,550
Cash flows from financing activities		
Repayment of long-term note	(19,000)	
Proceeds from shares issuance	182,200	
Dividends paid	(42,590)	
Net cash flows from financing activities		120,610
Net increase (decrease) in cash		57,500
Cash, January 1		250,000
Cash, December 31		$ 307,500

Disclosures:

Cash paid for income taxes	$38,880
(60,000 + 33,000 − 54,120)	
Cash paid for interest charges	11,400
(33,000 + 3,000 − 24,600)	
Cash received for dividend income	3,000

Note that the interest income of $2,000 reported in the income statement is not included in the additional disclosures shown above. This is because the interest income was accrued as an adjusting entry regarding the trading investments, so it was not a cash-received item.

20.3 Statement of Cash Flows: Direct Method

As mentioned earlier, the only difference when applying the direct method, as opposed to the indirect method, is in the operating activities section; the investing and financing sections are prepared exactly the same way. Typical reporting categories in the operating section for the direct method include:

- Cash received from sales
- Cash paid for goods and services
- Cash paid to, or on behalf of, employees
- Cash received for interest income
- Cash paid for interest
- Cash paid for income taxes
- Cash received for dividends

Recall that the categories above are based on the nature of the cash flows. Whereas with the indirect method the cash flows are based on the income statement and changes in each non-cash working capital (current) asset and liability account. Below is a comparison of the two methods:

Indirect Method		Direct Method	
Cash flows from operating activities:		Cash flows from operating activities:	
Net income	$$	Cash received from sales	$$
Adjust for non-cash items:		Cash paid for goods and services	($$)
Depreciation	$$	Cash paid to or on behalf of employees	($$)
Gain on sale of asset	($$)	Cash received for interest income	$$
Increase in accounts receivable	($$)	Cash paid for interest	($$)
Decrease in inventory	$$	Cash paid for income taxes	($$)
Increase in accounts payable	$$	Cash received for dividends	$$
Net cash flows from operating activities	$$	Net cash flows from operating activities	$$
(supplementary disclosures for interest, dividends and income tax are required)		(interest and income tax categories exist so no supplementary disclosures required)	

The direct method is straightforward due to the grouping of information by nature. This also makes interpretation of the statement more intuitive for stakeholders. However, companies record thousands of transactions every year and many of them do not involve cash. Since the accounting records are kept on an accrual basis, it can be a time-consuming and expensive task to separate and collect the cash-only data required for the direct method categories by nature. Also, providing disclosures about sensitive information, such as cash receipts from customers and cash payments to suppliers, is not in the best interest of the company. For these reasons, many companies prefer not to use the direct method. Instead, the indirect method may be easier to prepare because it collects much of its data directly from the existing income statement and balance sheet. However, it is less intuitive as evidenced by the accounts-based categories above.

20.3.1 Preparing a Statement of Cash Flows: Direct Method

As with the indirect method, preparing a statement of cash flows using the direct method is made much easier if specific steps are followed in sequence. Below is a summary of those steps to complete the operating section of the statement of cash flows using the direct method:

Direct Method Steps:

- Complete the headings and categories section of the operating activities. The example below includes seven categories based on the nature of the revenue and expenses.

- Create three additional columns: Income Statement (I/S) Accounts, Changes to Working Capital (WC), and Accounts and Net Cash Flows In (Out).

- Starting with the top of the income statement, record each income statement line item amount to the most appropriate direct method category in the I/S Accounts column. These would include sales, cost of goods sold, operating expenses, non-operating revenue, and various expenses items. Any non-cash items are also recorded, but only as memo items in the column. Examples of these would be depreciation, amortization, and most gains or losses. Such as gains or losses from the sale of assets, gains or losses from the redemption of debt, impairment losses, and from fair value changes reported in net income. The I/S Accounts column total must be equal to net income.

- Under the Changes to Working Capital Accounts, record the net change amount for each non-cash working capital account (current assets and current liabilities) except for the "current portion of long term debt" line item. As it is not a working capital account, it is added back to its corresponding long-term liability. Also, record as an adjustment any additional non-cash items found in net income arising from the analysis of the non-current asset, liability, and equity accounts. The obvious non-cash items were recorded as memo items only in Step 3, but other non-cash items can be uncovered when analyzing the non-current assets, liabilities, and equity accounts. When these are discovered, they must be recorded as an adjustment to net income in this column.

- Under the Net Cash Flows In (Out), calculate the net cash flows amount for each direct method category.

- Calculate the subtotal of the operating activities section and transfer the information to the statement of cash flows operating activities section.

Using the financial statements from Watson Ltd. presented previously, we will apply the steps below:

Applying the Steps:

Step 1 and Step 2. Headings, categories, and three additional columns.

Watson Ltd.
Operating Activities

	I/S Accounts	Changes to Working Capital Accounts	Net Cash Flow In (Out)
Cash flows from operating activities			
Cash received from sales			
Cash paid for goods and services			
Cash paid to employees			
Cash received for interest income			
Cash paid for interest			
Cash paid for income taxes			
Cash received for dividends			
Net cash flows from operating activities			

Step 3. Record each income statement line item amount to its respective direct method category under the I/S Accounts column (non-cash items are memo items only):

Step 4. Record the net change amount for each non-cash working capital account, except cash (also, record any adjustment amounts to net income resulting from analysis of non-current accounts):

Watson Ltd.
Income Statement
For the year ended December 31, 2015

Sales		$3,500,000	1
Cost of goods sold		2,100,000	2
Gross profit		1,400,000	
Operating expenses			
Salaries and benefits expense	800,000		3
Depreciation expense	43,000		4
Travel and entertainment expense	134,000		5
Advertising expense	35,000		6
Freight-out expenses	50,000		7
Supplies and postage expense	12,000		8
Telephone and internet expense	125,000		9
Legal and professional expenses	48,000		10
Insurance expense	50,000		11
		1,297,000	
Income from operations		103,000	
Other revenue and expenses			
Dividend income	3,000		12
Interest income from investments	2,000		13
Gain from sale of building	5,000		14
Interest expense	(3,000)		15
		7,000	
Income from continuing operations before income taxes		110,000	
Income tax expense		33,000	16
Net income		77,000	

Watson Ltd.
Operating Activities

	I/S Accounts	Changes to Working Capital Accounts	Net Cash Flow In (Out)
Cash flows from operating activities			
Cash received from sales	$ 3,500,000	1	
Cash paid for goods and services	(2,100,000)	2	
	(134,000)	5	
	(35,000)	6	
	(50,000)	7	
Cash paid to employees	(12,000)	8	
Cash received for interest income	(125,000)	9	
	(48,000)	10	
	(50,000)	11	
	(800,000)	3	
	2,000	13	
Cash paid for interest	(3,000)	15	
Cash paid for income taxes	(33,000)	16	
Cash received for dividends	3,000	12	
Memo items:			
Depreciation expense	(43,000)	4	
Gain on sale of building	5,000	14	
Net cash flows from operating activities			$ 77,000

Watson Ltd.
Balance Sheet
as at December 31, 2015

	2015	2014	Change	
Current assets				
Cash	$ 307,500	$ 250,000		
Investments – trading	12,000	10,000	$ (2,000)	17
Accounts receivable (net)	249,510	165,000	(84,510)	18
Notes receivable	18,450	22,000	3,550	19
Inventory	708,970	650,000	(58,970)	20
Prepaid insurance expenses	18,450	15,000	(3,450)	21
Total current assets	1,314,880	1,112,000		
Current liabilities				
Accounts payable	$ 221,000	$ 78,000	$ 143,000	22
Accrued interest payable	24,600	33,000	(8,400)	23
Income taxes payable	54,120	60,000	(5,880)	24
Unearned revenue	25,000	225,000	(200,000)	25
Current portion of long-term notes payable	60,000	45,000	N/A	
Total current liabilities	384,720	441,000	(216,660)	

Watson Ltd.
Operating Activities

Cash flows from operating activities	I/S Accounts		Changes to Working Capital Accounts		Net Cash Flow In (Out)
Cash received from sales	$ 3,500,000	1	$ (84,510)	18	
			3,550	19	
			(200,000)	25	
Cash paid for goods and services	(2,100,000)	2	(58,970)	20	
	(134,000)	5	(3,450)	21	
	(35,000)	6	143,000	22	
	(50,000)	7			
	(12,000)	8			
	(125,000)	9			
	(48,000)	10			
	(50,000)	11			
Cash paid to employees	(800,000)	3			
Cash received for interest income	2,000	13	(2,000)	17	
Cash paid for interest	(3,000)	15	(8,400)	23	
Cash paid for income taxes	(33,000)	16	(5,880)	24	
Cash received for dividends	3,000	12			
Memo items:					
Depreciation expense	(43,000)	4			
Gain on sale of building	5,000	14			
Net cash flows from operating activities	$ 77,000		$ (216,660)		

332 ■ Statement of Cash Flows

Note how items 13 and 17 on the operating activities statement, regarding the trading investments, cancel each other out. This is because the interest income from the trading investment was accrued and not actually received in cash.

In this simple example, no adjustments to net income resulting from analysis of non-current assets, liabilities, and equity are identified. However, this situation will be illustrated in the comprehensive example later in this chapter.

The change in each working capital account can be a positive or a negative cash flow (using brackets). To ensure that the cash flow is correctly identified as positive or negative, apply the principles using the accounting equation explained earlier:

$$\text{Cash} + \text{Assets} = \text{Liabilities} + \text{Equity}$$

Refer to the earlier section in this chapter for more details regarding this technique.

Step 5 and Step 6. Calculate the net cash flows amount for each category and calculate the subtotal for the operating activities section (transfer the information to the statement of cash flows):

Watson Ltd.
Operating Activities

Cash flows from operating activities	I/S Accounts		Changes to Working Capital Accounts		Net Cash Flow In (Out)
Cash received from sales	$ 3,500,000	1	$ (84,510)	18	
			3,550	19	
			(200,000)	25	$ 3,219,040
Cash paid for goods and services	(2,100,000)	2	(58,970)	20	
	(134,000)	5	(3,450)	21	
	(35,000)	6	143,000	22	
	(50,000)	7			
	(12,000)	8			
	(125,000)	9			
	(48,000)	10			
	(50,000)	11			(2,473,420)
Cash paid to employees	(800,000)	3			(800,000)
Cash received for interest income	2,000	13	(2,000)	17	0
Cash paid for interest	(3,000)	15	(8,400)	23	(11,400)
Cash paid for income taxes	(33,000)	16	(5,880)	24	(38,880)
Cash received for dividends	3,000	12			3,000
Memo items:					
Depreciation expense	(43,000)	4			
Gain on sale of building	5,000	14			
Net cash flows from operating activities	$ 77,000		$ (216,660)		$ (101,660)

20.3. Statement of Cash Flows: Direct Method

A comparison of the two methods, for the operating activities section for Watson Ltd., is presented below:

Watson Ltd.
Operating Activities – Indirect Method

Cash flows from operating activities		
Net income (loss)		$ 77,000
Non-cash items (adjusted from net income):		
Depreciation expense		43,000
Gain from sale of building		(5,000)
Cash in (out) from operating working capital:		
Increase in trading investments		(2,000)
Increase in accounts receivable		(84,510)
Decrease in notes receivable		3,550
Increase in inventory		(58,970)
Increase in prepaid expenses		(3,450)
Increase in accounts payable		143,000
Decrease in interest payable		(8,400)
Decrease in income taxes payable		(5,880)
Decrease in unearned revenue		(200,000)
Net cash flows from operating activities		$(101,660)

Watson Ltd.
Operating Activities – Direct Method

Cash flows from operating activities	
Cash received from sales	$ 3,219,040
Cash paid for goods and services	(2,473,420)
Cash paid to employees	(800,000)
Cash received for interest income	0
Cash paid for interest	(11,400)
Cash paid for income taxes	(38,880)
Cash received for dividends	3,000
Net cash flows from operating activities	$ (101,660)

The cash received for interest income of zero dollars was included in the direct method example for illustrative purposes only. This line item would normally be removed when preparing the actual statement of cash flows. Also, additional disclosures for interest, dividends, and income taxes discussed previously are required when using the indirect method. With the direct method, these additional disclosures are not required as they are already reported as cash-paid line items within the statement (as shown in the example above).

20.4 Interpreting the Results

This section will focus on interpreting the results using the indirect method statement of cash flows, as it is the method most widely used in business today. For convenience, the entire statement of cash flows indirect method for Watson Ltd. is reproduced below.

Watson Ltd.
Statement of Cash Flows – Indirect Method
For the year ended December 31, 2015

Cash flows from operating activities	
Net income (loss)	$ 77,000
Non-cash items (adjusted from net income):	
Depreciation expense	43,000
Gain from sale of building	(5,000)
Cash in (out) from operating working capital:	
Increase in trading investments	(2,000)
Increase in accounts receivable	(84,510)
Decrease in notes receivable	3,550
Increase in inventory	(58,970)
Increase in prepaid expenses	(3,450)
Increase in accounts payable	143,000
Decrease in interest payable	(8,400)
Decrease in income taxes payable	(5,880)
Decrease in unearned revenue	(200,000)
Net cash flows from operating activities	(101,660)
Cash flows from investing activities	
Purchase of HTM investments	(30,750)
Sales proceeds from sale of building	55,000
Sales proceeds from sale of patent	14,300
Net cash flows from investing activities	38,550
Cash flows from financing activities	
Repayment of long-term note	(19,000)
Proceeds from shares issuance	182,200
Dividends paid	(42,590)
Net cash flows from financing activities	120,610
Net increase (decrease) in cash	57,500
Cash, January 1	250,000
Cash, December 31	$ 307,500

Disclosures:	
Cash paid for income taxes	$38,880
(60,000 + 33,000 − 54,120)	
Cash paid for interest charges	11,400
(33,000 + 3,000 − 24,600)	
Cash received for dividend income	3,000

The cash balance shows an increase of $57,500 for the current year. On the surface, a hasty conclusion could be drawn that all is well with Watson Ltd., as their bottom line is a positive cash flow. However, there is, in fact, trouble ahead for this company. We know this because the operating activities section, which represents the reason for being in business, is in a negative cash flow position. In other words, a company is expected to earn a profit, resulting in positive cash flows reflected in the operating activities section. However, in this case there is a negative cash flow of $101,660 from operating activities. Why?

For Watson Ltd., both the accounts receivable and inventory have increased, resulting in a net decrease in cash of $143,480. An increase in accounts receivable may mean that sales have occurred but the collections are not keeping pace with the sales on account. An increase in inventory may be because there have not been enough sales in the current year to cycle the inventory from current asset, to sales/profit, and, ultimately, to cash. However, the risk of holding large amounts of inventory is the increased possibility that the inventory will become obsolete, damaged, and unsellable.

In this example, an additional reason for decreased net cash from operating activities is due to a decrease in unearned revenue. Recall that unearned revenue is cash received from customers in advance of the company providing the goods and services. In this case, the cash would have been reported as a positive cash flow in the operating activities section in the previous reporting period when the cash was actually received. At that time, the cash generated from operating activities would have increased by the amount of cash received for the unearned revenue. The entry upon receipt of the cash would have been:

	General Journal			
Date	Account/Explanation	PR	Debit	Credit
	Cash		225,000	
	Unearned revenue.....................			225,000

When the company finally provides the goods and services to the customer, the net income reported at the top of the operating activities section will reflect the portion of the unearned revenue that has now been earned. However, the company did not obtain actual cash for this revenue in this reporting period since the cash was received in the prior reporting period. Keep in mind that unearned revenue is not normally an obligation that must be paid in cash to the customer, and getting customers to pay in advance is always a good cash management strategy. That said, once the goods and services are provided to the customer, the obligation ceases.

Listed in the investing activities section, there was a sale of a building and a purchase of a long-term investment in Held to Maturity (HTM) Investments. The sales proceeds from the building may have been partially invested in the HTM to make a return on the cash proceeds until it can be used in the future for its intended purpose. However, more analysis would be required to confirm whether or not this was the case. The sale of the patent also generated a positive cash flow. There was no gain on the sale of the patent reported in the income statement, so the sales proceeds did not exceed its carrying value at the time it was sold. Ideally, the patent would not have been sold in a panic, in an effort to raise immediate additional cash at the expense of future cash flows it could have generated.

Looking at the financing activities section, it is clear that the majority of cash inflows for this reporting period resulted from the issuance of additional common shares worth $182,200. This represents an increase in the share capital of more than 25%. Increased shares will have a negative impact on the earnings per share, and possibly the market price as well, which may give investors pause. The shareholders were also paid dividends of $42,590, but this amount only just covers the preferred shareholders dividend of $30,000 (15,000 × $2) plus its share of the participating dividend. This leaves very little dividends for the common shareholders, a situation likely to cause concern amongst the common shareholder investors, made worse by the dilution of their holdings due to the large issuance of additional shares.

When looking at the opening and closing cash balances for Watson Ltd., they seem like sizeable amounts. However, we must look at where the cash originated from. In this case, the $250,000 opening balance was due almost entirely to the $225,000 unearned revenue received in advance, which is not an ongoing source of capital. The ending cash balance of $307,500 was due to the issuance of additional share capital of $182,200 (a one-time transaction), plus an increase in accounts payable of $143,000 that will eventually have to be repaid. Consider also that during the year, the cash from the unearned revenues was being consumed and the issuance of the additional capital had not yet occurred. It would be no surprise, then, if cash at the mid-year point was insufficient to cover even the current liabilities, hence the increase in accounts payable and, ultimately, the issuance of additional capital shares.

In summary, Watson Ltd. is currently unable to generate positive cash flows from its operating activities. The unearned revenue of $225,000 at the start of the year added some needed cash early on, but this reserve was depleted by the end of the reporting year. In the meantime, without a significant change in how the company manages its inventory and receivables, Watson Ltd. may continue to experience a shortage of cash from its operating activities. To compensate, it may continue to sell off assets, issue more shares, or incur more long-term debt in order to obtain the needed cash. In any case, these sources will eventually dry up when investors are no longer willing to invest, creditors are no longer willing to extend loans, and no assets remain worth selling. Watson Ltd.'s current negative cash position from operating activities is unsustainable and must be turned around quickly in order for the company to remain a going concern.

20.5 Disclosures

Throughout this chapter, various disclosures have been discussed. Below is a summary of the main required disclosures:

- The change in cash (including cash equivalents) must be explained.
- The components of cash and cash equivalents must be disclosed as well as the company policy used to determine its composition.
- Cash flows are to be classified as either from operating, investing, or financing activities.
- Cash flows from operating activities can be reported using the indirect or direct method.
- Cash flows from interest received or paid, dividends received or paid (IFRS and ASPE), and income taxes paid (IFRS) are to be reported separately, either within the statement of cash flows or as a supplemental disclosure.
- Major classes of cash flows in and out within the investing and financing section are to be separately reported.
- Non-cash transactions are excluded from the statement of cash flows but must be disclosed as a supplemental disclosure.

20.6 Analysis

Ratio Analysis – Overview

Ratio analysis occurs when relationships between selected financial data (presented in the numerator and denominator of the formula) provide key information about a company. Ratios from current year financial statements alone may not be as useful as when they are compared with benchmark ratios. Examples of benchmark ratios are a company's own historical ratio trends, future ratio targets set by management as part of its strategic plan, industry sector ratios from the sector that the company operates in, or ratios from competitors, if obtainable.

Care must be taken when interpreting ratios because companies within an industry sector may use different accounting policies, which affect the comparison of ratios. In the end, ratios are based on a company's current and past performance and are merely indicators.

Further investigation is needed to gather more business intelligence about the reasons why certain variances in the ratios occur.

Statement of Cash Flows Analysis

Not all companies who report profits are financially stable. This is because profits do not necessarily translate to cash. Looking at the statement of cash flows for Watson Ltd. above, we see that it reported a $77,000 net income (profit), but it is currently experiencing significant negative cash flows from its operating activities.

As previously discussed, one of the most important aspects of the statement of cash flows is the cash flows generated from the operating activities, as this reflects the business's day-to-day operations. If sufficient cash is generated from operating activities, then the company will not have to increase its debt, issue shares, or sell off useful assets to pay its bills. However, as we saw the opposite was true for Watson Ltd. as it increased its short-term debt (accounts payable), sold off a building, and issued 25% more common shares.

Another critical aspect is the sustainability of positive cash flows from operating activities. Perhaps Watson Ltd.'s negative cash flow from operating activities will turn itself around in the next reporting period, as this would be the company's best hope. Other companies who experience positive cash flows from operations must also ensure that it is sustainable and can be repeated consistently in the future.

In summary, it is critical to monitor the trends regarding cash flows over time. Without benchmarks, such as historical trends or industry standards, ratio analysis is not as useful. If trends are tracked, ratio analysis can be a powerful tool to evaluate a company's cash flows.

Statement of Cash Flows Ratios

Below are some of the cash flows ratios currently used in business.

Ratio	Formula	Purpose
Liquidity ratios – ability to pay short term obligations		
Current cash debt coverage ratio	$\dfrac{\text{Net cash flow from operating activities}}{\text{Average current liabilities}}$	ability to pay short term debt from its day-to day operations. A ratio of 1:1 is reasonable.
Financial flexibility – ability to react to unexpected expenses and investment opportunities		
Cash debt coverage ratio	$\dfrac{\text{Net cash flow from operating activities}}{\text{Average total liabilities}}$	the ability to pay debt from net cash from operating activities

For Watson Ltd., since the net cash flow from operating activities is a loss of $101,660, the two ratios above would be unfavourable. For example, the current cash debt coverage ratio would be a negative 26.4% ($101,660 loss ÷ $384,720) and the cash debt coverage ratio would be a negative 16.1% ($101,660 loss ÷ $630,720). Without the historical trends for these ratios, it is impossible to say if Watson Ltd. can turn things around or not.

Free Cash Flow (FCF) Analysis

Another way to assess a company's cash flow liquidity is the free cash flow. Free cash flow is the cash flow remaining from operating activities after deducting cash spent on capital expenditures, such as purchasing property, plant and equipment. Some companies also deduct cash paid dividends. The remaining cash flow represents cash available to the company to do other things such as expand its operations, pay off long-term debt or reduce the number of outstanding shares. Below is the calculation using the data from Watson Ltd.'s statement of cash flows.

Watson Ltd.
Free Cash Flow
December 31, 2015

Cash flow provided by operating activities	$(101,660)
Less capital expenditures	0
Dividends	(42,590)
Free cash flow	$(144,250)

It is no surprise that Watson Ltd. has no free cash flow and no financial flexibility, since its operating activities are in a negative position. Watson Ltd. met its current year dividend cash requirements by selling more common shares to raise additional cash, thus diluting the shareholders' investment position. When calculating the free cash flow, the capital expenditures amount should be limited to those that relate to daily operations that are intended to sustain ongoing operations, such as PPE expenditures. Meaning, capital expenditures purchased as investments are usually excluded from the free cash flow analysis.

20.7 Comprehensive Example: Both Methods

The example below will incorporate some different transactions that were discussed earlier in this course, or the prerequisite courses. These include more complex transactions such as long-term investments such as Available for Sale investments, long-term liabilities such as accrued pension liabilities, deferred income taxes payable or bonds issued at a discount and equity items such as convertible securities, stock options and reacquisition and retirement of shares.

Below are three financial statements for Ace Ltd., as on December 31, 2015.

Ace Ltd.
Statement of Income
For the year ended December 31, 2015

Sales		$1,400,000
Cost of golds sold		630,000
Gross profit		770,000
Operating expenses		
Depreciation expense	$ 43,000	
Salaries and benefits expense	120,000	
Utilities expenses	50,000	
Travel expenses	26,000	
Operating expenses, including rent expense	80,000	319,000
Income from operations		451,000
Other (non-operating) revenue and expenses:		
Investment income	3,000	
Interest expense	(30,000)	
Gain on sale of AFS investment	3,000	
Loss on sale of machinery	(15,000)	(39,000)
Income before taxes		412,000
Income tax expense	79,000	
Deferred tax recovery	(12,000)	67,000
Net income		$ 345,000

Ace Ltd.
Statement of Comprehensive Income
For the year ended December 31, 2015

Net income	$345,000
Other comprehensive income	
Items that may be reclassified subsequently to net income or loss:	
Increase in fair value, AFS investments (OCI)*	44,000
Removal of unrealized gain on sale of AFS investment*	(3,000)
Actuarial loss on defined benefit pension plan*	(20,000)
Comprehensive income	366,000

* In the interest of simplicity, income taxes have been ignored.

20.7. Comprehensive Example: Both Methods

Ace Ltd.
Balance Sheet
as at December 31, 2015

	2015	2014
Assets		
Current assets		
Cash	$ 50,000	$ 30,000
Accounts receivable (net)	110,000	145,000
Inventory	175,000	200,000
Prepaid insurance expenses	6,000	–
Total current assets	341,000	375,000
Investments – available for sale (OCI)	150,000	80,000
Property, plant, and equipment		
Land	380,000	200,000
Machinery	1,700,000	1,500,000
Accumulated depreciation	(363,000)	(400,000)
Total property, plant, and equipment	1,717,000	1,300,000
Goodwill	300,000	300,000
Total assets	$2,508,000	$2,055,000
Liabilities and Shareholders' Equity		
Current liabilities		
Accounts payable	$ 200,000	$ 300,000
Salaries payable	128,000	125,000
Income taxes payable	115,000	120,000
Total current liabilities	443,000	545,000
Long-term liabilities		
6%, convertible bonds payable, net	–	750,000
7.2% bonds payable, net	453,000	–
Deferred income tax payable	38,000	50,000
Accrued pension benefit liability	85,000	75,000
Total long-term liabilities	576,000	875,000
Total liabilities	1,019,000	1,420,000
Shareholders' Equity		
Paid-in capital		
Common shares	1,210,000	500,000
Contributed capital, bond conversion rights	–	35,000
Contributed capital, stock options	62,000	50,000
Total paid-in capital	1,272,000	585,000
Retained earnings	192,000	46,000
Accumulated Other Comprehensive Income, pension	(40,000)	(20,000)
Accumulated Other Comprehensive Income, investments	65,000	24,000
Total shareholders' equity	1,489,000	635,000
Total liabilities and shareholders' equity	$2,508,000	$2,055,000

Additional information:

- Issued additional 7.2%, $500,000, 10-year bonds payable for cash of $452,000.

- Cash dividends were declared and paid.

- An AFS investment (OCI) was sold for $50,000 cash on January 2, 2015. Its original cost was $47,000 and had a carrying value of $50,000 (fair value) at the time of the sale. All unrealized gains previously recorded to OCI/AOCI for the sold investment were reclassified to net income. AFS investments of $76,000 were purchased for cash.

- There is a stock option plan for senior executives. In 2015, stock options with a book value of $15,000 were exchanged for common shares, along with $40,000 in cash. The remaining increase in the stock options account is due to the compensation expense included in the income statement as salaries and benefits.

- The six percent convertible bond payable was converted into common shares at the beginning of 2015.

- Land was acquired for cash.

- Machinery, with an original cost of $100,000 and a net book value of $20,000, was sold at a loss of $15,000. Additional machinery for other activities was acquired in exchange for common shares.

- Common shares with an average original issue price of $430,000 were retired for $485,000.

- The accrued pension benefit liability was increased by $20,000, due to an actuarial revaluation, and $10,000, because of the difference between funding and the pension expense.

- The company's policy is to report dividends received, interest received, and interest paid as operating activities, and dividends paid as financing activities.

20.7.1 Preparing the Statement of Cash Flows: Indirect Method

Indirect Method Steps:

1. Headings
2. Record net income/(loss)
3. Adjust out non-cash items from the income statement
4. Current assets and current liabilities changes
5. Non-current asset accounts changes
6. Non-current liabilities and equity accounts changes
7. Subtotal and reconcile
8. Disclosures

Following the steps listed above, prepare a statement of cash flows using the indirect method. Details are provided below for each step, followed by the completed statement of cash flows.

Notes to the Solutions and Details About Calculations:

Step 1. Headings:

Insert headings and subheadings, leaving spaces within each section to record the relevant line items resulting from the subsequent steps.

Step 2. Record net income/(loss):

Net income (and not comprehensive income) is the starting point for a statement of cash flows with the indirect method. Comprehensive income will become relevant if any of the AFS investments are actually sold. Recall that upon sale, any unrealized gains or losses previously recorded to OCI will be realized and moved to retained earnings from AOCI.

Step 3. Adjustments:

When reviewing the income statement, non-cash items for depreciation, loss on sale of machinery, and realized gain on sale of AFS investments are reported. However, since this is a more complex example, there could be other hidden non-cash items that will become apparent when analyzing the non-current asset, liability, and equity accounts. Leave some space in this section in case other non-cash items are discovered in the accounts analysis.

Step 4. Current assets and liabilities:

Continue to use the accounting equation, A = L + E, to determine if the change amount for each non-cash working capital account is a positive number or a negative number (requiring a bracket).

Step 5. Non-current asset changes:

Analyze all the non-current asset accounts to determine the reasons for the changes in the accounts. Additional information taken from the various accounting records has been provided. Items 3, 6, and 7 pertain to non-current assets so this information will be incorporated into the step 5 analysis.

    a. AFS investment (OCI):

Long-term AFS investments		
80,000		
	50,000	sale of investment
76,000		purchase of AFS investment
X = 44,000		increase in fair value (OCI)
150,000		

AOCI, investments		
	24,000	
	44,000	increase in fair value (OCI)
3,000		remove realized gain on sale
	65,000	

Additional information in note # 3 states that $50,000 of AFS investments (fair value = carrying value) was sold for $50,000 cash, so there's no gain or loss on the actual sale. However, the original cost was $47,000, so there is an accumulated unrealized gain of $3,000 ($50,000 fair value − $47,000 original cost) for the sold investment that was reclassified from OCI/AOCI to net income. This is confirmed by reviewing the income statement. This non-cash entry has already been adjusted in operating activities in Step 3, so no further action is required.

Entry for the sale:

General Journal				
Date	Account/Explanation	PR	Debit	Credit
	Cash		50,000	
	Investment, AFS			50,000

Entry to reclassify:

General Journal				
Date	Account/Explanation	PR	Debit	Credit
	Realized gain on sale (OCI/AOCI)		3,000	
	Gain on sale of AFS investment			3,000

Note # 3 also states that there was also a cash paid investment of $76,000.

The T-account requires another debit for $44,000 to balance properly. This must be for fair value changes and that is confirmed by reviewing the comprehensive income statement. This non-cash entry is not included in the income statement so no further action is necessary.

Analysis result: enter the cash amounts for the sale ($50,000) and the purchase of AFS investments ($76,000) highlighted in red in the investing activities section of the statement of cash flows.

b. Land:

```
          Land
        200,000
  X =   180,000          purchase of land
        ───────
        380,000
```

Additional information in note # 6 states that land was purchased for cash.

There is no other information about the land account so the balancing amount of $180,000 must be the purchase price of the land.

Entry for the purchase:

General Journal				
Date	Account/Explanation	PR	Debit	Credit
	Land		180,000	
	Cash			180,000

Analysis result: enter the cash amount for the purchase of land ($180,000) highlighted in red in the investing activities section of the statement of cash flows.

c. Machinery:

```
           Machinery
         1,500,000
                         100,000   sale of machinery
         X = 300,000               purchase of machinery for shares
         1,700,000
```

```
     Accumulated depreciation
                         400,000
          80,000
                          43,000   sale of machinery
                                   X = current year depreciation
                         363,000
```

Additional information note # 7 states that there was a loss from the sale of machinery of $15,000 that originally cost $100,000. The carrying value at the time of the sale was $20,000. The cash amount for the sale would therefore be $5,000 ($20,000 carrying value − $15,000 loss). The accumulated depreciation for the sold machinery would be $80,000 ($100,000 original cost − $20,000 carrying cost).

Entry for the sale:

Date	Account/Explanation	PR	Debit	Credit
	Cash		5,000	
	Loss on sale of machinery		15,000	
	Accumulated depreciation		80,000	
	Machinery			100,000

General Journal

Accumulated depreciation requires another $43,000 credit to balance properly. This must be for the current year depreciation expense and that is confirmed by reviewing the income statement. This non-cash entry has already been adjusted in operating activities in Step 3, so no further action is required.

Note # 7 also stated that additional machinery was purchased in exchange for common shares. The balancing amount of $300,000 would account for this non-cash transaction which is not included in the SCF except as a supplemental disclosure required for non-cash items.

Analysis result: enter the cash amount for the sale of machinery ($5,000) highlighted in red in the investing activities section of the statement of cash flows.

Step 6. Non-current liabilities and equity changes:

Analyze all the non-current liability and equity accounts to determine the reasons for the changes in the accounts. Additional information taken from the various accounting records has been provided. Items 1, 2, 4, 5, 8, and 9 pertain to non-current liabilities and equity so this information will be incorporated into the step 6 analysis.

d. 6% bonds payable:

```
              6% Convertible bonds payable
                              |  750,000
                              |
       X = 750,000            |            conversion of bonds to shares
  _____|_____
                              |   —
                              |
```

Additional information note # 5 states that these bonds were converted into common shares in 2015. The equity portion for the conversion rights of $35,000 will also be removed from the contributed surplus account.

Entry for the conversion:

	General Journal			
Date	Account/Explanation	PR	Debit	Credit
	6% bond payable..........................		750,000	
	Contributed surplus, conversion rights.......		35,000	
	Common shares........................			785,000

This is a non-cash entry which is not included in the SCF except as a supplemental disclosure required for non-cash items.

Analysis result: no cash entries to record.

e. 7.2% bonds payable:

```
              7.2% Bonds payable
                              |    —
                              |
                              |  452,000   issuance of bonds
                              |    1,000   X = amortized discount
                              |  _____
                              |  453,000
```

Additional information note # 1 states that bonds with a face value of $500,000 were issued for cash of $452,000. The discount amount would be $48,000 ($500,000 − $452,000) which will be amortized.

Entry for the bond issuance:

	General Journal			
Date	Account/Explanation	PR	Debit	Credit
	Cash.....................................		452,000	
	7.2% bonds payable, net of discount.....			452,000

348 ■ Statement of Cash Flows

> The balancing amount of $1,000 must therefore be for amortization of the discount which will be included in net income as part of interest expense of $30,000. This $1,000 non-cash amount should be adjusted from net income in operating activities because it was not done in Step 3.

Analysis result: enter the cash amount for the bond issuance ($452,000) and adjust the $1,000 amortization expense highlighted in red in the financing activities section of the statement of cash flows.

f. Deferred income tax payable:

Deferred Income Tax Payable	
	50,000
X = 12,000	reduction of taxes
	38,000

There is no additional information regarding this account. The balancing amount of $12,000 must be for a deferred income tax recovery which is confirmed by a review of the income statement. This non-cash entry was included in net income but not adjusted in Step 3, so it should be adjusted in the operating section now.

Analysis result: enter the non-cash amount for the deferred tax recovery ($12,000) highlighted in red in the operating activities section as an adjustment to net income.

g. Accrued pension benefit liability:

Accrued Pension Benefit Liability	
	75,000
	20,000 actuarial revaluation
X = 10,000	funding amount greater than pension expense
	85,000

AOCI, Pension Benefits	
20,000	
20,000	actuarial revaluation
40,000	

Additional information note # 9 states that this liability was increased by $20,000 due to an actuarial revaluation. This non-cash adjusting entry to OCI/AOCI was not included in net income so it will be omitted from the SCF.

Note # 9 also states that the remaining difference was due to the difference between the funding (cash paid) and the pension expense.

Entries for pension benefit:

		General Journal			
Date	Account/Explanation		PR	Debit	Credit
	Pension expense............................			??	
	Accrued pension liability..................				??
	Accrued pension liability.....................			??	
	Cash......................................				?? (greater by $10,000)

The pension expense amount is not known but the funding (cash) amount is known to be greater than the pension expense by $10,000. Even though this is a non-current liability, it's purpose is to benefit employees and not as a source of financing cash flow. For this reason, it is more appropriate to record this non-current liability reduction as an operating activity instead of a financing activity.

Analysis result: enter the cash difference amount ($10,000) highlighted in red as an operating activity item for the reduction in the pension liability.

h. Common shares:

```
           Common shares
                    |  500,000
                    |  300,000   machinery in exchange for shares
                    |  785,000   6% bonds converted
         430,000    |            shares repurchase
                    |   55,000   options exercise for shares
                    |1,210,000
```

```
   Contributed Surplus – Stock Options
                    |   50,000
         15,000     |            options exercised for shares
                    |   27,000   X = compensation expense (non-cash)
                    |   62,000
```

Additional information note # 8 states that shares with an original price of $430,000 were retired for $485,000 cash. The difference is to be debited to retained earnings.

Entry for shares repurchase:

General Journal

Date	Account/Explanation	PR	Debit	Credit
	Common shares		430,000	
	Retained earnings		55,000	
	Cash			485,000

Additional information note # 4 states that $15,000 of stock options were exercised along with an additional $40,000 in cash for common shares. The difference in the contributed surplus account was due to compensation expense.

Entry for exercise of options:

General Journal

Date	Account/Explanation	PR	Debit	Credit
	Cash		40,000	
	Contributed surplus, stock options...........		15,000	
	Common shares			55,000

Entry for compensation expense:

General Journal

Date	Account/Explanation	PR	Debit	Credit
	Compensation expense		27,000	
	Contributed surplus, stock options			27,000

It is now evident that $27,000 of the compensation expense included in net income in salaries and benefits line item is a non-cash transaction that was not adjusted in Step 3. This amount should therefore be adjusted out of net income in operational activities now.

Analysis result: enter the cash amount for the shares repurchase ($485,000) and the cash amount for stock options ($40,000) highlighted in red in the investing activities section of the statement of cash flows. Also, enter the adjusting entry ($27,000) highlighted in red in the operating activities section of the statement of cash flows.

i. Retained earnings:

```
              Retained earnings
                           |  46,000
                           | 345,000   net income
              55,000       |           stock options
              X = 144,000  |           dividends paid
              ─────────────┼──────────
                           | 192,000
```

Additional information note # 2 states that dividends were declared and paid but no amount given. The balancing amount to retained earnings of $144,000 must therefore be the amount of the dividend.

Entry for dividends paid:

	General Journal			
Date	Account/Explanation	PR	Debit	Credit
	Retained earnings		144,000	
	Cash			144,000

Analysis result: enter the dividend amount ($144,000) highlighted in red in the financing activities section of the statement of cash flows.

Step 7. Subtotal and reconcile:

Calculate subtotals for each section and also for net cash flows. Reconcile the net amount to the opening and closing cash balances from the balance sheet.

Step 8. Required disclosures:

Prepare the additional disclosures for cash paid interest and income taxes.

Below is the prepared statement of cash flows based on the steps discussed above.

Ace Ltd.
Statement of Cash Flows – Indirect Method
For the year ended December 31, 2015

Step 1: Headings

Step 2: Net income

Step 3: Non-cash items from income statement

Step 4: Changes in working capital accounts from balance sheet

Step 5: Changes in non-current asset accounts from balance

Step 6: Changes in non-current liability and equity accounts from balance sheet

Step 7: Subtotal and reconcile cash

Cash flows from operating activities			
Net income			$ 345,000
Non-cash items (adjusted from net income)			
Depreciation expense			43,000
Loss on sale of machinery			15,000
Gain on sale of AFS investment			(3,000)
Interest expense, amortization of bond		e	1,000
Deferred tax recovery		f	(12,000)
Reduction in pension benefit liability		g	(10,000)
Compensation expense, stock option plan		h	27,000
Cash in (out) from operating working capital			
Decrease in accounts receivable			
($145,000 – 110,000)			35,000
Decrease in inventory			
($200,000 – 175,000)			25,000
Increase in prepaid insurance ($0 – 6,000)			(6,000)
Decrease in accounts payable			
($200,000 – 300,000)			(100,000)
Increase in salaries payable			
($128,000 – 125,000)			3,000
Decrease in income taxes payable			
($115,000 – 120,000)			(5,000)
Net cash flows from operating activities			358,000
Cash flows from investing activities			
Sale of AFS investment		a	50,000
Purchase of AFS investment		a	(76,000)
Purchase of land		b	(180,000)
Sale of machinery		c	5,000
Net cash flows from investing activities			(201,000)
Cash flows from financing activities			
Issuance of 7.2% bonds		e	452,000
Repurchase of common shares		h	(485,000)
Exercise of stock options for common shares		h	40,000
Dividends		i	(144,000)
Net cash flows from financing activities			(137,000)
Net increase in cash flows			20,000
Cash, January 1			30,000
Cash, December 31			$ 50,000

Step 8: Disclosures

Disclosures:

Cash paid for income taxes ($67,000 + $12,000 + $5,000) = $84,000

Cash paid for interest charges ($30,000 − $1,000 amortization) = $29,000

Machinery ($300,000) was purchased in exchange for shares.

Six percent convertible bonds ($750,000), and contributed surplus rights ($35,000), were converted to common shares.

Stock options ($15,000) and cash ($40,000) were exercised for common shares.

20.7.2 Operating Activities Section: Direct Method

We will once again use the comprehensive illustration above for Ace Ltd. to demonstrate the completion of the operating activities section using the direct method. The first example explained below demonstrates how to prepare a direct method statement on its own. The second example demonstrates a quick technique to convert an already prepared indirect statement of cash flows into a direct method format.

Direct Method Steps:

1. **Headings and categories**
2. **Three additional columns**
3. **Record each income statement reporting line amount to its respective direct method category under the Income Statement Accounts column. Non-cash items are shown as memo items only.**
4. **Record the net change amount for each non-cash working capital account. Also record any adjustment amounts resulting from the analysis of non-current accounts from the investing or financing sections (highlighted in blue below).**
5. **Calculate the net cash flow amount for each category.**
6. **Calculate the subtotal for the operating activities section.**

Ace Ltd.
Statement of Cash Flows – Direct Method
For the year ended December 31, 2015

	Step 3	Step 4		Step 5
		Changes to W/C		Net cash
Cash flows from operating activities	I/S Accounts	+/- add'l adjustments		flow
Cash received from sales	$1,400,000	$	35,000	$1,435,000
Cash paid for goods and services	(630,000)		25,000	
	(50,000)		(6,000)	
	(26,000)		(100,000)	
	(80,000)			(867,000)
Cash paid to or on behalf of employees	(120,000)		3,000	
		g	(10,000)	
		h	27,000	(100,000)
Cash received for interest income	3,000			3,000
Cash paid for interest	(30,000)	e	1,000	(29,000)
Cash paid for income taxes	(67,000)		(5,000)	
		f	(12,000)	(84,000)
Cash received for dividends	–		–	–
Memo Items				
Depreciation	(43,000)			
Gain on sale of AFS investments	3,000			
Loss on sale of machinery	(15,000)			
Net cash flows from operating activities	$ 345,000			$ 358,000
				Step 6

In this example, steps 1 and 2 are self-explanatory. Steps 3, 4, and 5 are represented by entries in each of the columns in the schedule above. Note that this example is more complex as some non-cash costs were embedded with other income statement expenses initially treated as cash items and left unadjusted. There was also a reduction in the non-current pension liability which was more appropriately reported as an operating activity. These items were discovered when the analysis of the non-current assets (investing activities), liabilities and equity (financing activities) were completed. As a result, there are four additional adjusting entries (e, f, g and h) that must be adjusted in Step 4 of the operating section above (highlighted in blue).

20.8 Specific Items

The comprehensive illustration above included many of the more complex accounting transactions from the intermediate accounting courses (e.g., investments involving OCI, bonds issued at a discount, conversion of bonds to shares, deferred income taxes, exercising stock options, and accrued pension liabilities with funding changes). Below, however, is a brief discussion of further items to consider:

- **Cash equivalents**

    Cash equivalents are short-term, highly liquid investments that are both readily convertible to cash and carry little risk. Treasury bills, and term deposits that mature within 90 days, are examples of financial instruments that meet these two criteria and, thus, can be treated as a cash equivalent and added to cash for purposes of a statement of cash flows. Other instruments, such as publicly traded stocks, do not meet both criteria. While they may be easily traded, they carry significant risk due to market price fluctuations. For this reason, they cannot be classified as a cash equivalent. However, companies can choose whether or not to include cash equivalents with cash when preparing a SCF. If they do not include them with cash, then they are to be treated the same as the other working capital accounts. In which case, the accounting policy is disclosed in the notes to the financial statements.

    Unrestricted cash and cash equivalents are treated as one reporting line item in a SCF. This means that changes between them are netted and are, therefore, not itemized. Simply speaking, the cash and cash equivalents accounts are added together and reported as a single amount for both the opening and closing balance.

- **Restricted cash or cash equivalents**

    These are to be reported separately in the SCF.

- **Bank overdrafts**

    Bank overdrafts are generally included in the opening and closing cash balances, provided that they are an integral part of the overall cash management for the company. However, depending on local practice or other conditions, they may be excluded. Line of credit accounts that are payable on demand are examples of accounts that would be netted with cash.

- **Discontinued operations**

    The SCF begins with income before discontinued operations. Items from discontinued operations are shown separately in the operating, investing, or financing activities according to their nature. For companies following IFRS, they can also disclose cash flow information about discontinued operations in the notes to the financial statements.

- **Impairments of identifiable tangible or intangible assets**

    Any impairment write-downs reported in net income are adjusted out of net income in the operating activities as non-cash items. This is also the case with impairment reversals.

- **Investments in associates**

The accounting treatment for investments in associates was discussed in the previous accounting courses. Companies that follow IFRS account for these investments using the equity method. With ASPE, a policy choice allows either the equity method or fair value through net income or cost, depending upon the type of investment. Since the SCF reports cash flows, the cash dividend income received would be included in the SCF. Any investment income accrued, or unrealized gains or losses included in net income, must be adjusted out of net income as a non-cash item in operating activities.

- **Comprehensive income**

   As discussed earlier in the chapter, only net income is relevant with regard to the SCF. Comprehensive income items are excluded since they are non-cash items. For example, investments classified as "available for sale," have fair value adjustments every reporting period which are recorded to OCI rather than to net income. It is only when an AFS investment is sold that its respective accumulated unrealized gains are reclassified from OCI/AOCI to net income. When this occurs, an adjustment to net income is required in operating activities, since the gain or loss on the sale of the AFS investment is a non-cash item, the same way that a gain or loss on the sale of a building or an equipment asset is a non-cash item.

- **Liabilities**

   Netting old and new debt in the SCF is not permitted and each individual debt instrument is to be individually reported. Amortization of a discount or premium is a non-cash component of interest expense, and since interest expense is reported in net income, amortization amounts are adjusted out of net income in operating activities.

- **Leases**

   The increase in assets and liabilities due to a new finance lease is treated as a non-cash transaction and is excluded from the SCF, although supplementary disclosures are required. Cash payments made or received regarding a lease obligation are reported as a financing activity for the lessee.

- **Complex financial instruments**

   Upon issuance of a hybrid instrument such as a convertible bond, only one cash inflow is recorded in the SCF for both the debt and the equity portion of the instrument. For more details regarding hybrid instruments, refer to the earlier complex financial instruments chapter.

- **Stock splits and dividends**

   As these are non-cash transactions, they are excluded from the SCF, although supplementary disclosures are required.

- **Estimate for uncollectible accounts**

In cases where the balance sheet shows accounts receivable as a gross amount with a separate AFDA contra account, the indirect method will net the two accounts together and reports this net change as a change in the accounts receivable working capital account. However, with the direct method, an analysis is done on the AFDA to determine the current period estimate for uncollectible accounts and adjusts this amount from sales to cash paid for goods and services. This is done because the estimate for uncollectible accounts is debited to bad debt expense, which is usually included as other expenses within the cash paid for goods and services category.

20.9 IFRS/ASPE Key Differences

Earlier, we identified differences in the reporting items between ASPE and IFRS. For a review, please refer to sections 20.2 and 20.5 of this chapter.

Chapter Summary

LO 1: Describe the statement of cash flows (SCF) in accounting and business.

The SCF reports on how a company obtains and utilizes its cash flows and how it reconciles with the opening and ending cash and cash equivalent balances of the statement of financial position. It is separated into operating, investing, and financing activities, and the combination of positive and negative cash flows from within each activity can provide important information about how a company is managing its cash flows. Large differences between reporting net income and the net cash flows from operations reduce the quality of earnings and the reliability of the financial statements, creating the need for further evaluation into the reasons for the differences.

LO 2: Explain the purpose of the statement of cash flows and the two methods used.

The statement of cash flows provides the means to assess a business's capacity to generate cash and to determine the source of their cash flows. The statement combines with the SFP/BS to evaluate a company's liquidity and solvency, which represents its financial flexibility. This information, based on past events, can be used to predict the future financial position and cash flows of the company. It can also shed light on a company's quality of earnings and whether there may be a disconnect between report earnings and net cash flows from operating activities.

The SCF can be prepared using either the indirect or direct method. With the indirect method, the statement is presented in three distinct sections: operating activities (net income, current assets and liabilities), investing activities (non-current assets), and financing activities (long-term debt and equity), which follows the basic structure of the SFP/BS classifications. The changes between the opening and closing balances of the SFP/BS items are reported in the SCF as either cash inflows or cash outflows. The three sections net to a single net cash inflow or outflow, when combined with the cash and cash equivalent opening balance results in the same amount as the ending balance reported on the SFP/BS. The only difference between the methods is the categorization of cash flows by nature in operating activities, as occurs with the direct method. The investing and financing sections are identical for both methods.

There are some reporting differences between IFRS and ASPE regarding interest received and paid, dividends received and paid, and income taxes paid. For simplicity's sake, the chapter focuses on reporting interest received and paid, dividends received in operating activities, and dividends paid in financing activities. Income taxes paid can be separately reported for ASPE but it is only mandatory for IFRS. Whereas, both accounting standards require that non-cash transactions be reported in the notes to the financial statements. Where transactions involve some cash flows, this portion of the transaction is included in the SCF with supplementary disclosures of the transactions in the notes.

When preparing a statement of cash flows using the indirect method, the operating activities section begins with the net income/loss amount from the income statement. Entries for non-cash items such as depreciation, depletion, amortization, and gains/losses from sale/disposal of non-current assets are shown as adjustments to net income in order to remove the effects of non-cash items. The remainder of the operating activities section lists each non-cash working capital account change from opening to closing balances and reports as either cash flow in or out (cash flow out is prefixed by a minus sign). The investing activities are the change amounts between the opening and closing balances for any non-current assets such as long-term investments, property, plant, equipment, and intangible assets. Each line item from the non-current assets section of the SFP/BS is analyzed to determine if any non-current assets were purchased or sold during the year, and to report the cash paid or received. These amounts are reported as cash flows in or out. The financing section uses the same method as the investing for non-current liabilities and equities, such as any long-term debt, issuance or repurchase of shares for cash and dividends paid. These amounts are reported as cash flows in or out. Finally, the three sections are netted to a single amount and added to the cash and cash equivalent opening balance. The resulting sum should match the ending cash and cash equivalent balance reported in the SFP/BS, and the required disclosures (as described above) need to be prepared.

LO 3: Describe the statement of cash flows using the *direct method* and explain the difference in format from the *indirect method*.

With the direct method, the operating activities section is composed of major categories of cash flows in and out (determined by nature). Categories can include cash received from sales, cash paid for goods and services, cash paid to or on behalf of employees, as well as separate categories for interest received and paid and dividends received.

To prepare a statement of cash flows using the direct method, the operating activities section begins with the income statement where each line item is assigned to the most appropriate category as either a positive cash flow in or a negative cash flow out. Non-cash items are recorded as a memo item only. Next, each non-cash working capital account change between its opening and closing balance is then assigned to the most appropriate category as either a positive or negative cash flow. The net cash flow from each category, and for operating activities, is calculated. The methods used to prepare the investing and financing activities are the same as with the indirect method.

LO 4: Describe how the results from the statement of cash flows are interpreted.

The SCF, using the indirect method, is the most commonly used format in business, and the most important section within it is the operating activities. This is because it shows the cash flows in or out that result from the company's daily operations, which allows us to determine if the company is solvent. If cash flows in this section are negative, then management must determine if this is due to a temporary condition or if fundamental changes are needed to better manage the collections of accounts receivables or levels of unsold inventory. In any case, if a company is in a negative cash flow position from operating activities, it will usually either increase its debt through borrowing, increase its equity by issuing more shares, or sell off some of its assets. If any of these steps are taken, they will be reported as cash inflows from either the investing or financing sections. While none of these options are ideal, they can be used for the short-term, but they are unsustainable in the long-run. Positive cash flows from operating activities must also be evaluated to determine if they are sustainable and to ensure that they will be consistent going forward.

LO 5: Describe the required disclosures for the statement of cash flows.

The main disclosures identified in this chapter included an explanation of the changes in the opening and closing cash balance (including cash equivalents) as well as the components and policy used to determine them. Cash flows in and out are classified as operating, investing, and financing–using either the indirect or direct method. The major classes of cash flows in and out are also to be separately reported within each of the three sections. Cash flows from interest, dividends, and income taxes are separately disclosed as explained above, while non-cash transactions require supplementary disclosure.

LO 6: Describe the types of analysis techniques used for the statement of cash flows.

While the statement of cash flows may report a positive net income, this does not guarantee a positive cash flow for that period. Also, determining which activity the positive cash flows originate from is critical analytical information for the stakeholders. At the end of the day, operating activities must be able to sustain a positive cash flow in order for the company to survive. There are ratios that assess the operating activities cash flow, but trends or industry standards are also needed in order for the results to be informative. Two of the common ratios used are the current cash debt coverage ratio and the cash debt coverage ratio. Free cash flow analysis is another technique used, and it calculates the remaining cash flow from the operating activities section after deducting cash spent on capital expenditures, such as purchasing property, plant and equipment. Some companies also deduct cash paid dividends. The cash flow remaining is available to the company for strategies such as expansion, repayment of long-term debt, or downsizing share holdings to improve the share price, reduce the amount of dividends to pay, and to attract future investors.

LO 7: Review and understand a comprehensive example of an indirect and direct statement of cash flows that includes complex transactions from intermediate accounting courses.

Examples of how to prepare a SCF using the indirect and direct method are explained previously in the chapter. The examples include complex transactions including investments classified as available for sale, accrued pension liabilities, deferred income taxes, bonds issued as a discount with amortization, bonds converted to shares, stock options, and reacquisition of shares.

LO 8: Discuss specific items that affect the statement of cash flows.

Several issues are identified, and discussed, in this section in terms of their effect on the SCF. These include what makes up cash equivalents, restricted cash or cash equivalents, bank overdrafts, discontinued operations, impairments of assets, investments in associates, comprehensive income, netting of old and new liabilities, leases, complex financial instruments, and stock splits and dividends.

LO 9: Summarize the differences between ASPE and IFRS regarding reporting and disclosure requirements of the statement of cash flows.

The differences are identified throughout the chapter.

References

CPA Canada. (2016). *CPA handbook*. Toronto, ON: CPA Canada.

Exercises

EXERCISE 20–1

Below is a list of independent transactions:

Description	Section	Cash Flow In (Out)
Issue of bonds payable of $500 cash		
Sale of land and building of $60,000 cash		
Retirement of bonds payable of $20,000 cash		
Redemption of preferred shares classified as debt of $10,000		
Current portion of long-term debt changed from $56,000 to $50,000		
Repurchase of company's own shares of $120,000 cash		
Amortization of a bond discount of $500		
Issuance of common shares of $80,000 cash		
Payment of cash dividend of $25,000 recorded to retained earnings		

Purchase of land of $60,000 cash and a $100,000 note (the note would be a non-cash transaction that is not directly reported within the body of the SCF but requires disclosure in the notes to the SCF)		
Cash dividends received from a trading investment of $5,000		
Increase in an available for sale investment due to appreciation in the market price of $10,000		
Interest income received in cash from an investment of $2,000		
Leased new equipment under an operating lease for $12,000 per year		
Interest and finance charges paid of $15,000		
Purchase of equipment of $32,000		
Increase in accounts receivable of $75,000		
Leased new equipment under a finance lease with a present value of $40,000		
Purchase of 5% of the common shares of a supplier company for $30,000 cash		
Decrease in a sales related short term note payable of $10,000		
Made the annual contribution to the employee's pension benefit plan for $220,000		
Increase in income taxes payable of $3,000		
Purchase of equipment in exchange for a $14,000 long-term note		

Required: For each transaction, identify which section of the SCF it is to be reported under and indicate if it is a cash in-flow (positive) or cash out-flow (negative). Hint: recall the use of the accounting equation $A = L + E$ to help determine if an amount is positive or negative. Assume that the company policy is for interest paid or received, and dividends received, to be listed as operating cash flows, and for dividends paid to be listed as financing cash flows.

EXERCISE 20–2

Below are the unclassified financial statements for Rorrow Ltd. for the year ended December 31, 2015:

Rorrow Ltd.
Balance Sheet
as at December 31, 2015

	2015	2014
Cash	$ 152,975	$ 86,000
Accounts receivable (net)	321,640	239,080
Inventory	801,410	855,700
Prepaid insurance expenses	37,840	30,100
Equipment	2,564,950	2,156,450
Accumulated depreciation, equipment	(625,220)	(524,600)
Total assets	$3,253,595	$2,842,730
Accounts payable	$ 478,900	$ 494,500
Salaries and wages payable	312,300	309,600
Accrued interest payable	106,210	97,180
Bonds payable, due July 31, 2023	322,500	430,000
Common shares	1,509,300	1,204,000
Retained earnings	524,385	307,450
Total liabilities and shareholders' equity	$3,253,595	$2,842,730

Rorrow Ltd.
Income Statement
For the year ended December 31, 2015

Sales		$5,258,246
Expenses		
Cost of goods sold	3,150,180	
Salaries and benefits expense	754,186	
Depreciation expense	100,620	
Interest expense	258,129	
Insurance expense	95,976	
Income tax expense	253,098	
		4,612,189
Net income		$ 646,057

Required:

a. Complete the direct method worksheet for the operating activities section for the year ended December 31, 2015.

b. Prepare the operating activities section for Rorrow Ltd. for the year ended December 31, 2015.

EXERCISE 20–3

Below is the unclassified balance sheet for Carmel Corp. as at December 31, 2015:

Carmel Corp.
Balance Sheet
as at December 31, 2015

Cash	$ 84,000	Accounts payable	$ 146,000
Accounts receivable (net)	89,040	Mortgage payable	172,200
Investments – trading	134,400	Common shares	400,000
Buildings (net)	340,200	Retained earnings	297,440
Equipment (net)	168,000		$1,015,640
Land	200,000		
	$1,015,640		

The net income for the year ended December 31, 2016 was broken down as follows:

Revenues	$1,000,000
Gain	2,200
Total revenue	1,002,200
Expenses	
Operating expenses	809,200
Interest expenses	35,000
Depreciation expense – building	28,000
Depreciation expense – equipment	20,000
Loss	5,000
	897,200
Net income	105,000

The following events occurred in 2016:

i. Investments in traded securities are short-term securities and the entire portfolio was sold for cash at a gain of $2,200. No new investments were purchased in 2016.

ii. A building with a carrying value of $225,000 was sold for cash at a loss of $5,000.

iii. The cash proceeds from the sale of the building were used to purchase additional land for investment purposes.

iv. On December 31, 2016, specialized equipment was purchased in exchange for issuing an additional $50,000 in common shares.

v. An additional $20,000 in common shares were issued and sold for cash.

vi. Dividends of $8,000 were declared and paid in cash to the shareholders.

vii. The cash payments for the mortgage payable during 2016 included principal of $30,000 and interest of $35,000. In 2017, the cash payments will consist of $32,000 principal and $33,000 interest.

viii. All sales to customers, and purchases from suppliers for operating expenses, were on account. During 2016, collections from customers totalled $980,000 and cash payments to suppliers totalled $900,000.

ix. Ignore income taxes for purposes of simplicity.

x. The company's policy is to classify interest received and paid, and dividends received in operating activities. Dividends paid are classified in financing activities.

xi. Changes in other balance sheet accounts resulted from usual transactions and events.

Required:

a. Prepare a statement of cash flows in good form with all required disclosures for the year ended December 31, 2016. The company prepares this statement using the indirect method.

b. Calculate the company's free cash flow, and discuss the company's cash flow pattern, including details about sources and uses of cash.

c. How can the information from the statement of cash flows be beneficial to the company stakeholders (i.e., creditors, investors, management, and others)?

EXERCISE 20-4

Below is the comparative balance sheet for Lambrinetta Industries Ltd.:

Lambrinetta Industries Ltd.
Balance Sheet

Assets:	December 31 2016	2015
Cash	$ 32,300	$ 40,800
Accounts receivable	79,900	107,100
Investments – trading	88,400	81,600
Land	86,700	49,300
Plant assets	425,000	345,100
Accumulated depreciation – plant assets	(147,900)	(136,000)
Total assets	564,400	487,900
Liabilities and Equity:		
Accounts payable	$ 18,700	$ 6,800
Current portion of long-term note	8,000	10,000
Long-term note payable	119,500	75,000
Common shares	130,900	81,600
Retained earnings	287,300	314,500
Total liabilities and equity	$ 564,400	$ 487,900

Additional information:

i. Net income for the year ended December 31, 2016 was $161,500.

ii. Cash dividends were declared and paid during 2016.

iii. Plant assets with an original cost of $51,000, and with accumulated depreciation of $13,600, were sold for proceeds equal to book value during 2016.

iv. The investments are reported at their fair value on the balance sheet date. During 2016, investments with a cost of $12,000 were purchased. No other investment transactions occurred during the year. Fair value adjustments are reported directly on the income statement.

v. In 2016, land was acquired through the issuance of common shares. There were no other land transactions during the year. The balance of the common shares issued were for cash.

vi. The company's policy is to classify interest received and paid, and dividends received, in operating activities, and to classify dividends paid in financing activities.

vii. Note that payable arose from a single transaction.

viii. Changes in other balance sheet accounts resulted from usual transactions and events.

Required: Using the indirect method, prepare the statement of cash flows for the year ended December 31, 2016, in good form, including all required disclosures identified in the chapter material. The company follows ASPE.

EXERCISE 20–5

Below is a comparative statement of financial position for Egglestone Vibe Inc. as at December 31, 2016:

Egglestone Vibe Inc.
Statement of Financial Position

	December 31	
Assets:	2016	2015
Cash	$ 84,500	$ 37,700
Accounts receivable	113,100	76,700
Inventory	302,900	235,300
Investments – available for sale (OCI)	81,900	109,200
Land	84,500	133,900
Plant assets	507,000	560,000
Accumulated depreciation – plant assets	(152,100)	(111,800)
Goodwill (net)	161,200	224,900
Total assets	1,183,000	1,265,900
Liabilities and Equity:		
Accounts payable	$ 38,100	$ 66,300
Dividend payable	19,500	41,600
Notes payable	416,000	565,500
Common shares	322,500	162,500
Retained earnings	374,400	370,200
Accumulated other comprehensive income	12,500	59,800
Total liabilities and equity	$1,183,000	$1,265,900

Additional information:

i. Net income for the 2016 fiscal year was $24,700.

ii. On March 1, 2016, land was purchased for expansion purposes. On July 12, 2016, another section of land with a carrying value of $111,800 was sold for $150,000 cash.

iii. On June 15, 2016, notes payable of $160,000 were retired in exchange for the issuance of common shares. On December 31, 2016, notes payable of $10,500 were issued for additional cash flow.

iv. Available for sale investments (OCI) were purchased during 2016 for $20,000 cash. By year-end, the fair value of this portfolio dropped to $81,900. No investments from this portfolio were sold in 2016.

v. At year-end, plant assets originally costing $53,000 were sold for $27,300 since they were no longer contributing to profits. At the date of the sale, the accumulated depreciation for the assets sold was $15,600.

vi. Cash dividends were declared and a portion were paid in 2016. These dividends are reported under the financing section.

vii. Goodwill impairment loss was recorded in 2016 to reflect an impairment of the cash-generating unit (CGU), including goodwill.

viii. The company's policy is to classify interest received and paid, and dividends received in operating activities, and dividends paid in financing activities.

ix. Changes in other statement of financial position accounts resulted from usual transactions and events.

Required:

a. Prepare a statement of cash flows in good form, including all required disclosures identified in the chapter material. The company uses the indirect method to prepare the statement.

b. Analyze and comment on the results reported in the statement.

EXERCISE 20–6

Below are unclassified financial statements for Bognar Ltd. at December 31, 2015, and selected additional information taken from the accounting records:

Bognar Ltd.
Comparative Statement of Financial Position
December 31, 2015

	2015	2014
Cash	$ 5,500	$ 21,000
Accounts receivable, net	297,000	189,000
Investments – held for trading	209,000	241,500
Inventory	809,600	663,600
Land	363,000	430,500
Building	1,144,000	1,176,000
Accumulated depreciation, building	(517,000)	(399,000)
Machinery	1,188,000	918,750
Accumulated depreciation, machinery	(240,900)	(222,600)
Goodwill	49,500	115,500
	$3,307,700	$3,134,250
Accounts payable	$ 57,200	$ 94,500
Bonds payable, due 2026 (net)	1,089,000	1,034,250
Deferred tax payable (non-current)	26,400	69,300
Preferred shares	1,152,800	885,150
Common shares	305,500	199,500
Common stock conversion rights	525,000	525,000
Retained earnings	151,800	326,550
	$3,307,700	$3,134,250

Statement of Income
For the year ended December 31, 2015

Sales	$1,852,400
Cost of goods sold	1,213,300
Gross profit	639,100
Depreciation, building	121,000
Depreciation, machinery	82,500
Goodwill impairment	66,000
Interest expense	126,500
Other operating expenses	342,100
Loss in held for trading investment	32,500
Gain on sale of land	(24,200)
Loss on sale of machine	10,800
Loss before income tax	(118,100)
Income tax, recovery	59,400
Net loss	$ (58,700)

Additional information:

i. No held for trading investments were purchased or sold. These investments are not cash equivalents.

ii. A partially depreciated building was sold for an amount equal to its carrying value.

iii. Cash of $50,000 was received on the sale of a machine that originally cost $125,000. Addtionally, other machinery was purchased during 2015.

iv. Bonds payable are convertible to common shares at the rate of 15 common shares for every $1,000 bond after August 1, 2017. No new bond issuances occurred in 2015.

v. Preferred shares were issued for cash on May 1, 2015. Dividends of $40,000 were paid on these shares in 2015.

vi. In 2015, 25,000 common shares were purchased and retired. The shares had an average issue price of $60,000 and were repurchased for $65,000. Also in 2015, 50,000 common shares were issued in exchange for machinery.

vii. The company's policy is to classify interest received and paid, and dividends received in operating activities, and dividends paid in financing activities.

viii. Changes in other statement of financial position accounts resulted from usual transactions and events.

Required:

a. Prepare the statement of cash flows three-step worksheet for Bognar Ltd. for the year ended December 31, 2015 using the direct method. Include supplemental disclosures, if any.

b. Using the information from part (a), prepare the statement of cash flows operating activities section.

c. Prepare the operating activities section of the statement of cash flows for Bognar Ltd. for the year ended December 31, 2015 using the indirect method. Include supplemental disclosures, if any.

EXERCISE 20-7

The following are a list of transactions for an ASPE company, Verdon Ltd., for 2015:

i. Land asset account increased by $98,000 over the year. In terms of activity during the year, land that originally cost $80,000 was exchanged, along with a cash payment of $5,000, for five acres of undeveloped land appraised at $100,000. Three months later, additional land was acquired for cash.

ii. Equipment asset account had an opening balance of $70,000 at the beginning of the year, and $60,000 closing balance at year-end. Accumulated depreciation opening balance was $20,000 and its closing balance was $6,600. Equipment which originally cost $15,000 (and was fully depreciated) was sold during the year for $2,000. There was also equipment that originally cost $4,000, with a carrying value of $1,200, that was discarded. During the year, there was new equipment purchased for cash.

iii. Half way through the current year, the company entered into a six year capital lease for some equipment. The lease term called for six annual payments of $20,000, to be paid at the beginning of each year. Upon signing the lease agreement, the first payment was made. The equipment will revert back to the lessor at the end of the lease term. The implicit rate for the lease was 8%, which was known to the lessee.

Required:

a. Prepare the journal entries for Verdon Ltd. that relate to each of the changes in each asset account for 2015. Include entries for current year cash payments, depreciation, and interest, if any.

b. Identify and classify the cash flows for each of the transactions identified in part (a).

c. Prepare a partial SCF: operating activities, using the indirect method, including supplemental disclosures, if any. Assume no other transactions occurred in the current year for this company other than those identified in this question.

EXERCISE 20-8

Below are unclassified financial statements for Aegean Anchors Ltd. at December 31, 2015, and selected additional information taken from the accounting records.

Aegean Anchors Ltd.
Comparative Statement of Financial Position
December 31, 2015

	2015	2014	Increase (Decrease)
Cash	$ 33,960	$ 53,280	$ (19,320)
Accounts receivable, net	1,015,680	920,040	95,640
Inventory	861,120	810,000	51,120
Equipment	3,679,680	3,439,680	240,000
Accumulated depreciation, equipment	(1,398,000)	(1,212,000)	186,000
Investment in Vogeller Ltd., at equity	345,600	319,200	26,400
Note receivable	301,800	0	301,800
	$ 4,839,840	$ 4,330,200	
Bank overdraft	$ 171,120	$ 87,480	$ 83,640
Accounts payable	904,320	977,520	(73,200)
Income tax payable	44,400	55,200	(10,800)
Dividends payable	78,000	102,000	(24,000)
Obligations under lease	324,000	0	324,000
Common shares	1,080,000	1,080,000	0
Retained earnings	2,238,000	2,028,000	210,000
	$ 4,839,840	$ 4,330,200	

Additional information:

i. Net income for 2015 was $288,000. The income taxes paid were $181,000.

ii. The amount of interest paid during the year was $18,000, and the amount of interest received was $11,300.

iii. On January 2, 2015, Aegean Anchors Ltd. sold equipment which cost $84,000 (with a carrying amount of $53,000) for $50,000 cash.

iv. On December 31, 2014, Aegean Anchors Ltd. acquired 25% of Vogeller Ltd.'s common shares for $319,200. On that date, the carrying value of Vogeller Ltd.'s assets and liabilities were $1,276,800, which approximated their fair values. Vogeller Ltd. reported net income of $105,600 for the year ended December 31, 2015, and no dividend was paid on their common shares during 2015.

v. On January 2, 2015, Aegean Anchors Ltd. loaned $350,000 to Vancorp Ltd. (the company is not related to Aegean Anchors Ltd.). Vancorp Ltd. made the first semi-annual principal repayment of $48,200, plus interest at seven percent, on December 31, 2015.

vi. The bank overdraft identified in the comparative statement of financial position is a line of credit, payable on demand.

vii. On December 31, 2015, Aegean Anchors Ltd. entered into a finance lease for equipment. The present value of the annual lease payments is $324,000, which equals the equipment's fair value. Aegean made the first payment of $57,000 on January 2, 2016 when it was due.

viii. Aegean Anchors Ltd. declared and paid dividends in 2014 and 2015. In 2014, a dividend for $102,000 was declared to the shareholders on record at December 15, 2014. This dividend was paid on January 10, 2015. In 2015, a dividend for $78,000 was declared on December 15, 2015 and was paid on January 10, 2016.

ix. The company's policy is to classify interest received and paid, and dividends received in operating activities, and to classify dividends paid in financing activities.

x. Changes in other statement of financial position accounts resulted from usual transactions and events.

Required: Prepare a statement of cash flows for Aegean Anchors Ltd. for the year ended December 31, 2015, using the indirect method. Include supplemental disclosures, if any.

Chapter 21

Changes and Errors

Cooking the Books?

In July 2013, retail book giant Barnes & Noble created some headlines in the business press that were less than welcome. Earlier in the month, the company's CEO resigned. By late July, the company released its annual report for the year ended April 27, 2013, and reported that financial statements for the previous two fiscal years were to be restated due to material errors resulting from inadequate controls over the accrual reconciliation process at its distribution centres. The audit report stated that the company had not maintained effective internal control over financial reporting. When the financial statements were released, the company's share price immediately dropped by 5% to $17.51.

While the admission of internal control problems is certainly worrying to investors, the restatements made in the prior years actually improved the reported results. Cost of sales was reduced by $8.5 million in 2011 and by $6.7 million in 2012, which improved the reported profit and earnings per share amounts. However, more interesting was the adjustment to previously reported retained earnings. The company increased retained earnings by almost $95 million at the start of the 2011 fiscal year and reduced accounts payable by a similar amount. This had a significant positive effect on the company's net equity position. However, despite the adjustments, the company was still experiencing current losses.

While an improvement in the balance sheet is generally viewed positively, in this case shareholders and regulators were not impressed. On December 6, 2013, the Securities and Exchange Commission (SEC) announced it would be investigating Barnes & Noble's accounting practices, causing an immediate 11% drop in the share price. Then, on December 19, 2013, a shareholder launched a lawsuit against the company, claiming that the company had not properly exercised its fiduciary duties to its shareholders. By the end of December 2013, the share price had dropped by 25% from the price in July when the financial results were first reported.

Accounting is no different than any other activity that involves human judgment: errors can occur. And when errors in reported financial results come to light the effects can be profound. As seen in the example of Barnes & Noble, readers of financial statements can react negatively to the news of errors in previously reported results. As such, accountants need to be acutely aware of their responsibility to correct such errors and of their requirements to fully disclose such information. Changes in reported financial results, even if positive, can still cause a loss of confidence by

> the readers, and those readers may begin to doubt the integrity of other disclosures.
>
> (Sources: Barnes & Noble, 2014; Dolmetsch, 2013; Solomon, 2013)

Chapter 21 Learning Objectives

After completing this chapter, you should be able to:

LO 1: Describe the different types of accounting changes.

LO 2: Apply the appropriate method of accounting for an accounting policy change.

LO 3: Apply the appropriate method of accounting for an accounting estimate change.

LO 4: Apply the appropriate method of accounting for an error correction.

LO 5: Identify the disclosure requirements for different types of accounting changes.

LO 6: Describe the key differences between IFRS and ASPE with respect to the treatment of accounting changes and error corrections.

Introduction

As we have discovered in our previous discussions, accounting and financial reporting are time-sensitive activities. While the balance sheet represents the financial position of a company at a single point in time, the income statement and cash flow statements represent results for a defined period of time, usually one year. In attempting to present the economic truth of a company within the limitations of time, accountants are required to make choices, judgments, and estimations. It can be as simple as the choice of which depreciation method to use or determining the appropriate useful life for a piece of equipment. It is possible, however, that when accountants apply their judgment to make choices or estimates their judgment may later prove to be incorrect. Despite the extensive professional training that accountants receive, they can still make mistakes. Additionally, the need to produce timely information to fulfill the requirements of financial statement readers may sometimes result in less reliable information. In this chapter, we will examine different types of situations that can lead to both the revision of previously published financial information and to changes in the presentation of financial statements in the current and future periods.

Chapter Organization

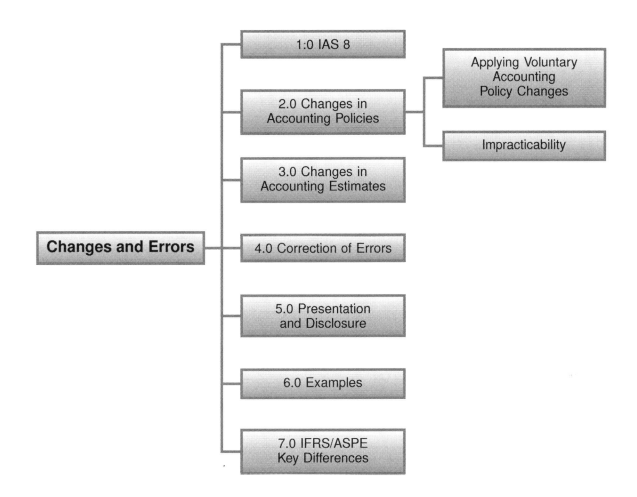

21.1   IAS 8

IAS 8 addresses the selection of accounting policies, changes in accounting policies, changes in accounting estimates, and corrections of errors. The standard is designed to ensure that the financial information is both relevant and reliable, but is also comparable with previous periods and with other entities. The standard is, thus, consistent with the objectives of the *Conceptual Framework*.

The standard indicates that the initial selection of accounting policies should follow the principles and guidance included in the IFRS, unless there is no IFRS that relates to the transaction in question. In such a case, management must apply judgment in selecting accounting policies that are both relevant and reliable. It is interesting that while the discussion of accounting policy choice in IAS 8 is generally consistent with the basic principles of the conceptual framework, an additional descriptor "prudent" is included. This would seem to place an additional level of responsibility on management to choose accounting policies that are not misleading. The initial discussion also states that accounting policies should be applied consistently for similar transactions, events, and conditions.

IAS 8 further describes three situations where changes to accounting information may be required:

- Changes in accounting policies
- Changes in accounting estimates
- Corrections of errors

We will examine each of these individually to determine the appropriate accounting treatment.

21.2 Changes in Accounting Policies

IAS 8 allows accounting policies to be changed in only two situations:

- The policy change is required by an IFRS.
- The new policy results in financial statements that are reliable and more relevant.

In the first case, the IFRS itself will usually provide guidance on how and when to implement the change. Sometimes these transitional procedures are quite complex, but IFRS generally allows reasonable amounts of time for companies to adapt to the new policies. As a general rule, the more complex the issues involved in the new policies, the longer the transition period allowed. For example, IFRS 15, the new revenue recognition standard, was published in May 2014, but companies are not required to implement it until January 1, 2018. Most new IFRSs allow for early adoption, that is, before the required transition date, and many companies will be proactive and implement the change early.

The second situation is referred to as a voluntary policy change. For this type of change the resulting information must still be considered sufficiently reliable and must also be more relevant. This condition obviously creates a situation where management must demonstrate logic and sound judgment. It is not generally sufficient to change accounting policies simply to create an effect in net income without providing any further justification. Management would need to demonstrate that the new policy better meets the needs of the financial statement readers in terms of helping them to understand the underlying economic reality of the company. As well, management would have to demonstrate that the level of reliability inherent in the information is still sufficient to meet the general requirement of representational faithfulness. A simple example of this type of change would be a company's decision to report certain property, plant, and equipment assets under the revaluation model rather than the cost model. The company may think that current value information is more helpful to financial statement readers than historical cost information. While this justification is quite reasonable, the company would have to make sure that the information on fair values had sufficient reliability to justify the change in policy. Note that the new level of reliability does not have to equal that of the old policy, but must simply be considered sufficient. In our example, while it is unlikely that fair value information would be as reliable as historical cost information, the new information could still be considered sufficiently reliable under the requirements of the fair value hierarchy.

Of course, it is not always easy to prove that one type of information is more relevant than another. Relevance is very subjective, and readers of financial statements will have different ideas of what information they require. As well, the question of relevance is unique to each business, and different companies may come to different conclusions about the accounting policy choices that they need to implement. In each case, management and the accountants advising them will need to use sound judgment and good sense in order to choose the best accounting policies suited to the circumstances facing the company.

21.2.1 Applying Voluntary Accounting Policy Changes

IAS 8 requires voluntary accounting policy changes to be treated **retrospectively**, meaning that after the new policy has been applied, the financial statements should appear as if the policy has always been in effect. The purpose of this approach is to maintain the comparability of current financial results with previous periods. Readers of financial statements need to make decisions regarding current results, and one of the criteria they may use is the change in performance from previous periods. Obviously, if an accounting policy was changed, and the prior periods were not restated, it would be impossible to make any meaningful comparisons.

Several steps are involved in retrospective application of policy changes:

1. The cumulative effect of the policy change on previous periods must be determined.

2. A journal entry is made to record the effect of this change. This adjustment will affect the appropriate category of equity and any other balance sheet amounts at the start of the current period.

3. Any financial statements that are presented for comparative purposes will also be restated to reflect the policy change. The opening balance of the relevant equity account on the earliest financial statement presented will need to be adjusted for

the cumulative effect at that time. As well, any earnings per share disclosures will need to be adjusted.

4. Disclosures are made to provide details of the reasons and effects of the policy change.

These steps can be demonstrated with the following example. Dameron Inc. purchased a piece of vacant land on January 1, 2015. The company intended to develop the property into a commercial shopping mall. The original purchase price was $2,000,000 and the company chose to apply the cost method to the property. However, in 2017, the company decided to then apply the fair value method as allowed under IAS 40, as management believed that this method would provide more relevant information to financial statement readers. No development work had yet been performed on the property, but the company was able to obtain independent, reliable appraisals of the fair value of the property as follows:

Appraisal Date	Appraised Value
31 December 2015	$1,850,000
31 December 2016	$2,100,000
31 December 2017	$2,275,000

On the 2015 and 2016 financial statements, the property was originally reported at its historical cost, which means there was no effect on the reported income in those periods. The company pays corporate income tax at the rate of 20%. The following information summarizes the effects of the change (take the income before tax figures as given):

Cost Method Applied	2017	2016	2015
Income Statement:			
Income before tax	$ 750,000	$ 720,000	$ 680,000
Income tax	150,000	144,000	136,000
Net income	$ 600,000	$ 576,000	$ 544,000
Retained Earnings Statement:			
Opening balance	$2,045,000	$1,469,000	$ 925,000
Net income	600,000	576,000	544,000
Closing balance	$2,645,000	$2,045,000	$1,469,000

Fair Value Method Applied	2017	2016	2015
Income Statement:			
Net income before tax	$ 925,000	$ 970,000	$ 530,000
Income tax	185,000	194,000	106,000
Net income	$ 740,000	$ 776,000	$ 424,000
Retained Earnings Statement:			
Opening balance	$2,125,000	$1,349,000	$ 925,000
Net income	740,000	776,000	424,000
Closing balance	$2,865,000	$2,125,000	$1,349,000

Recall that the effect of applying IAS 40 is that every year, any changes in the fair value of the investment property will be reported as a gain or loss directly on the income statement. For example, in 2015 the property's fair value drops by $150,000 ($2,000,000 – $1,850,000) during the year, so net income is reduced accordingly from $680,000 to $530,000. In 2016, the fair value increases by $250,000 ($2,100,000 – $1,850,000) so the income in that year is increased. Note as well that there is an income tax effect to the change each year. Although changes in fair value of an investment property are not usually directly taxable, there would still be an effect on the deferred taxes reported by the company.

In 2017, the company needs to record the effect of the change on opening balances. The books for 2015 and 2016 are already closed, but the books for 2017 are open. Thus, the cumulative effect up to the end of 2016 must be adjusted through retained earnings, net of the relevant tax effect. The fair value of the property on December 31, 2016 is $2,100,000 while the original cost is $2,000,000. A gain of $100,000 must be reflected in the carrying amount of the investment. The effect on the prior year's net income would be $80,000 ($100,000 gain less the tax effect) and the remaining $20,000 is reported as a deferred tax liability. The following journal entry will record this effect:

	General Journal			
Date	Account/Explanation	PR	Debit	Credit
	Investment in land		100,000	
	Deferred tax liability.....................			20,000
	Retained earnings			80,000

This journal entry corrects the land and deferred tax liability balances to the values that would have existed had the policy been implemented when the land was first purchased. As adjustments under IAS 40 flow to the income statement, the correct equity account to capture the net effect of the adjustment is retained earnings. In 2017, now that the policy has been implemented, the company will simply report the adjustment to fair value in the normal fashion as required by IAS 40.

If 2015 and 2016 are both being presented as comparative information in the 2017 financial statements, then the revised statements above would be presented with the heading "restated," along with note disclosures describing the change (this will be discussed later in the chapter). However, many companies only present one year as comparative information on current financial statements. If Dameron Inc. uses the former approach, then the retained earnings portion of the statement of changes in shareholders' equity would look like this:

	2017	2016 (Restated)
Opening balance, as previously stated		$1,469,000
Effect of accounting policy change, net of taxes of $30,000		(120,000)
Opening balance, restated	$2,125,000	1,349,000
Net income for the year	740,000	776,000
Closing balance	$2,865,000	$2,125,000

By identifying the effect of the change on opening retained earnings, the financial statements allow readers to compare the results to previously published financial statements. As well, IFRS requires the presentation of an opening restated balance sheet for the earliest comparative period. This presentation, along with the explanatory notes, should help maintain the consistency needed to satisfy the decision needs of those financial statement readers.

21.2.2 Impracticability

IAS 8 contemplates the possibility that it may be impracticable to apply an accounting change retrospectively. This may occur when, despite the accountant's best efforts, the information needed to determine the effect on prior periods is not available. Additionally, it is possible that in order to determine the effect assumptions need to be made about management's intentions in a prior period. Another possibility is that assumptions about conditions existing at the previous financial statement date need to be made in order to determine the effect. However, it is impossible for the accountant to determine if that information would have been available. When any of these circumstances occur, it is impossible for the accountant to reliably determine the effect of the policy change on prior period financial statements. It is important that the accountant not apply hindsight when determining the practicability of applying an accounting change. Information may have become available after a previous reporting period, but the accountant shouldn't use this information to make estimates for that period or to determine management intent if it wasn't available at the time.

Obviously, the accountant will need to apply reasoned judgment to determine if retrospective application is warranted or not. If, after careful consideration of all the facts, the accountant decides that retrospective application is impracticable, then the accountant can only apply the change to the earliest possible period where it is practicable. This means that the accountant may be able to partially apply the retrospective technique, that is to some previous years, but not to all. If there is no way to determine the effect of the change on prior periods, then the change will be applied **prospectively**, that is in the current year and in future years only. Additionally, full disclosure must be made for the reasons for not applying the change retrospectively.

21.3 Changes in Accounting Estimates

As we have seen in previous chapters, many accounting assertions require the use of estimates. Some more common estimates include the useful life of a piece of equipment, the percentage of accounts receivable that are expected to be uncollectible, and the net realizable value of obsolete inventory. The use of estimates is considered to be a normal part of the accounting process, and it is presumed that the accountant, when making an estimate, will take into account all the relevant information that is available at that time. However, new information can become available in later accounting periods that will cause accountants to reconsider their original estimates. If this information was not available at the time of the original estimate, it would be inappropriate to go back and restate prior period financial results. As such, changes in accounting estimates are treated prospectively, meaning financial results are adjusted to reflect the new information in the current year and in future periods. No attempt is made to determine the effect on prior years, and no adjustment to opening balances is necessary.

Consider the following example. Umbach Inc. purchased a machine to be used in its manufacturing facility on January 1, 2015. The machine cost $120,000 and was expected to be used for eight years, with no residual value. On January 1, 2017, an engineering review of the machine's performance indicated that its useful life is now six years instead of eight.

The machine would have been originally depreciated at $15,000 ($120,000 ÷ 8 years) per year. Thus, on January 1, 2017, the carrying amount of the machine would have been $90,000 ($120,000 − ($15,000 × 2 years)). On January 1, 2017, the remaining useful life is now four years (6 − 2). The new depreciation amount will therefore be $22,500 ($90,000 ÷ 4 years) per year. On December 31, 2017, the following journal entry will be made:

	General Journal			
Date	Account/Explanation	PR	Debit	Credit
	Depreciation expense........................		22,500	
	Accumulated depreciation			22,500

Note that we are simply recording the new depreciation amount in the normal fashion without making any attempt to restate prior depreciation amounts. This is the essence of prospective application: simply recalculating the amount based on the new information, and using this amount for current and future years only.

In some cases, however, it may not be clear if a change is a change in estimate or a change in policy. For example, changing from straight-line depreciation to declining balance depreciation may appear to be a change in policy. However, this change might, in fact, reflect a revision of management's view of how the pattern of benefits is being derived from the asset's use. In this case, the change would be treated as a change in estimate. If it is not clear whether a change is change in policy or a change in estimate, IAS 8 suggests that the change should be treated as a change in estimate.

21.4 Correction of Errors

Given the complex nature of some accounting transactions, it is inevitable that errors in reported amounts will sometimes occur. IAS 8 defines errors as both omissions and misstatements, and suggests that errors result from the failure to use or misuse of reliable information that was available and could have reasonably been expected to be obtained when the financial statements were issued. Thus, management cannot claim that a misstatement is simply a change in estimate if they did not take reasonable steps to verify the original amount recorded. IAS 8 also suggests that errors can include mathematical mistakes, mistakes in application of accounting policies, oversights, misinterpretations of facts, and fraud. We can see that there is quite a range of potential causes of financial misstatements. However, regardless of the cause, errors need to be corrected once they are discovered.

If the error is discovered before the financial statements are issued, then the solution is simple: correct the error. This is a normal part of the accounting and audit cycle of a business, and the procedure of correcting errors with year-end adjusting journal entries is quite common. However, if the error is not discovered until after the financial statements have been published, then the company faces a much larger problem. If the error is discovered soon after the financial statements are published, it may be possible to recall the documents and republish a corrected version. However, it is more likely that the error will not be discovered until financial statements are being prepared for a subsequent year. In this case, the error will appear in the amounts presented as comparative figures, and will likely also have an effect on the current year. In this case, the error should be corrected through a process of **retrospective restatement**, similar to the procedures used for accounting policy changes. Note that a subtle difference in terminology is used: accounting policy changes are retrospectively *applied*, while error corrections result in retrospective *restatements*. Despite the difference in terms, the basic principle is the same: a retrospective restatement results in financial statements that present the comparative and current amounts as if the error had never occurred.

Consider the following example. In preparing its 2017 financial statements, management of Manaugh Ltd. discovered that a delivery truck purchased early in 2015 had been incorrectly reported as a repair and maintenance expense in that year rather than being capitalized. The vehicle's cost was $50,000 and was expected to have a useful life of five years with no residual value. Assume that depreciation for tax purposes is calculated in the same way as for accounting purposes, and that the company's tax rate is 20%. Also assume that prior year tax returns will be refilled to reflect the correction of the error.

Prior to the discovery of the error, the company reported the following results on its 2017 draft financial statements:

	2017 (Draft)	2016
Revenue	$ 900,000	$ 850,000
Expenses	690,000	625,000
Income before tax	210,000	225,000
Income tax	42,000	45,000
Net income	168,000	180,000
Opening retained earnings	1,230,000	1,050,000
Closing retained earnings	$1,398,000	$1,230,000

In order to correct the error, we need to understand the balances of the relevant accounts prior to the error correction, and what they should be after the error is corrected. This analysis will need to be applied to all years affected by the error. Although there is no prescribed format for evaluating the effects of errors, a tabular analysis, as shown below, is often useful:

	2017	2016	2015
Repair expense incorrectly included			50,000
Depreciation expense, incorrectly excluded	(10,000)	(10,000)	(10,000)
Net effect on income before tax	(10,000)	(10,000)	40,000
Income tax expense over-(under) stated	2,000	2,000	(8,000)
Adjustment required to net income	(8,000)	(8,000)	32,000
Adjustment required to vehicle account	50,000	50,000	50,000
Adjustment required to accumulated depreciation	30,000	20,000	10,000
Adjustment required to income taxes payable	(2,000)	(2,000)	8,000

After analyzing the effects of the error, the following journal entry should be made in 2017 in order to correct the error:

General Journal				
Date	Account/Explanation	PR	Debit	Credit
	Vehicle		50,000	
	Depreciation expense		10,000	
	Accumulated depreciation			30,000
	Income taxes payable			4,000
	Income tax expense			2,000
	Retained earnings			24,000

Note that the adjustment corrects the balance sheet accounts, including retained earnings, to the amounts that would have been reported at December 31, 2017, had the error never occurred. The adjustment to retained earnings represents the net effect on income of the correction in 2015 and 2016, that is, $32,000 − $8,000. As well, because the books for 2017 have not yet been closed, we are able to adjust the two expense accounts, depreciation and income taxes, directly to the income statement. If, however, the books had already been closed for 2017, then these expense amounts would simply be added to the retained earnings adjustment.

After correcting the error, the financial statements will be presented as follows:

	2017	2016 (Restated)
Revenue	$900,000	$ 850,000
Expenses	700,000	635,000
Income before tax	200,000	215,000
Income tax	40,000	43,000
Net income	$160,000	$ 172,000

The retained earnings portion of the statement of shareholders' equity will include the following information:

	2017	2016 (Restated)
Opening balance, as previously stated		$1,050,000
Effect of error correction, net of taxes of $8,000		32,000
Opening balance, restated	$1,254,000	1,082,000
Net income for the year	160,000	172,000
Closing balance	$1,414,000	$1,254,000

The difference between the corrected closing retained earnings balance and the uncorrected balance ($1,414,000 − $1,398,000 = $16,000) can be derived directly from the journal entry by adding the prior period retained earnings adjustment to the current year expense adjustments ($24,000 + $2,000 − $10,000 = $16,000). Also note that the balance sheet will present the corrected amounts for the vehicle, accumulated depreciation, income taxes payable, and retained earnings with the 2016 comparative column labeled as "restated."

Analyzing and correcting errors is one of the most important skills an accountant can possess. This skill requires not only judgment, but also a very solid understanding of the operation of the accounting cycle, as the sources and effects of the errors may not always be obvious. Additionally, the accountant needs to be aware of the causes of the errors, as some parties may prefer that the accountant not detect or correct the error. In such cases of fraud or inappropriate earnings management, managers may deliberately try to hide the error or prevent correction of it. In other cases, management may try to offer explanations that suggest the error is just a change in estimate, not requiring retrospective restatement. Sometimes these justifications may be motivated by factors that don't reflect sound accounting principles. As such, the accountant must be prudent and exhibit good judgment when examining the causes of errors to ensure the final disclosures fairly present the economic reality of the situation.

21.5 Presentation and Disclosure

Because changes in accounting policies and errors may fall outside of the normal expectations of financial statement readers, it is not surprising that additional disclosures are required. When an accounting policy is changed, the following disclosures are required:

- If the change results from the initial application of an IFRS then disclosure must be made of the title of the new IFRS being applied, the nature of the change, a description of any transitional provisions, and the potential effect of those transitional provisions on future periods.

- If the change is a voluntary policy change then disclosure must be made of the nature of the change and the reasons why the change results in reliable and more relevant information.

- For both types of change, disclosure must be made of the effects on each financial statement line item and earnings per share in the current and prior periods, and the amount of adjustment that relates to periods prior to the earliest period presented.

- If it was impracticable to apply the change retrospectively to all previous periods, an explanation of the reasons why should be provided along with a description of how the change was applied.

- If the entity has not yet applied a new IFRS (that is, issued but not yet effective), the entity should disclose, where possible, an estimate of the future effects of the new IFRS on financial statements.

When a change in an accounting estimate is applied, the following disclosures are required:

- The nature and the amount of the change, including the effect on the current period and the expected effects on future periods, should be disclosed.

- If the effect on future periods cannot be determined, this fact should be disclosed.

It should be noted that, as with all accounting applications, the principle of materiality applies. As a practical matter, companies may not disclose all changes in estimates if the effects are not deemed to be material. However, companies are sometimes criticized for using immaterial estimate changes as a way to engage in creative earnings management. Obviously, careful consideration needs to be given to the required level of disclosures in cases like these.

For corrections of accounting errors, the following disclosures are required:

- The nature of the prior period error should be disclosed.

- Disclosure must be made of the effects on each financial statement line item and earnings per share in the current and prior periods, and the amount of adjustment that relates to periods prior to the earliest period presented.

- If it was impracticable to retrospectively restate all previous periods, an explanation of the reasons why should be provided along with a description of how the correction was applied.

21.6 Examples

Review the December 31, 2013 financial statements of Nestlé Group (taken from the company's annual report).

These financial statements provide a number of examples of how accounting changes are handled. First, in Note 1 on page 80, there is a general discussion of the use of estimates. The discussion identifies several areas where estimates are required—provisions, goodwill impairment, employee benefits, allowance for doubtful receivables, and taxes. The note also states that estimate changes are accounted for in the current and future periods to which the change affects, which is consistent with the prospective approach discussed previously in Section 21.3.

On page 117, Note 13.1 on provisions describes the revision of previous estimates by using the phrase "unused amounts reversed."

In addition to the estimate changes, the prior year comparatives were both "restated" and "adjusted." The restatement related to the application of two new IFRSs: IAS 19 and IFRS 11. The application of these new standards resulted in changes to both the income statement and the balance sheet of the previous year. A restated balance sheet on January 1, 2012 was also provided. As well, asset and liability accounts on the restated balance sheet were further adjusted due to a change in the provisional amounts of net assets obtained on the acquisition of a subsidiary company, as complete information was not available at the time of acquisition. This change is treated similarly to an error correction, and the comparative figures have been retrospectively restated. The disclosure of these restatements and adjustments can be found in Note 22 on pages 140 through 146 of the financial statements. As well, Note 2.2 on page 92 provides further details about the adjustments resulting from the acquisition of the subsidiary company.

These examples provide a good illustration of the detail required in the disclosure of accounting changes. This detail can help the readers make better comparisons with previous years' results as well as with other entities, both of which could have an impact on readers' decision-making processes.

21.7 IFRS/ASPE Key Differences

IFRS	ASPE
A voluntary accounting policy change can only be made if the new policy results in reliable and more relevant information.	A voluntary accounting policy change can be made if either: 1. The new policy results in reliable and more relevant information, or 2. It is a change between alternative methods specifically allowed in certain GAAP standards (investments in subsidiaries, jointly controlled enterprises and associates, intangible assets, defined benefit plans, income taxes, and financial instruments).
Errors should be corrected retrospectively, unless it is impracticable to do so.	Errors should always be corrected retrospectively. There is no recognition of the concept of impracticability for error corrections.

When applying a change retrospectively, a restated balance sheet at the beginning of the earliest comparative period must be presented.	When applying a change retrospectively, the effect on the opening balances of the earliest comparative period should be identified, but a restated opening balance sheet is not required.
Disclosure of the potential future effects of accounting standards issued, but not yet effective, needs to be made.	No disclosures for standards not yet implemented are required.

Chapter Summary

LO 1: Describe the different types of accounting changes.

There are three types of accounting changes: a change in accounting policy, which can be either voluntary if the change results in information that is reliable and more relevant, or required by the application of an IFRS; a change in accounting estimate, which presumes that the estimate was made with all the relevant information available at the time; and the correction of an accounting error, which means both omissions and misstatements and can include mathematical errors, mistakes in application of accounting policies, oversights, misinterpretations of facts, and fraud.

LO 2: Apply the appropriate method of accounting for an accounting policy change.

When applying an accounting policy change required by an IFRS, the IFRS will usually provide detailed transition provisions that outline the procedures. Voluntary accounting policy changes should be applied retrospectively, where all current and comparative information are restated as if the policy were always in effect. This means that opening balances will need to be restated, including the relevant equity accounts.

LO 3: Apply the appropriate method of accounting for an accounting estimate change.

Accounting estimate changes should be treated prospectively. This means that the new information is applied to the current year and any future years, if applicable. No attempt is made to restate prior periods, as it is assumed that the previous estimates were made with sound judgment based on all the information available at the time.

LO 4: Apply the appropriate method of accounting for an error correction.

When errors in prior period financial statements are discovered, the errors should be corrected retrospectively. This means that prior balances should be restated as if the error had never occurred. This will also require restatement of the relevant equity accounts.

LO 5: Identify the disclosure requirements for different types of accounting changes.

With retrospective restatement due to policy changes or error corrections, the reasons for the change must be identified and any transitional provisions disclosed. As well, the effects on each financial statement line item and earnings per share for current and prior periods should be identified. Comparative financial statements should be restated, and an opening balance sheet for the earliest comparative period should be presented. If retrospective application is impracticable, an explanation is required. The potential future effects of any IFRSs that are issued but not yet effective must also be disclosed. For estimate changes, the nature of the change and the effects on current and future periods should be disclosed. If the effects on future periods cannot be determined, this fact should be disclosed.

LO 6: Describe the key differences between IFRS and ASPE with respect to the treatment of accounting changes and error corrections.

IFRS only allows accounting policy changes if the new policy results in more relevant and reliable information. ASPE allows policy changes in the same circumstances, and also allows changes between acceptable alternatives identified for certain GAAP standards. ASPE requires errors to be corrected retrospectively, while IFRS requires retrospective restatement unless it is impracticable to do so. For a retrospective change, IFRS requires a restated balance sheet for the earliest comparative period, while ASPE only requires identification of the changes in the affected items. IFRS requires disclosure of the potential effects of accounting standards issued, but not yet effective, while ASPE does not require this disclosure.

References

Barnes & Noble. (2014). *2013 annual report*. Retrieved from `http://www.barnesandnobleinc.com/for_investors/annual_reports/2013_bn_annual_report.pdf`

Dolmetsch, C. (2013, December 18). Barnes & Noble shareholder sues over SEC investigation. *Bloomberg.com*. Retrieved from `http://www.bloomberg.com/news/articles/2013-12-18/barnes-noble-sued-by-shareholder-over-restatement`

Solomon, B. (2013, December 6). Were nook's books cooked? Barnes & Noble's accounting investigated by SEC. *Forbes.com*. Retrieved from `http://www.forbes.com/sites/briansolomon/2013/12/06/were-nooks-books-cooked-barnes-nobles-accounting-investigated-by-sec/#64fe44a048a8`

Exercises

EXERCISE 21-1

Identify if the following changes are an accounting policy change (P), an accounting estimate change (AE), or an error (E).

Item	Type of Change
The useful life of a piece of equipment was revised from five years to six years.	
An accrued litigation liability was adjusted upwards once the lawsuit was concluded.	
An item was missed in the year-end inventory count.	
The method used to depreciate a factory machine was changed from straight-line to declining balance when it was determined that this better reflected the pattern of use.	
A company adopted the new IFRS for revenue recognition.	
The accrued pension liability was adjusted downwards as the company's actuary had not included one employee group when estimating the remaining service life.	
The allowance for doubtful accounts was adjusted upwards due to current economic conditions.	
The allowance for doubtful accounts was adjusted downwards because the previous estimate was based on an aged trial balance that classified some outstanding invoices into the wrong aging categories.	
A company changed its inventory cost flow assumption from LIFO to FIFO, as the newly appointed auditors indicated that LIFO was not allowable under IFRS.	
A company began to apply the revaluation model to certain property, plant, and equipment assets, as it was felt that this presentation would be more useful to investors.	

EXERCISE 21-2

The financial controller of McEwan Limited, a publishing company, noted the following two items in a report to the finance director on the preliminary accounts for the year ended December 31, 2016:

- A copyright for a novel originally purchased for $100,000 in 2013 was being amortized over ten years with an expected residual value of $10,000. However, due to poor sales and a scandal earlier this year involving the author, it is now expected that the book will only be commercially viable for another year and the copyright will have no residual value.

- An insurance premium of $1,500 was paid on November 1, 2015, for a one-year policy. The payment was recorded as a debit to insurance expense in 2015.

Required:

a. Discuss the appropriate accounting treatment for two changes above.

b. Assuming the books are closed for 2015 and open for 2016, provide the journal entries required to address the two changes. Ignore income tax effects.

EXERCISE 21-3

The accountant of Swift Inc. was preparing for the audit of its financial statements for the year ended December 31, 2017, and discovered that an automobile was being incorrectly depreciated. The automobile was purchased on January 1, 2016, for $50,000 and the estimated residual value after five years was expected to be $5,000. The company uses the straight-line basis for depreciating vehicles, but the residual value was not considered when determining the depreciation amount. The financial controller informed the accountant that the company was switching to the double-declining balance method of depreciation for the current and future years, as it was believed this method would more accurately portray the consumption of benefits received from the asset's use.

Required: Prepare the journal entries required on December 31, 2017. Ignore income tax effects.

EXERCISE 21-4

Aldiss Ltd. currently uses the cost model for reporting its property, plant, and equipment assets. Management has decided to begin applying the revaluation model in the 2017 fiscal year to the company's office building, as it is believed that this will provide more relevant information to the shareholders. Although the company has been using the cost model, the following reliable valuations of the building were obtained:

> 31 December 2013 $800,000
> 31 December 2015 $825,000
> 31 December 2017 $740,000

The building was purchased on January 1, 2013, for $750,000. Straight-line depreciation is used and the estimated useful life is 30 years with no residual value.

Required: Prepare the journal entries required on December 31, 2017, to reflect the accounting policy change. Ignore income tax effects.

EXERCISE 21-5

Simic Distributors has been using the weighted average (WA) costing method to report its inventory and cost of sales amounts for several years. Early in 2016, management decided that the FIFO costing method would provide more relevant information to the financial statement readers. The following information regarding year-end inventory amounts has been determined:

Date	Inventory – WA	Inventory – FIFO
31 December 2013	$500,000	$530,000
31 December 2014	$590,000	$650,000
31 December 2015	$660,000	$730,000

Information for inventory amounts prior to the 2013 fiscal year cannot be obtained. The company's retained earnings balances prior to the change were $1,100,000 on December 31, 2014, and $1,375,000 on December 31, 2015. The company's tax rate is 30%.

Required:

a. Prepare the journal entry required in 2016 to reflect the accounting policy change. Assume the books have been closed for 2015 and for all previous years.

b. Prepare the comparative column of the retained earnings portion of the statement of shareholders' equity that will be presented in the 2016 financial statements. The net income previously reported in 2015 was $275,000.

EXERCISE 21-6

The auditors of Boyle Inc. have just completed the fieldwork of the company's first audit for the year ended December 31, 2016. The following potential errors have been identified:

- The balance of the salaries payable account, $52,000 has remained unchanged from the previous year. The controller indicated that the balance should be $45,000.

- On December 28, 2015, a fire destroyed one of the company's delivery vehicles. Insurance proceeds of $8,000 were received on January 16, 2016, and were credited to miscellaneous revenue. The delivery vehicle's original cost was $40,000, and at the time of the fire the accumulated depreciation was $26,000. Further depreciation of $5,000 was recorded in 2016, as the vehicle had not been removed from the equipment subledger.

- Based on deteriorating economic circumstances, the company decided that the allowance for doubtful accounts for 2016 should be 2% of the accounts receivable balance instead of the 1% that had been used in the previous year. The accounts receivable balances were $1,500,000 in 2016 and $1,750,000 in 2015. No entry has yet been made for the 2016 bad debts, and the balance in the allowance for doubtful accounts has remained unchanged from December 31, 2015.

- Due to a number of cut-off errors, the ending inventory balance on December 31, 2015, was overstated by $8,000 and was understated by $12,000 on December 31, 2016.

Required: Prepare the journal entries required to correct the above errors. The books for 2016 are still open, but the books for 2015 have been closed. Ignore income tax effects.

EXERCISE 21-7

Spark Ltd. has just completed preparing its financial statements for the year ended December 31, 2017. The assistant controller has brought the following items to the attention of the controller:

- In 2016, $9,000 of repairs expense was mistakenly charged to the equipment account. Depreciation has already been recorded in 2016 and 2017. The company uses straight-line depreciation and records half of the normal depreciation charge in the year of acquisition. The equipment's estimated useful life is six years with no residual value.

- No adjustment has yet been made for accrued interest on a loan receivable. Regular interest payments are made on February 28, May 31, August 31, and November 30, with interest revenue being recorded at the time of the payment. The balance of the loan receivable is $150,000 and the annual interest rate is 8%. The balance of the interest receivable account is $1,000, which is unchanged from the previous year.

- On July 1, 2015 a factory building was purchased for $1,000,000. The full amount of the purchase price was recorded in the building account, but 25% of the cost should have been allocated to land. The building is being depreciated on a straight-line basis with an estimated useful life of 50 years and a residual value of $50,000.

- On September 30, 2017, a fully depreciated factory machine was sold to a scrap metal dealer for $1,500. The original cost of the machine was $52,000. When the machine was sold, the proceeds were credited to the factory machine account.

Required: Prepare the journal entries required in 2017 to correct the above items. The books for 2017 are open, but the books for previous years are closed. Ignore income tax effects.

EXERCISE 21-8

You are the senior in charge of the audit of Rankin Ltd. for the year ended December 31, 2016. In the process of reviewing the audit working papers, you discovered the following:

- In 2015, an automobile purchase was incorrectly charged to the repair expense account. The cost of the automobile was $35,000, and its expected useful life was six years with a residual value of $5,000. The company uses double-declining balance depreciation with a full year of depreciation being charged in the year of acquisition.

- In 2014, a lawsuit was launched against the company for a product liability issue. The company's lawyers initially indicated that the company was likely to lose, and a provision of $750,000 was established. Late in 2016, the case was approaching a verdict, and the company's lawyers now indicated that the company would not lose the case and would, therefore, not be required to pay a settlement.

- Goods that were sold on credit for $18,000 on December 28, 2016, FOB destination were recorded as a sale on that date. The customer received the goods on January 4, 2017. The cost of the goods was $11,500.

- In December 2015, an advance deposit of $60,000 was received from a customer for work that was to be completed in 2016. When the deposit was received, it was a recorded as revenue.

Required: Prepare the journal entries required in 2016 to correct the above items. The books for 2016 are open but the books for previous years are closed. The company's income tax rate is 20%.

EXERCISE 21-9

You have been asked to provide an analysis of the reported net income of Hodgins Manufacturing Ltd. for the years ended December 31, 2016, and 2015. The reported net incomes were $1,200,000 in 2016 and $1,050,000 in 2015. You have also received the following information:

- A surplus building was rented to a tenant, starting on July 1, 2015. The lease term was 24 months and the annual rent was $60,000. The tenant paid the full amount required under the lease (i.e., $120,000) on July 1, 2015, and this amount was recorded as rental income.

- The company has never reported unused office supplies as an asset on its balance sheet. Office supplies have always been immediately expensed when purchased. The balances of office supplies on-hand were as follows:

31 December 2014	$18,000
31 December 2015	$13,500
31 December 2016	$19,200

- The company started offering a three-year warranty on its products in 2015. The warranty expense recorded was based only on actual expenditures made in each year. It was estimated, however, that warranty claims should eventually total 1% of revenue in each year. Sales and expenditures were as follows:

		Actual Warranty Costs for sales in:		
Year	Sales	2015	2016	Total
2015	$5,000,000	$12,000	–	$12,000
2016	$5,200,000	$30,000	$16,000	$46,000

- The manager is entitled to a performance bonus each year. The bonus is always paid in the February following the end of the fiscal year. The bonus has not been accrued at the year-end, but is simply recorded as an expense when paid. The following bonuses have been paid:

February 2015 (for 2014)	$50,000
February 2016 (for 2015)	$62,000
February 2017 (for 2016)	$27,000

Required: Complete the table below, analyzing the company's net income. Ignore income tax effects.

	2016	2015
Reported net income	$1,200,000	$1,050,000
Adjustment for rent		
Adjustment for office supplies		
Adjustment for warranty		
Corrected net income		

Chapter 22

Putting It All Together: Disclosures and Analysis Overview

Trading Has Been Suspended for SEHK: 0940

On December 4, 2015, a Hong Kong-listed animal drug company, China Animal Healthcare Ltd. (SEHK: 0940), announced a delay in the release of its financial statements. The firm alleged that a thief had stolen the truck in which the past five years of the company's financial records were being transported. The theft was alleged to have occurred during middle of a forensic audit, when the truck's driver, who was transporting the original financial documents from Qingyuan area to Hebel province, stopped and left the truck for a lunch break.

The company continues to be embroiled in the forensic accounting investigation, stalled as a result of the missing financials statements now labelled the "Lost Documents." As of March, 2016, the Hong Kong Stock Exchange suspended the company's shares trading when the firm missed its deadline for filing the 2014 financial results. The suspension is expected to continue until further notice, while the company continues its search for the stolen documents.

This situation has created more than a little angst for 20% shareholder Eli Lilly's Elanco company, which invested $100 million in the troubled China Animal Healthcare Ltd. in 2013. These recent events threaten to suspend Elanco's efforts to expand its presence in China, giving its competition a potential advantage.

If the issue is not resolved soon, Elanco may be on the hunt for another China-based partner to give it a stake in one of China's fastest growing markets for animal health.

(Sources: Business Insider, 2015; Weintraub, 2016)

Chapter 22 Learning Objectives

After completing this chapter, you should be able to:

LO 1: Discuss the rationale and methods of full disclosure in corporate reporting.

LO 2: Identify the issues and disclosure requirements for related parties.

LO 3: Describe the appropriate accounting and disclosure requirements for events occurring after the reporting period.

LO 4: Describe the purpose of the audit opinion and the contents of the auditor's report.

LO 5: Explain the various financial statement analysis tools and techniques.

LO 6: Explain the similarities and differences between ASPE and IFRS regarding disclosures and analysis of financial statements.

Introduction

The previous chapters of this text and the previous course text were focused on the individual aspects of financial reporting. For example, the previous intermediate financial accounting text covered how to prepare the basic core financial statements as well as the more complex aspects of current and long-term assets. In contrast, this text has discussed the complex issues regarding current and long-term liabilities and equity such as complex financial instruments, income taxes, pensions, leases, earnings per share, as well as an in-depth look at accounting changes, error analysis, and the direct method for preparing the statement of cash flows. This last chapter will focus on pulling together all of these individual topics into a cohesive overview of financial statement disclosures and analyses.

Chapter Organization

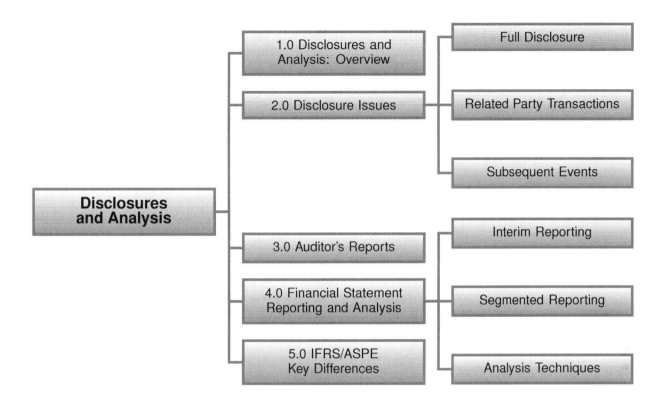

22.1 Disclosures and Analysis: Overview

The underlying purpose of the financial statements is to tell a story about the operations of a business from its inception to its dissolution. What stories could China Animal Healthcare's financials tell had they not been stolen, and how might this event affect investor and creditor decisions? Given the complexities in today's marketplace, decision-making for creditors and investors can be quite challenging. Financial statements only have meaning, and therefore appropriate influence, if they are complete and if users know how to interpret them. Appropriate disclosures and financial statement analysis are an important part of this evaluative process.

To aid users in understanding financial statements, most medium to large businesses prepare extensive disclosures in the notes to the financial statements. In addition, monthly or quarterly interim financial statements are often prepared that provide an early warning system for management and other select users, such as creditors, who monitor debt and compliance with restrictive covenants. Additionally, if business activities are diversified, segmented reporting is another financial report that separates business operations into segments such as geographical operations or various business lines. This allows stakeholders to determine which segments contribute the most to the overall business.

To assist with the task of a thorough financial statement assessment, there are several analytical techniques available to stakeholders. These include ratio, common size, and vertical and trend analysis. Actual results reported in the financial statements can be compared to the business's own strategic forecast and to industry competitors to see if it is keeping pace, growing, or shrinking.

Understanding a business, however, is more than just analyzing the core financial statements. Business stakeholders need to consider the quality of management, the overall industry climate, as well as projected economic developments. This information comes from many different sources such as the notes to the financial statements and the management discussion and analysis (MD&A) report, which presents information about the operations, company liquidity, capital resources, economic outlook, and any risks and uncertainties. Independently prepared reports such as auditor's reports, analysts' reports, economic reports, and news articles are also an important source of information.

The purpose of this chapter is to focus on the bigger picture of a business's overall current financial performance through the accurate interpretation of the financial statements and their disclosures.

22.2 Disclosure Issues

Recall from our previous discussions that the purpose of financial reporting is to provide financial information that is useful to investors, lenders, and other creditors in making decisions about providing resources to the company. In this text, we have focused on the preparation of financial reports to meet the usefulness criteria identified above. However, it is important to keep in mind a fundamental deficiency of financial reporting: it is backward looking. That is, financial statements report on events that have already occurred. For investors and creditors, the more relevant consideration is the financial performance in the future, as this is where profits and returns will be made. While the accounting profession has always assumed that historical financial statements are useful in making predictions about the future, users understand that the financial statements are only one of many sources of information required to make well-informed decisions. In this section, we will examine some of the other types of information used by investors, as well as some of the specific disclosures that enhance the financial statements themselves.

22.2.1 Full Disclosure

The concept of full disclosure is a well-established principle that has been broadly recognized as an essential component of financial reporting models. The principle is derived directly from the economic concept of the **efficient securities market**. A semi-strong efficient securities market is a market in which securities trade at a price that reflects all the information that is publicly available at the time. Although there have been many studies over the years that question the true level of efficiency in securities markets, strong evidence suggests that share prices do respond quickly to new information. Thus, from the perspective of a financial statement preparer, full and complete information should be disclosed in order to meet the needs of the readers. This will help engender a sense of confidence not only in the individual company, but also in the market as a whole, and will help alleviate the problem of information asymmetry.

One way that accountants contribute to the process of full disclosure is through the presentation of financial statement notes. The notes include additional explanations and details that provide further information about the numbers that appear in the financial statements. This additional information can help readers understand the results more fully, which can lead to better decisions. The notes also contain a description of significant accounting policies. These disclosures are very important to help readers understand how accounting numbers are derived. In making investment decisions, readers may wish to compare one company's performance to another's. Because accounting standards sometimes allow choices between alternative accounting treatments, it is important that the readers fully understand which policies have been applied. The concept of the semi-strong efficient market presumes that readers of financial statements can determine the effects of different accounting policy choices, as long as the details of those policy choices are disclosed. The principle of full disclosure also presumes that readers of financial statements have a reasonable knowledge of business methods and accounting conventions. Thus, the accountant is not required to explain the most basic principles of accounting in the note disclosures. As businesses have become more complex over time, note disclosures have become more detailed. The accounting profession is sometimes criticized for presenting overly complicated note disclosures that even knowledgeable readers have difficulty understanding. This criticism is a result of one of the trade-offs that the profession often faces: the need for completeness balanced against the need for understandability.

Most companies will disclose significant accounting policies in the first or second note to the financial statements. A retail company, for example, may disclose an accounting policy note for inventory as follows:

Merchandise Inventories

Merchandise inventories are carried at the lower of cost and net realizable value. Net realizable value is defined as the estimated selling price during the normal course of business less estimated selling expenses. Cost is determined based on the first-in-first-out (FIFO) basis and includes costs incurred to bring the inventories to their present location and condition. All inventories consist of finished goods.

Review the accounting policy notes of Canadian Tire Corporation's 2015 annual financial statements[1].

The significant accounting policy note begins on page 66 of the document and continues for ten pages. Canadian Tire Corporation has fully disclosed all the significant accounting policies to help readers understand the methods used to generate the amounts that appear on the financial statements.

Aside from descriptions of accounting policies, the notes to the financial statements contain further details of balance sheet and income statement amounts. For example, the property and equipment account on Canadian Tire Corporation's 2015 balance sheet is disclosed as a single item. However, Note 16 (page 86 of the document) contains further details of individual classes of assets and movements within those classes, including opening balances for each class of property and equipment, additions and disposals during the year, reclassification to or from the "held for sale" category, depreciation, impairment, and other changes. This level of disclosure helps readers better understand the asset composition and capital replacement policies of the property and equipment account.

Aside from the financial statements themselves, companies provide further disclosures in the annual report and in other public communications. Canadian Tire Corporation's *2015 Report to Shareholders* (Canadian Tire Corporation, 2016) is 118 pages long, including the financial statements. Aside from the financial statements, the annual report includes messages from the Chairman and the President/CEO, listings of the Board of Directors and Executive Leadership Team, and a section entitled "Management's Discussion and Analysis" (MD&A), on pages 3 to 54. The MD&A is required disclosure under Canadian securities regulations. Similar disclosures are required or encouraged in other jurisdictions, although they may bear different names, such as Management Commentary or Business Review. The purpose of MD&A, and similar disclosures, is to provide a narrative explanation from management's perspective of the year's results and financial condition, risks, and future plans. The guidelines encourage companies to provide forward-looking information to help investors understand the impact of current results on future prospects. MD&A should help investors further understand the financial statements, discuss information not fully disclosed in the financial statements, discuss risks and trends that could affect future performance, analyze the variability, quality and predictive nature of current earnings, provide information about credit ratings, discuss short- and long-term liquidity, discuss commitments and off balance sheet arrangements,

---

[1] http://s2.q4cdn.com/913390117/files/doc_financials/annual/2015/Canadian-Tire-Corporation_2015-Annual-Report_ENG.pdf

examine trends, risks and uncertainties, review previous forward-looking information, and discuss the risks and potential impact of financial instruments.

The objectives of MD&A are clearly aimed at helping investors link past performance with predictions of future results. Although this type of information is consistent with investors' needs, there are some limitations with MD&A disclosures. First, although the general elements are defined by securities regulations, companies have some discretion in how they fulfill these requirements. Thus, some companies may provide standardized disclosures that change little from year to year. Although the disclosures may meet the minimum requirements, the usefulness of these boilerplate, or generic and non-specific statements, may be questionable. Second, MD&A disclosures are not directly part of the financial statements, meaning they are not audited. Auditors are required to review the annual report for any significant inconsistencies with the published financial statements, but the lack of any specific assurance on the MD&A may result in investors having less confidence in the disclosures. Third, the MD&A contains more qualitative information than the financial statements does. Although this qualitative information is useful in analyzing past, and predicting future, financial results, it is not as easily verified as the more quantitative disclosures.

One interesting effect of the qualitative nature of MD&A is that companies may either deliberately or inadvertently provide signals to the readers. A number of studies have examined the use of language and the presence of tone in the narrative discussion of the MD&A. Although the research is not always conclusive, there is evidence to suggest that the word choice and grammatical structures present in the reports may provide some predictive function. The language choices may reflect something about management's more detailed understanding of the business that is not directly disclosed in the information.

Although there are sometimes suggestions of information overload levied against the accounting profession and securities regulators, the continually expanding volume of financial and non-financial disclosures does suggest that there is a demand for this information and that readers are finding some value in the disclosures.

22.2.2 Related Party Transactions

One area in particular where full disclosure is important is in the case of related parties. The accounting issue with related parties is that transactions with these parties may occur on a non-arms-length basis. Because the transactions may occur in a manner that is not consistent with normal market conditions, it is important that readers are alerted to their presence. IAS 24 provides guidance to the appropriate treatment of related party transactions and balances.

IAS 24 provides a detailed definition of related parties, as follows:

a. A person or a close member of that person's family is related to a reporting entity if that person:

   i. has control or joint control of the reporting entity;
   ii. has significant influence over the reporting entity; or
   iii. is a member of the key management personnel of the reporting entity or of a parent of the reporting entity.

b. An entity is related to a reporting entity if any of the following conditions applies:

   i. The entity and the reporting entity are members of the same group (which means that each parent, subsidiary and fellow subsidiary is related to the others).
   ii. One entity is an associate or joint venture of the other entity (or an associate or joint venture of a member of a group of which the other entity is a member).
   iii. Both entities are joint ventures of the same third party.
   iv. One entity is a joint venture of a third entity and the other entity is an associate of the third entity.
   v. The entity is a post-employment benefit plan for the benefit of employees of either the reporting entity or an entity related to the reporting entity. If the reporting entity is itself such a plan, the sponsoring employers are also related to the reporting entity.
   vi. The entity is controlled or jointly controlled by a person identified in (a).
   vii. A person identified in (a)(i) has significant influence over the entity or is a member of the key management personnel of the entity (or of a parent of the entity).
   viii. The entity, or any member of a group of which it is a part, provides key management personnel services to the reporting entity or to the parent of the reporting entity. (CPA Canada, 2016, Part I, Section IAS 24.9)

The standard further defines close family members as the children, dependents, and spouse or domestic partner of the person in question. However, the definition leaves some room for interpretation as it suggests that a close family member is any family member who is expected to influence, or be influenced by, the person in question.

In cases where complex corporate structures exist, it may be helpful to draw organization charts or other visual representations to determine who the related parties are. Correct identification of the related parties is important, as this will determine the disclosures that are required.

The key feature of IAS 24 is that it requires additional disclosures when related parties exist. Specifically, all related party relationships must be disclosed, even if there are no transactions with those parties. When transactions with related parties do occur, the amount of the transactions and outstanding balances must be disclosed, along with a description of the terms and conditions of the transaction, any commitments, security, or guarantees with the related party, the nature of the consideration used to settle the transactions, and the amount of any provision or expense related to bad debts of the related party. Additionally, the standard requires disclosure of details of compensation paid to key management personnel. The disclosure requirements are designed to help readers understand the potential effects of the related party transactions on the entity's results and financial position.

ASPE takes related party disclosures one step further by also requiring different measurement bases for the transaction, depending on the circumstances. In summary, related party transactions are normally reported at the carrying amount of the item or services transferred in the accounts of the transferor. This means that the transaction may need to be remeasured at a different amount than what was agreed upon by the parties. The only circumstances where the exchange amount (i.e., the amount agreed upon by the related parties, is used to measure the transaction is if the transaction is:

- a monetary exchange in the normal course of operations

- a non-monetary exchange in the normal course of operations which has commercial substance[2]

- an exchange not in the ordinary course of business where there is a substantive change in ownership, the amount is supported by independent evidence, and the transaction is monetary or has commercial substance.

These rules are intended to prevent related parties from reporting transactions at amounts that may not be representative of fair values. By requiring most related party transactions to be reported at the carrying amount, the standard may prevent gains or losses from being reported that represent the result of bargaining between arm's length parties. Only where the transaction is monetary, has commercial substance, or is the result of a substantial change of ownership interests, can the negotiated price be used.

Other disclosure requirements under ASPE for related parties are similar to those of IFRS, except ASPE does not specifically require the disclosure of key management compensation.

---

[2]This rule doesn't apply if the exchange is of assets held for sale in the normal course of operations that will be sold in the same line of business.

22.2.3 Subsequent Events – After the Reporting Period

Financial statements are defined very precisely in terms of time periods. Whereas balance sheets report financial position as at a specific date, income and cash flow statements report results for a period of time ending on a specific date. It would be understandable to think that events occurring after the reporting period are not relevant, as they do not occur within the precisely defined period covered by the financial statements. However, remember that investors and other readers often use financial statements to make predictions about the future. As such, if an event occurs after the reporting date, but before the financial statements are issued, and if the event could have a material impact on the future operations of the business, it is reasonable to expect that investors would want to know about it. For this reason, IAS 10 takes into account the reporting requirements where material events occur after the reporting period.

IAS 10 specifically defines the relevant reporting period as the time between the reporting date and the date when the financial statements are authorized for issue. Although the date of authorization will depend on the legal and corporate structure relevant to the entity, a common scenario is that the financial statements are authorized for issue when the board of directors approves them for distribution to the shareholders. This may be several weeks or even months after the reporting date.

The treatment of events after the reporting period will depend on whether they are adjusting or non-adjusting events. While adjusting events are those that provide further evidence of conditions that existed at the reporting date, non-adjusting events are those that are indicative of conditions that arose after the reporting date. As suggested by the nomenclature, when adjusting events occur, the accounts should be adjusted to reflect the effect of those events, while non-adjusting events will not result in any adjustments to the accounts.

The logic of this treatment is clear. If the event after the reporting date provides further evidence of a condition that existed at the reporting date, then the amount should be adjusted to reflect all available information. If the event only provides evidence of a new condition that arose after the reporting date, then adjustment would not be appropriate, as the condition didn't exist at the reporting date.

In many cases, the appropriate treatment will be obvious. For example, if a provision for an unsettled lawsuit were included in current liabilities on the reporting date, but the lawsuit was later settled for a different amount before the approval of the financial statements, it makes sense to adjust the provision to the actual settlement amount. Similarly, if an error in the accounts is subsequently discovered before the financial statements are approved, then the error should be corrected.

In some cases the treatment of non-adjusting events is clear. For example, if the company's warehouse burns to the ground after the reporting period, this is clearly not indicative of a condition that existed at the reporting date, and no adjustment should be made.

In other cases, however, the treatment is less clear. For example, if a significant customer goes bankrupt after the year-end, and no provision had been made for any bad debts, should the accounts be adjusted? Although the customer's bankruptcy occurred after the reporting date, there may have been prior evidence of the customer's financial difficulties. One would need to look at account aging, payment patterns, and other evidence that would have been available at the reporting date to determine if the condition existed. If the balance of evidence suggests that the customer's financial troubles already existed at the reporting date, then an adjustment would be appropriate. In cases like these, the accountant will need to apply sound judgment in evaluating all the evidence.

Even when an event is determined to be a non-adjusting event, disclosure may still be appropriate if the event is anticipated to have a material effect on future economic decisions. In our previous example, the destruction of a company's warehouse may have a serious impact on the company's future ability to deliver products and to earn profits. Thus, disclosure of the nature of the event, and the estimated financial effect of the event on future results, should be made.

In rare cases, a company's financial condition may deteriorate so quickly after the reporting period that it may be impossible for the company to continue operating. Although events after the reporting period may not necessarily provide evidence of conditions that existed at the reporting date, the going concern assumption will override the normal procedure. Because financial statements are presumed to be prepared on a going concern basis, any change in this fundamental assumption would create the need for a complete change in the basis of accounting. This would obviously have a profound effect on all aspects of the financial statements.

The guidance in IAS 10 provides another example of how the principle of full disclosure is employed to help financial statement readers make more informed decisions.

22.3 Auditor's Reports

So far we have focused on the role that the accountants and management play in providing useful information to investors. Another important component of a company's financial statements is the audit opinion. Audit opinions are prepared by firms of independent and professionally trained auditors whose job is to examine a company's financial statements and disclosures, internal control systems, and all other relevant data in order to express an opinion on the fairness of their financial statements. Audit opinions are required for any company that wants to trade its shares publicly; in some jurisdictions they may also be required of private companies.

The purpose of an audit opinion is to provide assurance to the readers that a company's financial disclosures have been prepared in accordance with the appropriate accounting standards and to ensure that they are not materially misstated. This assurance is important to the operation of capital markets, as investors need to have confidence in the information that they are using to make decisions.

Although auditing standards are regulated nationally, many jurisdictions have adopted the International Standards on Auditing (ISAs), which are issued by the International Auditing and Assurance Standards Board (IAASB). With over 80 nations globally now using the ISAs, there are still jurisdictions, such as the United States, which issue their own audit standards. However, they have recently made attempts to harmonize these standards with the ISAs.

The end product of the auditor's work is an audit report that is attached to the financial statements. This report may appear fairly simple but it is, in fact, the product of many hours of detailed testing and procedures carried out by audit professionals. An example of the standard form of the report used in Canada is featured below.

INDEPENDENT AUDITOR'S REPORT

[Appropriate Addressee, usually the Board of Directors]

Report on the Financial Statements

We have audited the accompanying financial statements of Sample Company, which comprise the statement of financial position as at December 31, 20X7, and the statement of comprehensive income, statement of changes in equity and statement of cash flows for the year then ended, and a summary of significant accounting policies and other explanatory information.

Management's Responsibility for the Financial Statements

Management is responsible for the preparation and fair presentation of these financial statements in accordance with International Financial Reporting Standards, and for such internal control as management determines is necessary to enable the preparation of financial statements that are free from material misstatement, whether due to fraud or error.

Auditor's Responsibility

Our responsibility is to express an opinion on these financial statements based on our audit. We conducted our audit in accordance with Canadian generally accepted auditing standards. Those standards require that we comply with ethical requirements and plan and perform the audit to obtain reasonable assurance about whether the financial statements are free from material misstatement.

> An audit involves performing procedures to obtain audit evidence about the amounts and disclosures in the financial statements. The procedures selected depend on the auditor's judgment, including the assessment of the risks of material misstatement of the financial statements, whether due to fraud or error. In making those risk assessments, the auditor considers internal control relevant to the entity's preparation and fair presentation of the financial statements in order to design audit procedures that are appropriate in the circumstances, but not for the purpose of expressing an opinion on the effectiveness of the entity's internal control.An audit also includes evaluating the appropriateness of accounting policies used and the reasonableness of accounting estimates made by management, as well as evaluating the overall presentation of the financial statements.
>
> We believe that the audit evidence we have obtained is sufficient and appropriate to provide a basis for our audit opinion.
>
> *Opinion*
>
> In our opinion, the financial statements present fairly, in all material respects, the financial position of Sample Company as at December 31, 20X7, and its financial performance and its cash flows for the year then ended in accordance with International Financial Reporting Standards.
>
> [Auditor's signature]
>
> [Date of the auditor's report]
>
> [Auditor's address]

Note that the final opinion states that these financial statements present fairly the financial position and financial performance of the company in accordance with IFRS. However, in some jurisdictions the term "present fairly" is replaced by the statement that the presentation gives a "true and fair view" of the company's affairs. These phrasings are generally considered to be equivalent in meaning. Also, in some jurisdictions, the audit report may provide more details of the auditor's procedures and further assurances regarding regulatory or legal issues. However, the basic elements of the report will be the same.

This audit opinion is sometimes referred to as a **"clean" opinion**, although this term is somewhat misleading. While the audit opinion is prepared to provide assurance to investors, it does not guarantee that the financial statements are 100% accurate.

In some cases, auditors may find it necessary to modify their opinion. This occurs when insufficient audit evidence is available or if material misstatements are included in the financial statements. If these effects are not considered pervasive, the auditor can then issue a qualified audit opinion. This type of opinion states that the financial statements are presented fairly except for the particular accounts for which insufficient evidence or misstatements are present. Further explanations for the reasons for the qualification will be required in the audit report.

In cases where the effects of insufficient evidence or misstatements are considered pervasive, the auditor will have to either deny an opinion, in the case of insufficient evidence, or issue an adverse opinion, in the case of misstatements. Effects are considered pervasive if they are not confined to specific elements or accounts in the financial statements, if they represent a substantial portion of the financial statements, or if they are fundamental to the users' understanding of the financial statements. In such cases, the auditor needs to exercise prudent judgment, as such opinions can prove harmful to a company. As these types of opinions essentially state that either the auditor cannot provide an opinion, or that the financial statements are not fairly presented, they will not provide assurance to investors. However, adverse opinions are rare, as management will try to correct any material misstatements.

In other situations, the auditor may determine that all the appropriate disclosures have been made, but that there is a particular disclosure that is critical to the readers' understanding of the financial statements as a whole. In this case, the auditor may include an **emphasis of matter** paragraph which highlights particular disclosures.

In summary, the audit report adds value to the package of full disclosures that companies provide to financial statement readers to enable them to make better decisions.

22.4 Financial Statement Reporting and Analysis

Financial statement analysis is the process of reviewing and interpreting a company's core financial statements in order to make better business decisions. While it sounds simple, it isn't. Many tools have been developed in the financial community to assess a business's financial performance. In simple terms, the process usually starts with a high-level liquidity, activity, profitability, and coverage ratio analysis of the core financial statements and of the various supplementary financial reports such as interim and segmented financial reports. The analyses of these financial reports can also incorporate other types of ratio analysis such as common size analysis and trend analysis. These analytical techniques have been covered in detail in previous chapters of this text and in the previous intermediate financial accounting text. A summary of the commonly used ratios is presented at the end of this chapter for review purposes.

22.4.1 Interim Reporting

In basic terms, interim reports cover periods that are less than one year. As previously stated, interim financial statements are often prepared on a monthly or quarterly basis. They are increasingly popular as more frequent disclosures are becoming the new norm in today's economy. While ASPE does not provide standards regarding interim reporting, IFRS does provide guidance that IFRS compliant companies are encouraged to follow and to disclose.

In many cases, the same headings, subheadings, and subtotals would be employed for both the interim and the annual financial statements. If segmented financial statements are employed by a business, reportable segments would also be applied to the interim financial statements.

IFRS supports the idea that each interim period is to be reported as separate and distinct. Also, the same policies that are used for annual financial statements are to be used for interim financial statements as well. This means that deferrals and accruals used in the interim statements would follow the same principles and tests as those that are used in the annual financial statements. Simply put, revenues would be recognized and reported when earned (revenue recognition) and expenses incurred to earn those revenues would be reported when goods and services were received (matching principle). Accounting policies such as depreciation, inventory cost formulas, and required disclosures, such as earnings per share from the annual financial statements, would also be applied equally for interim statements. IFRS requires the same five core financial statements for interim reporting as required for the annual reports. Interim reports can be condensed as long as they include the same headings, subtotals, and comparative columns as in the annual reports.

Review Suncor Energy Inc.'s 2015 Annual Report[3] and financial statements. The quarterly financial summary for each interim quarter can be found starting on page 120.

The financial data in the current Quarterly Financial Summary is comparative on a quarterly basis with the previous year, 2014, and is highly condensed. Note that the interim report also breaks down the interim reporting periods into four product line segments, namely oil sands, exploration and production, refining and marketing, and corporate (Suncor Energy Inc., n.d.). Segmented reporting will be discussed in the next section.

Interim reporting has several challenges. For example, what happens when there is a change in accounting principle? If this change were to occur in the second or third quarter, how would this affect the first quarter interim financial statements? The general consensus is that, even if the change of a particular accounting policy, such as a depreciation method, is prospective, the annual change should be prorated to each of the interim accounting periods so as not to over- or understate any specific quarter. This would lessen any tendency for management to manipulate accounting policies within a specific quarter in order to influence bonuses or operational results targets. As such, even though the change in policy is applied prospectively for the fiscal year, if interim statements are prepared, the change in policy would be applied proportionally between each quarterly period in order to smooth the results over each quarter of that fiscal year.

Further challenges to interim reporting are the cyclical and seasonal swings experienced by businesses within a fiscal year. While revenue intake can be concentrated over a limited number of months, expenses may continue to be incurred on a monthly basis.

---

[3] http://www.suncor.com/investor-centre/financial-reports/annual-disclosure

If IFRS guidelines are followed, the principles of revenue recognition and matching will continue to be applied within each of the interim periods and the same tests used for annual financial statements would be applied to interim reports. With seasonal swings, this can result in volatile earnings comparisons between quarters, which can be seen in the wide fluctuations of Suncor Energy Inc.'s quarterly earnings per share amounts as shown in the quarterly financial summary report referenced above.

Additionally, difficulties exist regarding certain allocations such as for income taxes and earnings per share. Under IFRS, each interim period is to be independent of each other and interim allocations are to be determined by applying all the same tests as those used for the annual reports.

Note that interim financial reports are unaudited, as evidenced by the "unaudited" notation under the title of Suncor Energy Inc.'s quarterly financial summary report. While some stakeholders continue to push for an examination of the interim reports in order to provide some assurance, auditors remain reluctant to express an opinion on interim financial statements. As a result, there will always be a trade-off between the need for assurance and the need to produce the interim report on a timely and cost effective basis.

22.4.2 Segmented Reporting

Structural analysis is the study of relationships between resources, people, activities, and products. Segmented, or disaggregated, financial reporting is an example of how structural analysis can be used for financial analysis purposes. As mentioned in the opening comments of this chapter, more and more businesses are diversifying their business lines. This creates the need for additional reporting about those business lines—how each contributes to the overall entity in terms of profits, growth, and risk.

Segmented reporting enhances decision making and analysis as it highlights business components that have strong financial performances over those that are weak, or even losing, performers. Management can then make decisions about which components to keep and which components to discontinue as part of their overall business strategy. Keep in mind, however, that not all business components that experience chronic losses should be automatically discontinued. There can be strategic reasons for keeping a losing component. For example, a company may retain a particular borderline, or losing component, that produces a particular part needed for the entity's manufacturing process. Keeping this business line guarantees a steady supply of these critical parts, thus ensuring a smooth and uninterrupted production process with resulting sales and profits.

As different components within a company can have different gross margins, profitability, and risk, segmented reporting can also assist in forecasting future sales, profits, and cash flows. With segmented reporting comes a better understanding of the company's performance and future prospects, resulting in better decision making overall.

Although there are many, the two most common segmented activities are by products (or by business lines) and by geography. Either the physical location of the company's assets or the location of its customers can be the geographic basis for segmentation.

For ASPE, there is currently no guidance regarding segmented reporting. As such, privately held corporations tend not to report segmented information. For IFRS companies, however, a segment must meet several characteristics and quantitative thresholds in order to be considered a reportable segment for the purposes of the published financial statements.

Reportable Segments

Reportable segments possess certain characteristics, such as having separate and distinct financial information that is regularly monitored by the senior operations management. These are then tested for materiality and are identified as a reportable segment if at least one of the following conditions is met:

1. Its reportable revenue, including intercompany sales and transfers, is 10% or greater than the company's combined revenue of all the segments.

2. Its reported profits or losses, in absolute amounts, are 10% or greater than the greater of:

    a. the combined reported profits
    b. the combined reported losses.

3. Its assets are 10% or greater than the company's combined assets of all the segments.

Below is some sample data from a fictitious company:

Segment	Possible Reporting Segments Data in $ millions			10% Revenue Threshold #1	10% Profit/loss Threshold #2	10% Assets Threshold #3
	Total Revenue	Reported Profit/loss	Assets			
Canada	$ 500	$ 50	$ 300	Y	Y	Y
US	800	16	100	Y	Y	Y
Central America	300	(5)	35			
South America	600	(6)	40	Y		
Europe	400	10	70			
Asia	900	36	200	Y	Y	Y
Middle East	700	25	150	Y	Y	Y
	$ 4,200	$ 126	$ 895			

> Tests:
>
> 1. Its reportable revenue is 10% or greater than company combined revenue of all segments (10% × 4,200) = $420 threshold
> 2. Its reported profits/losses (in absolute amounts) are 10% or greater than the greater sum of:
>   a. the combined reported profits = $137
>   b. the combined reported losses = $11
>
>   Profits are greater, so (10% × $137) = $13.7 threshold in absolute terms (ignoring + and - math signs)
>
> 3. Its assets are 10% or greater than the company's combined assets of all the segments (10% × $895) = $89.5 threshold

Based on the three threshold tests above, Canada, the US, South America, Asia, and the Middle East all meet at least one or more of the tests.

Once these segments are identified, IFRS recommends that reportable segments comprise 75% or more of a company's overall combined sales to unrelated customers. They also recommend that the number of reporting segments be limited to ten in order to lessen the possibility of information overload. In the example above, the 75% threshold is $3,150 ($4,200 × 75%), and all five segments meeting at least one of the three test criteria above total $3,500 ($500 + 800 + 600 + 900 + 700). As such, this test has been met. It is important to note that management can override all of these tests and report a segment if they consider the segmented information to be useful to the stakeholders.

There are several issues, however, with segmented reporting. For instance, accounting processes such as allocation of common costs and elimination of inter-segment sales can be quite challenging. For this reason, allocation of common costs is not required. As such, thorough knowledge of the business and of the industry in which the company operates is essential when utilizing segmented reports, otherwise investors may find segmentation meaningless or, at worst, they may draw incorrect conclusions about the performance of the business components. For example, a particular business line may repeatedly report segment losses causing shareholders to put pressure on management prematurely to discontinue that line even if the better long-term strategy is to keep it. Additionally, the company may be reluctant to publish segmented information because of the risk it poses to them by way of competitors, suppliers, government agencies, and unions potentially using this information to their advantage and to the detriment of the company.

Review Suncor Energy Inc.'s 2015 Annual Report[4] and financial statements. The information in the notes to the financial statements regarding segmented information can be found on pages 85 to 87.

---

[4] http://www.suncor.com/investor-centre/financial-reports/annual-disclosure

In the segmented reports, note that Suncor Energy Inc. provides general information about each of its reportable segments and policies regarding intersegment sales and profit. The segmented financial report is condensed, but provided that senior management regularly reviews them, the line items identified are the minimum required disclosures according to IFRS. The segmented reports must also be reconciled to the core financial statements for revenues and operating profits/losses. While IFRS also states that assets and liabilities are to be reconciled, the segmented report only shows a reconciliation of non-current assets to the core statement of financial position. Other IFRS disclosures identified for segmented reporting include revenues from external customers as well as Canada versus foreign revenue and capital assets. While this is not an exhaustive list of all IFRS required segmented reporting disclosures, it provides a sense that these disclosures are extensive.

22.4.3 Analysis Techniques

Many different types of ratios are used in the analysis of financial statements. For instance, ratios applied to the financial statements include liquidity ratios, profitability ratios, activity ratios, and coverage ratios. While other types of ratios exist, including vertical/common size analysis and horizontal/trend analysis, they have been covered in detail in previous chapters of this text and in the previous financial accounting text. However, a summary of the commonly used ratios, and a brief overview of common size and horizontal analysis, are presented below for review purposes:

Ratio	Formula	Purpose
Liquidity ratios – ability to pay short term obligations		
Current ratio	$\dfrac{\text{Current assets}}{\text{Current liabilities}}$	ability to pay short term debt
Quick ratio (or acid test ratio)	$\dfrac{\text{Cash, marketable securities and net receivables}}{\text{Current liabilities}}$	ability to pay short term debt using near-cash assets
Current cash debt coverage ratio	$\dfrac{\text{Net cash provided by operating activities}}{\text{Average current liabilities}}$	ability to pay short term debt from cash generated from its current fiscal year operations (statement of cash flows)

Ratio	Formula	Purpose
Profitability ratios – ability to generate profits		
Profit margin	$\dfrac{\text{Net income}}{\text{Net Sales}} \times 100\%$	net income for each dollar of sales
Return on total assets	$\dfrac{\text{Net income}}{\text{Average total assets}} \times 100\%$	overall profitability of assets
Return on common shareholders' equity	$\dfrac{\text{Net income} - \text{Preferred dividends}}{\text{Average common shareholders' equity (includes retained earnings/deficit)}} \times 100\%$	overall profitability of common shareholders' investment
Earnings per share	$\dfrac{\text{Net income} - \text{Preferred dividends}}{\text{Weighted average common shares outstanding (WACS)}}$	net income for each common share
Payout ratio	$\dfrac{\text{Cash dividends}}{\text{Net income}} \times 100\%$	percentage of earnings distributed as dividends

Ratio	Formula	Purpose
Activity ratios – ability to effectively use assets		
Accounts receivable turnover	$\dfrac{\text{Net sales}}{\text{Average net accounts receivable}}$	how quickly accounts receivable is collected
Days' sales uncollected	$\dfrac{\text{Accounts receivable}}{\text{Net sales}} \times 365$	average # of days that sales are uncollected (this can be compared to the credit terms of the company)
Inventory turnover	$\dfrac{\text{Cost of goods sold}}{\text{Average inventory}}$	how quickly inventory is sold
Days' sales in inventory	$\dfrac{\text{Ending inventory}}{\text{Cost of Goods Sold}} \times 365$	average # of days to sell inventory.
Accounts payable turnover	$\dfrac{\text{Cost of goods sold}}{\text{Average accounts payable}}$	how quickly accounts payable is paid
Asset turnover	$\dfrac{\text{Net sales}}{\text{Average total assets}}$	the ability of assets to generate sales

Ratio	Formula	Purpose
Coverage – ability to pay long-term obligations		
Debt ratio	$\dfrac{\text{Total liabilities}}{\text{Total assets}} \times 100\%$	percentage of assets provided by creditors*
Equity ratio	$\dfrac{\text{Total equity}}{\text{Total assets}} \times 100\%$	percentage of assets provided by investors*
Cash debt coverage ratio	$\dfrac{\text{Net cash from operating activities}}{\text{Average total liabilities}} \times 100\%$	the ability to pay current and long-term debt from net cash from operating activities (statement of cash flows)
Book value per common share	$\dfrac{\text{Common shareholders' equity}}{\text{\# of common shares outstanding}}$	the amount per common share if company liquidated at reported amounts.

* These two ratios can also be expressed as a single debt-to-equity ratio; Total assets ÷ Total liabilities.
A low debt-to-equity ratio indicates that creditors have less claim on the company's assets resulting in less financing risk.
A higher debt-to-equity ratio can mean a higher risk for financial difficulty if the debt and interest cannot be paid when due.

Common Size Analysis

Common size, or vertical, analysis takes each line item on a financial statement and expresses it as a percentage of a base amount. The base figure used in a balance sheet is usually total assets, while for the income statement, it is usually net sales.

Below is an example of common size analysis of an income statement:

Common Size Income Statement
as at December 31

	2015	2014
Revenue	100.00%	100.00%
Cost of goods sold	60.00%	58.00%
Gross profit	40.00%	42.00%
Operating expenses		
Rent	2.00%	2.00%
Salaries and benefits expense	6.00%	5.80%
Depreciation and amortization expense	2.00%	2.00%
Office supplies expense	0.50%	0.40%
Travel	1.00%	1.10%
Utilities expense	1.00%	1.00%
Other operating expenses	0.20%	0.20%
	12.70%	12.50%
Income from operations		
Other revenues and expenses		
Interest expense	0.40%	0.35%
Income before income taxes	26.90%	29.15%
Income tax expense	4.00%	3.80%
Net income	22.90%	25.35%

These percentages can then be compared to the previous years' data, competitors' financials, or industry benchmarks. An example of a typical common size ratio that is compared in this way is the gross margin percentage. A downside of ratio analysis, however, is its potential to foster an environment where management chooses accounting policies, such as inventory costing, in order to influence a favourable gross profit for personal reasons such as bonuses or positive performance evaluations. In the example above, the gross margin decreased from 42% to 40% over a two-year period. While this decline could be a realistic reflection of operations, it could also be the result of a change in estimates or of accounting policy in order to avoid income taxes. For this reason, any change in ratios should always be investigated further.

Horizontal Analysis

Horizontal, or trend, analysis examines each line item on a financial statement in order to see how it has changed over time. The line items that are of most interest tend to be the changes in sales, gross profit, and net income. If the company's operations are relatively stable each year, this analysis can prove to be quite useful.

Below is an example of common size analysis of an income statement:

Horizontal Analysis Income Statement
as at December 31

	2015	2014	2013
Revenue	105.20%	101.40%	100.00%
Cost of goods sold	102.80%	101.30%	100.00%
Gross profit	110.00%	101.50%	100.00%
Operating expenses			
Rent	110.00%	100.00%	100.00%
Salaries and benefits expense	106.00%	103.00%	100.00%
Depreciation and amortization expense	100.00%	100.00%	100.00%
Office supplies expense	96.00%	98.00%	100.00%
Travel	102.00%	101.00%	100.00%
Utilities expense	105.00%	103.00%	100.00%
Other operating expenses	81.00%	80.00%	100.00%
	102.00%	101.00%	100.00%
Income from operations			
Other revenues and expenses			
Interest expense	103.00%	101.00%	100.00%
Income before income taxes	102.00%	101.00%	100.00%
Income tax expense	100.00%	100.00%	100.00%
Net income	102.00%	98.00%	100.00%

Note that the percentages do not add up vertically as was the case with vertical analysis. Looking at sales, gross profit, and net income, we notice that all three have all increased, with gross profit increasing the most. This could be due to a change in the pricing policy as evidenced by the 5% increase in revenue over two years. However, more investigation would be necessary in order to determine if the increase is due to true economic events or if it was influenced by changes in policies made by management.

In summary, remember that when working with ratios analysis, ratios are only as good as the data reported in the financial statements. For instance, if quality of earnings is high, then ratio analysis can be useful, otherwise it may do more harm than good. Additionally, it is important to focus on a few key ratios for each category in order to avoid the risk of information overload. Those key ratios can then be investigated and tracked over time. It is also important to understand that industry benchmarks make no assurances about how one company compares to its competitors, as the basis for the industry ratio may differ from the basis used for the company. While ratios provide good indicators for further investigation, they are not the end-point if an evaluation is to be conducted properly.

22.5 IFRS/ASPE Key Differences

Item	ASPE	IFRS
Related Parties	In addition to disclosure of related party balances and transactions, some related party transactions may need to be remeasured to the carrying amount, rather than the transaction amount.	The presence of related parties needs to be disclosed, along with details of transactions and balances with related parties.
Key Management	There is no specific disclosure requirement for key management compensation.	Disclosure of compensation paid to key management personnel is required.
Subsequent Events	Subsequent events are considered up to the date that the financial statements are completed, which may require some judgment.	Periods after the reporting date must be considered up to the date that the financial statements are authorized for issue.
Interim Reporting	N/A	Provides guidance but no required disclosures. Accruals and accounting policies should be applied in the same way as is done in the annual financial statements.
Segmented Reporting	N/A	Reportable segments are defined by characteristics and significance tests. Disclosures can be extensive and include reconciliation of key line items such as revenue, profits/losses, assets, and liabilities to the core financial statements.

Chapter Summary

LO 1: Discuss the rationale and methods of full disclosure in corporate reporting.

The practice of full disclosure is motivated by the need to create information useful to financial statement readers in helping them make decisions. Full disclosure of relevant information can improve the efficiency of financial markets by lessening the information asymmetry problem, thus creating more confidence for financial statement users. Financial information, however, is backward-looking in nature, so disclosures beyond the financial statements are required. Financial statement notes provide additional details and explanations of amounts included in the financial statements, as well as descriptions of significant accounting policies. Complete disclosures of accounting policies are necessary in order to allow readers to make comparisons between companies. Outside the financial statements, companies will also make other disclosures, including the management discussion and analysis (MD&A) section of the annual report. This section provides a narrative review of the year's results from the perspective of management, as well as a discussion of risk factors, future plans, and other qualitative information that may be useful to readers. A well-written MD&A will help investors link past performance to predictions of future results.

LO 2: Identify the issues and disclosure requirements for related parties.

Related parties are either individuals or entities that are presumed to not deal with the reporting entity at an arm's length basis. Because related parties are assumed to have some influence over the reporting entity, there is a possibility that transactions with these parties may not be conducted under the same terms as with other market participants. The existence of related parties needs to be disclosed, even if there are no transactions with those parties during the reporting period. When transactions with related parties do occur, the amount of the transactions and outstanding balances must be disclosed, along with a description of the terms and conditions of the transaction, any commitments, security, or guarantees with the related party, the nature of the consideration used to settle the transactions, and the amount of any provision or expense related to bad debts of the related party. Details of compensation paid to key management personnel must also be disclosed. In certain circumstances, ASPE also requires remeasurement of related party transactions.

LO 3: Describe the appropriate accounting and disclosure requirements for events occurring after the reporting period.

Events that occur after the reporting period, but before the financial statements are authorized for issue, may require additional disclosures. If the event does not provide evidence of a condition that existed at the reporting date, then note disclosure would generally be the only required action. If the event does provide evidence of a condition that existed at the reporting date, then adjustments of the reported amounts are required. However, in some cases it may not be clear if the condition existed at the reporting date. In rare circumstances, the subsequent event may result in a reassessment of the going concern assumption, which would cause a complete revision of the reporting basis of the financial statements.

LO 4: Describe the purpose of the audit opinion and the contents of the auditor's report.

Audit opinions are prepared by independent, professional auditors in order to provide assurance to the readers of the financial statements that they have been prepared in accordance with the appropriate accounting standards and that those financial statements are not materially misstated. This assurance is intended to provide confidence to financial market participants that the information used to make decisions is relevant and reliable. A typical clean audit opinion would identify the auditor's and management's responsibilities, the financial statements being audited, and would provide an opinion that the financial statements are fairly presented. In cases where errors are identified, or audit evidence is unavailable, the auditor may issue a qualified opinion if the effects are not pervasive. Where the effects of errors or insufficient evidence are pervasive, the auditor will need to either deny an opinion or issue an adverse opinion.

LO 5: Explain the various financial statement analysis tools and techniques.

Techniques used to analyze financial statements include interim reporting, segmented reporting, and various other analysis techniques. The process usually starts with a high-level liquidity, activity, profitability, and coverage ratio analyses of the core financial statements and of the various supplementary financial reports, such as the interim and segmented financial reports. The analyses of these financial reports can also incorporate other types of ratio analysis such as common size analysis and trend analysis.

LO 6: Explain the similarities and differences between ASPE and IFRS regarding disclosures and analysis of financial statements.

Some differences exist between ASPE and IFRS regarding related parties disclosures and subsequent events. However, for interim and segmented reporting, ASPE is silent.

References

Business Insider. (2015, December 30). *China firm to investors: A thief took my financial statements.* Retrieved from http://www.businessinsider.com/afp-china-firm-to-investors-a-thief-took-my-financial-statements-2015-12

Canadian Tire Corporation. (2016). *Annual report 2015.* Retrieved from http://s2.q4cdn.com/913390117/files/doc_financials/annual/2015/Canadian-Tire-Corporation_2015-Annual-Report_ENG.pdf

CPA Canada. (2016). *CPA Canada handbook.* Toronto, ON: CPA Canada.

Suncor Energy Inc. (n.d.). *Annual Report 2015.* Retrieved from http://www.suncor.com/%7E/media/Files/PDF/Investor%20Centre/Annual%20Reports/2015%20AR/2015%20English/2015%20Annual%20Message%20to%20SH%20EN_FINAL.ashx?la=en-CA

Weintraub, A. (2016, January 7). *China Animal Healthcare creates embarrassment for stakeholder Lilly.* FiercePharma. Retrieved from http://www.fiercepharma.com/animal-health/china-animal-healthcare-creates-embarrassment-for-stakeholder-lilly

Exercises

EXERCISE 22-1

Determine if a related party relationship exists in each of the cases below and describe what disclosures would be required under IAS 24.

a. Kessel Ltd. sells goods on credit to Sterling Inc., a company owned by the daughter of Ms. Bender (Ms. Bender is a director of Kessel Ltd.). On December 31, 2016, trade receivables of $50,000, owing from Sterling Inc., were reported on Kessel Ltd's books. Management of Kessel Ltd. decided to write off $20,000 of this receivable and provide a full allowance against the remaining balance.

b. During 2016, Kessel Ltd. purchased goods from Saunders Ltd. for $175,000. Saunders Ltd. indicated that this amount represents the normal price it would charge to arm's length customers. Kessel Ltd. owns 35% of the shares of Saunders Ltd.

c. In late December 2016, a vacation property owned by Kessel Ltd. was sold to one of its directors, Mr. Chiang, for $325,000. The property had a carrying value of $150,000 and an estimated market value of $360,000. Kessel Ltd. also provided a guarantee on the mortgage that Mr. Chiang took out to acquire the property.

d. On December 31, 2016, Kessel Ltd. owed $120,000 to its major supplier, Rickert Ltd., for purchases made on account at regular commercial terms.

EXERCISE 22-2

In each of the cases below, determine if the relationships should be considered related party relationships under IAS 24.

a. Mr. Fowler is a director of both Goss Ltd. and Link Inc. Are these two companies related?

b. Rosen Ltd. and Chabon Inc. are both associated companies of Lethem Ltd. Are Rosen Ltd. and Chabon Inc. related parties?

c. Abernathy Ltd. and Beron Inc. each have a board containing seven directors, five of who are common. There are no common shareholdings. Are the two companies related?

EXERCISE 22-3

The following events occurred between December 31, 2017 (the reporting date) and March 22, 2018, the date that Ealing Inc.'s financial statements were approved for issue:

a. January 8, 2018: The local government approved the expropriation of one of the company's manufacturing facilities for construction of a new motorway. On December 31, 2017, the carrying value of the property, land and building, was $2,750,000. The company has determined that they will be able to move most of the manufacturing machines to other facilities. The company was not previously aware of the local government's plan, as the council discussions had been held in camera. The local government has not yet proposed a compensation amount. The appropriation will occur later in 2018.

b. January 27, 2018: The board of directors approved a staff bonus of $250,000. The terms of this bonus were included in the employment contracts of key management personnel and the bonus calculation was based on the reported financial results of the December 31, 2017 fiscal year.

c. February 3, 2018: The company received notice from the federal income tax authority that additional income taxes of $75,000 for the 2015 and 2016 fiscal years were payable. The company had previously disputed the calculation of these taxes, and had reported an accrual $30,000 on December 31, 2017.

d. February 21, 2018: The accounts receivable clerk was fired after it was discovered she had perpetrated a fraud in the accounts. The accounts receivable balance was overstated by $75,000 on December 31, 2017. The company has consulted legal counsel to determine if any action can be brought to recover the stolen funds, but no action has yet been filed.

e. March 16, 2018: The board of directors declared a dividend of $550,000 based on the results reported on the December 31, 2017 financial statements.

f. March 18, 2018: A fire completely destroyed one of the company's production machines. It is not expected that any insurance proceeds will be received on this asset.

Required: Determine what adjustments or disclosures, if any, should be made on the December 31, 2017 financial statements for the above items.

EXERCISE 22-4

On January 15, 2018, several pieces of plaster fell from the ceiling in the offices of Satterlee LLP, a firm of professional accountants, crushing several pairs of green eyeshades. Luckily, no accountants were injured. The management of the firm hired professional engineers to examine the problem. The engineers determined that there were, in fact, more serious problems in the overall structure of the building, and, in particular, the foundation. The engineers indicated that it appeared the foundation had been sinking for several years, although the evidence of the cracked ceiling only just appeared. The engineers indicated that the repair work to the foundation was essential to keep the building safe for occupation.

Required: Determine how this event should be dealt with on Satterlee LLP's financial statements for the year ended December 31, 2017.

EXERCISE 22-5

On November 12, 2017, the federal government filed a lawsuit against Magus Corp. The lawsuit contends that one of Magus Corp.'s factories has been dumping unfiltered effluent into a local river, resulting in contamination that has required the water treatment plant downstream to commit to additional procedures to keep the water safe for community residents. The lawsuit not only seeks compensation for the damage done, but also seeks a remedy that would force the company to install filtration equipment at the factory to clean the effluent before it reaches the river. The company has not accrued any provision for this lawsuit on December 31, 2017, as the company's legal counsel has indicated that the outcome cannot currently be determined. Management of the company has indicated that if they are forced to install the filtration equipment, that they will, instead, shut down the factory as the required equipment would render the entire operation economically infeasible. The factory in question is one of three factories that the company operates, producing approximately 40% of the company's output.

Required: Discuss the potential impact of the above situation on the auditor's report for the year ended December 31, 2017.

EXERCISE 22–6

Arburator Inc. has six business lines with the following information:

Business Line	Total Revenue	Operating Profit/(Loss)	Assets
1	$ 90,000	$ 18,000	$150,000
2	25,000	(7,000)	20,000
3	20,000	(4,000)	15,000
4	140,000	30,000	266,000
5	10,000	4,000	15,000
6	4,000	(3,000)	12,000
	$289,000	$ 38,000	$478,000

Required: Assuming that Arburator Inc. follows IFRS, determine which business lines, if any, qualify as a reportable operating segment for purposes of financial reporting.

EXERCISE 22–7

With regard to interim reporting, what accounting issues can occur? Is there a difference between IFRS and ASPE with regard to interim reporting?

EXERCISE 22–8

The condensed income statement for Egor Inc. is shown below:

	2016	2015	2014
Net sales	25,000	22,500	21,000
Cost of goods sold (COGS)	16,250	13,500	13,230
Gross profit	8,750	9,000	7,770
Selling and administration expenses	5,000	4,800	4,600
Income from continuing operations before income taxes	3,750	4,200	3,170

Required:

a. Analyze Egor Inc.'s statement using vertical and horizontal techniques.

b. What are some of the limitations of this type of analysis?

EXERCISE 22–9

Presented below is the balance sheet, including disclosures, of Hibertia Corp. for the year 2015:

Hibertia Corp.
Balance Sheet
December 31, 2015

Assets

Current assets			
Cash		$ 60,000	
Accounts receivable	$215,500		
Less allowance for doubtful accounts	2,400	213,100	
Inventory*		210,500	
Prepaid insurance		15,900	
Total current assets			$ 499,500
Long-term investments*			
Investments in shares*			320,000
Property, plant, and equipment			
Cost of uncompleted plant facilities:			
Land	$125,000		
Building in process of construction	220,000	345,000	
Equipment	325,000		
Less accumulated depreciation	180,000	145,000	490,000
Intangible assets			
Patents*			60,000
Total assets			$1,369,500

Liabilities and Shareholders' Equity

Current liabilities			
Notes payable to bank*		$ 112,000	
Accounts payable		215,000	
Accrued liabilities		66,200	
Total current liabilities			$ 393,200
Long-term liabilities			
Bonds payable, 11%, due Jan. 1, 2026		250,000	
Less discount on bonds payable		22,000	228,000
Total liabilities			621,200
Shareholders' equity			
Capital shares			
Common shares; 600,000 shares authorized,			
400,000 shares issued and outstanding		400,000	
Retained earnings		203,300	
Accumulated other comprehensive income		145,000**	748,300
Total liabilities and shareholders' equity			$1,369,500

Disclosures:

- Inventory — at lower of FIFO cost/NRV

- Long-term investments – fair value through OCI

- Investments in shares, of which investments costing $140,000 have been pledged as security for notes payable to bank.

- Patents (net of accumulated amortization of $20,000). Amortization is on a straight-line basis.

- Notes payable to bank, due 2016 and secured by investments which cost $140,000.

Additional information:

Net sales for 2015 are $550,000; Cost of goods sold is $385,000; Net Income is $125,000.

Required: Based on the information available above, identify and calculate:

a. One liquidity ratio

b. One activity ratio

Briefly discuss the results for this company. Also, use ending balances in lieu of averages when calculating ratios.

EXERCISE 22–10

Below is the balance sheet for Great Impressions Ltd. as at December 31, 2015.

Great Impressions Ltd.
Balance Sheet
As at December 31, 2015

Assets			
Current assets:			
Cash			$ 300,000
Accounts receivable		$ 900,000	
Allowance for doubtful accounts		(13,000)	887,000
Inventory			55,000
Spare parts supplies			1,500
Prepaid insurance			53,000
Total current assets			$1,296,500
Property, plant, and equipment:			
Land		300,000	
Equipment	$143,000		
Accumulated depreciation, equipment	(62,000)	81,000	381,000
Intangible assets:			
Patent			300,000
Total assets			$1,977,500
Liabilities			
Current liabilities:			
Accounts payable		265,200	
Unearned consulting fees		25,500	
Current portion of long-term note payable		100,000	
Total current liabilities			390,700
Long-term liabilities			
Long-term note payable			93,800
Total liabilities			$ 484,500
Equity			
Contributed capital:			
Preferred shares, authorized 5,000 shares;			
issued and outstanding 3,744 shares		93,600	
Common shares, unlimited authorized;			
issued and outstanding, 15,900 shares		159,000	
Total contributed capital		252,600	
Retained earnings		1,240,400	
Total equity			1,493,000
Total liabilities and equity			$1,977,500

Additional information:

Net sales for 2015 are $1,100,000; Cost of goods sold is $500,000; Net income is $544,960.

Market price per common share is currently $97.

Industry average ratios:
Accounts payable turnover	2 times
Current ratio	2:1
Days' sales in inventory	28 days
Debt ratio	26%
Profit margin	45%
Total asset turnover	1 times

Required: Calculate all the ratios listed above and comment on this company's performance. Identify each ratio as either being a liquidity, activity, solvency or profitability, or coverage ratio. Explain the purpose of the ratio selected and comment on the company's performance. Round your answers to the nearest two decimal places. Use the current year closing account balances in lieu of averages when calculating ratios requiring averages.

EXERCISE 22-11

Leo Creations Co. sells art supplies to retail outlets. Their financial statements are shown below:

Leo Creations Co.
Income Statement
For the Year Ended December 31, 2015

Sales		$1,500
Cost of goods sold		980
Gross profit		$ 520
Operating expenses:		
Depreciation expense	$ 48	
Other expenses	221	269
Operating income		$ 251
Other revenues and expenses		
Interest expense	$ 12	
Loss on sale of equipment	16	28
Net income		$ 223

Leo Creations Co.
Comparative Account Information
December 31, 2015 and 2014

	2015	2014
Accounts payable	$ 129	$ 115
Accounts receivable (net)	310	180
Bonds payable (due 2025)	610	100
Cash	75	42
Common shares	850	450
Equipment	1,360	500
Inventory	250	210
Accumulated depreciation	206	282
Long-term investment	400	400
Retained earnings	500	310
Salaries payable	100	75

Following are industry averages:

Current ratio	2.5:1
Inventory turnover	5.5 times
Acid-test (quick) ratio	1.4:1
Return on assets	13.4%
Accounts receivable turnover	8.2 times
Return on common shareholders' equity	18.3%

Required: (Round all calculations to two decimal places.)

a. i. Calculate the acid-test ratio for 2015. What type of ratio is this and what is its purpose?

ii. Is the company's acid-test ratio favourable or unfavourable, as compared to the industry average?

b. i. Calculate the accounts receivable turnover for 2015.

ii. Is the company's accounts receivable turnover favourable or unfavourable, as compared to the industry average in 2015?

c. Do Leo Creations Co.'s assets generate profits favourably or unfavourably, as compared to the industry average in 2015?

EXERCISE 22–12

The following information appeared on the alphabetized adjusted trial balance of Jill's Used Books Inc. for the year ended June 30, 2015. Assume all accounts have a normal balance.

Accounts payable	$ 1,800
Accounts receivable	29,000
Accumulated depreciation, equipment	3,800
Advertising expense	20,000
Allowance for doubtful accounts	1,400
Cash	10,000
Cost of goods sold	123,900
Delivery expense	4,875
Depreciation expense	5,000
Equipment	15,000
Interest income	2,000
Common shares	49,325
Preferred shares	40,000
Retained earnings	50,000
Cash dividends	46,000
Merchandise inventory	17,000
Notes payable ($3,000 is due by June 30, 2016)	7,000
Notes receivable (due in 2018)	14,000
Office supplies	750
Long-term investment	75,000
Copyright	25,000
Office supplies expense	1,200
Patent	2,500
Petty cash	500
Rent expense	17,900
Salaries expense	41,750
Salaries payable	950
Sales	314,000
Sales returns and allowances	22,000
Unearned sales	1,100

Additional information:

Assume total assets, liabilities, and equity at June 30, 2014 for Jill's Used Books Inc. were $120,000, $75,000, and $45,000, respectively.

Required: Explain whether the balance sheet was strengthened or not from June 30, 2014 to June 30, 2015.

EXERCISE 22–13

The following selected financial statement information is available for Yeo Company.

	(000's) December 31,	
	2015	2014
Cash	60	10
Accounts receivable (net)	80	70
Merchandise inventory	240	50
Equipment (net)	490	520
Accounts payable	180	75
Notes payable, due 2017	300	300

Required: Comment on the change in Yeo Company's ability to pay short-term debt. As part of your answer, include an explanation of the relationship between short-term debt paying ability and cash flow. Round to two decimal places.

EXERCISE 22–14

The following are comparative debt ratios for two companies in the same industry:

	2015	2014
Dilly Inc.	40%	35%
Kevnar Corporation	70%	83%

Required: Which company has strengthened its balance sheet? Explain your answer.

Manufactured by Amazon.ca
Bolton, ON